THIRD WORLD PR

Third World Protest

Between Home and the World

RAHUL RAO

OXFORD
UNIVERSITY PRESS

Great Clarendon Street, Oxford OX2 6DP,
United Kingdom

Oxford University Press is a department of the University of Oxford.
It furthers the University's objective of excellence in research, scholarship,
and education by publishing worldwide. Oxford is a registered trade mark of
Oxford University Press in the UK and in certain other countries

© Rahul Rao 2010

The moral rights of the author have been asserted

First published 2010
First published in paperback 2012

Impression: 1

All rights reserved. No part of this publication may be reproduced, stored in
a retrieval system, or transmitted, in any form or by any means, without the
prior permission in writing of Oxford University Press, or as expressly permitted
by law, by licence or under terms agreed with the appropriate reprographics
rights organization. Enquiries concerning reproduction outside the scope of the
above should be sent to the Rights Department, Oxford University Press, at the
address above

You must not circulate this work in any other form
and you must impose this same condition on any acquirer

British Library Cataloguing in Publication Data

Data available

Library of Congress Cataloguing in Publication Data

Data available

ISBN 978–0–19–956037–0 (Hbk.)
ISBN 978–0–19–965054–5 (Pbk.)

Printed in Great Britain by
MPG Books Group, Bodmin and King's Lynn

For my parents

Contents

Acknowledgements	ix
Abbreviations	xi
1. Introduction	1
1.1 An autobiography and anatomy of this book	1
1.2 Conceptions of cosmopolitanism: the everyday and the esoteric	9
1.3 Cosmopolitanism and its others	14
1.4 Subalternity, privilege, and the scope of justice	20
1.5 'Third World'	24
1.6 Methodological influences	30

PART I

2. The Dark Sides of Cosmopolitanism	35
2.1 Liberal cosmopolitanism and the construction of hegemony	37
2.2 Cosmopolitanism in the academy: between apology and utopia	58
3. The Dark Sides of Communitarianism	69
3.1 Pluralist rules, solidarist exceptions	74
3.2 Justifying pluralism	85
3.3 Criticizing pluralism	89
Intermezzo	105

PART II

4. Born Sneerers or Ironic Nationalists?	113
4.1 Rabindranath Tagore	117
4.2 Edward Said	127
4.3 Frantz Fanon	135
5. Indigenous Insurgents and Rioting Ryots	139
5.1 Class and nation in Marxist and Leninist thought	140
5.2 Contemporary anti-capitalist protest	146
5.3 Indigenous insurgents	150
5.4 Rioting ryots	158
5.5 Cosmopolitanism and nationalism in contemporary anti-capitalist protest	166

6. Queer in the Time of Terror 173
   6.1 Hangings in Iran: disaggregating the 'Gay International' 179
   6.2 Between malevolent enemies and condescending friends 189
   6.3 Cosmopolitanism and communitarianism in
       Indian queer activism 193

7. Conclusion 196

Notes 202
References 235
Index 263

Acknowledgements

This book emerged out of conversations and arguments with innumerable people, but four in particular deserve my most heartfelt thanks. Andrew Hurrell has taught me most of what I know about international relations. He was an extraordinary supervisor of the doctoral thesis on which this book is based and has been a deeply generous colleague in life after the thesis. Henry Shue's normative theory seminar in the autumn of 2002 made philosophical reasoning accessible in a way I had never previously thought possible, and laid out the conceptual apparatus that forms the point of departure for this book. The lucidity of his thinking and prose has set a standard that I have tried very hard to emulate. Ngaire Woods has been a tremendous intellectual and professional mentor, whose support and guidance have been critical at many junctures during the writing of this book. Finally, it is unlikely that I would have moved from the study of law to international relations, if I had not attended the political science lectures of Sitharamam Kakarala at the National Law School of India University, Bangalore.

A number of people have been crucial to the transformation of my doctoral thesis into this book. Fred Halliday and Kalypso Nicolaïdis were extraordinarily helpful thesis examiners, offering criticism that has been pivotal to this process. I am grateful to Duncan Bell for his incisive comments on the thesis manuscript, and for his invitation to a seminar at Cambridge whose participants commented helpfully on aspects of the overall argument. Thanks are also due to the many people at Oxford University Press who have been involved with different aspects of production, especially Dominic Byatt who has been a patient and supportive editor, and Aimee Wright, Louise Sprake, and Lizzy Suffling who have advised on, and assisted with, every step of the process.

I have been fortunate to have had the advice of a number of teachers and colleagues who have been extremely generous with their time, reading and commenting on draft chapters and responding to my incessant queries on the subjects of their expertise. In particular, I am grateful to Chris Bickerton, Michael Collins, Subir Datta, Frances Flanagan, Rosemary Foot, Shrimoyee Nandini Ghosh, Steve Hopgood, Lee Jones, Tarunabh Khaitan, Yuka Kobayashi, Leonardo Martinez-Diaz, Karma Nabulsi, Arvind Narrain and members of the queer law collective, Siddharth Narrain, Kerem Oktem, Mayur Patel, Jenni Quilter, Swagato Sarkar, Arash Sedighi, Keith Stanski, Marc Stears,

Kudrat Virk, and Jennifer Welsh. It is difficult to overstate the value of endless conversations with friends in my cohort of the graduate international relations programme at the Department of Politics & International Relations, University of Oxford. In addition to those already mentioned, I must thank Dan Baer, Tess Bridgeman, Arunabha Ghosh, Adam Humphreys, Priyanjali Malik, Sally McKechnie, Liat Ross, Sandeep Sengupta, and Christian Thorun. As a reflection on protest sensibilities, this book has been shaped in ways I have yet to fully appreciate by my involvement in political activism of various kinds, including the Narmada solidarity and queer rights movements in India, and anti-war groups such as Rhodes Scholars Against the War and the Oxford Students' Activist Network in the United Kingdom. I owe a great deal to the members of these groups and movements, too numerous to be named individually, whose political and intellectual comradeship has challenged and sustained me in my work.

In writing this book I have incurred a number of institutional debts. Funding for the doctoral thesis was provided by the Rhodes Trust and the Centre for International Studies at the Department of Politics & International Relations, University of Oxford. While at Oxford, Balliol and University Colleges were inspiring and congenial places in which to live and work. I am very grateful to my colleagues and students at the Centre for International Studies & Diplomacy, School of Oriental & African Studies, in whom I have found a lively and vibrant intellectual community in which to pursue my interests. I would particularly like to thank Par Engstrom and Amaia Sanchez-Cacicedo, whose tremendous teaching assistance over the academic year 2008–9 gave me the time and space within which to complete this book.

Elizabeth Angell, Antara Datta, Sameen Gauhar, Niharika Gupta, Sinead King, Nakul Krishna, Alex Luck, Niall O'Dea, Tamson Pietsch, Tina Piper, Bilal Siddiqi, Francois Tanguay-Renaud, Alice Wright, and the members of the 'lenjgang' deserve thanks in many different capacities as friends, critics, and family-away-from-family. Meeto Malik was enthusiastic about various aspects of this book, introducing me to people in Oxford with whom I could talk about my work and spending several hours on the telephone in Delhi one afternoon in the summer of 2005, attempting to do the same in India. Her work on historical syncretism in North India has a strong political resonance with my interest in contemporary post-colonial cosmopolitanism. She is deeply missed.

I owe my curiosity about the people and places in this book to my parents, who brought the world into our home in all sorts of ways. My father finds it difficult to nap without the sound of the news droning in the background, and is as exercised by events in the West Bank as by those in West Bengal. My mother seems to have had a world-atlas-buying fetish when my sister and I were children. I dedicate this book to them.

Abbreviations

ACIEZ	Alianza Campesina Independiente Emiliano Zapata (Emiliano Zapata Independent Peasant Alliance)
AMIS	African Union Mission in Sudan
ATTAC	Association pour la taxation des transactions pour l'aide aux citoyens
AU	African Union
BJP	Bharatiya Janata Party
BKU	Bharatiya Kisan Union
CEDAW	Convention on the Elimination of all forms of Discrimination Against Women
CERD	Convention on the Elimination of all forms of Racial Discrimination
Comintern	Communist International
EZLN	Ejército Zapatista de Liberacion Nacional (Zapatista Army of National Liberation)
FLN	Front de Libération Nationale
FRY	Federal Republic of Yugoslavia
GALA	Gay and Lesbian Alliance
GALHA	Gay and Lesbian Humanist Association
HIPC	Heavily Indebted Poor Countries
HRW	Human Rights Watch
ICC	International Criminal Court
ICCSR	Intercontinental Caravan of Solidarity and Resistance
ICISS	International Commission on Intervention and State Sovereignty
IFI	International financial institutions
IGLHRC	International Gay and Lesbian Human Rights Commission
ILGA	International Lesbian, Gay, Bisexual, Trans and Intersex Association
IMF	International Monetary Fund
KRRS	Karnataka Rajya Raitha Sangha (Karnataka State Farmers' Association)
LGBT	Lesbian, gay, bisexual, and transgendered
MCB	Muslim Council of Britain
MSM	Men who have sex with men
MUSLA	Makerere University Students' Lesbian Association

NAFTA	North Atlantic Free Trade Agreement
NAM	Non-Aligned Movement
NATO	North Atlantic Treaty Organization
NGLTF	National Gay and Lesbian Task Force
NGO	Non-governmental organization
NIEO	New International Economic Order
NSM	New social movement
OAU	Organization of African Unity
OECD	Organisation for Economic Co-operation and Development
OPEC	Organization of Petroleum Exporting Countries
PGA	Peoples' Global Action
PLO	Palestinian Liberation Organization
PRI	Partido Revolucionario Institucional
PT	Partido dos Trabalhadores
SADC	Southern African Development Community
SMR	Suicide mortality rate
SMUG	Sexual Minorities Uganda
SS	Shetkari Sangathan
WSF	World Social Forum

1

Introduction

> The clerk in my uncle's office, who grew up as our neighbour in Dariya Mahal 3, tells me that Dariya Mahal 2 is 'cosmopolitan.' This is how the real estate brokers of Nepean Sea Road describe a building that is not Gujarati-dominated. For a Gujarati, this is not a term of approval. 'Cosmopolitan' means the whole world except Gujaratis and Marwaris. It includes Sindhis, Punjabis, Bengalis, Catholics, and God knows who else. Nonvegetarians, Divorcees. Growing up, I was always fascinated by the 'cosmopolitan' families. I thought cosmopolitan girls more beautiful, beyond my reach.
>
> Suketu Mehta, *Maximum City: Bombay Lost and Found* (2004)

1.1 AN AUTOBIOGRAPHY AND ANATOMY OF THIS BOOK

On 15 February 2003, like millions of people all over the world, I marched on the streets of London to express my outrage at the Bush and Blair governments' eagerness to go to war in Iraq. There was something marvellously appropriate about chanting 'no more wars for oil' as we marched between Whitehall's impassive public buildings, visible testaments to an empire built on Indian indigo and Cairo cotton, on Ghanaian gold and Malayan rubber, on weavers' thumbs and opium wars. And yet the world does not stay the same. As an Indian in Britain, I was astonished and moved by the ferocity of the anti-imperial sentiment that was very much in evidence around me. In retrospect, the weeks and months of meetings, demonstrations, and direct actions that preceded the big march have come to feel like a moment in which I had begun to assimilate into a very particular segment of British society that felt tangibly post-imperial, even as the British state was embarking upon what many of us saw as a deeply imperialist venture.

But I was also filled with a sense of disquiet in February 2003. The slogans and chants on the left focused relentlessly on Bush, Blair, and the evils of Western imperialism. Few were talking about the brutality of Saddam Hussein's regime or what was to be done about it. Indeed, I had long been struck by the tacit alliance between a politically correct Western left, so ashamed of the crimes of Western imperialism that it found itself incapable of denouncing the actions of Third World regimes, and a hyper-defensive Third World mentality, exemplified by the nationalist historiography that suffused the pages of standard Indian history textbooks in which all the ills of the country were blamed on Western imperialism. Yet if few of the protesters were talking about human rights abuses in Iraq—of which the gassing of the Kurds in Halabja in 1988 is perhaps the most emblematic event—in the corridors of power in Whitehall and the White House, there was talk of little else. Written out of their narrative was the shameful record of official Western knowledge, silence, and complicity in these events and a complete lack of irony over the fifteen-year delay in any meaningful Western response to them.[1]

It seemed as if the stories told by voices of both power and resistance were informed by highly selective geographies and histories of culpability. Hardt and Negri have suggested that 'the first question of political philosophy today is not if or even why there will be resistance and rebellion, but rather how to determine the enemy against which to rebel'.[2] The public discourse of February 2003 suggested to me that no one had place for more than one enemy at any given time.

But what if things are more complicated, less dichotomous? Are the binary distinctions that we routinely draw—between proletariat and capital, multitude and empire, 'us' and 'them' in an array of different contexts—really up to the task of describing a world in which the evils and misfortunes of human rights abuse and bad governance may be the result of a more complex topography of agents linked to one another across territorial and non-territorial boundaries? What sorts of protest imaginaries and sensibilities might be more appropriate to this more complex world? Who has thought about this productively?

These concerns about the nature and focus of political resistance triggered by the events of early 2003 intersected with a number of theoretical questions that I had been puzzling over. Perhaps the most remarkable development in international relations in the previous decade had been the increasing proclivity of the 'international community' to intervene in the affairs of sovereign states if they were perceived as being unable or unwilling to protect the human rights of their citizens. As the roll-call of intervention in the 1990s suggested, this phenomenon typically took the form of Western states intervening in the putatively dysfunctional 'rogue' or 'failed' states of the Third

World. These interventions dramatically reconceptualized the meaning of sovereignty, which had long been understood as inviolable. Third World sovereignty began to be seen as problematic, functioning as a potentially repressive shield behind which states were able to kill, torture, and otherwise manipulate their citizens with impunity. The practice of humanitarian intervention and associated efforts to promulgate a norm of 'responsibility to protect' sought to reconstruct sovereignty as being contingent on the ability and willingness of states to protect the human rights of their citizens.[3]

Official Third World responses to the discourse of humanitarian intervention have been varied. While it is difficult to discern clear patterns in the responses of individual states to particular episodes of intervention, the collective response to the possibility of an emerging norm of intervention—as articulated through organizations such as the Non-Aligned Movement (NAM)—has been one of unremitting hostility. Many Third World states view intervention in their sovereignty as contemporary manifestations of imperialism and colonialism. By all indications, the perceived abuse and cynical manipulation of humanitarian justifications for the 2003 war on Iraq has set back prospects for wider acceptance of a norm of 'responsibility to protect', making its invocation in ongoing crises, such as the one unfolding in Darfur at the time of writing, deeply controversial and contested.[4]

Narratives of humanitarian intervention tend to focus on violations of particular kinds of rights—typically civil and political rights, which are construed as more fundamental than other sorts of rights such as subsistence rights.[5] My own practical political experiences as a researcher and activist with non-governmental organizations (NGOs) and social movements in India in the late 1990s suggested that these actors were rather more concerned with economic and social rights.[6] Perhaps this was because despite the guarantee of civil and political liberties by the Indian Constitution, economic and social deprivation tended to empty these of any meaningful content, rendering them formalistic and toothless. Be that as it may, these organizations and movements (many of which have now coalesced in the National Alliance of Peoples' Movements) tended to focus on the livelihood insecurities engendered by the Indian state's project of economic liberalization in the 1990s, as well as the more long-running phenomenon of development-induced displacement. In the course of my brief association with these actors, I was struck by what appeared to be a somewhat bifurcated attitude towards sovereignty. On the one hand, having themselves been victims of repression unleashed by the neo-liberal state, they were critical of unfettered sovereignty. On the other hand, they seemed desirous of a state that was robust enough to be able to stand up to, and refuse, the dictates of powerful international financial institutions (IFIs) such as the International Monetary Fund (IMF) and the World Bank, whose 'structural adjustment' prescriptions had stripped away the minimalist safety nets of overwhelmed but aspiring welfare states. They were also keen that their governments resist the demands of multinational corporations for increasingly lax labour and environmental regulation. This ambiguous stance on sovereignty was not experienced as a contradiction, given that the state was seen as the key implementing agent of the neo-liberal project unleashed by the Bretton Woods institutions and powerful donor states. 'Anti-globalization' social movements aimed to wrest the state away from neo-liberal capital so as to ensure that its coercive potential was utilized for welfare ends. Yet their awareness that the state was always vulnerable to capture by opposing special interests gave them an antipathy towards states with overdeveloped coercive abilities.

The different views on sovereignty expressed in each of the positions sketched above might be seen as a conversation about boundaries and what they signify. Attitudes towards boundaries are often premised on assumptions about interests and about the locus of threats to those interests. In the discourse of humanitarian intervention, the interests to be protected are those of individuals and these interests are seen to be threatened most seriously by the Third World state; hence the construction of sovereignty as contingent on the performance of 'good governance'. In the official Third World response to this discourse, it is states whose interests have to be protected from the neo-imperial incursions of other powerful states and institutions; hence the construction of sovereignty as inviolable. The social movements that I had occasion to observe were concerned about people—both as individuals and communities—whose interests were seen to be threatened both by the state and by powerful external actors; hence the desire for neither overly strong nor weak states, but for robust and representative ones.

This uncertain attitude towards sovereignty came back to me as I marched on 15 February, mulling over the plight of the Kurds who seemed to owe their misfortunes both to the actions of Saddam Hussein's regime and to the acquiescence and active connivance of Western governments that supported him as the lesser of two evils through the long and brutal war between Iraq and Iran from 1980 to 1988.[7] In contrast to the simplistic imaginaries of threat that underwrote cosmopolitan and Third World statist attitudes towards sovereignty, it seemed to me more reasonable to assume that threats to human rights emanated both from outside the state and from the state itself. Yet if this were the case, how ought sovereignty and boundaries to be conceived? More fundamentally, *what sort of protest sensibility would be appropriate to a world in which there is no singular locus of threat?* This is the question at the heart of this book.

Let me be clear about what I mean by a 'protest sensibility'. The *Oxford English Dictionary* defines 'sensibility' as the 'power or faculty of feeling, capacity of sensation and emotion as distinguished from cognition and will'.[8] T. S. Eliot used the phrase 'dissociation of sensibility' to refer to a separation of thought from feeling, which he held to be first manifested in the poetry of the late seventeenth century.[9] In many ways, Jane Austen's *Sense and Sensibility* is a critique of such a rigid separation, particularly in the character of Elinor in whom a depth of feeling is almost always concealed and rationalized behind a visage of eminent good sense.[10] Following Austen, my usage does not distinguish thought from feeling quite so starkly but is interested in the feelings that lurk beneath or behind thoughts, in the inarticulate assumptions, prejudices, and preconceptions that underpin normative world views. I have already alluded to some of these in contrasting the attitudes of advocates of humanitarian intervention, Third World states, and social movements. This is a book about the mindsets, orientations, and background assumptions of political protest in the Third World. It does not purport to offer specific guidance on what the goals and forms of protest ought to be in particular contexts. Its analytical ambition is to excavate and problematize the assumptions that inform attitudes towards the boundaries of Third World states. Its normative ambition is to call for a more nuanced and creative approach to Third World sovereignty that takes into account the dispersed nature of threats to human rights in the Third World.

The book proceeds in two parts. Part I is a critical exploration of two dominant ways of thinking about boundaries.[11] The first of these is cosmopolitanism, which considers individuals to be the ultimate units of moral and political concern and moreover regards all individuals as being of equal moral worth in the eyes of all others.[12] This has a number of implications for international relations, of which two in particular are worth noting. The first is that boundaries are not morally significant and worthy of respect in themselves, but might become so if they are of significance to individuals; this means that the inviolability of boundaries is contingent on their contribution to the welfare of individuals (the position taken by contemporary advocates of humanitarian intervention and, in a modified form, the 'responsibility to protect'). A second implication of cosmopolitanism is that in the choice of particular policies or institutional arrangements, the interests of all individuals who might be affected by such arrangements ought to be weighed equally (e.g., in determining its policy on climate change, the US government ought to place the welfare of Bangladeshis who might be impacted by rising sea levels on a par with that of its own citizens who might be adversely affected by the economic-growth-reducing impacts of efforts to mitigate climate change).[13]

A second dominant way of thinking about boundaries is provided by communitarians, who see community as a significant source of value in moral and political life. In their world view, communal boundaries are morally significant in themselves because life as we know it would be inconceivable without communal affiliations.[14] Communitarians see intervention in the affairs of political communities as undermining self-determination.[15] They also regard the cosmopolitan injunction to treat all individuals equally, regardless of communal membership, as being both undesirable and infeasible. For communitarians, part of what it means to belong to a community is to accord greater priority to the claims of fellow members.[16] In the context of state policy, this means that it is permissible to prioritize the claims of citizens over those of strangers.

I shall define and contrast these antagonistic world views in greater detail in sections 1.2 and 1.3 of this chapter. Suffice it to say that both sides in this debate address the question 'to whom is justice owed?'. Their contrasting responses might be understood as exercises in the justification of practices of inclusion and exclusion. Such practices are central to all aspects of political life. Governments choosing from amongst a set of policy options must evaluate the likely impacts of those options on people, and in doing so must decide whether to give equal consideration to the consequences of their policies for citizens and non-citizens. Protesters resisting the decisions of governments must decide whom they are fighting for and whom they will affiliate with. Cosmopolitan and communitarian commitments will be evident in all such decisions. As such, we should regard these contrasting views on the scope of justice as vocabularies in which state power is exercised and resisted.

The field of international normative theory has been marked by a sort of grand debate between partisans of these antagonistic world views. Part I of this book expresses dissatisfaction with both sides of this debate, focusing particularly on the ways in which these world views are expressed in the behaviour of states. One strand of the critique explores the 'sensibility' of hegemonic discourses of cosmopolitanism and communitarianism—the silences, elisions, and inarticulate assumptions particularly in the form of the spatial imaginaries of threat that underpin these different world views. Simplifying considerably for now, from a cosmopolitan perspective, the major threats to human rights in the Third World are often assumed to be domestic and to emanate from the Third World state. Conversely, the 'international' is a sanitized space populated by benevolent, knowledgeable, and heroic actors that are called upon to rescue dysfunctional states in the Third World from the consequences of their own decisions. Boundaries are seen as an inconvenience that ought not to be permitted to impede this noble mission. In the

Third World nationalist world view, the international is a predatory neo-imperialist realm against which the domestic must defend itself. Boundaries must be strengthened to protect the domestic against the depredations of the international. I have caricatured both positions of course, but putting them starkly in this fashion can help us to see the more subtle ways in which they are inscribed in the thought and practice of political actors.

A second strand of critique moves beyond unspoken assumptions to focus on the ways in which cosmopolitanism and communitarianism are invoked to justify the exercise of power by states, demonstrating the coercive logics inherent in both these world views. Chapter 2 analyses the role that cosmopolitanism plays in legitimating Western hegemony through the justifications it offers for two of the most intrusive practices vis-à-vis the Third World—humanitarian intervention and economic conditionality. It explores the increasingly close relationship between cosmopolitanism and power, demonstrating the extent to which the contemporary praxis of cosmopolitanism relies on, and reinforces, the existing distribution of power in the international system. Chapter 3 looks at the communitarian ideas underpinning state- and nation-building projects in the Third World. It demonstrates how and why the imperatives of community construction are used to justify the repressive behaviour of the Third World state. Cumulatively, Part I of the book is intended to make the case for a protest sensibility that is critical of hegemonic understandings of both cosmopolitanism and communitarianism.

Part II is a series of sketches of what protest sensibilities that are critical of both cosmopolitanism and communitarianism might look like.[17] The three chapters in Part II study different kinds of resistance anchored on different sorts of identities: nation, class, and gender. Chapter 4 explores the political thinking of four writers (James Joyce, Rabindranath Tagore, Edward Said, and Frantz Fanon), who were differently associated with anti-colonial nationalist movements at the same time as they were fierce critics of nationalism. Chapter 5 analyses the relationship between the universalist consciousness of class and particularist articulations of nation in the political activism of two 'anti-globalization' movements (the Zapatistas in Chiapas, Mexico, and the Karnataka State Farmers' Association in India). Chapter 6 explores hierarchies of nationality, race, and class in an emerging global queer rights discourse, with a focus on the dilemmas of queer activism in the Third World and amongst ethnic minorities in the West against the backdrop of the ongoing 'war on terror'.

It is difficult to generalize across these very different types of resistance, particularly given that the subjects of analysis occupy different temporal and socio-political locations. Nonetheless, what holds this part of the book together is the idea that the political thinking of the actors studied is underpinned by more complex spatial imaginaries of threat than those that typically animate hegemonic discourses of cosmopolitanism and communitarianism. These actors assume that threats to vital interests emanate from both outside and inside the nation-states with which they identity. This awareness induces a dual movement—a communitarian impulse to construct unified national political agency with a view to confronting an external threat, and a cosmopolitan inclination to deconstruct that community in an effort to civilize its exercise of disciplinary power vis-à-vis its own members. One might say that the complexity of their understanding of the locus of threat induces them to occupy a space between cosmopolitanism and nationalism.[18] The normative project of this book is to suggest that the unresolved tension between cosmopolitanism and nationalism in their thought and practice is constitutive of a protest sensibility appropriate to our time, given the architecture of threat described in Part I.

In addition to these core lines of argument, the book has a number of subsidiary themes. The most important of these is a concern to interrogate the relevance of cosmopolitanism to the articulation of protest in the Third World. Indeed this question constitutes the point of departure for the book. There are several reasons for beginning from here. For anyone interested in human rights there is something intuitively attractive about cosmopolitanism as a way of thinking about boundaries, precisely because it accords the interests of individuals a higher moral priority than those of other entities or institutions. Cosmopolitanism takes seriously the notion that the interests of individuals can sometimes be threatened by the groups or institutions to which they belong and which they might themselves normally value. This is a normative position that, in the context of Iraq, would have placed the interests of the victims of Saddam Hussein's regime at the heart of any account of what needed to be done. But as the subsequent course of the international community's engagement with Iraq demonstrates, cosmopolitan discourses have also been picked up by powerful actors in the international system and deployed at particular times for particular purposes, in ways that have not always prioritized the interests of individuals on whose behalf they purport to act. In addition, critics have lampooned cosmopolitanism as an elite perspective, as a mindset that is the prerogative of the privileged. The first two chapters of the book therefore set out to explore the ambiguous appeal of cosmopolitanism for the Third World.

This chapter does five things. First, in section 1.2, it introduces the idea of cosmopolitanism as it is conventionally understood, both in an everyday sense and in the literature of political philosophy and the social sciences. Second, in section 1.3, it maps normative thinking in international relations with a view to locating cosmopolitanism in relation to its antonyms. This mapping exercise is conducted around one of the central questions of international normative theory: 'to whom is justice owed?'. The cosmopolitan response to this question is 'everyone'. Against this are a number of positions that argue for a more limited conception of the scope of justice and defend the moral significance of boundaries that demarcate this scope. After sketching the contours of this debate briefly, I endeavour to relate the debate over the scope of justice to problems of articulation of political protest. In doing so, I explain why the cosmopolitan–communitarian dichotomy is of central importance to the argument of the book—even though the contestation of this dichotomy is one of its major endeavours. Section 1.4 commences a prima facie exploration of a key subsidiary theme, namely whether subaltern resistance tends to be informed by cosmopolitan or communitarian sensibilities. Section 1.5 defines and defends an adjectival category used throughout the book: 'Third World'. Finally, section 1.6 discusses some important methodological choices and influences.

1.2 CONCEPTIONS OF COSMOPOLITANISM: THE EVERYDAY AND THE ESOTERIC

Suketu Mehta's racy account of his return to the city of his youth begins, appropriately enough, with a vignette about house-hunting. Yet house-hunting is a rather ironic note on which to begin a discussion of cosmopolitanism. Diogenes the Cynic whose apocryphal utterance 'I am a citizen of the whole world' is credited with 'inventing' cosmopolitanism, cared little for where he lived, sleeping out of doors even in cold weather, and spending much of his life in a tub. For the Gujaratis of Dariya Mahal, however, home is a temple, its sanctity guarded by means of an elaborate set of understandings about purity and pollution. Cosmopolitanism at home is a threat. It portends the invasion of all sorts of destructive external influences, bringing in its wake miscegenation, meat eating, and mishmash. This outside world fascinates the adolescent Mehta. For him, 'cosmopolitan' girls are unattainable, in a different class. This cosmopolitanism reeks of sophistication and glamour. It is a world of exotic cocktails and magazines with leggy blondes on glossy covers. It is elite, well travelled, and jet-setting. Yet in addition to being all of these things, for the non-Gujaratis[19] of the world that Mehta describes, whatever their class—for the Bombay that is peopled by the likes of Salman Rushdie's Everyman Saleem Sinai, or the Parsi residents of Rohinton Mistry's Firozsha Baag, for Christians, Sikhs, Buddhists, Jains, and the last remaining Bene Israel, for non-vegetarians and divorcees—cosmopolitanism is a refuge, an ethic that permits a sense of belonging in a place that no one fully owns. It is an ethic that has broken down with frightening consequences in the past—but even then, not entirely, so that Hindu householders have still hidden their Muslim neighbours from bloodthirsty mobs. Sometimes in Bombay, this quotidian cosmopolitanism has made the difference between life and death.

The term 'cosmopolitanism' might be understood as an instance of what W. B. Gallie called an 'essentially contested concept'.[20] According to Gallie, essentially contested concepts are appraisive or value-laden, internally complex in the sense that they have a number of constituent elements that are variously describable and differently valued by rival users of the concept, and open to modification in the light of changing circumstances. The essential contestedness of cosmopolitanism might be traced to two ideas lying at the heart of the concept that tend to be variously emphasized in its different usages. The first of these is universality or the quality of being all-embracing. This is the sense in which John Stuart Mill noted that 'capital is becoming more and more cosmopolitan'.[21] In almost identical terms in the very same year, his contemporary Karl Marx observed that the bourgeoisie had, through its exploitation of the world market, 'given a cosmopolitan character to production and consumption in every country'.[22] The second element of the concept of cosmopolitanism is egalitarianism. When Diogenes declared himself to be a citizen of the world, he was not describing an existing state of affairs so much as expressing a moral aspiration of belonging to an imagined political community that regarded all human beings as members of equal standing in a universal polity. Derived from the Greek words *cosmos* (world) and *polis* (city, people, citizenry), the term 'cosmopolitan' was first uttered by Stoic and Cynic philosophers to describe such a moral stance rooted in a belief in the equal worth of humanity in all persons, in virtue of their capacity for reason. This was to be accompanied, or reinforced, by an affective attitude of universal love for humanity as a whole, regardless of the particular polis of which one claimed membership.[23]

A number of usages of cosmopolitanism imply both the dimensions of universality and egalitarianism, although these are manifested in different ways and accorded varying weight in different usages. For instance, both universality and egalitarianism tend to be implied in the use of the term to describe particular conceptions of world moral or political community— whether these take the form of a world state, or a model of relations between members of the world's actually existing political communities. Both dimensions are also implied in the occasional use of the term as a rough analogue to 'multiculturalism' (e.g. 'Bombay is a cosmopolitan city'). As an ethic that insists on the possibility of political coexistence and cooperation despite cultural difference, multiculturalism aims at fostering egalitarian relations between all cultures encompassed by a polity. But in contrast to usages of cosmopolitanism that imply both universality and egalitarianism, the adjectival form 'cosmopolitan' has also come to acquire the connotation of worldliness, of being 'widely diffused over the globe; found in all or many countries'.[24] To be cosmopolitan is to be worldly-wise or to know about the world as a whole. In this guise, the term might attach as easily to an imperial administrator, a frequent-flying business executive, or a gap-year backpacker as to an international drug smuggler, an al-Qaeda operative, or a United Nations employee. In such usages, the descriptive dimension of universality—or, perhaps more accurately, of cross-border experience and knowledge—seems to have edged out any normative content implied in other usages of the term.

We might therefore distinguish between a *normative* usage of the term cosmopolitanism and a more *empirical–analytic* usage intended to describe phenomena of cross-border interaction and identity formation.[25] While normative cosmopolitanism is a moral view of how relations between all human beings ought to be ordered, empirical–analytic cosmopolitanism describes the cross-border ontologies that are brought into being by all manner of human activity—conquest and commerce being perhaps the most significant.[26] It would be a mistake to assume that these ontologies are of recent provenance. As Ulrich Beck notes, 'the (forced) mixing of cultures is nothing new in world history; on the contrary, it has been the rule through all the plunder and conquests, the migrations, slave trade and colonisation, ethnic cleansing, settlements and expulsions'.[27] In a similar vein, the editors of a recent collection of essays, seeking to move from a normative to a more epistemological usage of the term 'cosmopolitanism', frame their task as one of 'look[ing] at the world across time and space [to] see how people have thought and acted beyond the local'.[28] This collection treats phenomena such as the circulation of Sanskrit literature from Central Asia to the South China Sea in the pre-colonial era, or the melange of architectural styles that characterized pre-war Shanghai, as cosmopolitan practices. 'Cosmopolitanism' in this sense refers to the potentially infinite 'ways of living at home abroad or abroad at home'[29] that have developed as a result of human migration and the global circulatory networks of goods and ideas that have developed in conjunction with these movements.

Differences between normative and empirical cosmopolitanism notwithstanding, there are a number of ways in which the two may be linked. It *may* be the case that the cosmopolitanization of culture, even if occasioned by some initial act of coercion, fosters a greater habituation to—possibly even respect for—cultural difference and diversity. 'Multiculturalism', for example, has been a normative accommodative response by Western liberal democracies to the influx of immigrants from their former overseas colonial empires. Or as Beck notes, the cosmopolitanization of risk occasioned by increasing interdependence *might* generate the pressure to cooperate in the fashioning of cosmopolitan norms and regimes.[30] While remaining sensitive to these potential connections, this book is concerned chiefly with normative cosmopolitanism.

In an essay entitled 'Conceptions of Cosmopolitanism', Samuel Scheffler identifies two strands in cosmopolitan thinking, both of which may be seen to have explicit normative commitments.[31] First, cosmopolitanism as a doctrine about justice posits that the scope of justice ought to be universal. It rejects more particular views (discussed in section 1.3), which hold as a matter of principle that norms of justice cannot apply universally but only within bounded groups comprising some subset of the global population.[32] As I have already mentioned, in the cosmopolitan world view, boundaries are morally arbitrary and have no intrinsic significance. Second, cosmopolitanism as a doctrine about culture and the self posits that the well-being, identity, or capacity for effective human agency of individuals does not require membership in a determinate cultural group whose boundaries are clear and whose stability and cohesion are secure. Instead, cultures are seen to be constantly in flux, influenced by, and in their turn influencing, other cultures. At first glance this cultural conception of cosmopolitanism might appear to be a manifestation of empirical–analytic cosmopolitanism discussed above. Yet it is crucial to recognize that Scheffler's second strand of cosmopolitanism is both a descriptive view of how cultures evolve (all cultures simply *are* cosmopolitan mixtures, evolving in interaction with other cultures, so that we are all 'naturally' hybrid and it is purification that is taught and imposed[33]) and a normative view of how they ought to evolve (see for instance some of the more explicitly celebratory writing on cultural miscegenation[34]).

Again, it is possible to see potential (but not inevitable) connections between normative views about justice and culture. For example, it is precisely because many critics of cosmopolitanism see tradition, social context, and culture as the source of moral and political reasoning *and* because they (implicitly) see cultures as discrete entities boxed off from one other, that they deny the possibility of universal norms of justice.[35] But equally it is possible to identify views that see culture as the source of some, but not all, norms of justice, thereby endorsing a thin universalism but insisting on the cultural specificity of other standards of justice.[36] Other normative world views might see justice and culture as essentially distinct concerns. Multicultural nationalists, for example, would appear to be cosmopolitan on the question of culture, but not justice. Given the possible linkages between thinking about culture and justice, this book is interested in both the cultural and justice-oriented strands of normative cosmopolitanism and in the frequently difficult relationship between the two (this theme is central to chapter 4).

If culture serves as a source of norms about justice, we might expect a variety of cosmopolitan conceptions of justice, reflecting the diversity of cultures that exist in the world. Many Western writers claim that three elements are shared by all cosmopolitan positions: individualism (the ultimate units of concern are individual human beings), universalism (the status of ultimate unit of concern attaches to every human being equally regardless of the groups to which they belong), and generality (individuals are ultimate units of concern, equally, for everyone).[37] Yet in its very individualism, this is a peculiarly liberal form of cosmopolitanism that cannot claim to exhaust cosmopolitan conceptions of justice. Consider for example the possibility of 'socialist cosmopolitanism',[38] for which the unit of analysis is class, and the privileged unit of concern the proletariat class, but whose ultimate telos is quintessentially cosmopolitan in its vision of a classless society open to all. Liberalism and socialism, being of Western provenance, cannot claim to monopolize cosmopolitan conceptions of justice. Writing about Indian conceptions of order and justice, Kanti Bajpai mentions both 'Gandhian cosmopolitanism'[39] (a world view in which individuals are the irreducible subjects of social and political life, whose needs must be met in radically decentralized fashion through the devolution of power to small community governments) and a more chauvinistic 'Hindu notion of cosmopolitan justice'[40] (a world order in which relations between distinct states or civilizations would be regulated by Hindu dharmic rules of behaviour, given the assumed superiority of Hindu culture). In a similar review of Islamic perspectives on international society, Sohail Hashmi distinguishes 'Islamic cosmopolitanism' from more statist and internationalist varieties of Muslim thought.[41]

Even this brief survey suggests a wide and often unacknowledged diversity of cosmopolitan conceptions of justice, which can be seen as such because the norms of justice that they posit transcend the state system and are universal in their scope (albeit unevenly egalitarian in their content). They describe what Hedley Bull would have called 'world orders' of different kinds, as distinct from an 'international order' in which the primary units of membership are states.[42] While they all share a universal scope or range of concern, they differ with respect to the content of that concern. Specifically, the ultimate units of concern are different in each case (individuals, classes, civilizations) and different sorts of relations are posited between those units (hierarchical and non-hierarchical). Strictly speaking, the term cosmopolis should be understood as signifying simply a universal polity, with the nature of relations within that polity being described by a qualifying adjective (liberal, socialist, Hindu, Islamic, etc.).

This book engages primarily with liberal cosmopolitanism. There are a number of reasons for this focus. Liberalism as a political philosophy is globally hegemonic, both in the sense that the current international order is heavily informed and structured by liberal principles,[43] and in the sense that its assumptions dominate much of the social science literature particularly on issues of globalization.[44] Within the academy, champions of liberal cosmopolitanism have claimed for it an extraordinary emancipatory potential on the basis of its promises of universal inclusion and egalitarianism. But critics have lampooned it as an elitist and even imperial perspective. In the world at large, liberal cosmopolitan discourses have underpinned practices such as humanitarian intervention and economic conditionality that have occasioned much controversy.[45] Supporters justify them as exercises in rescue, liberating vast numbers from the misfortunes of bad governance; critics point to the allegedly devastating consequences of such practices. These disagreements will be developed in more detail in the rest of this introduction and chapter 2, but their very existence invites us to critically interrogate the emancipatory claims of liberal cosmopolitanism. One way of doing so would be to ask whether liberal cosmopolitanism offers a vocabulary in which the globally most disadvantaged might advance their claims.

1.3 COSMOPOLITANISM AND ITS OTHERS

Having considered the range of meanings with which cosmopolitanism has become encrusted both in everyday language and in the literature of political philosophy and the social sciences, it is appropriate to focus more specifically on what liberal cosmopolitanism has to say about questions of justice. This is best done by contrasting it with the philosophical positions against which its claims are typically advanced. As I mentioned at the start of this chapter, this book is a critical examination of two dominant ways of thinking about boundaries: cosmopolitanism and communitarianism. But communitarians are not the only critics of cosmopolitanism. This section therefore attempts to map the field of international normative theory, before going on to explain why the cosmopolitan–communitarian dichotomy is central to the book's concerns about the articulation of political protest.

Recall that the debate between cosmopolitanism and its antagonists is one about the scope of justice. It addresses the question 'to whom is justice owed?'. For cosmopolitans the answer to that question is 'everyone'. The scope of justice is universal. Practically speaking this means, amongst other things, that boundaries are only of contingent significance and that in the choice of policies or institutional arrangements, all individuals who might be affected ought to be weighed equally regardless of the communities to which they might belong. Cosmopolitan accounts of justice are impartial, universalist, individualist, and egalitarian. But while cosmopolitans agree that everyone is due the same concern, they disagree amongst themselves about the foundational basis for this belief and advance different accounts of the moral minima that all are due. At least three kinds of cosmopolitan positions can be distinguished.

For utilitarians, the morally most worthy courses of action are those that promote the greatest happiness for the greatest number. Consequences or outcomes, rather than intentions or fidelity to categorical principles, are the basis of moral judgment here. In making choices about what policies to pursue, individuals are undifferentiated in the sense that no individual's utility is to count for more or less than that of any other.[46]

Entitlement-based theories seek to provide an account of what individuals are due in virtue of their humanity. In this category we find theories of basic rights that ground such rights on the claim that they protect human interests that are sufficiently weighty from a moral point of view to justify imposing duties on all other individuals to promote them. Such rights are basic in the sense that their fulfilment is a precondition for the enjoyment of all other rights.[47] Other entitlement theories prefer to begin with duties rather than rights, arguing that rights tend to be meaningless unless they specify the allocation of their counterpart obligations. Such theories often imply that some kinds of obligations are more easily allocated than others, thereby appearing to set up a hierarchy of corresponding rights.[48] A third variant of entitlement theory is the neo-Aristotelian capabilities approach, which attempts to articulate a bare minimum conception of the good life through an intuitive grasp of the goods that are required for human flourishing.[49]

Social contractarian cosmopolitan approaches envisage society as a contract for mutual advantage that human beings will enter into when the 'circumstances of justice' obtain (i.e. when people are so placed that it makes sense for them to exit the state of nature and make a compact for mutual advantage). As originally devised by John Rawls, such approaches take the form of a thought experiment in which human beings are imagined to contract behind a 'veil of ignorance'—a state of mind in which they are divested of knowledge of morally arbitrary characteristics such as race, gender, wealth, education, etc. The theory argues that the principles resulting from such a bargain would be just, given its egalitarian starting point and fair procedure.[50] Although Rawls himself was not a cosmopolitan, his work has been taken in a cosmopolitan direction by theorists arguing that nationality ought to be considered a morally arbitrary characteristic, from which contracting individuals should abstract themselves.[51] Global contractarians argue that the result of such a procedure would be the endorsement of Rawls's difference principle (first articulated in a domestic context) on a global scale, so that global inequalities would be permissible only if they were to the benefit of the least advantaged.

Each of these positions is far more complex than I have been able to do justice to here. Suffice it to say that while these theories offer distinct responses to the questions of what justice entails and why, they share a consensus on the issue of whom justice is owed to: the scope of justice, in their view, is universal. Ranged against this view are a number of positions that insist on a more limited scope of justice. Again, while there is much to distinguish them from one another, they converge on the notion that boundaries are not morally arbitrary features of political life and that it is permissible (even obligatory, in stronger versions of the argument) to accord ethical priority to members of one's community over outsiders. I shall sketch some of these positions briefly before focusing more specifically on those that are relevant to this book.

First, there are communitarians, for whom the norms, traditions, and values of a community are a source of meaning in ethical and political life, generating a web of obligations and a sense of justice. Such a view might stem from a methodological claim about the importance of tradition and social context for moral and political reasoning, from an ontological claim about the inescapably social and embedded nature of the self, or from a normative claim about the value of community.[52] Shades of all three are visible in the work of Michael Walzer, who sees the enterprise of moral argumentation as that of providing an account of the actually existing morality 'because it is only by virtue of its existence that we exist as the moral beings we are'.[53] In this vein, Walzer argues that distributive justice is relative to 'shared social meanings' associated with the goods to be distributed. If we understand what the good is and what it means to those for whom it is a good, we will understand how, by whom, and for what reasons it ought to be distributed. Different goods, being invested with different social meanings, ought to be distributed for different reasons, in accordance with different procedures by different agents—for example, careers ought to be distributed to the talented, health care to the sick, and salvation to the faithful. Crucially, for Walzer, the scope of distributive justice cannot be universal because the 'shared social meanings' relative to which distribution must occur exist only within political communities.[54]

David Miller is interested in a particular kind of community—the nation—and his account of boundaries as limiting the scope of justice rests largely on the substantive functions that they perform. Like Walzer, Miller begins with the observation that people tend to have strong national allegiances and attachments and argues that philosophy ought to leave such commonplace sentiments in place unless strong reasons can be found for rejecting them.[55] In Miller's view, we have good reason to support such everyday sentiments. The sense of solidarity felt by those who share a national identity generates mutual trust among individuals who are otherwise strangers to one another, thereby making it more likely that they will cooperate in endeavours such as the resolution of collective-action problems, schemes of redistributive justice, and the practice of deliberative democracy. Partiality to fellow nationals has provided the social cement necessary to allow liberalism and social democracy to flourish.[56] Impartial accounts of justice fail to acknowledge the role of community and boundaries in enabling the enjoyment of these goods. Further, in overlooking the tight link between identification with others and willingness to make sacrifices for them, universalist accounts of justice are also psychologically over-demanding and infeasible.[57]

Philip Petit's account of republicanism as 'freedom as non-domination' similarly provides an implicit justification for community on the basis of the political goods that it enables. Arguing that republican laws must be supported by norms of civility if they are to be effective, Petit finds such civility in norms of solidarity with others and in the ability to identify with larger groups and to adopt group-level points of view.[58] Crucially, Petit's argument does not require boundaries to be drawn in a particular way (he does not, for example, argue that actually existing national or state boundaries are best placed to enable republicanism). Indeed, James Bohman has argued that in conditions of contemporary capitalism, the republican ideal of freedom as non-domination demands the creation of political community beyond the nation-state.[59]

In contrast to communitarian arguments that restrict the scope of justice because they regard community as a source of value in ethical and political life, a second category of theorists defends the differential treatment of citizens and strangers on premises that are nonetheless claimed to be impartial. I shall refer to this category of arguments as 'institutionalist' because they arise from a felt need to justify the existence of institutions that impact the life prospects of individuals in profound ways. Crucially, they take the existence of institutions such as the international state system as their point of departure. They do not ask historical or constitutive questions about how or why such institutions exist or whether they are inevitable, but see the task of normative theory as one of rendering these institutions tolerable.

Thus, Michael Blake argues that the state has to offer different guarantees to citizens from those it offers strangers, not because it cares more about the former but because it relates to these different categories of persons in different ways.[60] The state coerces its citizens through the operation of its criminal and civil law. Such coercion violates their autonomy and therefore needs to be justified in a way that might appeal to all who are coerced. One way of doing this is to demonstrate that the coercive practice in question could elicit the consent of the affected parties if they were fully reasonable. For the exercise of coercion to be justified, those affected must be able to hypothetically consent to the pattern of entitlements that result from its application. The only pattern of entitlements that could conceivably be consented to by the entirety of persons so coerced would be one in which any departures from egalitarianism served to better the position of the worst off. The state must therefore concern itself with relative equality as between all those encompassed by its coercive apparatus (citizens). It need not adopt similarly egalitarian policies towards those it does not coerce (strangers), although it would still have obligations to respect the minimal preconditions of their autonomous functioning as persons. In a similar argument, Thomas Nagel argues that citizens have obligations to address domestic inequalities in a way that they do not in respect of international inequalities, because they are joint authors of the coercively imposed apparatus of the state and of the inequalities that follow from such coercion. What is objectionable about domestic inequalities and what generates unique obligations amongst citizens to address them, is that they are all fellow participants in a collective enterprise of coercively imposed legal and political institutions that generate such inequalities.[61]

These arguments rest on the potentially controversial empirical premise that international institutions do not coerce individuals in ways that demand similar justification. For Andrea Sangiovanni, the fact of coercion is a sufficient but not a necessary condition for restricting the scope of egalitarian concern to fellow citizens. In a hypothetical non-coercive state (say, in the immediate aftermath of a terrorist attack that deprived the state temporarily of its coercive capacity), the institutions of the state would remain in need of justification, not on account of their coerciveness (now temporarily suspended), but on account of their non-voluntariness. Conversely, joint authorship is a necessary but insufficient condition for restricting the scope of egalitarian concern because we could be joint authors of the rules of a number of institutions where a concern for egalitarianism would nonetheless not be considered important (the local tennis club, for instance), simply because membership in such institutions is voluntary. Again, it is the non-voluntariness of the state that stands in need of justification. Yet a justification for restricting the scope of egalitarian concern to fellow citizens cannot be grounded solely on the non-voluntariness of the state, because subjection to

Introduction 19

international rules and institutions is also not voluntary in any meaningful sense in many cases (particularly where the costs of exclusion are prohibitive). Arguing that both coercion and voluntarism are red herrings in the debate about the scope of justice, Sangiovanni suggests instead that we owe obligations of egalitarian reciprocity to fellow citizens and residents of the state because it is they (rather than strangers) who contribute to the provision of the basic conditions and guarantees necessary for human flourishing. When it is functioning well, it is the state—rather than the global order—that provides security, access to legally regulated markets, and a system of property rights that enable individuals to develop and act upon conceptions of the good life. Such state capacities are enabled by the contributions of fellow citizens and residents. Accordingly, obligations of egalitarian concern are owed to this class of persons and no other. Like Blake and Nagel, this argument claims to be impartial in that it restricts the scope of concern, not on the basis that some individuals are of greater moral worth than others, but on grounds of reciprocity: some individuals (specifically fellow citizens and residents) contribute more to our enjoyment of the good life than others, and accordingly it is to them that we owe obligations of egalitarian concern.[62]

In addition to communitarian and institutionalist defences of the bounded scope of justice, realists might be thought to offer a third account of the restricted scope of justice. Realists espouse a scepticism of morality in international relations. In part, this scepticism arises from a belief in the relativity of all thought including utopian thought, and from a healthy suspicion that it is the special interests of the powerful that tend to masquerade as universal principles.[63] But in large part, the denial of morality in international politics also stems from the perceived security implications of the international state of anarchy. The lack of an overarching authority is thought to necessitate a perpetual preparedness for war on the part of all states. In an environment in which states constantly fear for their survival, the state's highest moral obligation is to ensure the survival of its people. When this imperative conflicts with international moral principles, the latter must give way. This is not an amoral view of international politics because it regards the state as a moral force, enabling the existence of an ethical community at the domestic level. Rather, it makes prudential action in defence of that community the supreme moral obligation.[64]

In the foregoing paragraphs, I have provided a relatively high-altitude view of the normative landscape of thinking on the scope of justice. On the one hand, I identified three major strands of cosmopolitan thinking (utilitarian, entitlement-based, and contractarian) that insist, in various ways, that the scope of justice ought to be universal. Against this, I set out a number of arguments (communitarian, institutionalist, and realist), which argue for a more restricted conception of justice. Because of its overriding preoccupation with political protest, this book interests itself in only a small part of the conversation on the scope of justice, namely the dichotomy between cosmopolitanism and communitarianism. This is interesting and relevant because of communitarianism's claim that cosmopolitanism fails to recognize the value of community in political life. Although we have looked at a number of suggestions regarding the values or goods that community enables (redistributive justice and deliberative democracy in Miller's account, republicanism in Petit's account), one potential contribution of community that has gone unmentioned so far is its role in political resistance.

The construction of community has been central to subaltern contestation of oppression and marginalization. Resistance has often been about asserting long-suppressed identities and creating safe spaces within which such identities can be expressed freely and defiantly. It might be described, in the words of Manuel Castells, as a process of 'exclusion of the excluders by the excluded'.[65] Such resistance reverses the value judgments implicit in dominant norms and institutions of society by privileging once marginalized identities, while reinscribing the boundary between privileged and marginalized identities. Indeed boundaries are valued as defensive mechanisms that keep the threat of renewed oppression at bay, securing the subaltern enclaves that have been carved out of hostile territory and protecting the hard-won freedoms of the struggle. This is a crude but plausible description of the normative thinking that informs not only nationalist resistance with a territorial dimension, but all forms of collective subaltern resistance based on identities of class, caste, gender, race, sexual orientation, etc. But if community and boundaries are such central features of the imagination of subaltern resistance, this seems to pose a challenge to cosmopolitanism's insistence on the universality of the scope of justice and the moral arbitrariness of boundaries. Or is it the case that cosmopolitanism can find a way to justify and accommodate subaltern communitarianism? Can these apparently antagonistic ways of thinking about boundaries coexist?

1.4 SUBALTERNITY, PRIVILEGE, AND THE SCOPE OF JUSTICE

These questions intersect with an ongoing debate in which many participants voice a growing scepticism of cosmopolitanism's relevance to subaltern politics. The problem, stated in a nutshell, looks something like this. Viewed as a doctrine about justice, cosmopolitanism appears to be extraordinarily hospitable to subaltern concerns; yet as a doctrine about culture, cosmopolitanism appears elitist and inaccessible to subalterns. Cosmopolitanism's appeal as a doctrine about justice comes across clearly in its promise of universal inclusion and egalitarianism, manifest in its insistence that the interests of all individuals affected by policies and institutional arrangements ought to be weighed equally regardless of their nationality and other morally arbitrary characteristics.[66] Conversely, the communitarian claim that it is permissible—even necessary—to give priority to one's compatriots appears to be a profoundly selfish one in a world of grossly unequal political communities that increasingly affect each other's life prospects in diverse ways.[67]

Yet in evaluating ethical world views, it is imperative that we do more than simply examine the prescriptive content of their norms. Reviewing the potentials of Enlightenment thinking, Fred Halliday has called for a linking of the domains of speculative political theory, which is concerned with reasserting the values of the Enlightenment, and historical sociology, which asks whether purposive action in pursuance of those values is possible within the constraints of the contemporary world.[68] In deciding whether a reassertion of Enlightenment values is warranted in our own time, it is important to consider the historical and sociological contexts in which such norms were crafted. The contemporary legitimacy of these norms may be shaped to a large extent by perceptions of their provenance and praxis. Where have they come from? What has been done in their name?

Genealogical accounts of cosmopolitan thinking that move beyond its prescriptive content to examine the socio-historical conditions of its production reveal its deep implication in the conception and practice of empire and capitalism. Anthony Pagden has argued persuasively that Cynic and Stoic ideas of cosmopolitanism emerged in tandem with the spread of Greek and Roman empires. He reminds us that Cicero was writing about cosmopolitanism at the very moment that the Roman republic was being replaced by the Roman Empire, and Zeno at the time that the independent Greek city states were being absorbed into Alexander's 'world' empire. He also remarks that one of the greatest of the Roman Stoics (Marcus Aurelius) was an emperor, while another (Seneca) advised one (Nero).[69] Similarly, he writes that it was European Enlightenment cosmopolitans who often advanced moral justifications for later exercises in European imperialism.[70] Stoic, Cynic, and Enlightenment cosmopolitanisms may have emerged in tandem with the spread of empires, partly because the ideas of universal moral community that they recommended seemed practicable at precisely those times and in those places where universal political communities (i.e. empires) were being constructed, and partly also because those ideas provided attractive justifications for projects of empire-building. The notion that ideas of cosmopolitan ethics enjoy a resurgence at those historical moments when their proponents sense the political power to take them forward, might explain a great deal about the provenance and timing of particular conceptions of cosmopolitanism. It might explain why non-Western universalist discourses seem to have emerged largely in the pre-colonial period. And, as I shall demonstrate in chapter 2, it might explain why liberal cosmopolitan discourse flourished in the unipolar moment afforded by the end of the Cold War.

In a similar vein, Craig Calhoun writes that the culture of cosmopolitanism has flourished in locations created by empire and capitalism—imperial capitals, trading cities and, in our own time, the top management of multinational corporations, consulting firms, and international organizations of all kinds.[71] Calhoun suggests that the notion of world citizenship has been championed by, or at least comes most readily to, elites who are able to experience a sense of inhabitation of the world as a whole thanks to their ability to enter and exit polities and social relations around the world, armed with visa-friendly passports and credit cards.[72] These material privileges provide an unacknowledged grounding for the intellectual positions and sensibilities of liberal cosmopolitans, distorting them in very particular ways. The material self-sufficiency of elite cosmopolitan theorists confirms them in their individualism and enables them to recommend the repudiation of particularistic attachments such as ethnic solidarities. Conversely, such attachments are often a resource for effective collective action and mutual support among the less powerful.[73] If inclusion in the polis has usually had to be fought for, the subaltern as individual would appear to stand little chance in that fight. Subaltern inclusion seems more likely as a result of the strengthening of collective consciousness and subaltern community.[74] Historically, it is communitarianism—and more particularly nationalism—that has been the instinctive vocabulary of grievance and resistance (one thinks here of Isaiah Berlin's view of nationalism as 'a response to a wound inflicted upon a society'[75]).

As I suggested at the start of this section, one way of describing the ambiguous appeal of cosmopolitanism, harking back to Scheffler, might be to say that when viewed as a doctrine about justice, cosmopolitanism appears conducive to subaltern interests; but as a doctrine about culture and the self, cosmopolitanism seems inaccessible to subalterns. Misrepresented as the view from nowhere (or everywhere), the cosmopolitan perspective is in reality one that is advanced from privileged social locations that are uninhabitable by subalterns. Yet even as a doctrine about justice, cosmopolitanism is not wholly unproblematic from a subaltern perspective. If resistance is primarily about securing justice and if community and boundaries have historically been integral components of subaltern struggles for justice, then cosmopolitanism as a doctrine about justice must find a way to reconcile this insight with its insistence that boundaries are morally arbitrary. It must at the very least offer an account of when boundaries are morally defensible and when they are arbitrary. The problem seems to be that although cosmopolitan utopias promise better subaltern futures, their failure to acknowledge the role of community and boundaries in subaltern resistance means that they neglect to offer a credible account of the agency that subalterns themselves might exercise in realizing those futures. In short, although the praxis of cosmopolitanism by elites seems to be good for subalterns, subalterns themselves can never *be* cosmopolitan in their subaltern condition.

But it would be simplistic to reduce cosmopolitanism to a perspective of elite benevolence, and conversely to align communitarianism with subaltern resistance. For one thing, we know from the work of James Scott that the resistance of the very weak is usually unorganized and highly individualized.[76] Even more organized subaltern resistance does not invariably take classic communitarian forms. Marx and Engels's declaration that 'the working men have no country',[77] echoed by Virginia Woolf in respect of women,[78] might be regarded as exhortations to cosmopolitan resistance addressed to subalterns. Yet, as subsequent sections of this book will go on to show, what makes class- and gender-based internationalisms interesting is precisely the difficulty of their categorization as classically cosmopolitan or communitarian forms of protest. They might be seen as varieties of communitarianism in the sense that they are efforts to forge new forms of community cutting across pre-existing ones. Their communitarian sensibility is evident in their practices of inclusion and exclusion as movements of people of particular classes and genders. But they appear cosmopolitan in their attempts to forge alliances across national boundaries with a view to contesting the policies of nation-states. And, in some variants, they are profoundly cosmopolitan in the normative destinations of classless or gender-blind societies towards which they aspire. And yet, complicating the task of categorization still further, such movements often bear very particular national inflections, reflected in their idioms of protest or in the way they instrumentalize the nation-state. The nation often rears its head in these ostensibly non-national forms of protest. Subaltern protest therefore frequently defies attempts at categorization as either cosmopolitan or communitarian.

As for the political economy of the cosmopolitan gaze, we might further disrupt the dichotomies constructed earlier in this section by noting the possibilities for subaltern access to cosmopolitan scripts in conditions of contemporary capitalism. In an argument that essentially adapts Benedict Anderson's classic account of the origins of nationalism[79] to the current conjuncture, Arjun Appadurai has suggested that we are beginning to witness the emergence of 'postnational' communities. Just as New World nations were imagined in particular ways corresponding to the migratory and professional mobility options of Creole elites conjoined with the phenomenon of 'print capitalism', global migration and global mass media now provide the infrastructural basis for the imagination of postnational communities.[80] As in Calhoun's argument, mobility is key in shaping the cosmopolitan imaginary, but importantly in Appadurai's view, mobility is not the prerogative of the privileged. The demographic basis for a postnational world is provided as much by refugees, exiles, migrant labour, trafficked women, and illegal aliens, as by wealthy frequent flyers. One might still object that the link between cosmopolitanism and mobility (even subaltern mobility) leaves serious questions about the possibilities for cosmopolitan identification by the subaltern immobile.[81] Yet even if human mobility is policed ever more stringently by nation-states, flows of capital and information might be seen as foisting a sort of 'forced cosmopolitanism' on rooted subalterns, albeit unevenly. If anyone could live in locales entirely of their own creation, it is the powerful—though even that is doubtful, as post-colonial work on the mutual constitution of identities has shown.[82] The weak find it harder to resist the encroachment of external influences and the consequent cosmopolitanization of their lives. We might say, then, that hybridity and the possibilities of cultural cosmopolitanism emerge first on the terrain of the weak.[83]

Rather than reaching definitive conclusions, the discussion in this section has attempted to unsettle facile dichotomies that would align privilege with cosmopolitanism and subalternity with communitarianism, and to propose instead that these relationships are more uncertain and open-ended than the literature sometimes suggests.[84] Indeed this open-endedness invites us to consider the nature of the sensibilities of subaltern protest in the Third World.

1.5 'THIRD WORLD'

I have been speaking of human rights, protest, and social movements in the 'Third World', but what—or where—is the Third World? I use this category, acutely conscious of the fact that many consider it to be somewhat outdated on one of two grounds: first, the contemporary political relevance of the category is questionable given the end of the Cold War tripartite division of the world into capitalist, communist, and non-aligned blocs; second, the analytical utility of the category is questionable given its size and heterogeneity. I will deal with each of these objections in turn and, in doing so, hope to say something about the geographical scope of this book.

As Vijay Prashad has written, the 'Third World' was not a place but a political project pursued by a group of recently decolonized states between the mid-1950s and the early 1980s, aimed at mitigating interstate inequality in the international system. The outlines of this project first became evident in gatherings of anti-colonial activists at meetings such as the 1920 Baku Congress of the Peoples of the East and the 1927 conference of the League Against Imperialism at Brussels, the Communist Internationals, and the numerous Pan-African Congresses held in the first half of the twentieth century.[85] From the time of the 1955 Bandung Afro-Asian Conference and as decolonization proceeded apace, the vehicles of this project were increasingly sovereign states, acting in concert within existing international institutions like the United Nations or establishing new ones such as the NAM and the Group of 77 (G77). The term 'Third World' first seems to have been used in French (*tiers monde*) by the demographer Alfred Sauvy in 1952, to suggest a parallel with the *tiers etat* (Third Estate) of the French Revolution.[86] The implication seems to have been that like the proletariat and bourgeoisie of the French Revolution, the newly decolonized states would play a progressive and radically transformational role in international politics. The original connotations of 'Third World' are, for this reason, far more attractive than those of 'developing', which suggests a slavish, unimaginative teleology in which developing states strive to resemble the developed.[87]

The Third World project took the form of an attack on the global hierarchical structures in which Third World states found themselves. As Bull noted, it was a 'revolt against the West',[88] championing norms of self-determination, sovereign equality, and territorial integrity in a world that had been incompletely decolonized.[89] The provision of moral, diplomatic, and sometimes material support to 'wars of national liberation' was a key element of this agenda, with the occupation of Palestine and apartheid in South Africa functioning as lightning rods for collective mobilization and protest. Third World states advocated new norms of racial equality, economic justice, and cultural liberation that presaged an end to their subordinate status.

The Third World as a conceptual entity was as much a creation of the Cold War as it was the result of decolonization. From the perspective of the superpowers, the Third World comprised those parts of the world that were to be courted and intervened in if necessary for the prosecution of their material and ideological struggle against one another; from the perspective of the Third World, these were areas that had a common interest in resisting such intervention.[90] Given this context, the notion of non-alignment had a powerful attraction for Third World states—even if its rhetoric was almost always undermined by an enduring structural dependence of peripheral states on one of the superpowers or the erstwhile colonial power. Attacking such dependence through demands for a comprehensive renegotiation of the economic relationship between Third and First Worlds therefore constituted a key component of the Third World agenda. In its most radical versions, this agenda called—somewhat inconsistently—both for a delinking from the global economy via policies of import-substitution industrialization and infant-industry protection, and for assurances of preferential access to markets, technology, and credit from the industrialized world. Third World assertiveness reached its peak in the confrontational cartelism of 1973, when oil-producing states increased the price of oil fourfold, much to the consternation of the industrialized world. The confidence engendered by this moment spawned the radical rhetoric of the Declaration of a New International Economic Order (NIEO) in 1974, which codified many of the Third World's long-standing demands.[91] In retrospect, this would turn out to be the highpoint of the Third World project.

By the time the debt crisis erupted in 1982, the Third World as a project of states was largely dead—although its infrastructure would linger on and its echoes would continue to be heard in smaller groups of states bargaining around particular issues. Although the debt crisis affected a large number of countries in Latin America and sub-Saharan Africa, the debtors did not organize collectively in their dealings with creditor institutions such as the Paris Club. In 1980, the very term 'Third World' was replaced by the anodyne and apolitical 'South' in the language of the Brandt Commission, which had been charged with studying international development issues.[92] The shift in terminology seemed to obscure the hierarchical relationship between rich and poor by re-presenting it in apparently egalitarian spatial terms, although critics of Mercator projection maps have long pointed out that the North is still always on 'top'. Whatever the political and cognitive implications of this shift in discourse, it seemed to confirm that the Third World had ceased to exist, killed by both failure and success. The failures were painfully evident in economic stagnation and crushing indebtedness. The demands of the NIEO had been emphatically rejected by the conservative Western governments of Reagan, Thatcher, and Kohl. A vicious 'second' Cold War had broken out in Nicaragua, Afghanistan, Angola, and Cambodia, demonstrating that the superpowers had lost none of their appetite for intervention. But it was the spectacular economic success of some Third World states—the 'Asian Tigers'—that induced many of its constituents to abandon the old *tiersmondiste* political critique of the economic order, and to begin the process of dismantling trade barriers and radically downsizing the role of the state from that of Keynesian demand management to the more limited one of managing the money supply and controlling inflation.[93] In some cases, reforms were adopted voluntarily and enthusiastically; in others they were the reluctant price that heavily indebted countries paid for being 'rescued' by the IFIs. Most of the time, structural adjustment was neither straightforwardly consensual nor coercive, with Third World elites using circumstances of crisis to push through reforms that they had long been advocating.[94]

The Third World as a state-led project is dead, but one has only to glance at the demands of 'Southern' states in intergovernmental negotiations across issue areas to see that much of its unfinished agenda is still with us. There is still the old impassioned defence of sovereignty and territorial integrity, the prickliness over Western intervention, the demands for fairer terms of trade, more aid, debt cancellation, and above all equity in issue areas as varied as climate change and nuclear proliferation. Membership of a notional Third World has no doubt changed over time: think not only of the Asian Tigers but also of elites in countries like Mexico, Brazil, and India who would doubtless like to think of themselves as having 'graduated'. But there is still a large group of states (one thinks here of the World Bank's Heavily Indebted Poor Countries) that advances many of the old demands, albeit not in the collective and combative fashion of the 1970s. In that sense, changes in membership require a tightening of the boundaries around the category rather than its abandonment.

Much of the unfinished Third World agenda is also pushed forcefully by non-state actors—NGOs, 'civil society', and social movements—protesting against what they see as the injustices of global imperialism and capitalism.[95] Meetings of the IFIs and the G8 have been magnets for such protest. Some commentators have seen, in arenas like the World Social Forums, striking parallels with Bandung in their ability to bring together disparate causes protesting against different aspects of global injustice but united in their opposition to the current US-led hegemony.[96] The comparison cannot be pushed too far. Although much of the rhetoric sounds like the unfinished business of *tiersmondisme*, made more urgent by the preponderance of a single superpower and the interconnectedness forged by capitalist globalization, it is underpinned by a radical disillusionment with the institution of sovereignty as the key vehicle of resistance. Nonetheless, given these resonances it seems premature to announce the death of the Third World as a political project: it would be more accurate to see the project as being carried forward by a different set of agents. This book uses the term 'Third World' because it is interested in the new agents at the forefront of this continuing project. Its main subjects of interest are Third World protest movements. As outlined in section 1.1, it is interested in their constructions of threat and their attitudes towards boundaries and sovereignty.

But I shall also continue to use the term 'Third World' to refer to a particular group of states. My argument for doing so is that the demise of the Third World, as a purposive project pursued by a group of states acting in concert with one another, does not preclude the use of the term as an analytical category to describe what are still in many respects similarly situated states. That is to say, these states still have much in common, even if those commonalities do not induce the same levels of political cooperation and organization that they once did. Indeed the ubiquity of various problematic substitutes for 'Third World' such as 'global South' and 'developing world', suggests a continuing analytical demand for macro-categories that capture what is still a major axis of interstate inequality.[97] It is difficult to frame disagreements over many issues central to world order—climate change, arms control and non-proliferation, democracy and human rights, and intervention—without reference to this axis of inequality.[98] Critics of these macro-categories have suggested that they ought to be reconceptualized as social rather than geographical terms, given widening income disparities within most states.[99] Yet as long as the life prospects of individuals and their ability to access the benefits of globalization are mediated by the states to which they belong, it will still be relevant to distinguish between strong and weak states on the basis of their ability to secure the basic interests of their people.[100] The usefulness of a global *binary* distinction between rich and poor states is of course highly contextual—there will be many contexts in which such macro-level categories are simply too crude to be analytically useful. The fundamental point here is that the demise of the Third World as a political actor need not preclude the use of the term as an analytical construct that may sometimes be useful in capturing the challenges faced by a similarly situated set of states in the international system.

In what ways are these states 'similarly situated'? Attempts to define the Third World have sometimes compiled extensive lists of quantifiable socio-economic criteria (one thinks here of the components of the world development and human development indices). My understanding of the category is more attentive to the nature of state–society relations and political culture. Mohammed Ayoob highlights two factors, both of which follow from the colonization of Third World states: their relatively late entry as full members into a society of juridically sovereign states, and the incompleteness[101] of their state- and nation-building processes. These factors, in his view, account for the basic characteristics of 'the prototypical Third World state':

> lack of internal cohesion, in terms of both great economic and social disparities and major ethnic and regional fissures; lack of unconditional legitimacy of state boundaries, state institutions, and governing elites; easy

susceptibility to internal and interstate conflicts; distorted and dependent development, both economically and socially; marginalisation, especially in relation to the dominant international security and economic concerns; and easy permeability by external actors, be they more developed states, international institutions, or transnational corporations.[102]

Of course not all Third World states embody these 'prototypical' characteristics to the same degree. Latin American states have had relatively uncontested interstate boundaries and relatively little interstate war for at least the past century,[103] yet arguably possess other characteristics of Third Worldness (great economic and social disparities, dependent development, and marginalization from the core of international society) to a sufficient degree to qualify for membership. The oil-producing states of the Middle East enjoy incomes per capita approaching those of the First World, but possess virtually all other characteristics of Ayoob's 'prototypical Third World state'. Thus, any definition of the Third World must allow for unevenness in the extent to which its constituents meet its criteria.

One implication of this understanding of the Third World state is that a key assumption underlying many schools of international relations (IR) theory—namely that the international is the domain of anarchy and the domestic the domain of hierarchical order[104]—might apply with rather less force to the Third World. The weaker capabilities of Third World states and their relatively late entry into a society of sovereign states with already well-developed institutions suggest a hierarchical positioning vis-à-vis the more established members of this society. The relative incipience of state- and nation-building suggests either an anarchic domestic realm in which no single actor has yet monopolized the means of violence, or a hierarchical realm in which the legitimacy of the monopolizer is deeply contested. Given this structural position, one would expect Third World societies to be vulnerable to two sets of disadvantages. First, they suffer the disadvantages of belonging to states that are at the bottom of the international hierarchy (doing less well in the interstate distribution of goods and bads in the international system, being vulnerable to penetration by more powerful external actors, etc.). Second, they bear the highly uneven consequences of state builders' invariably conflictual attempts to persuade rival aspirants to state control to accept their legitimacy. Both sets of disadvantages will be developed in more detail in chapters 2 and 3.

The above is a relatively broad-brushed attempt to sketch a definition of the Third World as an analytical construct. To attempt to say something about as vast and variegated a landscape as this is of course a risky endeavour. Much of the discussion in the book, particularly in Part II, is rooted in specific geographical and historical contexts. Where it generalizes about the Third

World as a whole, it tries to do so in a way that takes into account Onora O'Neill's distinction between abstraction and idealization.[105] O'Neill argues that abstraction is an innocuous and unavoidable feature of ethical reasoning. We abstract whenever we make claims that bracket some predicates and that are indifferent as to their satisfaction or non-satisfaction. We can of course disagree about which predicates to bracket, but the act of bracketing itself is uncontroversial. It is idealization—the denial of certain predicates or the assertion that absent predicates obtain—that is argumentatively problematic. In thinking about a category as large as the Third World, I have abstracted certain features of the structural position of Third World states in the international system and considered a set of normative dilemmas following from these structural constraints that many social movements in such states will find familiar. 'Many' in the preceding sentence is a crucial qualification: I do not claim that all social movements everywhere in the Third World will be able to identify with the issues discussed here, only that many will. In sum, I can be criticized for having abstracted and foregrounded the wrong features of 'Third Worldness', but not for the intellectual sin of idealization.

1.6 METHODOLOGICAL INFLUENCES

Abstraction brings its own challenges. My conviction that this book describes a set of normative dilemmas that are very widely experienced by Third World social movements has led me to construct an argument in Part I at a level of generality comparable to, say, Rawls' *The Law of Peoples*. Yet I am also concerned by the occasional failure of normative theorists to appreciate the complexity of many empirical debates and the instability of empirical 'facts' on which their normative premises are often contingent. This can result in an opportunistic use of empirical evidence to support preferred positions.[106] In attempting to strike a balance between the empirical and the normative, this book tries to be more empirically informed than work that is typical of the field of international normative theory; but it necessarily falls well short of the sort of 'thick description' that area studies scholars working in disciplines like sociology and anthropology might aim for. The ambition has been to steer a path between providing too much empirical detail to be able to do justice to the normative questions that are the book's central concern, and too little to offer a nuanced description of the politics of so vast and internally complex a canvas as the Third World.

The book draws on a number of different bodies of literature in its study of Third World protest. Its engagement with the debate between cosmopolitanism and communitarianism makes it centrally a work of normative political theory. Yet it is also interested in the relationship between normative ideas and the projection of power to implement those ideas in the state system, making it also a work of IR theory. Within the field of IR theory, strictly rationalistic approaches proved unhelpful given their relative lack of interest in normative questions. In contrast, the 'international society' approach, sometimes misleadingly called the English School of IR theory, has provided a more hospitable methodological environment in which to combine an interest in the ethical content of norms with attention to the political mechanisms by which norms are held in place or undermined.[107] Part I of the book draws substantially on this approach to describe the operation of cosmopolitanism and communitarianism as vocabularies in which states exercise power.

Like most schools of IR theory, international society thinkers have not—for the most part—seen the Third World as generating IR theory in its own right.[108] Key concepts have been elucidated with reference to the development of the European state system, with the non-European world being added on as a result of the supposed 'expansion of International Society'.[109] The tacit premise here is that the frameworks and ideas that have been developed to understand the practices of European or Western states are sufficient to understand international relations as a whole, with non-Western states differing merely in the success with which they approximate the norms of what was once a largely European society of states. In contrast, post-colonial theory takes the experiences of Third World states and societies as its starting point and subject matter.[110] It also pays a great deal more attention to state–society relations than most variants of IR theory. Accordingly, this book draws frequently on the insights of post-colonial theorists.

Post-colonial theory in turn grew out of the academic study of post-colonial literature, which has provided a rich and sometimes startling source of inspiration and confirmation for the arguments in the book. Each chapter begins with an epigraph from a work of post-colonial literature. In most cases the epigraph sets the tone or provides an orientation to the chapter, sometimes it suggests an idea around which the chapter is structured, and occasionally it takes on a life of its own to do something more substantive. Taken together, the epigraphs seem to confirm that writers of post-colonial fiction have long been aware of the structural constraints within which Third World societies are entrapped and have been moved to create characters that are constantly seeking ways out of these confines. It may be that imaginative literature is able to anticipate normative political theory precisely because it is not constrained by the actual and has the luxury, but also the obligation, of thinking beyond what is to what might be.

Part I

2

The Dark Sides of Cosmopolitanism

> The conquest of the earth, which mostly means the taking it away from those who have a different complexion or slightly flatter noses than ourselves, is not a pretty thing when you look into it too much. What redeems it is the idea only. An idea at the back of it; not a sentimental pretence but an idea; and an unselfish belief in the idea—something you can set up, and bow down before, and offer a sacrifice to . . .
>
> Joseph Conrad, *Heart of Darkness* (1902)

It has become something of a truism in international relations to note that there has been an enormous proliferation of norms and institutions in international society since the end of the Second World War. Different schools of IR theory have attempted to capture this intuition in their distinctive vocabularies. Liberals have described the increasing enmeshment of states in explicit and implicit regimes fashioned to manage their growing interdependencies.[1] Constructivists have remarked on the growing density of transnational relations and have explored the interaction of power and norms in the creation of international regimes.[2] International society theorists have described a thickening in the scope of consensus on the norms that govern the society of states, from a minimalist 'pluralist' agreement on the norms required for mere coexistence (sovereignty, territoriality, non-intervention) to a more ambitious 'solidarist' agenda comprising norms about the substantive goals of that society (human rights, democracy, capitalism).[3] Poststructuralists have deployed the Foucaultian notion of 'governmentality' to describe an explosion in the mechanisms of international surveillance and control to which states are increasingly subject.[4] While there are significant ontological and epistemological differences between these approaches, they all express a sense of a shifting balance between the international and the domestic. The 'international' has become more intrusive, so that the scope of 'matters which are essentially within the domestic jurisdiction of any state'—to use the language of Article 2(7) of the UN Charter—has steadily shrunk.

From the perspective of Third World states, two practices in the post-Cold War era have come to be seen as emblematic of this trend: humanitarian intervention and economic conditionality. Both might be understood as disciplinary practices intended to enforce conformity with a set of liberal political and economic norms. In this chapter, I read humanitarian intervention and economic conditionality as liberal cosmopolitan practices by demonstrating the ways in which liberal cosmopolitan norms and teleologies are invoked to justify them. In his book entitled *The Dark Sides of Virtue*, legal theorist David Kennedy writes that although humanitarians are accustomed to thinking of their efforts to promote humanitarianism as marginal and weak—as speaking truth to power from outside power—in fact, 'state power is now routinely exercised in the vocabularies of these helping professions. As is economic power.'[5] What Kennedy says of humanitarianism is applicable to liberal cosmopolitanism, which provides the moral underpinning for many ostensibly humanitarian practices including intervention by force. Liberal cosmopolitanism provides a vocabulary that has frequently been appropriated by states to justify the exercise of their power. This chapter explores this process of appropriation, as well as the response thereto from cosmopolitans within the academy. It may therefore be read as a critical account of the contemporary praxis and theory of liberal cosmopolitanism.

The chapter is divided into two parts. The first part argues that the praxis of liberal cosmopolitanism today assists in the consolidation of Western hegemony. It begins by explaining the notion of 'hegemony' that underpins the analysis. It then outlines the ways in which liberal cosmopolitanism is invoked to justify humanitarian intervention and economic conditionality, before going on to demonstrate the power-political relations that the moral justification of these practices tends to obscure. If the argument is convincing, we should be able to see why the contemporary praxis of liberal cosmopolitanism justifiably arouses resistance in the Third World. The second part of the chapter relates these practices to the writings of cosmopolitans within the academy. The history of ideas literature identifies an inherent dual tendency within cosmopolitan thought towards the justification of imperial governance on the one hand, and a critique of empire on the other. I attempt to trace these tendencies within contemporary cosmopolitan thought and identify what may be called—following Martti Koskenniemi—'apologist' and 'utopian' lines of thinking. The apologists, I will argue, have made liberal cosmopolitanism complicit in contemporary imperialism. The utopians, while critical of imperialist practices, have failed to navigate the argumentative paths necessary to realize cosmopolitanism's anti-imperial potential.

2.1 LIBERAL COSMOPOLITANISM AND THE CONSTRUCTION OF HEGEMONY

Critics of realism have frequently commented on its neglect of norms and values and its consequently impoverished view of its central concept: power. As Andrew Hurrell has written, 'a great deal of the struggle for political power is the quest for legitimate and authoritative control that avoids costly and dangerous reliance on brute force and coercion'.[6] Robert Cox, deploying a Gramscian understanding of 'hegemony', suggests that:

> force will not have to be used in order to ensure the dominance of the strong to the extent that the weak accept the prevailing power relations as legitimate. This the weak may do if the strong see their mission as hegemonic and not merely dominant or dictatorial, that is, if they are willing to make concessions that will secure the weak's acquiescence in their leadership and if they can express this leadership in terms of universal or general interests, rather than just as serving their own particular interests.[7]

At the end of the Cold War, the West—and the United States in particular—found itself in a position of unprecedented power, which it has sought to maintain. It has found in the language of liberal cosmopolitanism, a philosophical vocabulary in which to represent its particular interests as universal interests, thereby eliciting the acquiescence of lesser actors in the international system in its continued dominance. The argument in this section attempts to do two things: first, to demonstrate the ways in which the West's coercive interventions in the Third World in the form of humanitarian intervention and economic conditionality are legitimated in the universalist vocabulary of liberal cosmopolitanism; and second, to reveal the particular interests that such legitimation tends to mask. In doing so, I hope to demystify the power relations on which the contemporary praxis of liberal cosmopolitanism rests.

2.1.1 Humanitarian intervention

As explained in chapter 1, for liberal cosmopolitans it is individuals who are the ultimate repositories of moral worth in political life. Institutions such as boundaries and sovereignty are worthy of respect only to the extent that they are of value to individuals. When they cease to be of value—in a situation where a state is abusing the human rights of its citizens, for example—they no longer warrant international respect. In such circumstances, liberal cosmopolitans argue, it is permissible (or, in stronger versions of the thesis, obligatory) for other actors in international society to ignore the prohibition on intervention in the affairs of sovereign states in order to protect individuals at risk of human rights abuse.[8] One might see humanitarian intervention as *the* paradigmatically liberal cosmopolitan practice in international society today. Much of the contemporary debate on intervention centres on the questions of when (i.e. at what threshold of rights abuse) it is permissible to intervene, who can authorize and execute intervention, and what the limits of such intervention ought to be.[9]

The mobilization of humanitarian reasons to justify the use of force is not new. Western powers frequently intervened in the affairs of the Ottoman Empire, for example, to defend the humanity of Christians.[10] Yet the practice seems to have taken something of a hiatus in international society in the years after the Second World War. Writing in 1984, Bull noted that intervention in the Third World had become much more difficult in this period than it had been in the interwar years or, of course, in the heyday of European imperialism. Bull attributed the increasing difficulty of intervention to five factors: the growth of a Third World will and capacity to resist intervention, the weakening of the West's will to intervene, the growing power of the Soviet Union, the operation of the general balance of power and fear that intervention by either of the superpowers or their allies outside their respective spheres of influence might escalate Cold War hostilities, and finally the emergence of a new normative climate that was unfavourable to intervention.[11] This last factor was due in no small measure to an emphasis on the more statist commitments of the UN Charter[12] in state practice and in numerous resolutions reaffirming those commitments.[13] Bull correctly notes that the normative consensus against intervention was particularly hostile to Western intervention in the Third World, which was seen as portending a regression to colonialism.

In practice, both superpowers intervened frequently and flagrantly in their respective client states—the United States in accordance with the perceived imperatives of 'containment', and the USSR under the terms of the so-called Brezhnev Doctrine. Nor did the apparent normative consensus against intervention prevent intervention by Third World states in each other's affairs (e.g. India in East Pakistan (1971), Vietnam in Cambodia (1979), and Tanzania in Uganda (1979)). Crucially, none of these interventions were justified in humanitarian terms—even though they might plausibly have been, given the massive human rights abuses that could be said to have occasioned them. Nicholas Wheeler argues that the fact that humanitarian justifications were not invoked in any[14] of these cases despite the plausibility that such a claim might have enjoyed suggests that 'humanitarian claims were not accepted as a legitimate basis for the use of force in the 1970s'.[15] Indeed as recently as 1986, the British Foreign Office could categorically assert that:

> [The] overwhelming majority of contemporary legal opinion comes down against the existence of a right of humanitarian intervention for three main reasons: First, the UN Charter and the corpus of modern international law do not seem to specifically incorporate such a right; secondly, state practice in the past two centuries, and especially since 1945, at best provides only a handful of genuine cases of humanitarian intervention, and, on most assessments, none at all; and finally, on prudential grounds, the scope for abusing such a right argues strongly against its creation... in essence, therefore, the case against making humanitarian intervention an exception to the principles of non-intervention is that its doubtful benefits would be heavily outweighed by its costs in terms of respect for international law.[16]

Evidently, states can change their minds rather quickly. Had Bull lived to see the end of the Cold War, he would no doubt have commented on the seismic shifts that heralded a new era that was far more receptive to claims of humanitarian intervention. Most obviously, the Soviet Union had collapsed, making way for what many saw as a unipolar world. In a 1993 speech widely regarded as setting out US priorities for that world, the then US National Security Advisor Anthony Lake declared that 'the successor to a doctrine of containment must be a strategy of enlargement... of the world's free community of market democracies'. The speech promised that US policy would focus on strengthening and expanding the 'core of major market democracies', while minimizing the ability of states outside this core to threaten it.[17]

The collapse of the Soviet Union and the end of the Cold War also triggered a wave of security crises that appeared to beseech some form of international intervention and amelioration. Mary Kaldor described the moment as representing a shift from old, 'Clausewitzean' wars fought over territory for geopolitical or ideological objectives and financed by state-controlled autarchic economies, to newer wars fought over identity and fuelled by the economic opportunities opened up by globalization.[18] Critics responded that the distinction between so-called old and new wars was overplayed, and that the geostrategic and ideological preoccupations of the superpowers during the Cold War had obscured other forms of conflict which had become newly visible.[19] States that had long suffered internal crises of legitimacy but were propped up by superpower patronage, now began to collapse as their strategic significance waned and aid flows dried up (the classic example is Somalia). In parts of the former Communist world such as Yugoslavia, economic precariousness combined with the stresses of democratization, as elites sought to mobilize power on ethnic lines, with devastating consequences for the body politic.[20]

In addition to the systemic changes that seemed both to demand and enable Western military intervention, changes within Western societies and electorates also prompted a renewal of the interventionist impulse. As David Chandler notes, centre-left parties increasingly saw the articulation of 'Third Way' policies that rejected traditional political programmes of the Left and Right and focused instead on ethics and morality, as the most effective means of connecting with a citizenship alienated from party politics. One consequence was that ethical foreign policies began to be seen as a central component of domestic legitimacy.[21] In light of these systemic and state-level changes, powerful Western states faced a dramatically altered set of incentives in deciding whether and how to respond to humanitarian crises in other parts of the world.

The result was a series of military interventions—explicitly justified as 'humanitarian'—in countries such as Iraq, Somalia, Haiti, the former Yugoslavia, and East Timor. Not all interventions were by Western states, as the example of Nigeria leading interventions in Liberia and Sierra Leone under the imprimatur of the Economic Community of West African States (ECOWAS) demonstrates. Nonetheless, the broad pattern was one of Western states intervening in the putatively dysfunctional states of the Third World. The latter were effectively put on notice that the manner in which they treated their own citizens would now be considered a legitimate matter for international scrutiny and remedial action by force if necessary.

As a particular species of coercive action, humanitarian intervention is governed by a legal regime on the use of force that has remained largely unaltered (in letter, if not in spirit) since the end of the Second World War. Article 2(4) of the UN Charter prohibits the use of force 'against the territorial integrity or political independence of any state, or in any other manner inconsistent with the Purposes of the United Nations'. This general rule is subject to two exceptions—Article 51, which recognizes the inherent right of states to individual or collective self-defence in case of armed attack, and Article 42, which permits the Security Council to authorize the use of force should this be necessary to maintain or restore international peace and security. The earliest humanitarian interventions of the post-Cold War era in Iraq, Somalia, Bosnia, and (very belatedly) Rwanda, all took place under cover of explicit authorization for the use of force from the Security Council.[22]

The North Atlantic Treaty Organization (NATO)'s intervention in Kosovo in March 1999 marked a decisive break from this pattern because it did not receive the prior authorization of the Security Council.[23] The Council had passed two resolutions (1160 and 1199) addressing the human rights situation in Kosovo. But neither of these authorized the use of 'all necessary means' (generally considered the diplomatic trigger phrase for the use of force) in the event of Serb non-compliance with the Council's demands, reflecting the reluctance of Russia and China to countenance a war against Serbia. The ensuing legal debate was split between supporters of the intervention arguing either that the existing resolutions provided implicit authorization for NATO intervention,[24] or (in the view of a minority) that no authorization was needed since the human rights provisions of the UN Charter permitted unilateral humanitarian intervention.[25] Opponents of the intervention argued that it could not be considered legal without the explicit authorization of the Security Council.[26]

Quite apart from this legal argument, there was a more significant political debate that juxtaposed the notion of a rule of law in international relations with other competing considerations. A number of intellectuals and a minority of state elites candidly acknowledged the illegality of the intervention, while nonetheless defending its legitimacy. The Independent International Commission on Kosovo concluded that 'the NATO military intervention was illegal but legitimate'.[27] Jürgen Habermas controversially endorsed the moral legitimacy of the intervention, while expressing the hope that cosmopolitan legal institutions could be developed so as to make future derogations from the law unnecessary.[28] Scholars like Allen Buchanan welcomed the intervention both for its immediate value in halting the slaughter of Kosovar Albanians,[29] and for its more enduring contribution 'to the development of a new, morally progressive rule of international law according to which humanitarian intervention without Security Council authorisation is sometimes permissible'.[30] In essence, these views set up an opposition between legality and morality and emphasized the primacy of the latter. The requirements of procedural legality were seen as impediments to moral progress and the unilateral recourse to force by powerful states regarded as morally preferable, given the urgency of the imperative of halting human rights abuse.[31] What is significant here is that when legality was found wanting, cosmopolitan moral arguments became even more crucial to the legitimation of intervention.

Arguably, the Kosovo precedent emboldened the United States and the United Kingdom to attack Iraq in 2003, again without explicit Security Council authorization, on grounds that were weaker and more controversial than in the case of Kosovo. This war was justified primarily on grounds of preventive self-defence, relying on the false claim that Iraq possessed weapons of mass destruction with which it could attack the United States directly or in collaboration with a terrorist network.[32] Nonetheless, liberal cosmopolitan arguments were also pressed into service as a subsidiary justification for the war via frequent references to the lack of democracy and human rights abuses in Iraq, particularly after other justifications for the war were discredited. In the wake of the attack on Iraq in 2003, opponents of the Kosovo intervention seemed vindicated in their argument that the prioritization of cosmopolitan morality over legality had significantly loosened the procedural constraints on the use of force, giving powerful states a greater propensity to wage war. It should be noted, however, that the inability of the United States and the United Kingdom to build a broad international consensus in favour of the 2003 war on Iraq suggests that the discourse of cosmopolitan morality is not infinitely elastic. Where the conduct of states departs substantially from their professed justifications, their credibility becomes suspect. In such circumstances, the exercise of hegemony tends to become more coercive and less consensual.

The question that concerns us here is how the cosmopolitan legitimation of humanitarian intervention assists in the maintenance of Western hegemony. Realists have long argued that the claim to be acting in defence of universal morality usually turns out to obscure the pursuit of very particular interests. Carl Schmitt's observation that 'whoever invokes humanity wants to cheat' is frequently cited in this regard,[33] as is E. H. Carr's evisceration of the tendency of dominant groups to conflate their interests with those of the community as a whole and to proclaim them as such.[34] In the context of Kosovo, for example, Danilo Zolo has suggested that lurking beneath the cosmopolitan moral justifications for the intervention were a host of power-political considerations—an opportunity for the United States to demonstrate its indispensability in the maintenance of European security, to obtain access to the resources of the Caspian Sea and the Caucuses, to establish new raisons d'être for NATO given the end of the Cold War, and so on.[35] Critics on the left have made analogous arguments in respect of virtually every humanitarian intervention in the post-Cold War era.

Liberal proponents of intervention have urged that motivation ought not to be considered a defining test for the humanitarian credentials of an intervention. Wheeler suggests that this treats the intervening states as the referent object for analysis rather than the victims.[36] Michael Ignatieff advances a pragmatic consequentialist argument for ignoring motivation: 'if good results had to wait for good intentions, we would have to wait forever'.[37] While a great deal of the moral argument around humanitarian intervention has focused on the issue of motives, an obsession with the nature of motivations for particular interventions misses the ways in which intervention as a persistent practice in international society has assisted in the consolidation of Western hegemony. Recall that hegemony rests, to a significant extent, on the acquiescence of lesser actors in the international system in their own domination. In the context of humanitarian intervention, this acquiescence has been elicited, first, by creating a broad consensus on the need for international intervention, and second, by insisting on satisfying the demand for intervention in ways that maintain and reinforce a distribution of power in the international system that grossly favours the West in general and the United States in particular.

Egregious human rights abuses are an undeniable feature of our contemporary world, but the clamour for *international* intervention to deal with them is the result of a set of representational practices[38] in which failures of governance are attributed primarily to local dynamics *internal* to putatively dysfunctional states. This is a crucial element of the hegemonic cosmopolitan sensibility. Anne Orford offers a compelling critique of what she calls 'the imaginative geography of intervention, according to which the international community is absent from the scene of violence and suffering until it intervenes as a heroic saviour'.[39] In contrast to readings of the humanitarian crises in Yugoslavia and Rwanda as exemplars of 'ancient tribal hatreds',[40] Orford argues that international economic institutions and development agencies were present and actively interventionist in these regions well before the eruption of security crises. Relying on Susan Woodward's account of the dissolution of Yugoslavia for example,[41] she draws attention to the detrimental impact of economic austerity measures foisted on the Yugoslav state in the 1980s by foreign creditors and Western governments, which weakened the federal government at precisely the moment when greater state capacity was needed to ensure civil order and to enable people to cope with the shocks of transition from a state to a market economy. Orford's analysis radically unsettles the false dichotomy between international intervention and inaction that is usually presented at the moment of crisis to justify the imperative that 'something must be done'. In her reading of these cases, the international had already intervened in the domestic in ways that rendered it deeply culpable for the security crises that allegedly beseeched (more) intervention.

Working in conjunction with imaginative geographies are imaginative histories, whereby security crises are represented as failures of *post*-colonial governance, with the causal implication of colonial governance being eclipsed or retrospectively whitewashed.[42] Robert Jackson's work on 'quasi-states' is illustrative in this regard, for its insinuation that decolonization heralded a significant deterioration in the quality of governance experienced by Third World peoples and for its silencing of the historical and contemporary *global* relationships that contribute to state failure.[43]

One corollary of the practice of constructing failures of governance as primarily local and *post*-colonial is that the function of the international human rights regime is conceived in extremely narrow terms as facilitating the intervention of the international in the domestic. Prominent liberal cosmopolitan philosophers have been complicit in these constructions. According to Charles Beitz, for example, 'the role of human rights in international political discourse has two aspects: first, human rights may serve to justify interference in the internal affairs of states or other local communities; second, they may argue for various external agents, such as international organizations and other states, to commit the resources required for effective interference'.[44] Similarly, the liberal international lawyer Michael Reisman views the function of human rights as being 'the international control of the essential techniques by which governments manage and control their peoples internally'.[45] In an influential 1992 article on a putative 'emerging right to democratic governance', Thomas Franck saw the most significant threats to democracy as internal to states, emanating from coups, dictators, and totalitarianism.[46] The notion that human rights or democracy could be threatened by powerful external actors (other states, IFIs, multinational corporations) or global structures (capitalism) and that international human rights regimes ought to protect against such eventualities does not even enter into these formulations. It is not as if this literature is blind to these possibilities; rather, it is informed by an implicit hierarchy of threats and a corresponding set of priorities. 'Human rights' are the instruments that protect individuals from the depredations of their own states; 'sovereignty' is supposed to shield them from the depredations of the international. Yet human rights are treated as absolute and non-derogable, while sovereignty has become conditional—thereby betraying a sense that it is the local that is likely to be the more serious locus of threat.

We should note, parenthetically, that these assumptions also infect the thinking of Western communitarians, where they serve a radically different purpose. Rawls, relying on the work of David Landes, asserts that 'burdened societies' owe their travails primarily to features of their domestic political culture.[47] Miller has similarly relied on the empirical assumption that successful economic development reflects prudent domestic choices, to deny that Western states have global obligations of distributive justice.[48] For Western communitarians, the attribution of Third World underdevelopment to domestic dysfunctionality is used to deny or restrict the claims of global distributive justice. Cosmopolitans use the very same assumption to bolster the authority of the international to intervene in Third World states. Despite beginning from shared empirical premises, the antagonists in this debate reach radically different conclusions because of a fundamental normative disagreement. For communitarians, obligations of justice are tied to causality: those who are responsible for bringing about a certain state of affairs must remedy any injustices that result from it. For cosmopolitans, obligations of justice arise out of a putative shared humanity, tempered perhaps by the capacity to assist.

The selective geographies and histories of culpability that underpin cosmopolitan narratives of intervention are essentially exercises in constructing the authority of the international, premised on its putatively superior knowledge, expertise, and clean hands. Having established a relatively consensual basis (a 'demand') for intervention as the best method of dealing with security crises, the West—and the United States in particular—insists on supplying security in ways that reinforce its crushing dominance in international society. Referring to Lake's 1993 'From Containment to Enlargement' speech setting out US priorities for the post-Cold War world, Andrew Bacevich finds it instructive for what it did not mention—worldwide disarmament and the creation of an effective global security organization, both of which had long been central to the liberal internationalist agenda. Neither figured explicitly in Lake's strategy of enlargement because each would diminish US authority and freedom of action.[49] Rather than taking seriously alternative methods of global security provision, the United States has unilaterally assumed the mantle of 'guardianship of human rights everywhere',[50] and has tended to seek exemption from a number of rules on that basis. It has sought to legitimate unrestrained power by setting itself up as the driving agent of the liberal cosmopolitan project (even if not explicitly in those terms).

It is possible to cite several instances of this sort of mindset. Justifying his refusal to sign the Convention on the Prohibition of the Use, Stockpiling, Production and Transfer of Anti-Personnel Mines and on their Destruction, US President Bill Clinton said: 'Our nation has unique responsibilities for preserving security and defending peace and freedom around the globe.... As Commander-in-Chief, I will not send our soldiers to defend the freedom of our people and the freedom of others without doing everything we can to make them as secure as possible.'[51] In a similar vein, attempting to explain the decision of the first George W. Bush administration not to become a party to the Rome Statute of the International Criminal Court, Marc Grossman, the then Under Secretary for Political Affairs said:

> The US has a unique role and responsibility to help preserve international peace and security. At any given time, US forces are located in close to 100 nations around the world conducting peacekeeping and humanitarian operations and fighting inhumanity. We must ensure that our soldiers and government officials are not exposed to the prospect of politicized prosecutions and investigations. Our President is committed to a robust American engagement in the world to defend freedom and defeat terror; we cannot permit the ICC to disrupt that vital mission.[52]

Performing the very rhetorical manoeuvre that Schmitt and Carr were so scathing of, Condoleezza Rice—National Security Adviser to the same administration—memorably proclaimed: 'America's pursuit of the national interest will create conditions that promote freedom, markets and peace... the triumph of these values is most assuredly easier when the international balance of power favours those who believe in them.... America's military power must be secure because the US is the only guarantor of global peace and stability.'[53] What ties these statements together is the self-perception of successive US administrations that their country bears the unique responsibility for 'fighting inhumanity' and that it must be freed from all restraint in the interests of effectively discharging this role.[54] In effect, the United States sees itself as a kind of arsenal for cosmopolitan right, as the force that must stand outside the law in order to uphold the law.[55]

Let me sum up the argument so far. Humanitarian intervention is a quintessentially cosmopolitan practice, underpinned by the premise that individuals are the ultimate repositories of moral worth and that it is permissible to disrespect the sovereignty of states when they violate the human rights of their citizens. Although it has undoubtedly saved lives, the practice of humanitarian intervention has often been deeply self-interested, with liberal cosmopolitanism furnishing a vocabulary in which particular interests have been able to masquerade as universal ones. The imperatives of cosmopolitan morality have been elevated over those of legality, undermining the rule of law and loosening procedural restraints on the resort to war. Yet as a hegemonic practice, humanitarian intervention has also sought to build a consensual basis for itself and for the power structure on which it rests. It has done this through a set of representational practices in which international intervention is seen as the most appropriate response to crises that are constructed as 'local'. The United States has taken the further step of arguing that its crushing preponderance offers the best means of responding to such crises and assuring global security. In this way, the most powerful actor in the international system has used its supposed pursuit of cosmopolitan purpose to argue for its further aggrandizement.

2.1.2 Economic conditionality

Since at least the signing of the Atlantic Charter in 1941, it has been the declared policy of the United States, the United Kingdom, and their allies to create an open international trading system and to promote liberal capitalism as the best means of organizing international economic relations. For much of their post-colonial history, most Third World countries resisted full incorporation in this system, attempting to pursue policies of import-substitution within protected economies with a view to reducing their vulnerability to external economic shocks.[56] It was the debt crisis of the 1980s that provided an opportunity for powerful capitalist states to prise open the hitherto relatively protected markets of Latin America and sub-Saharan Africa and to disseminate an Anglo-American model of capitalism through the instrument of conditional lending by the IFIs, which they dominated. In this section, I explain briefly what conditionality entailed. I then demonstrate the ways in which liberal cosmopolitanism has been used to legitimate the global spread of capitalism, before going on to analyse the power relations and interests that it helps to obscure.

The political story of economic conditionality begins with the oil shocks of 1973, when members of the Organization of Petroleum Exporting Countries (OPEC) virtually quadrupled the world price of oil in an attempt to increase their leverage vis-à-vis oil companies. Commercial banks flush with petro-dollars and looking for ways to profitably recycle this money, found ready customers in oil-importing developing countries, which now faced huge oil import bills. As a result, lending and debt soared through the 1970s. When the US Federal Reserve hiked interest rates in 1979 in an attempt to control inflation through contractionary monetary policies, debtors suddenly faced exponentially higher interest rates and found themselves unable to comply with repayment schedules. Creditor banks were unwilling to extend new loans, and politically conservative administrations then in power in Western states were loath to extend economic assistance to Third World debtors. Yet the scale of the crisis, the extent to which large international commercial banks were overexposed and the consequent vulnerability of the international financial system as a whole made some sort of state intervention imperative.[57]

The IMF became the lead agency in managing the debt crisis. In return for providing credit (together with banks and Western governments) to enable debtors to meet their repayment schedules, it demanded that indebted countries undertake 'stabilization' measures. In the short term, these aimed at reversing acute balance of payments deficits by requiring governments to reduce public sector expenditure and investment, eliminate subsidies, increase taxes, increase interest rates to discourage capital flight and control inflation, and (often) devalue the national currency in order to boost exports and improve the trade balance. Simultaneously, the IMF's sister institution—the World Bank—recommended policies of 'adjustment', which were concerned with promoting longer-term economic recovery and institutionalizing elements of the IMF's stabilization efforts. Broadly, adjustment was intended to reduce and redirect state economic intervention and increase reliance on the market for the allocation of scarce resources and commodities. It typically comprised major fiscal policy reform, trade, and financial sector liberalization and privatization. Economist John Williamson would subsequently label this package of policy measures the 'Washington Consensus'.[58] Debt management has essentially been a bargaining process in which borrower countries pursuing significant reform along the lines of the Washington Consensus, were 'rewarded'—with debt rescheduling (1982–5), fresh inflows of money under the Baker Plan (1985–9), some degree of market-based writing-down of debt under the Brady Plan (1989–96) and more comprehensive debt-cancellation under the Heavily Indebted Poor Countries (HIPC) initiative (1996 onwards).[59] In this way, conditional lending has been used as a tool to disseminate a particular model of capitalism to indebted countries.

While liberal cosmopolitan arguments are foregrounded very clearly in the justification of humanitarian intervention, they play a more discreet role in the legitimation of capitalism. Capitalism is typically justified in frankly self-interested terms by reference to the profit motive. By the same token, its global dissemination via free trade is usually justified in terms of mutual self-interest using David Ricardo's theory of comparative advantage. Conditionality in particular was justified as being necessary to curb profligacy and encourage greater fiscal responsibility on the part of Third World governments. But liberal cosmopolitanism has always played something of a supporting role in the justification of capitalist social relations. For one thing, capitalism and cosmopolitanism share a sensibility that is resolutely individualist. As I mentioned in chapter 1, critics like Calhoun have written that the individual material self-sufficiency of elite theorists might, in some subliminal way, account for their ethical repudiation of particularistic solidarities.[60] But it is possible to make the case for a more explicit link between cosmopolitanism and the global dissemination of capitalism.

Proponents of liberal capitalism have long argued that individual freedom—the core concern of liberalism as a political philosophy—entails the freedom to engage in economic exchange. The intellectual pedigree of this belief in the essential inseparability of political and economic freedom is traced to John Locke's affirmation of the natural rights of all men to life, liberty, and property.[61] Early Enlightenment thinkers such as Grotius, Pufendorf, and Vattel dwelt extensively on the psychological basis of universal affect, doing much of the work in linking cosmopolitanism and capitalism. They tended to see the cultivation of cosmopolitan sentiments of universal love for humanity as being motivated primarily by egoistic considerations. In their view, human beings' desire for survival (but also their greed for superfluities) necessitated trade and commerce, which in turn demanded the cultivation of universal sociability. Commerce was seen to play a civilizing role in international relations, with the result that the promotion of trade and commerce became both rational and a matter of moral duty. Because trade was enabled by the institution of private property, the moral imperative to promote trade was in effect one to impose property rights—by force if necessary—on those parts of the world that did not yet recognize them. The language of individual liberal rights and duties was ultimately an expression of this effort to reorganize human relations as market relations. Universal community in this view was not an end in itself, but a means to the end of business, with cosmopolitan sociability functioning as the ideological superstructure of a world capitalist market.[62]

In his wide-ranging survey of contrasting ideological attitudes towards capitalism, Albert Hirschman informs us that the notion that commerce was a civilizing agent—what he calls the 'doux-commerce thesis'—was propounded by a veritable deluge of eighteenth-century writers including Montesquieu, Condorcet, William Robertson, Thomas Paine, David Hume, and Adam Smith.[63] To this list can be added Immanuel Kant, whose essay *Perpetual Peace* invokes the 'spirit of commerce' as one motivational device by which the 'cunning' of nature will lead selfish men towards peaceful interaction.[64] Kant was not in favour of unrestricted economic globalization, criticizing 'the inhospitable conduct of...the commercial states, the injustice which they display in visiting foreign countries and peoples (which in their case is the same as conquering them)' and commending the behaviour of states resistant to being drawn into relations of unrestricted trade ('China and Japan, having had experience of such guests, have wisely placed restrictions on them').[65] Nonetheless, contemporary invocations of the 'spirit of commerce' can be found in the literature of democratic peace theory, which views economic interdependence between liberal states as providing additional material incentives for peaceful relations with one another.[66]

This putative relationship between capitalist social relations, human rights, and world peace has been elevated into a staple of US foreign policy, with policy pronouncements frequently reiterating the theme that free markets and free peoples go together. As the 2006 National Security Strategy proclaims: 'Promoting free and fair trade has long been a bedrock tenet of American foreign policy. Greater economic freedom is ultimately inseparable from political liberty. Economic freedom empowers individuals, and empowered individuals increasingly demand greater political freedom.'[67] Whatever the truth of this view, my argument here is simply that the ideals of universal human rights and world peace—paradigmatic cosmopolitan goals—are frequently pressed into service in the dissemination of capitalism. Even conditionality's fiercest critics have conceded the great *moral* appeal of the drive to harmonize the economic systems of states around the world under the aegis of supranational institutions such as the IFIs. Peter Gowan, for example, has acknowledged that this development 'could appear to respond to the great power of the idea of establishing a cosmopolitan system of global governance for it responds to deep, wide and thoroughly justified yearnings in the contemporary world to overcome nation-state rivalries'.[68] Nonetheless, it is imperative that we probe beneath the surface of justificatory discourse to investigate the power-political interests that it might serve.

Theorists of capitalism have noted its perpetual vulnerability to crises of over-accumulation, a state of affairs in which surpluses of labour and capital pile up side by side without any apparent means of bringing them together profitably. David Harvey argues that in such circumstances, surplus capital is typically absorbed by means of a 'spatio-temporal fix'.[69] Capital surpluses can either be temporally displaced through investment in long-term capital projects or social expenditures; or they can be spatially displaced through opening up new markets, new production facilities, etc. Over-accumulation emerged as a problem in the late 1960s, when competition from German and Japanese industry impeded the ability of the United States to absorb surplus capital, thereby necessitating the opening up of new markets.

But increasing competition within the capitalist core of the world economy also brought about more far-reaching shifts. As Harvey argues, US hegemony can be understood as standing on the three pillars of military power, productive capacity, and money. The first of these pillars has only grown stronger since the end of the Second World War particularly after the demise of the Soviet Union, with the crucial qualification that the United States has always had trouble fighting small imperial wars. The second of these pillars began to weaken in the late 1960s, prompting the United States to re-establish its hegemony on the basis of financial power. The Nixon administration accomplished this in two ways. First, it abandoned the gold standard in August 1971 and established a dollar standard in its stead, effectively seizing control of world monetary policy. Second, it reportedly colluded with the oil-producing states in the price hikes of 1973, in the knowledge that German and Japanese industry would suffer more given their heavier reliance on Middle Eastern oil supplies. It insisted on the recycling of petrodollars through US banks and abolished capital controls in 1974 with a view to liberalizing international financial markets. The rationale for these measures was to compensate for the loss of productive supremacy by preserving the privileged global financial position of the United States and the dollar's central role in international monetary relations.[70] But the effective exercise of financial power required markets in general and capital markets in particular to be opened to international trade.

The debt crisis provided a golden opportunity both to relieve the more general crisis of over-accumulation in the core of the capitalist system and more specifically to enable the exercise of US financial power. The immediate priority from the point of view of creditor states was to stabilize the private commercial banks that had been overexposed to Third World debt as a result of lax regulation and profligate lending to oil-importing states. There is a virtual consensus amongst analysts that structural adjustment programmes in the 1980s prioritized the interests of the banks over those of the populations of indebted countries.[71] While the debt crisis was over by 1985 from the perspective of the banks, Third World debt spiralled out of control as governments continued to borrow heavily to meet interest repayment schedules. The result was a net negative transfer of resources from debtor to creditor countries, setting back growth in the former by at least a decade.[72]

In the longer term, the debt crisis provided an opportunity for core capitalist states, working through the IFIs, to restructure the economies of indebted countries in ways that favoured their penetration by foreign capital. Structural adjustment was foisted on borrowing countries primarily on grounds of fostering greater fiscal responsibility and stimulating growth, and secondarily with reference to the pacifying effects of the spread of global capitalism. In fact it had a negative impact on both growth and development, and left many of its beneficiaries newly vulnerable to the exercise of US financial power and to the gyrations of global capitalism thanks particularly to the lifting of capital controls.

If growth is the standard by which the success of structural adjustment is to be evaluated, the evidence is very worrying indeed. One study reported that between 1960 and 1980 (a period during which most Third World countries were highly protectionist and interventionist), GDP per capita grew by 75% in Latin America and 36% in sub-Saharan Africa; in the 1980–98 period, when stabilization and adjustment policies were implemented in these countries, the corresponding figures were 6% and −15%, respectively.[73] The only region that grew faster in the latter period was East Asia—but this was largely fuelled by growth in China, a country that has hardly been a practitioner of the Washington Consensus.

Indeed many have pointed out that East Asian success was not achieved via adherence to the orthodoxy that the IFIs preached. Far from being laissez-faire, governments in the region intervened actively and imaginatively, using a variety of policy instruments, to develop specific industries that they saw as having a high potential for growth and job creation.[74] Far from liberalizing trade across the board, they were initially export-oriented and selectively protectionist (maintaining an openness to inputs but not imports per se and liberalizing imports only after there had been a transition to high growth). The Washington Consensus, as it stands, barely acknowledges these heterodox routes out of marginality. In Dani Rodrik's words, 'today's globalisers would be unable to replicate these experiences without running afoul of the IMF or the WTO'.[75] From a more historical perspective, Ha-Joon Chang demonstrates that today's wealthy countries engaged in high levels of infant industry protection (using such instruments as tariffs, subsidies, and public-private partnerships) during the early phases of their industrialization. In his view, by prohibiting Third World countries from pursuing similar policies through the exercise of conditionality, they are in effect 'kicking away the ladder' that these countries hope to climb.[76]

One aspect of structural adjustment that deserves special attention is financial liberalization, because it illustrates the ways in which the United States exercises power on the strength of its financial hegemony. A number of states (including East Asian countries which had emerged relatively unscathed from the debt crisis of the 1980s) began to lift capital controls under pressure from the United States, becoming vulnerable to large flows of speculative 'hot money' that had a tremendously destabilizing effect on their currencies and economies. Harvey has gone so far as to suggest that capitalism survives its crises of over-accumulation not only via the spatio-temporal fix but also through periodic devaluations of capital visited on vulnerable territories by means of what he calls 'accumulation by dispossession'. This essentially entails the release of assets into the market at very low or no cost, so that they can then be seized by over-accumulated capital and turned to profitable use. In its crudest and most obvious manifestations this might take the form of what is typically called the 'enclosure of the commons'. In the global financial system, Harvey argues, 'accumulation by dispossession' takes the form of speculative attacks on currencies by hedge funds and other major financial institutions, which often results in capital flight from the state concerned and a consequent devaluation of assets that can then be bought up by foreign and local capitalists at bargain prices.[77] Gowan has written of how financial crises in the Third World can actually boost Wall Street through capital flight: 'when a financial crisis hits a country, large funds would flee not only that country but others fearing contagion and the funds would flee to the Anglo-American financial nexus, boosting liquidity, lowering interest rates and having a generally healthy impact'.[78] Because of the ever-present danger that such crises can become generalized, it is the function of state interventions and of international institutions, in Harvey's view, 'to orchestrate devaluations in ways that permit accumulation by dispossession to occur without sparking a general collapse'.[79]

Former World Bank chief economist Joseph Stiglitz corroborates the view that something like this occurred in the aftermath of the East Asian financial crisis of 1997–8. Accusing the IMF of safeguarding the interests of Wall Street above all else, he demonstrates how policies imposed by the Fund in response to the crisis systematically prioritized the repayment of foreign creditors over all other considerations.[80] Massive bailout packages to countries like South Korea enabled governments to provide money to firms that were in debt to Western banks. The IMF was, in effect, bailing out the banks, which were thereby relieved of having to assume responsibility for bad lending decisions. The bailouts also allowed countries to sustain artificially high exchange rates for a brief period, giving foreign investors and domestic capitalists the opportunity to convert their money into dollars on favourable terms before whisking it abroad. The IMF prescription that countries build up financial reserves by cutting expenditure, increasing interest rates, and reducing imports, made sense from the perspective of repaying foreign creditors, but had the consequence of exacerbating domestic recession, increasing unemployment, and exporting the economic downturn to trading partners. Lurking behind each of the IMF's prescriptions was a clear hierarchy of interests in which creditors (most of whom were located in the IFIs' most powerful shareholding countries) came first.

This brief review of the critical literature on conditionality reveals some striking similarities with the discussion of humanitarian intervention in the previous section. Like humanitarian intervention, conditionality is a practice that is deeply interventionist in the affairs of Third World states. It is typically legitimated in universalist terms (the mutual benefits of comparative advantage, the pacifying effects of economic interdependence, etc.) but serves very particular interests including the maintenance of US hegemony. But the argument is vulnerable to the criticism that it offers an impoverished view of agency in its insinuation that the content of conditionality is shaped almost single-handedly by the most powerful capitalist state in the system—the United States—or, in subtler analyses, by that formation that some commentators have referred to as the 'Wall Street-Treasury-IMF complex'. Such a claim would be exaggerated, and is not essential to my argument.

Conditionality has been implemented primarily through the IMF and the World Bank, within which it is certainly the case that powerful capitalist states have the greatest voice. Voting power in both institutions is unequal and weighted, in accordance with a country's shareholding in the case of the Bank[81] and its relative weight in the world economy in the case of the IMF.[82] This results in a situation where one country—the United States—with 4.6% of the world's population has a 17.1% voting share, giving it a veto over decisions requiring a majority of 85%. On the other hand, 44 of the 45 sub-Saharan African members of the IMF (with roughly 10% of the world's population) have a voting share of 4.4%. The 40 HIPC countries—in whose affairs the IMF is most intrusive—have a combined voting share of 2.29% in the IMF.[83] Three-quarters of the member states of the IMF and the World Bank are not directly represented on the Board of Executive Directors or in the senior management of either institution, and many have virtually no nationals working on the staff.[84]

Some critics have taken these facts as suggesting that the IFIs are simply instruments of their most powerful shareholders (Gowan sees them as 'façade-cosmopolitan agencies for advancing the interests of American capitalism').[85] Others like Ngaire Woods have qualified this view in important ways. Woods argues that the attitudes of borrowing Third World governments as well as the bureaucracy of the IFIs themselves are crucial additional variables shaping their output. In her view, the IFIs are most effective in deploying coercive power to implement their technical advice when they are able to work with sympathetic interlocutors within borrowing countries who are willing and able to put conditionality into effect.[86] This is an important point because it underscores once again the consensual basis for hegemony. Normative justifications for conditionality as being in the borrowing countries' interests are not *simply* smokescreens for the power-political interests of creditors, even if they also perform this function. The US claim that the global spread of capitalism is in the universal interest retains a degree of plausibility because sufficient benefits flow to capitalists in all countries. Conditionality is often welcomed by domestic capitalists for its ability to unleash economic opportunities that were hitherto closed to them.[87] Indeed, some sectors of domestic capitalism benefit even in circumstances of financial crisis: money capital escapes to Wall Street, domestic capitalists with access to funds can snap up state industries being privatized to restore state finances, and export sectors can benefit given the export-orientation of conditionality packages.[88]

The consensual basis for intervention in the economic affairs of Third World states has also been established through a claim to greater knowledge and expertise on the part of the IFIs and a representation of economic crisis as the consequence of ill-advised or 'politicized' local decision-making. That the expertise of IFI personnel is acknowledged by their sympathetic interlocutors in borrowing countries should come as no surprise, given the common class interests and intellectual provenance of these two groups.[89] As for the representation of crisis, once again an analogy can be drawn with the construction of humanitarian crises as stemming from primarily local factors. The World Bank's 1982 Berg report, widely seen as a manifesto for the application of Washington Consensus policies in Africa and published on the eve of the debt crisis, consistently discounted the significance of external factors[90] in accounting for Africa's disappointing economic performance and focused largely on what African governments ought to be doing differently (with some genuflection in the direction of greater aid from the donor community). Its conclusion that 'African governments must lead the way because domestic policy issues are at the heart of the crisis'[91] was somewhat belied by its own observation that lack of growth in Africa was to some extent a result of vulnerability to external shocks and constraints (declining terms of trade as a result of oil price hikes, a decline in demand for primary commodities, trade restrictions, etc.).

Although the rhetoric of responsibility has changed, with an acceptance by both donor and recipient countries of their respective obligations,[92] the attitudes that underlay this initial spatial attribution of culpability for poor growth performance remain today. IMF-designed stabilization packages focus almost exclusively on the domestic causes of balance of payments deficits, largely ignoring exogenous factors that make it difficult for countries to increase their export earnings such as short-term fluctuations in commodity prices, and volatility among key currencies, etc. The Fund incurred sharp criticism for its relative neglect of exogenous factors in its management of the East Asian financial crisis.[93] Woods argues that the IMF has tended to focus on factors internal to deficit countries for institutional reasons: it has the tools and the leverage to exact promises of policy reform from borrowing governments, but no leverage over creditor governments in respect of their trade and macroeconomic policies and currency arrangements. Closely related to this is the power-political reality that if it were to turn its attention to exogenous factors, the Fund would run up against the preferences of its most powerful shareholders. The US Treasury has pushed strongly for rapid capital-account liberalization despite criticism that premature liberalization renders countries vulnerable to speculative attacks on their currencies and destabilizing capital flight. It has also fought against such measures as short-term capital controls, despite their evident success in countries like Malaysia and Chile.[94] Proponents of the Washington Consensus have tended to interpret the East Asian and other financial crises as evidence of rotten local institutions and 'crony capitalism', rather than as following from IFI advice in the first place.

In this section, I have offered a reading of economic conditionality as a liberal cosmopolitan practice that helps to shore up US hegemony. Conditionality is typically justified primarily as a means of curbing the profligacy of Third World governments and encouraging growth, and secondarily as laying the foundations for economic interdependence in ways that will foster peace between states. The latter has been a central element of the cosmopolitan agenda. In fact, conditionality has been motivated primarily by the need to alleviate capitalism's periodic crises of over-accumulation and to accommodate the shifting material bases of US hegemony. It has had deeply damaging impacts on growth and equity in many Third World states. Nonetheless, it is more appropriate to view conditionality as a hegemonic rather than a purely coercive practice. In addition to the moral claims that it makes for itself, it has legitimated itself by distributing benefits to propertied classes all over the world. Finally, it has bolstered its claim to authority through its construction of the international as the domain of expertise and the local as the domain of ignorance, rent-seeking, and corruption.

2.1.3 Historical memory and resistance

Only by historicizing the experience of intervention in the Third World can we begin to appreciate the depth of hostility and resistance that its contemporary manifestations arouse. Moral argumentation over humanitarian intervention and economic conditionality bears a striking resemblance to the normative controversies that attended the practice of imperialism in the nineteenth and early twentieth centuries. Writing in 1902, the British political economist J. A. Hobson commented on the extraordinary mixture of actors and interests that drove the imperialist impulse. He testified to the existence 'in a considerable though not a large proportion of the British nation [of] a genuine desire to spread Christianity among the heathen, to diminish the cruelty and other sufferings which they believe exist in countries less fortunate than their own, and to do good work about the world in the cause of humanity'.[95] Alongside this, he wrote extensively about the self-interested motivations of imperialist politicians, soldiers, and specific trading and financial sectors. He criticized the first group for their belief 'that religion and other arts of civilisation are portable commodities which it is our duty to convey to the backward nations, and that a certain amount of compulsion is justified in pressing their benefits upon people too ignorant at once to recognize them'; but he was more scathing of the second group, who 'simply and instinctively attach to themselves any strong, genuine elevated feeling which is of service, fan it and feed it until it assumes fervour, and utilize it for their ends'.[96] In a critique that struck an eerily contemporary note when I first read it in the months before the 2003 Iraq war, he says:

> ...politicians, in particular, acquire so strong a habit of setting their projects in the most favourable light that they soon convince themselves that the finest result which they think may conceivably accrue from any policy is the actual motive of that policy. As for the public, it is only natural that it should be deceived. All the purer and more elevated adjuncts of Imperialism are kept to the fore by religious and philanthropic agencies: patriotism appeals to the general lust of power within a people by suggestions of nobler uses, adopting the forms of self-sacrifice to cover domination and the love of adventure.... It is precisely in this falsification of the real import of motives that the gravest vice and the most signal peril of Imperialism reside. When, out of a medley of mixed motives, the least potent is selected for public prominence because it is the most presentable, when issues of a policy which was not present at all to the minds of those who formed this policy are treated as chief causes, the moral currency of the nation is debased. The whole policy of Imperialism is riddled with this deception.[97]

Like the 'genuine desire to spread Christianity' of nineteenth-century missionaries, liberal cosmopolitanism today enables self-interested exercises of power to masquerade as fantasies of rescue. Critics of economic conditionality will find no less striking parallels in the work of the Italian political economist Achille Loria:

> When a country which has contracted a debt is unable, on account of the slenderness of its income, to offer sufficient guarantee for the punctual payment of interest, what happens? Sometimes an out-and-out conquest of the debtor country follows. Thus France's attempted conquest of Mexico during the second empire was undertaken solely with the view of guaranteeing the interest of French citizens holding Mexican securities. But more frequently the insufficient guarantee of an international loan gives rise to the appointment of a financial commission by the creditor countries in order to protest their rights and guard the fate of their invested capital. The appointment of such a commission literally amounts in the end, however, to a veritable conquest. We have examples of this in Egypt, which has to all practical purposes become a British province, and in Tunis, which has in like manner become a dependency of France, who supplied the greater part of the loan....[98]

There is a resonance between contemporary practices that invoke liberal cosmopolitan justifications and classical imperialism, not only in the material practices that they entailed and the moral arguments that were used to buttress them, but also in the identity of the actors at the forefront of both developments. The states in the vanguard of humanitarian intervention and economic conditionality happen to be those with imperial pasts or sharing close cultural affinities with former imperial powers. This is not surprising given the role of capitalism in driving both imperialism and contemporary coercive interventions in the Third World, and given also the brute fact that liberal capitalist states are the most powerful in the world. I include within this characterization not only the core states of the EU with histories of formal imperialism, but also the United States which, despite its foundation in an anti-colonial act of revolution and its frequent protestations of anti-colonialism, is justifiably seen as an imperial and colonial power. (One thinks here of its continent-wide expansion by means of conquest and extermination of native inhabitants, its highly unequal relations with its Latin American neighbours under the Monroe Doctrine, its practice of formal colonialism between 1898 and 1946, its consistent support to colonial powers attempting to suppress nationalist movements during the Cold War wherever these were perceived to be Communist-influenced, etc.)[99]

The participation of 'non-imperial'[100] states such as the smaller powers of the EU, Canada, Australia, New Zealand, and even Southern Cone states like Argentina[101] and Chile in liberal cosmopolitan ventures does little to weaken perceptions of continuity between historic imperialism and contemporary coercive interventions in the Third World. The incremental expansion of what international society theorists might call the 'liberal solidarist vanguard' to include mostly states that have strong cultural affinities with the former imperial powers seems to acknowledge an implicit cultural hierarchy in international society. The message to those not included is that they must either undergo dramatic cultural revolutions of their own, or remain permanent outliers. This point is further reinforced by the fact that economic success does not appear to be a sufficient condition for entry into this vanguard. Witness the difficulties faced by Japan in persuading the World Bank (despite being one of its largest shareholders) to modify its approach to conditionality by taking into account the developmental experiences of East Asian states.[102] Think also of the difficulties that East Asian countries as a group have faced in setting up an Asian Monetary Fund as an alternative to the US-dominated IMF. Despite their impressive economic success, these states do not yet appear to be significant norm-entrepreneurs.

The striking parallels between historic imperialism and contemporary coercive interventions in the Third World—or what might now appropriately be called neo-imperialism—coupled with the fact that both sets of practices were spearheaded by virtually the same states, severely undermines the credibility of invocations of liberal cosmopolitan arguments by states today. There is a considerable literature on the ways in which social memory—and particularly the memory of empire and imperialism—informs contemporary resistance to Western power. Analysts of Chinese foreign policy have often remarked on the extent to which Chinese elites' perception of a 'century of humiliation' suffered under the boot of Western imperialism between 1840 and 1949 informs their present-day world view.[103] Writers on the Middle East have noted that the memory of relatively recent imperial rule in that region may account for the high degree of scepticism with which Anglo-American justifications for the 2003 invasion of Iraq were greeted.[104] In Chapter 3, I will argue that this memory of imperialism informs collective Third World responses to contemporary liberal cosmopolitan interventionism. But I will also be interested in exploring the coercive logics of this Third World response.

2.2 COSMOPOLITANISM IN THE ACADEMY: BETWEEN APOLOGY AND UTOPIA

There is a rather polarized debate in the literature on the history of ideas about whether cosmopolitanism is an imperial or an anti-imperial world view. As I mentioned in chapter 1, Pagden's genealogical analysis of cosmopolitanism

The Dark Sides of Cosmopolitanism

reminds us of the difficulties of disentangling it from the history of European universalism and its civilizing mission. Sceptical of the contemporary revival of Stoic cosmopolitanism in the Western academy,[105] he offers a more sobering reading of some of its key figures, drawing attention to the potentially ethnocentric nature of their claims: 'in calling upon all men to belong to a common *deme* or polis, Zeno was also making all men members of the *deme* or polis to which *he* belonged'.[106] Calhoun's criticisms are more oblique. Cosmopolitanism per se is not responsible for empire and capitalism, but it has flourished in locations created by those enterprises (imperial capitals, trading cities, and a transnational capitalist class) and bears the imprint of their sensibilities. The failure to acknowledge that the imagination of cosmopolitanism was enabled by these oppressive material preconditions makes it woefully inadequate to the task of attacking those structures.[107] On the other side of the argument, Sankar Muthu has argued that eighteenth-century Enlightenment thinkers such as Diderot, Kant, and Herder espoused a decidedly anti-imperialist notion of cosmopolitanism, one that understood 'humanity' as a capacity for cultural agency that expressed itself differently in different environments. The view that what makes us human also makes us different from one another, accounted for their understanding of human societies as radically incommensurable (i.e. impossible to rank against one another) which in turn provided the basis for a defence of non-European peoples against European imperialism that is frequently articulated in their work.[108]

There are a number of difficulties with making a judgment about this debate. Its participants tend to focus on different figures in the cosmopolitan canon, and they are not all equally interested in the relationship between theory and praxis. Indeed it is precisely by paying attention to this relationship that we might begin to see how both sides of this argument make valid claims. Cosmopolitanism has always had an inherent dual tendency towards both the justification and critique of empire. But how can this be possible?

Some scholars have suggested that cosmopolitanism in the thought of the early Stoics was simply a philosophical ideal committed to the essential equality of all human beings. It was a critical normative standard against which the conduct of actually existing polities was to be judged, rather than a political blueprint for the organization of power. When Zeno, Diogenes, and Socrates amongst others spoke of being citizens of the world, they did not mean to imply the existence of a world state or the need to bring one into being. Rather, their primary concern was that human beings give each other equal respect in their dealings with one another regardless of the communities to which they belonged, *as if* they were fellow citizens of a universal polity. The language of citizenship was used in an entirely metaphorical fashion. Derek Heater surmises that they may have chosen to express this moral stance in a political vocabulary simply because they lacked any other. Or they might have believed that if people were to understand this philosophical ideal and act in accordance with it, their behaviour would so approximate the ideal of Greek and Roman civic life that 'citizenly' seemed the appropriate description.[109]

Whatever the reason, when the Greek city states were absorbed into the Macedonian and later the Roman empire something quite different started to happen. As Costas Douzinas argues, Stoic ideas of universal morality proved to be of great use to empire builders, particularly in the construction of a law common to all imperial subjects—what the Romans called *jus gentium*. The metaphorical notion of world citizenship was transformed into the actuality of membership in a rapidly expanding polity with pretensions to world statehood. Cosmopolitanism was no longer a tool of resistance that mobilized the spirit of the cosmos against the order of the polis. Instead, the law of the polis had been elevated to rule the cosmos with Stoic ideas of universal moral community being invoked in legitimation. As Douzinas puts it, 'cosmopolitanism starts as moral universalism but often degenerates into imperial globalism'.[110]

In fact, both tendencies can be apparent contemporaneously and can help us understand the state of thinking on cosmopolitanism in the Western academy today. Much of this chapter has demonstrated the ways in which cosmopolitanism is used to legitimate imperial globalism. Far from attacking the hegemonic capture of cosmopolitanism, many writers have called upon Western states to act as a vanguard for the achievement of liberal cosmopolitan goals.[111] Francis Fukuyama famously argued that Kant's project for perpetual peace could best be accomplished through the forceful and concerted action of the United States and other democracies to preserve, and where possible expand, the sphere of democracy.[112] Martin Shaw has called for Western states to take the lead in dealing with global crises 'since only the West has the economic, political and military resources and the democratic and multinational institutions and culture necessary' for this purpose. In his view, 'the west has a historic responsibility to take on this global leadership, not because it should impose itself on the rest of the world, but because so many people in the rest of the world look to it for support'.[113] It is in this context that we can understand the nostalgia for US hegemony expressed by Michael Doyle (in an era when the thesis of declining US hegemony was perhaps more credible).[114] Some like Ignatieff have recognized the frankly imperial—even hypocritical—character of Western claims to be waging war for human rights, but have nonetheless endorsed these ventures as the best hope for realizing cosmopolitan purposes.[115] These writers are untroubled by a balance of power in the world today that grossly favours the West. Far from recognizing the implications of such a state of affairs—its culpability for what Johan Galtung called 'structural violence'[116]—they regard the Western advantage as a means of achieving liberal cosmopolitan goals. In effect, they function as apologists for neo-imperialism.

But there is another significant body of work in the academy that has been deeply critical of the policies of Western states. Liberal cosmopolitan philosophers Charles Beitz and Thomas Pogge have long argued for the global application of Rawls' difference principle, whereby resources would be distributed globally in such a way as to maximize the condition of the least well-off—a prescription that would have radical distributive implications if it were ever implemented.[117] Pogge has excoriated Western economic policies for causing poverty in the Third World rather than merely failing to alleviate it.[118] Henry Shue's demolition of the distinction between so-called positive and negative rights seriously undermines one of the traditional Western justifications for failing to accord equal priority to economic and social rights such as a right to subsistence.[119] Martha Nussbaum earned the censure of a wide swath of the US academy for arguing that it was morally arbitrary to accord citizens a higher priority than strangers.[120] Peter Singer has long been accused of making unreasonable demands on human generosity by insisting that one is obliged to contribute to the alleviation of the suffering of distant strangers to the point where one is in danger of losing something of moral significance comparable to what one's intended beneficiaries lack.[121] Far from being apologists for the policies of Western states or the moral intuitions of Western societies, these philosophers are amongst their fiercest critics.

But their work might also be considered utopian in the pejorative sense of being ineffectual or inadequate to the task of combating a Western-led imperialist globalism. In at least one respect, these philosophers are the intellectual heirs of the early Stoic tradition, which saw cosmopolitanism as a philosophical standard of judgment rather than an ideal of political organization. That distinction is encoded in a contemporary differentiation between moral and institutional cosmopolitanism, which all of them make and which lies at the heart of their thinking about the possibilities for the praxis of cosmopolitanism in the world today. It is also what makes them utopian in the pejorative sense of that word.

As Beitz explains it, institutional cosmopolitanism is concerned with the way political institutions ought to be designed so as to give effect to cosmopolitan precepts. Although it could conceivably take a wide variety of forms, from 'world government' at one extreme to looser networks of regional arrangements at another, 'the distinctive common feature is some ideal of world political organisation in which states and state-like units have significantly diminished authority in comparison with the status quo and supranational institutions have more'.[122] In contrast, moral cosmopolitanism is concerned, not with institutions themselves, but with 'the basis on which institutions, practices, or courses of action should be justified or criticized. It applies to the whole world the maxim that answers to questions about what we should do, or what institutions we should establish, should be based on an impartial consideration of the claims of each person who would be affected by our choices.'[123] Beitz sees moral cosmopolitanism as more fundamental than institutional cosmopolitanism because it provides the basis for arguments on behalf of cosmopolitan institutions as well as for the specification of institutional design.[124] He also sees no necessary link between moral and institutional cosmopolitanism:

> Someone who adopts the point of view of moral cosmopolitanism is not necessarily committed to the belief that the world should be reorganised as a unitary or stateless political and legal order. Indeed, it might be argued that a state-based world order is more likely to be justifiable from a point of view that includes everyone—at least under contemporary conditions.... Two points follow from this. First, the widely alleged undesirability of world government is not a good reason to reject the ethical aspiration it represents. If advocacy of world government is a mistake, this is more likely because it exhibits political naivety than philosophical error. More importantly, what moral cosmopolitanism requires of political institutions is a complex question—more complex than both the friends and the opponents of cosmopolitan views have sometimes appreciated.[125]

To illustrate the possibility of giving effect to the precepts of moral cosmopolitanism in a world that is not institutionally cosmopolitan, Beitz gives the example of the doctrine of universal human rights, which is cosmopolitan in its foundations without being cosmopolitan in its institutional requirements. Universal human rights are founded on the cosmopolitan idea that conceptions of individual well-being are not fundamentally relative to culture or geographical location and that, in the assignment of responsibility for satisfying basic individual needs, national (or cultural or ethnic) boundaries do not necessarily play a limiting role. At the same time, human rights doctrine does not prescribe any particular institutions for the world as a whole: it does not insist on universal institutions; merely that institutions everywhere, whatever form they might take, protect universal interests. Accordingly in Beitz's view, 'human rights doctrine does not rule out the possibility—indeed, it trades on the hope—that its institutional requirements can be satisfied within a political structure containing nation-states more or less as we know them today'.[126]

The primacy accorded to moral cosmopolitanism does not mean that these theorists see no role for institutions in their proposals for global justice. Indeed Beitz, Nussbaum, Pogge, and Shue are unanimous on the point that institutions must play the primary role in giving effect to duties of global justice, given the problems of collective action, fairness, and capacity that would arise were such duties to be left to individuals.[127] The point of the distinction between moral and institutional cosmopolitanism is to insist that institutions for global justice ought not, and need not, take a cosmopolitan form. In part this insistence comes out of a belief, echoing Kant, in the undesirability of a world state—a hypothetical institution that is seen to be fraught with the prospect of inescapable global tyranny.[128] As Shue advocates, 'rather than global institutions, which may be dangerous and are in any case most unlikely, we would pursue minimal global standards for national institutions'.[129] In part, it comes out of a belief in the moral worth and defensibility of the nation-state, with the crucial proviso that such states satisfy a certain threshold of legitimacy.[130] And in part, it may stem from a desire to insist on the possibilities for the practice of cosmopolitanism in the world as it is rather than a deferral of such praxis to a hypothetical uncertain future in which a world state has been ushered into being. While these are all commendable reasons, the disavowal of institutional cosmopolitanism is nonetheless problematic for three reasons.

First, much of this work appears to set up a false opposition between a tyrannical world state on the one hand and a system of sovereign states on the other. In a highly reductive move, institutional cosmopolitanism is equated with world statehood,[131] only to be summarily dismissed by raising the spectre of global tyranny from which there would be no escape. Shue's opposition between dangerous global and actually existing national institutions is unhelpful because it offers a somewhat impoverished view of what institutional cosmopolitanism *might* look like (recall Beitz's recognition that it might take a variety of forms, of which world government is only the most extreme).[132] There is an emerging literature on cosmopolitan democracy that attempts to think through what these alternative forms might be. I will explain why this literature is unsatisfactory in its own way. But I first need to make a case for why the utopians are wrong not to take institutional cosmopolitanism more seriously.

As I mentioned earlier, moral cosmopolitans agree that institutions rather than individuals ought to be the primary bearers of duties of global justice, with individuals being under an obligation to create and support such institutions. Yet despite this recognition that institutions will have to do the heavy lifting, the disavowal of institutional cosmopolitanism seems to impose constraints on the extent to which existing institutions can and ought to be redesigned to ensure that they give effect to moral cosmopolitan precepts. To put this slightly differently, the fear of world government seems to result in an endorsement of the institutional status quo[133] and a reliance on a heroic degree of voluntarism to make existing institutions deliver better results. Nussbaum's latest work on global justice is a case in point. After rehearsing a familiar litany of arguments against institutional cosmopolitanism, she says:

> If these arguments are good ones, the institutional structure at the global level ought to remain thin and decentralised. Part of it will consist, quite simply, of the domestic basic structures, to which we shall assign responsibilities for redistributing some of their wealth to other nations. Part of it will consist of multinational corporations, to which we shall assign certain responsibilities for promoting human capabilities in the nations in which they do business. Part of it will consist of global economic policies, agencies, and agreements, including the World Bank, the IMF, and various trade agreements. Part will consist of other international bodies, such as the UN, the ILO, the World Court and the new world criminal court, and of international agreements in many areas, such as human rights, labour, and environment. Part of it will consist of non-governmental organizations of many kinds, ranging from the large and multinational (such as OXFAM) to the small and local.[134]

In other words, institutionally, the world ought to look very much as it does today. But existing institutions ought to take on ethical obligations to promote the capabilities that Nussbaum argues are essential for human flourishing. It is curious that in Nussbaum's view, the process of assigning and assuming new ethical responsibilities in her preferred world order does not seem to entail radical revision of institutions or the incentive structures within which they operate. Arguing that multinational corporations ought to assume responsibility for promoting human capabilities in the regions in which they operate, she says:

> To some extent corporations can be controlled by domestic laws in each country. But the difficulty is that all countries want to attract them [thereby potentially setting off a 'race to the bottom'] so the main responsibility must rest on the members of the corporation themselves, their lawyers, and, very importantly, their consumers, who may bring pressure to bear on a corporation to perform better than it has been performing.[135]

This is not the appropriate place to enter into a debate over the merits of voluntary corporate social responsibility programmes, although critics of these would probably find Nussbaum's proposal vacuous. Suffice it to say that this approach to reform of the current global order reveals the deep conservatism of a moral cosmopolitanism that refuses to acknowledge, first, that moral cosmopolitanism might be inconceivable without deep and radical reform of existing institutions, and second, that such reform *might* push us in the direction of institutional cosmopolitanism.

A third reason why the disavowal of institutional cosmopolitanism is problematic is that it seems to rest on a view of the world that betrays the elite theorist's vantage point and may not be widely shared. There is something ontologically quaint about Shue's hope, expressed in the mid-1990s, that 'rather than global institutions...we would pursue minimal global standards for national institutions'[136] (implying that we live in a world of mainly national institutions), or Nussbaum's more recent argument that 'the institutional structure at the global level ought to *remain* thin and decentralised'[137] (as if that institutional structure *were* thin and decentralized). One of the central questions in the debate on 'globalization' concerns the impact that its constituent processes have had on state sovereignty. David Held offers a useful typology of views on this question, distinguishing between 'hyperglobalists' who see globalization as eclipsing the state, 'sceptics' who see states as being in the driving seat of globalization, and 'transformationalists' who see states as key actors but ones that increasingly have to share the regulatory space with other actors in ways that transform the nature and exercise of sovereignty.[138] The problem with the first two sets of views is that it is simply impossible to generalize about what globalization is doing to the state. Perspective is everything here. From the point of view of the United States or perhaps even states like India, Brazil, and South Africa, we do indeed live in a world of sovereign states where the state largely possesses a monopoly over the legitimate use of coercion within its territory, can control the pace of its integration into the world economy, and demonstrates other attributes of sovereignty. From the point of view of states like Afghanistan, Liberia, Sierra Leone, or the Democratic Republic of Congo, where the state lacks a monopoly over the legitimate means of coercion, or maintains one only with considerable external assistance, or where it is so heavily penetrated by IFIs, donors, NGOs, and other actors as to enjoy very little meaningful sovereign space, it is not at all clear *pace* Shue that we live in a world of national institutions, or *pace* Nussbaum that the international is thin and decentralized. From here, the world looks very different indeed.

But we do not even have to adopt the perspective of this emerging 'Fourth World' to discern the outlines of a world state. Following Schmitt's understanding of the sovereign as 'he who decides on the exception'[139] and referring specifically to the wars on Kosovo and Iraq, Douzinas has argued that by deciding to except itself from the rule of law on those occasions, the United States effectively placed itself in the position of the sovereign in the new world order.[140] Indeed these are only the most spectacular occasions on which it has done so. Nico Krisch has demonstrated a more long-running tendency on the part of the United States to formalize a position of superiority for itself in the law (what he calls the 'legalisation of inequality') or to except itself from a number of provisions of international law, either by entering extensive reservations or by simply refusing to sign or ratify treaties (what he calls the 'inequality of legalisation'). Krisch suggests that the United States displays many features of a world sovereign, given the numerous ways in which it unilaterally exercises legislative, executive, and judicial functions, albeit often in the name of an amorphous 'international community'.[141] In a similar vein, reacting with surprise to Hardt and Negri's understanding of empire as a decentralized and de-territorialized apparatus of rule, Tarak Barkawi and Mark Laffey have spoken of the creation of an international state dominated by the United States.[142]

These pronouncements should not induce us to take a view of the United States as omnipotent. The point is simply that far from living in a world of sovereign states enveloped by a thin and decentralized international order, we inhabit a hierarchical imperial system in which sovereignty—rather than eroding for all—has flowed from some states to others. No one put this more clearly than Richard Haass, Director of Policy Planning in the US Department of State under the first George W. Bush administration:

> What you are seeing in this administration is the emergence of a new principle or body of ideas... about what you might call the limits of sovereignty. Sovereignty entails obligations. One is not to massacre your own people. Another is not to support terrorism in any way. If a government fails to meet these obligations, then it forfeits some of the normal advantages of sovereignty, including the right to be left alone inside your own territory. Other governments, including the US, gain the right to intervene. In the case of terrorism, this can even lead to a right of preventive... self-defence. You essentially can act in anticipation if you have grounds to think it's a question of when, and not if, you're going to be attacked.[143]

The zero-sum logic of this way of thinking about sovereignty is very clear: some states lose, other states gain. When hegemony is exercised coercively, the centre of sovereign power in the international system comes into sharper focus. When hegemony reverts to more consensual means of exercising its power (as the Obama administration looks set to do), it is harder to discern a centre. Yet as long as power continues to be distributed as unevenly as it is in the world today, and in the absence of radical changes in the purposes for which power is used, the shift to more consensual forms of hegemony will offer only the consolation of tyranny without a tyrant from the perspective of less powerful actors in the system.

If we are ever to wake up and find ourselves in a world state, it will not have had a formal inaugural moment. Instead, it will have come about through the gradual and insidious accretion of norms, institutions, networks, and other novel and complex forms of governance that encode new forms of hierarchy and power—a process that is already well under way.[144] Whether moral cosmopolitans like it or not, imperial cosmopolitan institutions are being—have been—constructed. The choices now can only be to roll them back, or to democratize them. Rolling back international institutions *in toto* seems increasingly unlikely, although one could regard the new rhetoric of 'ownership' espoused by donors and IFIs as a case of rolling back the international and widening the sovereign space in a very specific context. Nonetheless, roll back on a macro scale is difficult to envisage and might even be undesirable in many cases, given the range of problems generated by interdependence that demand cooperation across borders and given also the gross abuses that the institution of sovereign statehood has enabled (the subject of chapter 3).[145] If that is the case, then there can be no escape from the task of engaging with the possibilities of institutional cosmopolitanism, an endeavour that would entail radically reshaping international institutions in ways that ensured that they took seriously the cosmopolitan premise that the claims of all individuals who inhabit our planet ought to be regarded equally.

There is a literature that has begun to think through the implications of the fact that the locus of power is no longer primarily national—namely, that people are increasingly implicated in what Held calls 'communities of fate' where their life chances are shaped by forces that lie beyond the nation-states to which they belong, and that the emergence of these new spaces and communities demands new democratic political institutions. Democracy, it is argued in this literature, must exist not only within and between states but also in these new global spaces where its exercise will involve more than simply scaling up democratic institutions and procedures that have been developed within nation-states. These new institutions of 'cosmopolitan democracy' would coexist with the state system but would override states in certain clearly defined spheres.[146]

These are interesting lines of enquiry, but this literature has not lived up to its promise for a number of reasons. For one thing, it is still mainly speculative or normative in its spirit without thinking very deeply about the historical-sociological conditions under which its objectives could be accomplished. Critics have also pointed out that it adopts a sociologically thin notion of democracy, neglecting to provide an account of the social bases of solidarity and public discourse and of how these can be developed at levels above and beyond the nation-state.[147] This literature is also narrowly political, failing to confront the social and economic realities of contemporary capitalism, much less offering an account of how it can be brought to heel.[148] And beyond vague genuflections before the altar of civil society (a concept that is itself aspirationally defined, if at all),[149] it says little about the role of popular agency in bringing about cosmopolitan democracy, threatening to replicate the problems of 'democratic deficit' that are a familiar feature of the European institutional landscape. The question of how we ought to think about institutional cosmopolitanism is beyond the scope of this book. Suffice it to say that we cannot indulge in the luxury, enjoyed by the early Stoics, of maintaining an arm's length from the ongoing construction of cosmopolitan institutions. If cosmopolitanism is to realize its anti-imperialist potential, it must engage with the difficult political question of what a non-imperial institutional cosmopolitanism might look like.

Martti Koskenniemi has argued that international legal discourse is structured by an opposition between two vulnerabilities. If it hews too closely to the interests of states, it risks becoming an apology for state behaviour. If it departs too much from state interest, it risks politicization in the quite different sense of being based on a utopian morality that pre-exists the wills and interests of states. Koskenniemi's broader point is that international legal discourse is inherently unstable. Although envisaged by its mainstream inhabitants as an arena onto which political disputes can be displaced to be resolved in accordance with technical rules, it simply cannot avoid being political.[150]

Something similar can be said about cosmopolitanism in the academy today. Its promoters seem to be polarized between apologists for Western hegemony, who view the existing distribution of power as a resource to be utilized for cosmopolitan ends rather than as a problem in itself; and utopians, who mobilize abstract philosophical principles to criticize Western imperialism, but who resist the institutionalization of these principles for fear of creating a global Leviathan—oblivious, like the proverbial ostrich with its head buried in the sand, to the ongoing construction of such a behemoth. A cosmopolitanism that sidesteps the question of redistributing power in the international system and, equally importantly, of institutionalizing this redistribution, can do little for the globe's most disadvantaged inhabitants.

3

The Dark Sides of Communitarianism

'I think I should take the advantage of this forum to propound the new radicalism which I believe we should embrace.' Applause of expectation. 'First and foremost, this radicalism must be clear-eyed enough to see beyond the present claptrap that will heap all our problems on the doorstep of capitalism and imperialism....Please don't get me wrong. I do not deny that external factors are still at the root of many of our problems. But I maintain that even if external factors were to be at the root of all our problems we still must be ready to distinguish for practical purposes between remote and immediate causes, as our history teachers used to say.' Smiles of recognition. 'May I remind you that our ancestors —by the way you must never underrate those guys; some of you seem too ready to do so, I'm afraid. Well, our ancestors made a fantastic proverb on remote and immediate causes. If you want to get at the root of murder, they said, you have to look for the blacksmith who made the matchet.' Loud laughter. 'Wonderful proverb, isn't it? But it was only intended to enlarge the scope of our thinking not to guide policemen investigating an actual crime.' Laughter.

Chinua Achebe, *Anthills of the Savannah* (1988)

Memories of empire have sharpened the ongoing experience of neo-imperialism legitimated by liberal cosmopolitanism, arousing the resistance of Third World states. This chapter explores the nature and forms of such resistance as well as the justifications offered for them. But more significantly, it is concerned with the coercive logics of resistance to neo-imperialism by Third World states, and the implications thereof for Third World societies. It should be read as complementing chapter 2 in describing an alternative locus of threats to human rights in the Third World, underwritten by a distinctively communitarian logic.

To describe this Third World response, I draw substantially on two key concepts from the vocabulary of international society theorists. At the heart of this approach to the study of international relations is a view of states as forming a society amongst themselves, evidenced by their mutual recognition of common rules and participation in common institutions, and emerging out of a consciousness of common interests and perhaps even values.[1] Much of the debate within this field of IR theory is centred on an analytical disagreement over the extent of actually existing consensus on common norms and institutions, and a normative disagreement over how much consensus would be desirable and how it might be achieved.[2] In the view of 'pluralists', international society is what Terry Nardin calls a 'practical association' that permits its members to pursue their own conceptions of the good life, united only by a procedural consensus on norms such as sovereignty, territorial integrity, and non-intervention that impose certain minimal constraints on how each might pursue its distinctive projects.[3] In contrast, 'solidarists' see international society as a 'purposive association' held together by a substantive consensus on the value of jointly pursuing goals beyond that of mere coexistence, such as the enforcement of human rights or the promotion of democracy or capitalism.[4]

Much of chapter 2 can be understood as an account of the efforts of powerful Western states to push international society in a liberal solidarist direction by attempting to enforce compliance with a range of norms of liberal political and economic organization—a phenomenon that Hurrell has described as 'coercive solidarism'.[5] I argue in this chapter that the neo-imperial nature of this process has reinforced a Third World attachment to quintessentially pluralist norms of sovereignty and non-intervention. The perception of renewed imperial incursion revives anxieties about the incipience of Third World state- and nation-building. These processes of community construction and reproduction are seen as central goals of political life, providing a source of political values, a locus for the exercise of self-determination, and a defence against a reversion to a position of subservience in a hierarchical, imperial system. Pluralism is justified as a method of ordering international relations that is most conducive to the imperatives of community construction. The justification of pluralism, therefore, typically rests on communitarian assumptions.

This chapter attempts to do three things. First, it assesses the extent to which Third World states have demonstrated a preference for pluralism in their international relations during and after the Cold War. Second, it examines moral justifications for pluralism, identifying a three-step argument that is typically made: (*a*) community enables the enjoyment of a number of political goods; (*b*) the institution of sovereign statehood enables life in community; (*c*) pluralism as a method of ordering international relations offers a more conducive environment for community construction (understood as state- and nation-building). Other justifications of pluralism, rather than beginning from communitarianism, rest on the putative contribution of a system of territorial sovereign states to global order and justice. These claims are contested in the third section of the chapter, which argues that pluralism licenses deeply arbitrary and illegitimate exercises of authority in the name of state- and nation-building. Although justified on communitarian grounds, the praxis of pluralism seems to undermine the values that communitarians are so keen to defend. In addition, the brittle and authoritarian states established by these practices seem an inadequate foundation for the global order values that non-communitarian justifications of pluralism allude to.

Pluralism and solidarism should be understood, not as static alternative conceptualizations of international society, but as being in a dynamic, historical, and mutually constitutive relationship—as political responses to one another. In the conventional historical narrative of international society, the procedural consensus underwriting pluralist international society derives from the practices that European states developed in their relations with one another. The Peace of Westphalia, concluded in 1648, is considered a symbolic 'pluralist moment' in this process, marking the transition from what Jackson calls 'a *universitas* based on the solidarist norms of Latin Christendom, to a *societas*, based on the pluralist norms of state sovereignty, on political independence'.[6] In his view, pre-Westphalian medieval diplomacy in Europe was a quasi-domestic dialogue conducted between subjects of the same overall political community, conducted within the framework of *respublica Christiana* and subject to the papal monarchy—in principle, if not always in fact. The Peace of Westphalia recognized the territorial sovereignty of an assortment of 300 states and statelets, the rights of these entities to enter into treaty relations with one another, as well as the rights of their rulers to determine which particular variant of Christianity would be practised within their realms in accordance with the principle *cujus regio ejus religio*.[7] In retrospect, this has come to be seen as the first explicit recognition of the rights of states to territorial integrity, sovereignty, and non-intervention.

In Jackson's view, international society has been essentially pluralist from the seventeenth century onwards. It has been subject to numerous (ultimately unsuccessful) solidarist challenges from the monarchical and imperial ambitions of Louis XIV and Napoleon respectively, the revolutionary aspirations of Lenin and Stalin, and the fascist agendas of Hitler, Mussolini, and Hirohito. But each of these was defeated or socialized into the rules of pluralist international society.[8] In this narrative, the originally European society of states was of course universalized into an international society by the admission of non-Western states, but their entry is not seen as having disrupted the essential pluralism of that society. Indeed, Jackson sees an enduring pluralism stretching unbroken from the Westphalian 'pluralist moment' to the present day, tempered only very marginally by a reinvigoration of solidarist principles in Western states in a limited and voluntary fashion following the Second World War.[9]

Virtually all international society theorists writing about the 'entry' of non-Western states have commented on the alacrity with which these states embraced pluralist norms of sovereignty, territoriality, and non-intervention. Yet this view misses the extraordinarily bifurcated nature of the experience, for non-Western political communities, of entering the society of states as *states*. For such communities, the moment of entry into a society of states whose relations were ordered in accordance with European practices marked a dramatic departure, not only from their established practices of ordering external relations with other political communities, but also from their particular forms of political subjectivity. Although Western and non-Western regional societies of political communities had interacted with one another for centuries, prior to the incorporation of the latter into Western-dominated international society on Western terms, each construed its relations with the other in accordance with its own notions of world ordering. For example, Onuma Yasuaki explains that the Qing dynasty 'understood' the Treaty of Nanjing that it was forced to conclude with European states after its defeat in the First Opium War within the terms of its Sinocentric world view. Consular jurisdiction for the Europeans was seen as a case of 'allowing' the barbarians to settle their own disputes, and most-favoured-nation status as an expression of the benevolent intent of the emperor to treat all subjects under Heaven as equal. Yasuaki traces how Chinese elites were forced to shed elements of this Sinocentric world view and adopt the practices of European society, first in their relations with European states and subsequently in relations with states like Japan that had once been subsidiary members of the Sinocentric system, as a result of successive military defeats. It was only with the secession of Korea (hitherto China's most faithful tributary) from the Sinocentric tribute system following a war with Japan in 1894, that Chinese elites realized they could no longer delude themselves into thinking that Sinocentric notions of world ordering were still consequential.[10]

The creation of *international* society was the result of a number of such interactions between the European society of states and other regional societies (or individual political communities), in which the former emerged triumphant and imposed its methods of ordering inter-communal political relations on the latter. The creation of international society entailed an extraordinary convergence of norms, in which multiple forms of political subjectivity were supplanted by one kind of political subject—the territorial state—and in which a plurality of forms of ordering inter-communal relations were swept aside by a particular set of 'pluralist' rules of Westphalian pedigree. In this sense, the creation of a universal international society must be seen as a *solidarist* moment.[11] Of course, there is no founding 'moment' as such because the society of states was universalized over an extended period of time. But for every non-Western political community entering the society as a *state*, the moment of entry is a solidarist one in which the scope for constituting oneself politically in forms alternative to the Westphalian territorial state has been extinguished.

Upon entry into international society, the creation of which I have suggested must be seen as a solidarist achievement, non-Western states—and more particularly weaker Third World states—seized upon those rules of international society that seemed most conducive to bolstering their fragile autonomy. The pluralist norms of sovereignty, territorial integrity, and non-intervention, which had developed as a functional response to a situation of stalemate between states enjoying rough parity in Western Europe, now seemed extraordinarily valuable to the weakest members of international society. In Hindu cosmology, the world is supposedly held aloft on the backs of four elephants, which in turn stand on a giant turtle. If the elephants represent the pluralist norms of contemporary international society, then the turtle is the solidarist achievement of norm convergence whereby the territorial state becomes the only acceptable form of political subjectivity in international society. Third World acceptance and affirmation of pluralist norms must be seen as riding on the back of a more fundamental solidarist norm convergence.

The entry of Third World states into international society was an extraordinarily ambiguous moment for each of the new entrants. On the one hand, there was a passionate embrace of juridical equality as something long overdue; on the other hand, an awareness that the form in which one had finally been accorded equal recognition had not been entirely of one's choosing.[12] Third World adherence to, and advocacy of, pluralist norms of international society has to be understood as a political response to the historical memory of the defeat, trauma, and loss of self entailed by the solidarist achievements of European imperialism—achievements that, as I have argued above, made international society possible. This relationship is important because, as I will demonstrate later in this chapter, Third World pluralism derives much of its political capital and legitimacy by setting itself up as a bulwark against a renewal of neo-imperialist solidarism: Third World pluralism is the post-colonial 'never again'.

The dynamic interaction between solidarism and pluralism does not stop there. The phenomenon of coercive solidarism discussed in chapter 2 is itself justified as a response to the impairment of human security by the putative abuses of pluralism. And coercive solidarism in turn has generated apparently pluralist responses, some of which have taken the form of so-called anti-globalization movements, which I discuss in chapter 5. Thus, pluralism and solidarism cannot be understood as abstract alternative conceptions of international society, but must be viewed in a dynamic, historical, and mutually constitutive fashion as political responses to one another. The following section offers an empirical assessment of the extent to which Third World states may be said to have exhibited a preference for pluralism in the Cold War and post-Cold War periods. This provides the political context for a deeper engagement with the ethics of pluralism as a method of ordering international relations, in the sections that follow.

3.1 PLURALIST RULES, SOLIDARIST EXCEPTIONS

Because solidarism entails purposive action, it is possible to identify solidarist 'projects' pursued by identifiable agents with particular interests. Even where the notion of a 'project'—with its implications of coherent and teleological agency—is misleading, solidarist norms usually operate at a higher degree of specificity than pluralist norms. Pluralism is not a 'project'. It is a permissive state of affairs, a licence for the pursuit of multiple projects taking a potentially infinite variety of forms. As such, while solidarist behaviour seems more amenable to identification and description, pluralism is rather more difficult to describe.

Nevertheless, it is possible to discern a concerted Third World effort from the very moment of entry into international society, to sustain and reinforce the norms that make pluralist behaviour possible—sovereign equality, non-intervention, and territorial integrity. The Latin American republics were the first states to advocate a norm of non-intervention in the form of the Calvo doctrine, formulated by the Argentinean jurist Carlos Calvo in 1868. Prompted partly by French intervention in Mexico to recover the pecuniary claims of French nationals in that country, the doctrine sought to protect Latin American states from diplomatic or armed intervention by other states to recover debts owed to their nationals. In 1902, in response to the German, Italian, and British blockade of the Venezuelan coast, another Argentinean—Luis Drago—would formulate the Drago doctrine, prohibiting coercive intervention to force a state to pay its public debt. Between 1826 and 1936, Latin American states struggled to enshrine a norm of non-intervention within the inter-American system, in an effort to delegitimize the US assumption of a prerogative to intervene in their affairs for the purpose of maintaining an exclusive sphere of influence in the Western hemisphere in accordance with the Monroe Doctrine. Having progressively institutionalized the norm of non-intervention within their regional system, Latin American states were later at the forefront of the effort to elevate it to the status of a general principle of the United Nations during the process of drafting its Charter.[13]

3.1.1 Cold War

As decolonization proceeded apace following the Second World War, the Latin Americans were joined in their support for the norms of sovereignty and non-intervention by the newly independent states of Africa and Asia. Taking advantage of their numerical strength in arenas like the UN General Assembly, Third World states repeatedly affirmed the centrality of these norms in landmark resolutions such as the Declaration on the Granting of Independence to Colonial Countries and Peoples (1960)[14] and the Declaration on the Inadmissibility of Intervention in the Domestic Affairs of States and the Protection of their Independence and Sovereignty (1965).[15] Yet the implications of sovereignty and non-intervention would have remained unclear without agreement on the territorial limits within which these were to operate. Accordingly, we might view the frequently reiterated Third World insistence on respect for territorial integrity and the inviolability of existing territorial boundaries as a further manifestation of pluralist behaviour.

African states played a leading role in the institutionalization of this norm, pledging 'to respect the borders existing on their achievement of national independence' at one of the earliest meetings of what was then called the Organization of African Unity (OAU) in Cairo in 1964.[16] Christopher Clapham explains that the very artificiality of frontiers in Africa made them more, not less, central to the identity of the states they constituted. It was precisely because there was no 'idea' of, say, Mali or Zambia which preceded the existence of their frontiers and which could have been invoked to challenge them, that African rulers were more agreeable to the mutual recognition of existing frontiers, however arbitrarily they may have been drawn by the erstwhile colonial power.[17] There were of course states where identity preceded frontiers (Somalia, Ethiopia), which would—for that very reason—be more vulnerable to ethnic secessionist and irredentist claims.[18]

Notwithstanding collective Third World affirmations of the bedrock norms of pluralism, it would be inaccurate to characterize these states as exclusively pluralist during the early post-colonial decades. A politics of Third World *solidarity* was clearly visible around the goals of ending colonialism and white minority rule in Africa, and Israeli occupation of Palestinian territories.[19] Article 3(6) of the OAU Charter explicitly pledged 'absolute dedication to the total emancipation of the African territories which are still dependent' and a Liberation Committee based in Dar-es-Salaam was set up to further this end. 'Frontline states' bordering white minority regimes provided bases and sanctuary for liberation movements operating across the border, and training facilities were often hosted by states further afield.[20] Whilst recognizing the *de jure* independence of apartheid South Africa, the fourteen east and central

African signatories to the Lusaka Manifesto of April 1969 explicitly justified their disregard of pluralist norms of sovereignty and non-intervention in the following terms:

> On every legal basis its internal affairs are a matter exclusively for the people of South Africa. Yet the purpose of law is people and we assert that the actions of the South African government are such that the rest of the world has a responsibility to take some action in defence of humanity, self-determination and non-racialism.[21]

It is worth dwelling on this remarkable pronouncement for a moment, if only to note that perhaps here too, a Schmittian scepticism of invocations of humanity is warranted. For although apartheid was rightly seen as a crime against humanity, the post-colonial behaviour of many African states suggested an extraordinary narrowing of vision in which 'humanity' was only ever under threat from white minority rule. Theirs was an emphatically black solidarism premised on a racialized notion of self-determination. Once black majority rule was established, states were deemed to qualify for the absolutist protections of pluralist norms regardless of how governments treated their people. This accounted for the extraordinary tolerance that African and other states evinced for regimes that were known for their murderous and kleptocratic tendencies, such as those of Idi Amin in Uganda, Jean-Bédel Bokassa in the Central African Republic, and Mobutu Sésé Seko in what was then called Zaire.[22] As the Tanzanian government noted in an official statement protesting the hosting of the 1975 OAU Summit in Kampala, Uganda, 'Africans lose their right to protest against state-organised brutality on the day that their country becomes independent through their efforts. For on all such matters the OAU acts like a trade union of the current Heads of State and Government, with solidarity reflected in silence if not in open support for each other.'[23] In a similar vein, Tanzanian President Julius Nyerere, in a speech delivered in December 1978 prior to Tanzania's invasion of Uganda, observed:

> ... there is a strange habit in Africa: an African leader, so long as he is an African, can kill Africans just as he pleases, and you cannot say anything. If Amin was white, we would have passed many resolutions against him. But he is black, and blackness is a licence to kill Africans.[24]

Nyerere's bitterness accurately summed up the dual standard then in operation, under which racial solidarism against white minority regimes was staged against the 'normal' backdrop of pluralist relations vis-à-vis all other states. Combinations of pluralist and solidarist behaviour were also evident in early Third World attempts to restructure international economic relations. Informed by economic theories of dependency and political strategies of non-alignment, in the early post-colonial decades many Third World countries used their pluralist space to experiment with various forms of economic nationalism (initially entailing simply the replacement of foreign with native proprietors, but later involving nationalization of key industries), import-substitution industrialization, etc. The minimal success of these developmental strategies fuelled an uneasy realization amongst Third World states that political independence did not necessarily imply economic autonomy and that they needed tangible assistance from the external environment. This prompted a move from non-alignment to what Robert Rothstein has called 'international class war'.[25]

Third World states exhibited clear signs of solidarist behaviour in this interstate confrontation. Working in solidarity with one another through organizations such as the Non-Aligned Movement (NAM) and the Group of 77 (G77) and converging around specific normative demands, their efforts to reorder their relations with powerful industrialized states carried all the hallmarks of a purposive project.[26] Yet a closer perusal of their demands reveals both pluralist and solidarist elements. Much of the 1974 Declaration on the Establishment of a New International Economic Order, which, in retrospect, appears to have been the high watermark of the 'international class war', has a strongly pluralist tenor. This is evident in the opening affirmations of sovereign equality, territorial integrity, and non-intervention, but also in more specific declarations of the 'right of every country to adopt the economic and social system that it deems the most appropriate', of the 'full permanent sovereignty of every State over its natural resources and all economic activities ... including the right to nationalisation', and of the right to regulate and supervise the activities of transnational corporations. Alongside this, one sees a much more solidarist realization of 'the reality of interdependence', of the fact that 'the interests of the developed countries and those of the developing countries can no longer be isolated from each other, that there is a close interrelationship between the prosperity of the developed countries and the growth and development of the developing countries, and that the prosperity of the international community as a whole depends upon the prosperity of its constituent parts'. In the politics of the NIEO, we might view the Third World as acting as a solidarist vanguard, seeking to promote acceptance of new norms governing relations between industrialized countries and themselves. Note the demands for a just and equitable relationship between the prices of imports and exports and an improvement in unsatisfactory terms of trade, for 'active assistance to developing countries ... free of any political or military conditions', for 'preferential and non-reciprocal treatment for developing countries', for transfers of financial resources, technology, etc.[27]

This combination of pluralism and solidarism in Third World interstate behaviour appears less puzzling when one realizes that both tendencies operated to buttress the position of Third World state elites. Third World solidarism was intended to alter the *interstate* power balance in favour of Third World states (in the case of racial or anti-colonial solidarism, it was intended to facilitate the logically prior step of bringing those states into existence as independent entities). Third World pluralism was intended to preclude external scrutiny of, and interference in, state–society relations within the Third World: it was intended to give Third World state elites greater room for manoeuvre vis-à-vis their own societies. Of course both solidarist and pluralist politics were justified as being in the interests of 'the people', but whether or not they actually benefited Third World *societies* depended on the nature of the state–society compact that existed within individual states. Yet, crucially, the nature of that compact was also claimed by Third World states as a subject that legitimately belonged within the pluralist space, as a matter that remained 'essentially within the domestic jurisdiction' of states, in the language of Article 2(7) of the UN Charter.

These intensive normative efforts on the part of Third World elites to fend off external scrutiny of their state–society relations were of course a response to—and constantly undermined by—the structural conditions of the Cold War. Both superpowers, seeking to maintain or improve upon their position in the international system, intervened regularly in their respective spheres of influence to stabilize client regimes in danger of collapse or to remove regimes that threatened to alter external alignments or internal state–society relations in ways that were detrimental to their geopolitical objectives. More fundamentally, as dependency theorists emphasized, the political sovereignty of Third World states had been grafted on to a productive structure that had been constructed in the colonial era to serve the needs of colonial powers for raw material and markets. Protestations of pluralism notwithstanding, the persistence of this productive structure deprived Third World states of their autonomy, locking them into subservient and dependent positions at the bottom of production chains from which many found it difficult to extricate themselves.[28]

Yet where Third World elites were able to stabilize their relations with one or the other superpower, the structural conditions of the Cold War operated quite effectively to insulate them from their own societies. Colonialism tended to create disarticulated economies on the periphery characterized by vast 'traditional' sectors and smaller 'modern' sectors developed to serve the needs of the colonial power. The latter were closely integrated with the metropolitan and world economies and were typically operated by native elites, on whom the colonial power relied for the purpose of maintaining order and extracting revenue from the colony. In many cases the Cold War preserved this structure, replacing the colonial power with one of the superpowers, which might have offered 'security assistance' in return for the allegiance of client states in the global geopolitical confrontation of the period. One could update this narrative further by examining patterns of assistance and allegiance in the ongoing 'war on terror'. In every phase of this enduring structural relationship, the fact of external patronage obviates the need for native elites to bargain with their societies to stabilize their power, thereby reproducing the oppressive class structures and conditions of unrepresentative governance that have prevailed since colonial times.[29] We can see now how Third World pluralism and solidarism articulated against the backdrop of these structural conditions, operated to strengthen the position of Third World elites vis-à-vis other states *and* their own societies.

3.1.2 Post-Cold War

To what extent has the Third World preference for pluralism persisted in the post-Cold War era? Third World positions on humanitarian intervention or the new notion of 'responsibility to protect' championed by the International Commission on Intervention and State Sovereignty (ICISS) could serve as a proxy for their attitude towards pluralism, given that both concepts attempt to reshape the meaning of sovereignty. ICISS invested considerable effort in distinguishing its conception of 'responsibility to protect' from ongoing controversies about humanitarian intervention. The language of responsibility sought to reframe a debate that had been about the prerogatives of powerful states as one about the collective responsibility of all. The emphasis on protection was intended to refocus attention from the intervening states to the victims of human rights abuses, and to underscore the need for preventive and not merely reactive action. In addition, the Commission sought to underscore its respect for state sovereignty by emphasizing that the primary responsibility for protection lies with states in the first instance and devolves on the international community only in the event that states are unable or unwilling to fulfil their responsibilities.[30]

Despite strenuous efforts to assuage concerns about perceived imperial continuities in the 'responsibility to protect', the collective Third World response to the proposed norm has been one of outright hostility. NAM has consistently reiterated its opposition to 'the so-called "right" of humanitarian intervention' and has expressed concern at the 'similarities between the new expression "responsibility to protect" and "humanitarian intervention"'.[31]

Some analysts have argued that Third World states have in fact responded in a variety of different ways to particular instances of humanitarian intervention, suggesting that there is no unified Third World perspective on the issue.[32] Ramesh Thakur has observed that African states appear to have gone the furthest in rejecting an absolutist position on state sovereignty, Latin American states seem open to intervention based on universal principles and under regional or international authority, and Asian states continue to be the most stubbornly resistant to external interference.[33] I will look briefly at attitudes towards intervention in each of these regions as a prelude to making the case that while analysts are right to point to variations in Third World attitudes towards intervention, it is still possible and meaningful to speak of a strong Third World preference for pluralism.

African specialists have noted the breaking of two post-colonial taboos in Africa after the Cold War. First, the inviolability of inherited colonial boundaries has been undermined by military interventions in Lesotho, Liberia, Congo-Brazzaville, and the Democratic Republic of Congo, to cite only a few instances, undertaken by regional organizations such as ECOWAS and the Southern African Development Community (SADC), and led by regional hegemons such as Nigeria and South Africa. Second, the secession of a group from a state through armed struggle, thwarted in the cases of Katanga and Biafra, succeeded in the creation of Eritrea from Ethiopia in April 1993.[34] Commentators have also noted the OAU's strong stand against unconstitutional changes of government in Africa (evident, for example, in its refusal to permit the military regimes of Côte d'Ivoire and Comoros from attending its 2000 Lomé summit), and the new African Union's (AU) institutionalization of 'the right of the Union to intervene in a Member state pursuant to a decision of the Assembly in respect of ... war crimes, genocide and crimes against humanity' enshrined in Article 4(h) of its Constitutive Act.[35]

Yet *against* these signs of departure from absolutist pluralism, it should be pointed out that ECOWAS's actions in Liberia and Sierra Leone are susceptible to more conservative readings that suggest that they might not have been 'interventions' at all.[36] We should also note South Africa's denunciation of NATO's unilateral intervention in Kosovo, even as it condemned the ethnic cleansing policies of the Milosevic government.[37] More recently, attempts to institutionalize a norm of 'responsibility to protect' at the 2005 World Summit received enthusiastic support from only Botswana, Mauritius, Rwanda, and Tanzania and more cautious endorsement from South Africa; Egypt and Zimbabwe were explicitly opposed, while all other African states remained non-committal.[38]

Finally, it is worth noting that the AU Constitutive Act licenses intervention only by the Union itself in the affairs of its member states.[39] This is in consonance with its broader philosophy of African solutions to African problems, suggesting that African states are still extraordinarily sensitive to Western intervention in their affairs. This attitude was expressed very clearly in the final communiqué of an African 'mini-summit' on Darfur convened at Tripoli in October 2004, which rejected 'any foreign intervention by any country, whatsoever in this pure African issue'.[40] Even the official spokesman for the Sudanese National Democratic Alliance (the umbrella opposition group that includes actors like the Sudanese Peoples' Liberation Army, which might have been expected to welcome foreign assistance in its struggle against the Sudanese government), has been quoted as saying 'we are against foreign military intervention. We have before us the example of Iraq.'[41] Yet 'foreign' in these statements seems to mean 'non-African', and it is the case that many of the actors opposed to Western intervention in Sudan have nonetheless been willing to countenance the presence of the AU Mission in Sudan (AMIS). This is in itself a significant departure from the absolutist pluralism previously operating between independent black African states that Nyerere found so deeply frustrating.

The Latin American situation is also more differentiated than Thakur's broad generalization implies. Monica Serrano argues that amongst Latin American countries, Mexico and to a lesser extent Brazil (and, one might add, Venezuela under Chavez and Bolivia under Morales) have been relatively more resistant to perceived intrusions into their domestic affairs. Conversely, Argentina and Chile have questioned absolutist interpretations of sovereignty and have strongly supported the international protection of democracy and human rights through regional and global institutional mechanisms. The foreign policy preferences of this latter group arguably stem from a desire to consolidate their recent transitions to democracy from military rule by locking themselves into international structures of accountability. This is also true of Central American countries such as Nicaragua, El Salvador, and Guatemala, where international involvement of different kinds has helped resolve intractable conflicts, leaving a legacy of more flexible attitudes towards sovereignty.[42] These intra-regional distinctions notwithstanding, Latin American states were prominent among those that embraced the notion of a responsibility to protect at the 2005 World Summit, although Cuba and Venezuela made statements in opposition.[43]

It is doubtful whether an Asian perspective can be identified on any issue. Lacking the racial solidarism of Africa or the shared history and legacies of Latin colonization in Central and South America, 'Asia' simply does not have a coherent regional identity at the continental level, although it does encompass a number of self-identifying regions.[44] Nevertheless, one prominent manifestation of pluralist behaviour at the continental level occurred in the run up to the 1993 World Conference on Human Rights, when representatives of more than forty Asian states met on the sidelines of the conference to endorse what came to be known as the Bangkok Declaration. The Declaration was widely seen as institutionalizing what some of its signatories publicly called 'Asian values', although it did not actually use this terminology anywhere. It expressed concerns about the unbalanced nature of the global rights agenda, which was seen to relate 'mainly to one category of rights' (civil and political); it warned against 'confrontation and the imposition of incompatible values' or the use of human rights 'as a conditionality for extending development assistance'; most significantly, it offered the following convoluted observation on the relationship between human rights and culture: 'while human rights are universal in nature, they must be considered in the context of a dynamic and evolving process of international norm-setting, bearing in mind the significance of national and regional particularities and various historical, cultural and religious backgrounds'.[45]

I return to the use of 'culture' and to the debate over 'Asian values' in a later section of this chapter. Here I only wish to note that it is difficult to identify any enthusiastic proponents of humanitarian intervention in Asia. China's opposition is well known and frequently reiterated. India has been wedded to a rigid interpretation of the UN Charter, seeing the use of force without Security Council authorization as illegal and unmitigated by any humanitarian considerations whatsoever.[46] Even when Council authorization has been solicited it has acquiesced rather grudgingly, in the case of Somalia because of the perceived exceptionality of a situation of a state without a sovereign,[47] and when UN involvement was sought in Liberia following the ECOWAS intervention because the Foreign Minister of Liberia himself had requested UN action.[48]

Few Muslim-majority states[49] have been supportive of a right of humanitarian intervention in principle. In the wake of NATO's intervention in Kosovo, a resolution co-sponsored by Russia, Belarus, and India seeking to condemn the intervention was defeated by twelve votes to three (Russia, China, and Namibia). Of the twelve votes supportive of the intervention, two came from Muslim countries—Bahrain and Malaysia. Given Malaysia's credentials as a strong defender of pluralist norms, Wheeler speculates that it was a sense of Muslim solidarity with the Kosovar Albanian victims of Milosevic's ethnic cleansing, rather than a universalistic liberal solidarism, that elicited Malaysia's supportive vote.[50] Yet Muslim-majority countries were themselves deeply ambivalent about the intervention, with some like Egypt and Jordan protesting Milosevic's persecution of Muslims and others such as Algeria, Iran, Iraq, and Libya more concerned about NATO's disregard of the role of the UN and norms of state sovereignty.[51] It is surely no coincidence that states enjoying relatively good relations with the United States supported the intervention, while those that did not opposed it: attitudes towards intervention were shaped more by the state of relations with the intervening countries than by abstract principles.

Among the few Asian countries to endorse the 'responsibility to protect' at the 2005 World Summit were Japan, South Korea, Singapore, Jordan, and Sri Lanka; Indonesia offered qualified support, noting that the use of force had to be a last resort; Malaysia's individual position was ambiguous; and of the eight countries that explicitly rejected the 'responsibility to protect', four were Asian (China, Iran, Pakistan, and Vietnam).[52]

The purpose of this overview has been to acknowledge the range of perspectives on humanitarian intervention that exists within the contemporary Third World, but also to insist that there is still a great deal of opposition to the institutionalization of a responsibility to protect. Sarah Robinson uses the notion of a two-level game to explain the phenomenon of variegated individual positions on humanitarian intervention juxtaposed with a collective Third World opposition to the practice. Collective opposition impedes, or at least decelerates, the proposed institutionalization of humanitarian intervention in the normative fabric of international society, yet the variety of individual attitudes surveyed above leaves open the possibility for individual states to support the practice on a case-by-case basis if they feel a sense of solidarity with the victims or if their national interests so demand.[53]

It seems fair to say that in the wake of the perceived abuse of humanitarian justifications for the war on Iraq in 2003, opposition to the institutionalization of a norm permitting intervention for humanitarian purposes—even in the language of a 'responsibility to protect' that is more deferential to state sovereignty—has only grown. Indeed it is not clear that the change in language has done anything to change the underlying political preferences of states. As Alex Bellamy reports, in the debates over intervention in Sudan, opponents of Western intervention including key members of the AU, the Arab League, and Sudan itself seem to have appropriated the language of the 'responsibility to protect', but used it to argue that the primary responsibility for protection still lay with Sudan and that the circumstances in which such responsibility might shift to other actors did not yet obtain.[54] Finally, it is worth noting that when UN Secretary General Ban Ki-moon sought to appoint Edward Luck as his Special Advisor on the Responsibility to Protect in early 2008, Latin American, Arab, and African delegates to the UN's budget committee went on record as saying, variously, that 'the World Summit rejected R2P in 2005', that 'the concept of the responsibility to protect has not yet been adopted by the General Assembly', and that 'the responsibility to protect itself ... was not accepted or approved as a principle by the General Assembly'.[55] This suggests that Third World states continue to have a strong attachment to pluralist norms of sovereignty and non-intervention and resist any perceived modification of these norms.

Interestingly, these fiercely pluralist commitments do not manifest themselves as strongly when it comes to economic issues. Humanitarian intervention poses a frontal challenge to the interests of those Third World elites who do not enjoy congenial relations with powerful Western states. In contrast, the spread of capitalism via conditionality has been more consensual from the perspective of such elites because it has distributed sufficient benefits to them. This is not to suggest that capitalism and conditionality have not been contested; merely, that the degree of *elite* contestation has been far less than in the case of humanitarian intervention. As I have mentioned in previous chapters, disillusioned with the attempts of the early post-colonial decades to achieve economic self-reliance and impressed by the tremendous success of the Asian Tigers, elites in many Third World states abandoned policies of economic nationalism and welcomed IFI conditionality as an opportunity to persuade recalcitrant groups in their societies of the need for deep and radical structural reform. In other words, Third World elites have acquiesced far more readily in the shrinking of the scope for economic pluralism,[56] even as they have remained fiercely pluralist in the political realm.

This is reflected very clearly in NAM statements, which, in contrast to vociferous condemnations of humanitarian intervention, express a clear acceptance of capitalist conditionality. The Final Document of the XIV Ministerial held in 2004 at Durban notes that 'the increasing interdependence of national economies in a globalising world and the emergence of rule-based regimes for international economic relations have meant that the space for national economic policy ... is now often framed by international disciplines, commitments and global market considerations'. There is little in the document to suggest a desire to rollback these constraints or otherwise disengage from them. Rather, the thrust of the entire statement is in the direction of enabling Third World states to 'participate in and benefit from globalisation' and calling for special measures to draw into this process those who are most marginalized.[57] More radical pluralist voices, questioning both the ends and means of neo-liberal economic policy now come increasingly from the non-state actors of 'anti-globalization' movements, although the rise to power of left-wing regimes such as those of Chavez and Morales serve as reminders that they *could* still come from states.

3.2 JUSTIFYING PLURALISM

The normative defence of pluralism typically takes the form of a three-step argument. Most justifications of pluralism begin with an account of community as enabling the enjoyment of a host of political goods. Second, the state is said to provide an appropriate protective and nurturing environment for the development of community. Third, pluralist international relations are argued to be most conducive to state- and nation-building. Not all proponents of pluralism move explicitly through each of these stages. Nonetheless, it would be useful to understand the links between these claims to better appreciate the criticism of pluralism that I advance in section 3.3.

As I mentioned in the introduction, the defence of community[58] might stem from a methodological claim about the importance of tradition and social context for moral and political reasoning, as in Walzer's claim that standards of distributive justice are relative to the 'shared social meanings' associated with the good to be distributed.[59] It might stem from an ontological claim about the inescapably social and embedded nature of the self, a view that Daniel Bell has advanced in his account of how identity is constituted by the communities to which we belong.[60] Or it might stem from a normative claim about the value of community. Miller, for example, defends the nation as a particular kind of community that has provided the social cement necessary for the generation of trust and cooperation between individuals who are otherwise strangers to one another, enabling the resolution of collective action problems as well as practices of redistributive justice and deliberative democracy.[61] Likewise, Petit's account of republicanism as 'freedom as non-domination' emphasizes the need for republican laws to be supported by norms of civility, which have historically developed amongst fellow members of a community.[62] (In practice, most communitarian writers combine methodological, ontological, and normative claims in their defence of community.)

Having made a set of claims about the value of community, many of these writers go on to make the further claim that only the institution of sovereign statehood can guarantee the autonomy necessary to realize the potential goods inherent in community. Thus, Miller has argued that nations need states because only when a nation is politically autonomous can it implement schemes of social justice, protect and foster its common culture, and collectively determine its common destiny.[63] Similarly, Walzer has defended what he calls the 'presumptive legitimacy' of states in international society with the argument that politics depends upon shared history, communal sentiment, and accepted conventions; communal life and liberty in turn require the existence of the 'relatively self-enclosed areas of political development' that are provided by the institution of sovereignty.[64]

Other writers have defended the state more directly without appealing to some underlying notion of community. For example, Philip Cunliffe has criticized the notion of a 'responsibility to protect' devolving on an amorphous international community, arguing that the locus of responsibility is clearer in a system of sovereign states and the possibility of holding power to account therefore correspondingly greater.[65] Still other writers advance multi-pronged justifications for the institution of sovereignty, some of which rest on an appeal to the value of political life in community and some of which do not. Doyle has usefully summarized the case for sovereignty by underlining its expressive, protective, and productive functions (enabling the expression and protection of community, but also providing a regulatory framework for the production of wealth).[66]

Having defended the institution of sovereign statehood, it is then a short step to defending pluralism as a method of ordering international relations that is most conducive to the imperatives of state- and nation-building. Ayoob has made this argument most explicitly, highlighting additionally the acute difficulties faced by Third World states in this regard. I shall therefore focus most closely on his defence of pluralism in the remainder of this section. Recall that for Ayoob, the 'incompleteness' (or what I prefer to call incipience) of state- and nation-building is a constitutive feature of the Third World. In his view, Third World states are undergoing processes of state- and nation-building that are no more bloody and brutal than those of their European counterparts which took several centuries to reach their current levels of stability.[67] Yet the Third World experience of these processes has been complicated by three sets of factors, which underscore the need for a non-interventionist pluralist international order.

First, in contrast to European states, which took three to four centuries to consolidate their power and monopolize the instruments of coercion within their territories, Ayoob argues that Third World political elites are compelled to accomplish these processes in a much shorter period of time. In his view, 'The demands of competition with established modern states and the demonstrated effectiveness of socially cohesive, politically responsive, and administratively effective states in the industrialised world make it almost obligatory for Third World states to reach their goal within the shortest time possible or risk international ridicule and permanent marginalisation within the system of states.'[68] The imperative of speed intensifies the sense of dislocation and trauma that inevitably accompanies the twin processes of state- and nation-building. Second, nation-state building in the Third World is complicated by a host of colonial legacies—arbitrary boundaries drawn by colonial authorities for purposes of administrative convenience rather than with reference to the identities of the populations they enclosed, ethnically heterogeneous societies lacking a sense of community and consequently vulnerable to secessionist or irredentist claims, disarticulated economies subservient to and dependent on metropolitan capital, etc.[69] Third, European state-builders were unencumbered by the normative restraints to which Third World political elites are subject. Chief among these are the advent of mass politics and democratization and the post-war emphasis on individual human rights. As Ayoob explains, while European state-makers 'could single-mindedly pursue their goals of accumulating power and extracting resources without being distracted by demands for economic redistribution and political participation', Third World state-makers have had to operate in the shadow of the example set by already established and successfully functioning liberal-democratic welfare states. The existence of these states exerts a sort of teleological pull, compelling Third World elites to conduct their state- and nation-building processes in as humane, 'civilised', and consensual a fashion as possible. Yet 'satisfying popular demands can frequently run counter to the imperatives of state making, because state making, as the European experience has demonstrated, is a rather unsavoury task and often involves levels of coercion that are bound to be unacceptable to populations that have been influenced by notions of human rights, political participation, and social justice'.[70]

These three sets of factors—abbreviated timeframes, colonial legacies, and new norms of civility—combine to make state- and nation-building vastly more difficult in the Third World than they were in Europe. As Ayoob repeatedly stresses, the conjunction of these factors has 'overloaded' the political capacities of Third World states, exacerbating disorder within and outside them. From an analytical point of view, Ayoob's argument has two merits. First, by placing Third World state formation in historical perspective and demonstrating the common rationales underpinning state formation in Europe and the Third World, his work challenges the arguments of those who attribute Third World disorder to a putative lack of readiness for self-government in the more 'backward' parts of the world.[71] Further, by demonstrating the complex spatial and temporal interplay of internal and external as well as historical and post-colonial factors in generating Third World insecurity, he destabilizes the selective geographies and histories of culpability characteristic of neo-imperialist accounts of state failure discussed in chapter 2. We can begin to see that the apparently 'internal' processes of state- and nation-building are powerfully shaped by their interactions with colonialism, imperialism, and globalization.

From a prescriptive point of view, Ayoob argues that in order to successfully replicate the European experience of state-building, Third World state-builders need 'lots of time and a relatively free hand to persuade and coerce the disparate populations under their nominal rule to accept the legitimacy of state boundaries and institutions, to accept the right of the state to extract resources from them, and to let the state regulate important aspects of their lives'.[72] This is essentially a demand for an expansion of the pluralist space and for the withdrawal of whatever surveillance and disciplinary mechanisms the contemporary human rights regime is able to wield. As he speculates acerbically, 'One wonders if West European and North American states would have successfully completed their state-building endeavours and eventually emerged as liberal, democratic states, if they had the United Nations Human Rights Commission, Amnesty International and now the UN Security Council breathing down their necks during the crucial early phases of their state making endeavours.'[73]

Ayoob's argument for a relaxation of human rights norms and a moratorium on the practice of humanitarian intervention is built on two kinds of narratives: first, a historical–sociological narrative that underscores the inevitability of violence and coercion during the state-making process, as evidenced by the European experience; second, a moral narrative that justifies the (presumably temporary) relaxation of human rights norms in the interests of state-building, on the ground that the protection of human rights itself presupposes relatively well-functioning, viable states. Writing in 1995, he characterizes state failure as the worst fate that human beings could suffer:

> The recent Lebanese and the current Somali, Afghan, Liberian, and Zairean experiences demonstrate clearly that the failure of the state in the Third World is a much greater source of human tragedy than the repression of their own people by even the most autocratic but functioning states such as Iraq and Syria.[74]

I shall return to this ranking of suffering later. Here I only want to underscore the essential import of Ayoob's argument that order—even of the kind provided by Saddam Hussein's Iraq—is a precondition for justice. More specifically, he argues that domestic order must have priority over international order because the former 'is an essential ingredient on which the foundations of international order are based.... a well ordered international system is constituted by well-ordered states where sovereigns are both powerful and legitimate because this prevents the exportation of domestic anarchy to interstate relations and vice versa'.[75] The underlying assumption here is that there is little prospect of regulating the use of coercion internationally in the absence of its monopolization at a more local level by sovereign states. 'Powerful *and* legitimate' of course elides the difficult questions, yet the thrust of Ayoob's argument seems to be that legitimacy must *follow* the monopolization of power. In sum, domestic state- and nation-building (using all necessary means) must have chronological as well as normative priority over international intervention for the protection of human rights.

All communitarians in the normative political theoretic literature are pluralists in international relations, but the reverse is not necessarily true. Thus Ayoob's defence of pluralism makes no reference to the value of community to individuals, resting instead on its putative contribution to global order and justice. Nevertheless, my critique of pluralism in section 3.3 should give pause to both communitarians and pluralists (who may not necessarily be communitarians). To the first group, I argue that pluralism in international relations licenses a host of practices that undermine the very values that communitarians are so keen to defend (preserving rich menus for moral choice, accountability, and self-determination). To the latter group, I argue that pluralism's inattention to questions of legitimacy means that it can, at best, deliver a world order of coercive, brittle states—hardly an enduring basis for global order, much less justice.

3.3 CRITICIZING PLURALISM

One of the more striking features of Ayoob's defence of pluralism is its curiously Eurocentric insistence that Third World states be given the pluralist space within which they might successfully replicate the European experience of state-building. Although the argument has the merit of undermining orientalist views of the Third World as deviant or backward, it seems to condemn Third World states to a historical trajectory down which European states have already travelled. As Michael Barnett argues, there is:

> no reason to presume that because Western state formation was violent, Third World state formation also must be so. It is one thing to argue that some amount of violence and repression accompanies most state-formation projects, but quite another to insist that any level is functionally necessary and therefore normatively justifiable. Not only is this morally objectionable, but it also represents historical determinism at its teleological and simplest.... Third World state formation will be different from Western state formation precisely because Third World state formation is occurring in a different historical context ... there is no historically invariant path toward state formation, and Third World state formation might demonstrate distinctively violent and pathological tendencies as a consequence.[76]

Indeed although Ayoob relies on Charles Tilly's celebrated aphorism that 'war makes states and states make war', Tilly himself is keen to stress the 'great contingency of European state formation [and] of the national state's ultimate triumph over other forms of political organisation'.[77] In fact, Tilly is at pains to point out that Third World states are *not* replicating the European experience. A key paradox of that experience, as he sees it, was that the 'pursuit of war and military capacity, after having created national states as a sort of by-product, led to a civilianisation of government and domestic politics'. Writing in 1990, Tilly observed a contrary tendency—a growing militarization of politics—in the Third World and attributed this to superpower competition for Third World allegiance, which he saw as strengthening military organizations within these states at the expense of other interest groups.[78] Ayoob of course recognizes that Third World state-building is occurring in a fundamentally different historical context. He is keen to point out the particular features of that context that make Third World state-building more difficult and to call for a restoration of those conditions (particularly non-interference) that would more closely replicate the international context in which European state-building proceeded. Yet such a response misses Tilly's larger and more significant point about historical contingency, which, in the context of European state-building refers to the kinds of wars that called European national states into being, and to the specific combinations of capital and coercion that made them possible. In the absence of such conditions, it seems futile to expect that something like European nation-states will, or can, be built in the contemporary Third World. Indeed some of the more empirically inclined research seeking to test the application of Tilly's ideas to the Third World have argued that 'war makes states' only under certain very specific conditions, in the absence of which it is more likely to be state-destroying.[79]

3.3.1 The problem of elite (il)legitimacy

Even accepting Ayoob's apparent assumption that something like European nation-states *ought* to be constructed in the Third World, Barnett is rightly sceptical of our ability to distinguish between 'state repression for the purposes of consolidation of state authority' and predatory behaviour.[80] This is surely a matter of perspective: what appears to some as gratuitous predatory violence is, from the point of view of the putative state builders, a legitimate attempt to coerce or persuade recalcitrant groups to acknowledge their authority. Yet the legitimacy of this use of violence is contested precisely because actors differ over definitions of state and national identity, membership, and inclusion and more fundamentally over the issue of who has the authority to drive this process.

The issue of legitimacy is crucial, but extraordinarily difficult to discuss in the abstract because the determinants of legitimacy are always multifarious, contextual, and historical. One staggering blind spot in Ayoob's work is his failure to consider the sources of legitimacy of actors driving the state-building effort in the Third World. His writing is full of references to 'Third World state makers', 'Third World state elites', and 'leaders of Third World states', but *who are these people*? What gives *them* the authority to build states and nations, as opposed to the 'recalcitrants' they seek to bring in line? In most accounts of political legitimacy, the monopolization of the means of coercion by the state is legitimized by a social contract. This is of course a fictional construct that one never sees in practice in the chaotic transition from state-of-nature to full-fledged state, yet it must still be possible to locate functional analogues of the social contract that give one or another set of actors less or more legitimacy to manage the state-building process. In the context of decolonization for example, we might think that mass participation in a national liberation struggle gives the leadership of that movement some legitimacy to claim the mantle of state- and nation-building. This is of course an inchoate and unstable sort of legitimacy, but it may suffice for the duration of a transition period in which mechanisms and institutions for the explicit legitimation of power are created.[81]

Because Ayoob's work lacks any account of elite legitimacy, one is left with the impression that he would have international society recognize whichever strongman has seized the initiative of state- and nation-building, grateful that someone—anyone—has taken on this unpleasant but necessary task. In effect, Ayoob is asking international society *not* to enquire too deeply into the legitimacy of state-builders since, whatever their methods and whomever they may be, they are laying the foundations for domestic and international order and indeed for the eventual protection of human rights. International society is asked to facilitate the work of these allegedly beleaguered state elites by expanding the pluralist space within which they may more effectively accomplish the state-building process.

Ayoob adds to the urgency of this imperative by raising the spectre of state failure, which, he argues, is 'a much greater source of human tragedy than the repression of their own people by even the most autocratic but functioning states such as Iraq'.[82] This ranking of suffering says a great deal about Ayoob's perspective and priorities. The insecurity of failed states tends to be generalized and dispersed, while the repression of predatory states is often precise and targeted at specific communities or individuals. From a systemic utilitarian perspective, the former may certainly be more destabilizing than the latter; from a deontological perspective that treats individuals as ends in themselves, this is less clear.[83] I am not sure how a Kurd faced with the prospect of extermination in Saddam Hussein's Iraq could have thought of the state as 'autocratic but functioning', even if it collected taxes, cleared garbage, and built palaces. In any case, by raising the spectre of state failure as the most likely outcome if authoritarian state elites are not given the pluralist space they demand, Ayoob seems to be presenting us with a false choice between predatory states and state failure.

Perhaps most ominously, Ayoob seeks to insulate Third World elites not only from the external interference of other states, but also from the internal demands of Third World societies. His work betrays a nostalgia for the environment in which European state-builders 'could single-mindedly pursue their goals of accumulating power and extracting resources without being distracted by demands for economic redistribution and political participation', and an exasperation with the new imperatives of mass politics, democratization, and human rights because 'satisfying popular demands can frequently run counter to the imperatives of state making'.[84] A more specific manifestation of this view can be found in the literature on development, where an influential current of thought argues that authoritarianism is more conducive to rapid economic development than democracy. As Pranab Bardhan summarizes it, the claim is that while democracies are susceptible to pressures for immediate consumption and other particularistic demands that may hamper long-run investment, authoritarian leaders are better insulated from the ravages of short-term pork-barrel politics.[85] Authoritarianism is said to increase the government's ability to extract resources, provide public goods (solving collective action problems by administrative fiat), and impose the short-term costs associated with efficient economic adjustment.[86]

Although this view describes the role of authoritarianism in enabling 'adjustment' to the imperatives of the world-market economy, it should be noted that the defence of authoritarian planning has tended to be agnostic as to the ideological content of the plan. It has featured in both socialist propaganda about the necessity for sacrifices for a 'common good' specified from above, as well as in the economic conditionality of the capitalist IFIs counselling the virtues of insulating 'rational' economic policymaking from capture by rent-seeking groups. In fact it is better viewed as a characteristic of what James Scott has called 'high-modernist ideology'—a world view that fuses a supreme self-confidence in continued linear 'scientific' progress, an optimism about the possibility of the rational design of social order, and a conviction that 'political interests can only frustrate the social solutions devised by specialists with scientific tools adequate to their analysis'.[87]

The defence of authoritarian planning has acquired respectability from the developmental successes of East Asian states, where a number of significant reforms were made possible by labour repression and other authoritarian exercises of power. While he is candid about the relationship between authoritarianism and high growth rates in East Asia, Stephan Haggard is sceptical of the possibility and/or likelihood of this example being successfully emulated elsewhere.[88] He writes that high-performing Asian economies enjoyed dictatorships that were relatively enlightened, at least in respect of economic policy, and that such rule is generally in short supply. Thus, autocratic rule notwithstanding, East Asian political elites delegated authority to relatively insulated technocratic agencies, in order to signal to business elites a willingness to make policy decisions on the basis of economic criteria. Further, they sought to stabilize their rule by ensuring that the poorer social strata shared in the benefits of growth and provided at least tacit support to the government. This was accomplished through land reform in Korea and Taiwan, the provision of low-cost housing in Singapore and Hong Kong, and policies favouring indigenous ethnic groups in Malaysia and Indonesia. Although state–society bargaining characteristic of democratic polities was absent in these countries, the state was nonetheless attentive to the interests of various groups.

The notion of 'enlightened dictatorship' does not negate the strong element of coercion in East Asian authoritarianism, but it does suggest that the category of 'authoritarianism' is a broad one encompassing significant variations. Authoritarianisms vary in the levels of coercion used, but also in the purposes for which coercion is employed. Here one might distinguish between dictatorships for purely personalized ends and those where power is employed no less coercively, but for more generalized goals over and above that of personal survival and enrichment.[89] Whether the latter are preferable depends of course on the nature of those goals and on how widely they are endorsed. The point I am trying to make is that the centralization of power and the insulation of political elites from their societies leaves the field wide open for dictatorships of both the developmental and predatory varieties and there is no guarantee that a society will be 'blessed' with the former rather than the latter.

More significantly, while authoritarian rule *of a particular kind* may have been a crucial element in boosting East Asian growth rates, scholars have failed to detect any consistent correlation between political regime type and economic growth.[90] The authors of one quantitative study of the relationship between these variables over the period 1950–90 reported that they 'did not find a shred of evidence that democracy need be sacrificed on the alter of development', and noted also that 'the few countries that had developed spectacularly during the past fifty years were as likely to achieve that feat under democracy as under dictatorship'.[91] Amartya Sen has gone further, eloquently describing the role of democracy *in* development as enabling both state cognizance of popular economic needs and the guaranteeing of their fulfilment.[92]

Ayoob's assumptions about the prerequisites for successful state-building are therefore clearly contradicted by a wealth of evidence. In seeking to insulate Third World elites from both the external interference of international society and the internal demands of Third World societies, he effectively justifies absolutist and unaccountable concentrations of power in the hands of those elites. The central problem with Ayoob's defence of pluralism lies in the way it defers state–society bargaining to a vaguely specified time horizon when the 'crucial early phase of state making' has been completed.[93] A more legitimate form of pluralism (from the perspective of Third World societies) might have recognized that such bargaining has often been hindered by external linkages between elites of metropolitan and client states. It might have objected more specifically to those forms of external intervention or linkage that have prevented, delayed, or otherwise skewed state–society bargaining in ways that favour the interests of state elites.

3.3.2 The anti-pluralism of pluralism

Ayoob defends pluralism on the basis of its ability to provide an international environment that is more conducive to state-building, the need for which is justified with reference to its contribution to global order and justice. In contrast, the emphasis in Jackson's work is on pluralism's ability to better accommodate the diversity of human values in international society.[94] This is a justification of pluralism that rests on much more explicitly communitarian foundations, sharing as it does the communitarian desire to preserve rich menus of options for moral and political reasoning. Yet if we were to pay attention to the history, sociology, and anthropology of state- and nation-building, we would begin to see the irony of such a defence of pluralism, given the very considerable extent to which these processes entail the elimination of pluralism and value diversity.

It is probably correct to suppose that value-diversity in international society is better ensured by a multiplicity of political communities. Yet the pluralist desire for an absence of any norms about how such communities might legitimately be constructed, licenses a quite considerable elimination of value diversity in the course of state- and nation-building. As Ernest Gellner reminds us:

> nationalism is, essentially, the general imposition of a high culture on society, where previously low cultures had taken up the lives of the majority, and in some cases of the totality, of the population. It means that generalised diffusion of a school-mediated, academy-supervised idiom, codified for the requirements of reasonably precise bureaucratic and technological communication. It is the establishment of an

anonymous, impersonal society, with mutually substitutable atomised individuals, held together above all by a shared culture of this kind, in place of a previous complex structure of local groups, sustained by folk cultures reproduced locally and idiosyncratically by the micro-groups themselves. This is what *really* happens.[95]

What really happens can be contrasted with the narrative that nationalisms and nationalists construct for themselves: namely, that *they* are the authentic bearers of a putative folk culture, struggling to overthrow an alien yoke. This is not inaccurate, particularly in imperial and colonial settings. The crucial point is that upon eliminating the alien high culture, successful nationalisms do not usually replace this with a plurality of local low cultures, but tend to revive or invent a local high culture of their own, though admittedly using pre-existing local folk styles and dialects as their raw material.[96] Particular groups that have dominated nationalist movements (Ayoob's nation-building elites), tend to be disproportionately represented in the newly invented high-vernacular culture. They take on the status of the 'core' model citizen, while other groups tend to be relegated to a sort of deviant, hyphenated form of belonging, if they are incorporated within the nationalist narrative at all.[97]

No single story can be told about how and why the new high vernaculars tended to edge out the variety of low vernaculars on which they were parasitic. In Benedict Anderson's account, print capitalism plays a central role in the rise of the linguistic nationalisms of eighteenth-century Europe. While the actual diversity of spoken languages was immense, Anderson points out that if print capitalism had sought to exploit each potential oral vernacular market, it would have remained a capitalism of petty proportions.[98] Because it did not, the imagined (solidarist) community of Latin Christendom was eventually fragmented (pluralized) into a limited number of communities each based on a print-language. These print-languages laid the bases for national consciousnesses, most importantly by creating unified fields of exchange and communication below Latin and above the spoken low vernaculars, thereby enabling mutual comprehension, communication, and the beginnings of solidarity amongst millions of people—but also clearly demarcating the outer limits of such solidarity. Dialects that were closer to the 'languages-of-power' created by print-capitalism tended to dominate their final forms; those more distant 'lost caste … because they were unsuccessful in insisting on their own print-form'.[99] *Which* dialects were elevated by print-capitalism to the status of languages-of-power often had less to do with numerical than political weight. As Eric Hobsbawm points out, although French was essential to the concept of France, only 50% of Frenchmen spoke the language in 1789 and only 12–13% spoke it 'correctly'; and although the Italian language was the only basis for Italian unification, at the moment of unification in 1860 only 2.5% of the population used the language for everyday communication.[100] If language is read as a metaphor for culture more broadly, the successful 'nationalization' of high vernaculars at the expense of low vernaculars should serve as a reminder of the significant loss of value pluralism entailed by nation-building.

If this particular account of the interaction between print-capitalism and political elites suggests one route for the disappearance of low vernaculars, we also need to consider the conscious elimination of low vernaculars as a result of state policy. This sometimes took the form of conservative, reactionary policies by dynastic states anticipating and pre-empting popular nationalist identification by re-imagining themselves as nations by 'stretching the short, tight, skin of the nation over the gigantic body of the empire' in Anderson's wonderfully evocative phrase.[101] One thinks here of such coercive (and obviously anti-pluralist) policies as the Tsarist empire's Russification of its domains, analogues of which might be found in a great many polyglot, multinational states today. As state interests (particularly with regard to success in warfare) came to depend increasingly on the participation and sacrifices of their citizens, states extended rights to citizens but also sought to hold them captive by attempting to formulate and inculcate new forms of civic loyalty and striving to ensure that these would trump other sorts of political identification. Nationalisms independent of the state (most likely to come from unauthorized low cultures) were potentially powerful assets if they could be integrated into state patriotism, but potentially subversive—and therefore best eliminated—if they were not.[102]

States tend to eliminate pluralities of low cultures not only in the course of crafting official nationalisms to give themselves legitimacy, but also—as Scott has shown—simply in the business of *being* states. All states—colonial and post-colonial and ruled by whatever sort of regime—have had certain fundamental objectives: appropriation of resources (through extraction, taxation, and sometimes conscription), and political control and manipulation of their subjects. With the move from tribute and indirect rule to taxation and direct rule, the effective pursuit of these objectives entailed not only an enormous expansion in state capacity and power, but also in knowledge. It became imperative for states to understand their societies better, to render them 'legible'. Towards this end, states devise schemes of simplification, abstraction, and standardization that enable them to apprehend the complex realities of their societies by filtering out those aspects of reality that are not of immediate interest to them. But crucially, states have also continually attempted to create a terrain and population that correspond to these abstractions and simplifications, making them easier to count, assess, monitor, and manage. As Scott puts it:

> The utopian, immanent and continually frustrated goal of the modern state is to reduce the chaotic, disorderly, constantly changing social reality beneath it to something more closely resembling the administrative grid of its observations.... The aspiration to such uniformity and order alerts us to the fact that modern statecraft is largely a project of internal colonization, often glossed, as it is in imperial rhetoric, as a 'civilizing mission'. The builders of the modern nation-state do not merely describe, observe and map; they strive to shape a people and landscape that will fit their techniques of observation.[103]

The continual reshaping of complex social realities to better approximate simplified cognitive frameworks has radically anti-pluralist implications. Scott provides fascinating glimpses of these—in the austere urban environments that residents of high-modernist planned cities such as Brasilia and Chandigarh are condemned to, in the destruction of the plurality of cultivation techniques traditionally practised by peasants in the Soviet Union and Tanzania as a result of collectivization schemes pursued by those states, etc. He attributes the enthusiasm for such state schemes to 'high-modernist' thinking (discussed earlier)—a mindset that post-colonial elites, who perceive in the moment of liberation an opportunity to drag their 'backward' societies out of stagnation, are particularly prone to.

In describing the anti-pluralist tendencies of nation- and state-building, I have been trying to suggest that defences of pluralist international society that emphasize its ability to accommodate value diversity rest on philosophically incoherent foundations. Pluralists and communitarians can of course offer the weak response that pluralist international society accommodates *more* diversity than a universal liberal solidarist international society would. But it would be impossible to defend the *content* of the plurality that characterizes international society at any given time, which is nothing but the sum total of high vernaculars that have triumphed over pluralities of low vernaculars in the multiple jurisdictions that comprise the society of states. Without norms of international society that determine how these intra-state contests are to be managed, the outcomes of these contests are largely a function of the power of the various contestants. It is not clear why one should celebrate the diversity —or 'pluralism'—that results from such outcomes.

3.3.3 The selectivity of pluralism

Third World elites tend to be highly selective in their choice of issue areas in which to be pluralist. Note that pluralism as a method of ordering international relations gives state elites room for manoeuvre, which can be used in a variety of ways. We have come to think of pluralism as enabling the assertion of difference and particularity; but equally, nothing prevents elites from using the pluralist space to mimic, borrow from the outside, or accede to norms promulgated by foreign norm entrepreneurs. Although it is impossible to generalize about the ways in which Third World state elites have used the pluralist space available to them, it may be possible to discern certain patterns in their tendencies to appropriate from the outside in some respects, while maintaining a detached particularity in others. We might consider cultural relativism an appropriate proxy for pluralist particularism and make a stab at discerning these patterns by thinking about the issue areas in which cultural relativist arguments are most frequently voiced.

I mentioned earlier that Third World political elites embraced the Westphalian nation-state, albeit with varying degrees of enthusiasm, despite its obviously *European* provenance. Indeed, anti-colonial nationalist and liberation movements often aspired to replicate within their countries the political institutions of their colonial oppressors. For virtually all of their post-colonial existence, Third World elites have perceived their developmental choices through the prisms of two *Western* modes of economic organization: capitalism and communism. Today, one rarely hears these elites articulate cultural relativist objections to the spread of *Western* medicine or banking practices (with the exception of Iran, in countries where Islamic banking is available, it operates in parallel with the conventional (read: Western) banking system).[104] Both the 'today' and 'elites' in the previous sentence deserve emphasis: we cannot forget that contemporary elite acceptance of these ubiquities is, to a large extent, a legacy of colonial exercises of power; we cannot also ignore contemporary non-elite resistance to the spread of these norms. Nonetheless, since I am interested in contemporary Third World state elite behaviour, I believe I can safely make the observation that cultural relativist objections—while they may have been articulated historically in a great many issue areas—are today most frequently raised in opposition to human rights.

Even within the area of human rights, the cultural relativist objection is selectively deployed. It is not seen to have any relevance to the issue of racial discrimination, for example, but is most frequently articulated in interstate conversations about gender discrimination. As a result, the norm against gender discrimination has had a much bumpier ride in international society than that against racial discrimination. Both the Convention on the Elimination of all forms of Racial Discrimination (CERD) and the Convention on the Elimination of all forms of Discrimination Against Women (CEDAW) were initially promulgated as declarations and acquired the status of binding conventions upon receiving the required number of ratifications. While CERD became a convention within 2 years, CEDAW took 13.[105] One analysis of reservations to the two conventions concluded that while 3.1% of states party to CERD had entered what were classified as 'substantive' reservations to the convention, the corresponding figure for CEDAW was 22%.[106] Even a quick perusal of the reservations is sufficient to reveal that some of the most fundamental objections to CEDAW are advanced on grounds of religion or tradition.[107] A comparison of the legislative progress of the two norms (both prohibiting discrimination on the basis of an unchosen characteristic) demonstrates strikingly that while there has been a remarkable convergence around a norm against racial discrimination, states continue to remain stubbornly pluralist on the issue of gender discrimination. As feminist legal scholars have commented, the privileged status of *jus cogens* norms 'is reserved for a very limited, male-centred category' and reflects 'a male perspective of what is fundamental to international society that may not be shared by women or supported by women's experience of life'.[108]

Battles over culture within Third World states further illuminate the state's highly selective preferences for cultural pluralism. The efforts of queer rights campaigners in India to challenge the constitutionality of the law criminalizing homosexuality in that country were opposed by the government on cultural grounds (specifically citing 'the current societal context and opinion' and 'public morality').[109] Yet the use of arguments about cultural patrimony by adivasi ('original inhabitants') communities protesting their displacement from the Narmada valley as a result of the construction of the Sardar Sarovar dam, has fallen on deaf ears. Indeed in this latter case, cultural arguments received a particularly unsympathetic hearing from the state. Overruling objections to the construction of the dam, a senior judge of the Supreme Court of India noted that:

> The displacement of the tribals [sic] ... would not *per se* result in the violation of their fundamental or other rights.... At the rehabilitation sites they will have more and better amenities than which they enjoyed in their tribal hamlets. The gradual assimilation in the mainstream of the society will lead to betterment and progress.[110]

Confronted with demands for the recognition of queer rights, the Indian state hides behind the cultural bogey; yet it launches an explicit attack on the culture of adivasis using a *universalist* modernist narrative of 'betterment and progress'. How do we understand these highly selective preferences for cultural pluralism? One explanation would stress contingency—the state simply reaches for whatever arguments are politically feasible in confrontations with different constellations of interests, no matter how inconsistent those arguments appear when juxtaposed with one other. A more convincing explanation, I would argue, is that the post-colonial state continues to work with frameworks for the selective appropriation of Western modernity that were developed in the course of anti-colonial nationalist politics.

Partha Chatterjee offers a compelling account of the construction of this framework. Although illustrated with reference to anti-colonial politics in India, he argues that it has been a fundamental feature of anti-colonial nationalisms in Asia and Africa. Briefly, the argument is that the encounter between the colonial state and the nationalist elite produced a perception (in the minds of both) of an essential cultural difference between East and West.[111] The nationalist response to this encounter was one of mimicry *and* rejection, corresponding to a division between the material and the spiritual. The material was the domain of the 'outside', of the economy, statecraft, science, and technology. It was in these domains that the West was thought to be superior to the East and therefore most worthy of emulation. Overcoming Western domination was thought to necessitate an appropriation of superior Western knowledge and techniques and an erasure of difference between colonizers and colonized in the external, material sphere. Yet wholesale mimicry risked a complete loss of identity; moreover, it was unnecessary. The nationalist compensated for his (and we are mostly talking about men here) impotence in the material domain with an assertion of Eastern superiority in the 'inner' spiritual domain, which bore the 'essential' marks of cultural identity. This was the domain of language, literature, art, education, and—above all—the family. 'What was necessary was to cultivate the material techniques of modern Western civilization while retaining and strengthening the distinctive spiritual essence of the national culture.'[112]

In matters of practical quotidian existence, the inner–outer distinction translated into the social spaces of the home and the world, typically seen as female and male domains, respectively. The world was a treacherous terrain of competitive, material pursuits, in which men had to learn to imitate the West in order to beat it at its own game. Indeed in the world outside, men made every effort to erase the markers of their difference with the West, attacking with particular ferocity that most odious and galling of distinctions: race. But at home, women were to function as repositories and transmitters of cultural distinctiveness.[113] Prior even to their political struggle against the colonial state, nationalists claimed the 'spiritual' domain as their sovereign territory, resisting all encroachments of the state in these areas.[114] This did not mean that the 'spiritual' was left unchanged—on the contrary, there was a ferment of nationalist activity directed towards the goal of fashioning a culture that was distinctly modern without being Western. Women had to be educated, but in a way that ensured that they did not become Westernized. The point was that in matters 'spiritual', reform was the prerogative of the nationalists, to be undertaken at their initiative and on their terms. The intervention of outsiders—and of course the colonial state was perceived as an outsider—would not be tolerated.

I would argue that the filters through which anti-colonial nationalist elites engaged with Western modernity continue to structure their relations with post-colonial international society. With decolonization, the boundary in the nationalist imagination between the self and the colonialist other acquires the tangible fixity of a state boundary, reinforced by the protections that pluralist international society affords. Yesterday's anti-colonial nationalist elites as today's post-colonial state elites remain enthusiastic mimic men[115] in the domain of the 'material'. In this respect they have long been Western modernity's sympathetic interlocutors in the Third World, seeing themselves as midwives to their societies' painful transitions to *Western material* modernity. Culture—whether in the guise of indigenous groups resisting displacement or peasants resisting the collectivization or commodification of agriculture—cannot be allowed to become an obstacle in this venture. It must be reformed, modernized, battered down.

Yet in the domain of the 'spiritual' (understood as those residual domains of life that are thought to have no bearing on the rate of accumulation of capital), 'culture'—understood in a highly selective, reified fashion—must be preserved as a mark of distinctiveness. Indeed, a distinctive culture is the very rationale for existence as an independent political community. Reform in this domain is the prerogative of the post-colonial state.[116] The intervention of international society is unwelcome. This persistence in the post-colonial era of frameworks for the selective appropriation of Western modernity that were crafted in the course of anti-colonial resistance, helps explain the highly selective manner—including the choice of particular issue areas—in which Third World state elites deploy the vocabulary of cultural relativism. When the arbitrariness of these choices is coupled with the fact of their illegitimacy, Third World societies might justifiably ask what authority their states have to make such choices for them.

3.3.4 Oppression in resistance

One of the most interesting observations that Chatterjee makes is that the greater the success in imitating Western skills in the material domain, the greater the nationalists' need to preserve the distinctiveness of their spiritual culture.[117] This suggests that as norms converge in the materialist sphere, we might expect to see elites emphasize pluralist cultural difference *more*, rather than less, strongly. It should come as no surprise that one of the most emphatic recent articulations of cultural relativism has come from a group of states whose material modernizing credentials are widely acknowledged: I refer to the 'Asian values' thesis disputing the universality of Western conceptions of human rights, advanced by elites in countries such as Singapore,[118] Malaysia, and Indonesia.[119] While these countries suggest potentially fertile contexts in which to study Chatterjee's material–spiritual tensions, I want to make a slightly different point here using three vignettes, of which the first concerns 'Asian values'. I lack the space in which to contextualize these vignettes adequately, but I attempt to draw a singular point from all three, which I hope will shed some light on the nature of authoritarian discourse.

Vignette 1: In the early 1990s, East Asian political elites challenged the notion that civil and political rights were absolute and inviolable, arguing that this reflected a specifically Western vision of the good life. They insisted that some rights might need to be curtailed in the interests of economic development, but more fundamentally that Asian cultures prioritized communal order over individual well-being. The articulation of 'Asian values' was, in part, an assertion of sovereignty and a protest against conditionality,[120] and a demand for the recognition of the contribution of local values and knowledge to East Asian success.[121] But local and Western critics saw it as an assault on individual freedom and a justification of state authoritarianism. Thus, while Malaysian Prime Minister Mahathir Mohamad was a forceful advocate of 'Asian values', his deputy Anwar Ibrahim (while still in office, but soon to fall from grace) could not have been more critical:

> It is altogether shameful, if ingenious, to cite Asian values as an excuse for autocratic practices and denial of basic rights and civil liberties. To say that freedom is Western or un-Asian is to offend our own traditions as well as our forefathers who gave their lives against tyranny and injustices. It is true that Asians place greater emphasis on order and societal stability. But it is certainly wrong to regard society as a kind of false god upon whose altar the individual must constantly be sacrificed. No Asian tradition can be cited to support the proposition that in Asia the individual must melt into the faceless community.[122]

Bell has argued that the fact that the debate was led by Asian leaders who seemed to be motivated primarily by political considerations made it easy to dismiss the 'Asian values' challenge as a self-serving ploy by elites to justify their authoritarian rule in the face of demands for democracy. Yet he cautions that the anti-democratic views of leaders such as Singapore's elder statesman Lee Kuan Yew are shared by intellectuals and other groups in society that have no obvious personal interest in justifying undemocratic rule, and therefore form part of the ideological apparatus that helps to sustain such rule.[123] As with imperial power, it is too simplistic to see local authoritarianism as being held in place by coercion alone.

Vignette 2: In a study of political rhetoric in Syria, Lisa Wedeen points to the curious disjunction between the cult of mass deference that surrounded former President Hafiz al-Asad and the reality of an absence of belief in, or emotional commitment to, the regime amongst a significant section of the population. She argues that Asad's cult operated as a disciplinary device, generating a politics of public dissimulation in which citizens acted *as if* they revered their leader even though they did not actually do so. In her analysis, one of the ways in which the official vocabulary functioned as a mechanism of political control despite broadcasting patently absurd falsehoods was by blending consensual understandings with obviously false statements, or by representing widely shared convictions about political life (such as the view of Zionism as a neo-colonial enterprise or the need to wrest the Golan Heights back from Israel), but in stark Manichean terms that simplified the range of complex and differentiated visions expressed by Syrians in private.[124]

Vignette 3: In Zimbabwe, President Robert Mugabe located his offensive against domestic opponents such as the Movement for Democratic Change within a broader anti-imperialist and pan-African discourse. The regime has been able to place land and economic redistribution at the centre of the crisis of governance that has engulfed the country, representing land seizures as a legitimate redress for colonial injustice and racially stratified property relations. This language resonated strongly within sections of Zimbabwean society, giving Mugabe's Zanu-PF almost half the vote in the elections of March 2008.[125] It also won the regime the backing of the governments of South Africa and Namibia, and more cautious support from Nigeria. Some commentators have pointed out that Mugabe's efforts to clothe the actions of his government in anti-colonial liberationist garb were assisted—no doubt unwillingly—by the Blair government's 1997 disavowal of any responsibility for colonial injustices in Zimbabwe as well as its pursuit, in other parts of the world, of policies that are widely regarded as neo-imperialist. Behind the rhetorical shield of anti-imperialism, they claim, 'the Zanu-PF government has effectively suspended the rule of law as it attempts to bludgeon its opponents into silence'.[126]

Although the three vignettes outlined above describe quite different state–society relationships, they share two common features. The first is that in all three, authoritarian claims to power are embedded within popular discourses (East Asian communitarianism, anti-Zionism, land hunger). Authoritarianism stabilizes itself by being populist. The second is that where the regime can displace the source of grievance on to an external other, it may succeed in deflecting attention from internal criticism of itself. By casting the international–domestic as the primary axis of confrontation, the state is able to obscure other sorts of conflicts.[127] Yet the crucial point here is that the existence of legitimate grievances against the external other functions as an enabling condition for such internal authoritarian practices. In other words, to the extent that there *is* a bone to pick with the hostile outside, the regime's claim to be the authentic agent of resistance retains considerable credibility in the eyes of its people, despite its self-evident brutality and authoritarianism.

A similar claim could be made in respect of pluralism more generally. As I have argued in this chapter, the normative justification of pluralism rests on a set of claims about the value of community in political life, the need for states to enable life in community, and the conduciveness of pluralism as a method of ordering international relations to the tasks of community construction. In fact, pluralism licenses a host of state- and nation-building practices that frequently trap Third World societies within jurisdictions that seek to reproduce themselves through arbitrary and illegitimate exercises of power. Notwithstanding their oppressiveness, these processes are justified as a necessary means of keeping at bay the neo-imperialist incursions of powerful states, IFIs, corporations, and a host of other invasive actors in the Third World. For all its authoritarianism, pluralism legitimates itself as the post-colonial 'never again', deriving its urgency and moral authority from the spectre of an ongoing coercive solidarism. The abuses of authoritarian pluralism in turn are used to justify coercive solidarism. One could say that authoritarian pluralism and coercive solidarism are their own best friends.

Intermezzo

'But what about the purges? Here: in this very university?' whispered a quiet voice in her head. 'What about the concentration camps? The torture of both the leftists and the Muslim Brotherhood?' I don't know. I don't know. Maybe he never knew of it. How can one man know everything? 'What about Salah Nasr and the Mukhabarat, the huge intelligence organisation that has been turned against the people?' What do I know of government? How do I know what he knows? He nationalised the Canal, he got rid of the British Occupation, he gave us back our dignity—and at home, what about the clinics he's building everywhere? What about the High Dam? What about electricity for the peasants and land reform and education? He has to be a good man.

Ahdaf Soueif, *In The Eye of the Sun* (1992)

Part I of this book explored two dominant ways of thinking about boundaries: cosmopolitanism and communitarianism. In contrast to the prevailing discussion within the field of international normative theory, which sets itself up as a grand debate between these contrasting world views, Part I has been critical of both sides of this debate. It has drawn attention to the impoverished spatial imaginaries of threat that underpin these world views, highlighting the selective geographies and histories of culpability that legitimate cosmopolitan intervention in the Third World, as well as an equally simplistic even if opposite Third World communitarian tendency to portray the international as a realm of neo-imperialist predation to be contrasted with the safety and security of the domestic community. Part I has also been critical of the expression of these normative world views in the practices of states, demonstrating the coercive logics inherent in both cosmopolitanism and communitarianism when they manifest themselves as coercive solidarism and authoritarian pluralism respectively. Indeed, the position of Third World societies in the current conjuncture might well be understood as one of entrapment between coercive solidarism and authoritarian pluralism. In sum, Part I has tried to make a normative case for a protest sensibility that is critical of hegemonic understandings and practices of both cosmopolitanism and communitarianism.

Part II comprises a series of sketches of what such sensibilities might look like. It picks up again on the theme of the inarticulate assumptions underpinning normative world views, focusing particularly on the idea that attitudes towards boundaries are premised on assumptions about the locus of threats to basic interests. In contrast to the simplistic imaginaries of threat that underpin hegemonic understandings of cosmopolitanism and communitarianism, the actors studied in Part II operate with more complex assumptions about the locus of threat. They assume that threats to basic interests in human rights and self-determination emanate from both within and outside the political communities with which they identify. This assumption induces them to occupy a space between cosmopolitanism and communitarianism. Cumulatively, Part II is intended to illustrate the possibility, but also the difficulties, of inhabiting such a space.

The transition from Part I to Part II entails a shift in levels and subjects of analysis. While Part I is concerned with patterns of behaviour in the international society of states, Part II studies individual thinkers and practitioners of Third World protest. This shift is animated by a number of considerations. The first is an interest in understanding how Third World societies cope with the coercive dynamics of the state system, particularly the conflictual interaction between coercive solidarism and authoritarian pluralism described in chapter 3. This is something that can only be done by departing from the systemic level of analysis (adopted for the most part in the first half of the book) to examine how such dynamics appear from the vantage point of particular societies and how individuals and groups within these societies respond to them.[1]

'Societies' offer a potentially infinite number of vantage points from which to study these questions. As explained in the introduction, one of the key subsidiary themes of this book is a concern to understand the extent to which subaltern resistance is informed by cosmopolitan and/or communitarian world views. This ambition is very incompletely realized in Part II of the book. As a work of political theory, the analysis focuses disproportionately on the sorts of actors within protest movements who are most closely associated with the production of theory. Protest movements need and produce 'theory' for a variety of purposes—as a guide to action for movement members, but also as a way of rendering their claims abstract, modular, and universally recognizable so as to enable their diffusion and sympathetic reception outside the locales in which they were generated.[2] Yet the actors responsible for these tasks tend to be leaders and/or elite theorists sympathetic to the movement but typically originating from a wealthier class than the rank-and-file. Because Part II focuses on such actors, it does not claim to be a work of subaltern normative theory.[3] It is perhaps better read as an account of how cosmopolitanism and communitarianism are deployed by elite theorists on behalf of subalterns.[4]

A second reason for the shift in scale from systemic dynamics to individuals associated with particular protest movements arises from a sense that constellations of perceived external and internal threat will manifest themselves in very different ways in different places and will accordingly demand different responses. The perceived balance of gravity between external and internal threats may vary. In addition, the relationship between these different loci of threat may vary. In some contexts, external and internal threat may be locked in Manichean confrontation (chapters 4 and 6); in others, the relationship may be one of collaboration (chapter 5). Both sorts of relationships may have deeply disenfranchising implications for subaltern social movements, but they will demand different sorts of responses. It would be futile, misguided, even arrogant, to attempt to describe a 'model' protest sensibility capable of grappling with these widely differing constellations of threat.

Finally, the actors studied in Part II are deliberately chosen from widely varying geographical, historical, and political contexts with a view to substantiating the intuition that this book describes a protest dilemma that is very commonly felt across the Third World in the articulation of many different kinds of resistance. The shift in scale enables the analyst to ascertain the scope of applicability of the argument by planting his or her feet, for a time, in many places so as to test the plausibility of the central thesis from different vantage points. In this sense, the book aims at a methodological cosmopolitanism that offers, not a view from nowhere (or what typically turns out to be an unacknowledged privileged location), but a view from many places that might corroborate a putatively universal claim.

It is important to be clear about the relationship between Parts I and II precisely because of the shift in focus and scale from one to the other. Part I pieces together the architecture of threats that confront human rights in the Third World in order to establish an 'ought': namely, that the structural position of the Third World in the current conjuncture demands protest sensibilities that adopt more complex imaginaries of threat than those that underpin hegemonic understandings of cosmopolitanism and communitarianism. Part II does two things. By describing constellations of external and internal threat as perceived in a number of particular contexts, it reinforces the 'ought' of Part I by making visible the political stakes involved in adopting such a normative stance. It becomes easier to appreciate the need for protest sensibilities underpinned by complex imaginaries of threat when one is confronted with the political costs and benefits of doing so in specific contexts. Secondly, 'ought' implies 'can'—normative theorists cannot demand the impossible. The sketches in Part II therefore also endeavour to demonstrate the *possibility* of adopting the sorts of protest sensibilities logically demanded by the argument of Part I.

But 'can' does not imply that the adoption of such sensibilities will be easy or will guarantee success (however that is defined). As such, the sketches in Part II are also intended to illustrate the difficulties of adopting such protest sensibilities, the tragedies and trade-offs inherent in them—in a word, their untidiness. Further, these illustrative sketches should not be read as uncritical endorsements of the political projects they describe. It is worth repeating that they are of interest to the larger argument of this book because of the complex imaginaries of threat that underpin them and the consequently interstitial location of their view of boundaries in a space between cosmopolitanism and communitarianism. The actors studied may be elitist, self-serving, hypocritical, unrepresentative, prejudiced, ineffectual, and a great many other unsavoury things—but this does not affect their value as illustrations of the central argument of the book. Indeed the sketches try to be attentive to the less complimentary aspects of the subjectivities they describe.

The relationship between theory and praxis offers another way of understanding the link between Parts I and II. This book was provoked, in part, by an intuition that the polarized debate in normative theory between cosmopolitanism and communitarianism failed to capture the actuality of the combinations of these world views in the practice of resistance. As such, Part II of the book may be understood as an exercise in listening to individuals associated with protest movements, with a view to complicating theoretical understandings of the moral standing of boundaries—or having praxis speak back to theory.

As with the first half of the book, post-colonial literature continues to be a rich source of insight into, and illustration of, the protest sensibilities that the book attempts to describe. One of the most acute representations of this sensibility can be found in the novel *In The Eye of the Sun* by the Egyptian-born author Ahdaf Soueif. The epigraph to this chapter describes the conflicted emotions of the protagonist—Asya al-Ulema—towards Gamal Abdel Nasser as she watches him striding into her university auditorium. The threats to her vision of the good life come not only from the British Occupation, which robbed Egyptians of their dignity and much else, but also from the torture and concentration camps of 'Salah Nasr and the Mukhabarat'. 'He has to be a good man',[5] she concludes, but it is more in the nature of an effort to convince herself of something about which she is not quite sure. What she *is* sure about is that the nationalization of the Canal and the termination of the British Occupation have restored her sense of dignity. Not just her dignity, but 'ours' including that of the leftist and Muslim Brotherhood prisoners rotting in Nasser's jails. In Asya's imagined community, even Nasser's most fervent opponents acknowledge the indispensability of post-colonial sovereignty towards the end of restoring their tattered dignity. The trouble is that the very institution that restored dignity and continues to be partly constitutive of it, now also tramples over it.

Part II

4

Born Sneerers or Ironic Nationalists? Joyce, Tagore, Said, Fanon

–Now that you have signed the petition for universal peace, said Stephen, I suppose you will burn that little copybook I saw in your room.
  As Davin did not answer, Stephen began to quote:
–Long pace, fianna! Right incline, fianna! Fianna, by numbers, salute, one, two!
–That's a different question, said Davin. I'm an Irish nationalist, first and foremost. But that's you all out. You're a born sneerer, Stevie.
–When you make the next rebellion with hurleysticks, said Stephen, and want the indispensable informer, tell me. I can find you a few in this college.
–I can't understand you, said Davin. One time I hear you talk against English literature. Now you talk against the Irish informers. What with your name and your ideas. . . . Are you Irish at all?
–Come with me now to the office of arms and I will show you the tree of my family, said Stephen.
–Then be one of us, said Davin. Why don't you learn Irish? Why did you drop out of the league class after the first lesson?
  [. . .]
  A tide began to surge beneath the calm surface of Stephen's friendliness.
–This race and this country and this life produced me, he said. I shall express myself as I am.
–Try to be one of us, repeated Davin. In heart you are an Irishman but your pride is too powerful.
–My ancestors threw off their language and took another, Stephen said. They allowed a handful of foreigners to subject them. Do you fancy I am going to pay in my own life and person debts they made? What for?
–For our freedom, said Davin.
  [. . .]
  Stephen, following his own thought, was silent for an instant.
–The soul is born, he said vaguely, first in those moments I told you of. It has a slow and dark birth, more mysterious than the birth of the body.

> When the soul of a man is born in this country there are nets flung at it to hold it back from flight. You talk to me of nationality, language, religion. I shall try to fly by those nets.
> Davin knocked the ashes from his pipe.
> –Too deep for me, Stevie, he said. But a man's country comes first. Ireland first, Stevie. You can be a poet or a mystic after.
> –Do you know what Ireland is? asked Stephen with cold violence. Ireland is the old sow that eats her farrow.
>
> James Joyce, *A Portrait of the Artist as a Young Man* (1916)

When a signature petition in support of world peace, disarmament, interstate arbitration, and a host of other worthy internationalist causes starts doing the rounds in his college, Stephen Dedalus—the protagonist of James Joyce's semi-autobiographical bildungsroman *A Portrait of the Artist as a Young Man*—is not impressed. At first the lofty goals of the campaign elicit only his weary disinterest, but he is also angered by the absurdity of their being urged on the world by one of its absolutist monarchs—Tsar Nicholas II of Russia. Historians have speculated that in proposing in 1898, a conference on disarmament at The Hague, which eventually established the Permanent Court of Arbitration, Nicholas's pretentions to playing the role of world statesman may have concealed a gnawing fear that Russia was losing the arms race in an increasingly fractious multipolar Europe. Less aware of these international political developments, Dedalus's friend Davin—described in the text as a simple-minded peasant boy, steeped in the language and myths of Ireland and widely thought of in the college as a 'young fenian'—has signed the petition. When Dedalus, bemused and scornful, asks him whether this means that he has turned his back on Irish nationalism, it is Davin's turn to be perplexed. Confounded by Dedalus's refusal to support pacific internationalism and his insistent mockery of Irish nationalism, it seems to Davin as if Dedalus cannot give his allegiance to anything or anyone. 'I can't understand you', he bursts out. 'One time I hear you talk against English literature. Now you talk against the Irish informers. What with your name and your ideas. ... Are you Irish at all?'[1] Davin's repeated entreaties to Dedalus to 'be one of us', provokes the latter to a bitter denunciation of Irish nationalism, citing its persistent betrayal of its most loyal sons and its unceasing suppression of individual freedom. It is difficult to imagine a more damning indictment of communitarianism than that offered by Dedalus's vision of the community devouring the individual: 'Ireland is the old sow that eats her farrow.'[2]

Yet contrary to the conventional reading of Dedalus as wanting to leap out of a stultifying provincialism into a liberating post-national identity, Marjorie Howes has drawn attention to the extent to which he continues to inhabit the very intellectual structures that he rejects. Even as he rejects the prevailing forms of cultural nationalism, vowing to 'fly by' the 'nets' of nationality, language, and religion (in an allusion to the classical tale of Daedalus and Icarus), he continues to think of the 'nation' in precisely the terms those forms offer him.[3] The novel closes with his determination to 'forge in the smithy of my soul the uncreated conscience of my race'[4]—an enterprise that many nationalists would be happy to claim as their own. In a similar vein, while discussing an argument that he had had with his mother over his refusal to take Easter Communion, Dedalus's immersion in Christian theology is so evident that his friend Cranly is moved to observe: 'It is a curious thing... how your mind is supersaturated with the religion in which you say you disbelieve.'[5]

Something similar might be said of Joyce's relationship to the Irish Literary Revival, of which he was a critical member—both in the sense of being important and dissenting. Kevin Barry locates Joyce in a group of cultural renegades that included such figures as John Eglinton, Thomas Kettle, James Connolly, Thomas McDonagh, R. W. Lynd, and the contributors to a short-lived literary journal called *Dana*, who were deeply critical of the exclusivist 'Irish Ireland' current of the Revival and called for its broadening beyond national boundaries and a recognition of the diversity of Irish life.[6] But Joyce also had much in common with leading figures of the Revival such as W. B. Yeats, Lady Gregory, George 'A. E.' Russell, J. M. Synge, and others. Like them, he was deeply engaged in 'narrating the nation', working in a literary mode—the novel—that had long been a key site for the production of national identity. David Lloyd has written that the autobiographical form has been central to nationalist discourse, typically telling the story of a nationalist hero who disavows his actual roots and then struggles to discover, identify with, and embody 'the spirit of the nation'. Emer Nolan reads *A Portrait* in just such a fashion, arguing that although Dedalus is devoted to the elaboration of a narrative that is diametrically opposed to the aspirations of contemporary cultural nationalism, 'none the less the aestheticist self-creation offered by Dedalus offers a structural homology to the artistic mission to which it is ostensibly opposed. In his resolutely individualistic self-fashioning, Dedalus ironically re-enacts the self-making and self-discovery of the nationalist cultural project.'[7]

While Joyce was deeply critical of what he saw as the caricature of Irishness being produced by the Revival, Ireland or an idea of Ireland continued to play a central role in his work. But as Seamus Deane has written, whereas for the revivalists the idea of Ireland was an invigorating and positive force, for Joyce (and other émigré Irish writers like Oscar Wilde and George Bernard Shaw), it was a negative place which threatened artistic freedom and integrity and squandered the talents of its people. The ends of liberation were best served, in Joyce's view, not by drawing flattering portraits of this society by romanticizing its rural and peasant life or the idea of the Celt and his lost language, but by subjecting it to the gaze of an unflinching realism that rendered Irish life in all its desperation, poverty, and ugliness. Defending the text of *Dubliners* from charges of indecency and demands for revision, Joyce wrote to the publisher Grant Richards: 'It is not my fault that the odour of ashpits and old weeds and offal hangs round my stories. I seriously believe that you will retard the course of civilisation in Ireland by preventing the Irish people from having one good look at themselves in my nicely polished looking-glass.'[8] Deane adroitly captures Joyce's ironic relationship with Irish nationalism, arguing that:

> Joyce set himself up as the anatomist of Irish illusions, but this did not in any sense inhibit him from believing that, under the 'lancet of my art', 'the cold steel pen'. . . , the soul of the country would be revealed. . . . If Ireland was to be seen, it would be in the full light of an Ibsenite dawn, not in the glimmer of a Celtic twilight. . . . The mirror held up to Culture was going to reflect a reality no-one had presented before. Dublin would find it an unwelcome sight, but Dublin and Ireland would be liberated by it.[9]

Irish nationalism was only one of many ideological formations subjected to Joyce's withering gaze. In 'After the Race', Jimmy, an Irishman, cavorts with a group of Continental and other acquaintances after a day spent watching cars race each other. When at the after-race dinner party, Jimmy gets into a political argument with the Englishman Routh, threatening to strain the atmosphere of cosmopolitan camaraderie, the host attempts to diffuse the situation by proposing a toast 'to Humanity'.[10] Later they drink toasts to Ireland, England, France, Hungary, and the United States, as if to bury their material differences in an imagined comity of nations. A card game ensues in which Jimmy loses heavily and Routh emerges the winner. There is an insinuation of cheating ('they were devils of fellows') and the outcome of the game seems to reinforce the essential inequality between the Irish and English members of the group. Howes has read this story as suggesting that 'cosmopolitanism and universalist ideals can function as a covert European nationalism, and can help to sustain imperialism rather than to dismantle it'.[11]

How do we understand Joyce's mockery of both cosmopolitanism and nationalism? It is difficult to pin down the political beliefs of a writer as given to parody, satire, and irony in his fiction as Joyce was. Nonetheless, it is possible to discern the spatial imaginaries of threat that inform his thinking about freedom and liberation in his more explicitly political writings. In an important essay entitled 'Ireland: Island of Saints and Sages', he is categorical about the culpability of the English in reducing Ireland to its present state, declaring that 'Ireland is poor because English laws destroyed the industries of the country, notably the woollen one; because, in the years in which the potato crop failed, the negligence of the English government left the flower of the people to die of hunger; because, while the country is becoming depopulated and, through criminality is almost non-existent, judges under the present administration receive the salaries of a Pasha'.[12] And he is clear that the Irish have a right to resist their subjection: 'If a victorious country tyrannises over another, it cannot logically take it amiss if the latter reacts. Men are made that way; and no one, unless he were blinded by self-interest or ingenuity, can still believe that a colonising country is prompted by purely Christian motives when it takes over foreign shores.'[13] But he is equally scathing about the local conditions that shackle the creativity and initiative of the Irish people, singling out the Catholic Church for especially severe condemnation. As he puts it: 'I do not see what good it does to fulminate against English tyranny while the tyranny of Rome still holds the dwelling place of the soul.'[14] Deane elaborates on Joyce's understanding of the relationship between these tyrannies:

> The remodelling of the national character, undertaken by groups like Sinn Fein and the Irish Revival, is indeed a heroic enterprise, but it is a futile one unless it accepts that the remodelling has to begin with the problem of fidelity to Rome rather than with the problem of fidelity or infidelity towards the British system. It is Rome, not London, which rules the Irish mind. London will readily use Rome for its purposes. But the Roman imperium is the more subtle and pervasive because it encroaches on the territory which should be ruled by the artist.[15]

Convinced that Irish freedom was shackled by Rome and London, Joyce struggled against these dual tyrannies, ruthlessly parodying both the narrow-minded provincialism of Irish nationalism and the civilizing pretensions of British imperialism.

4.1 RABINDRANATH TAGORE

In the same year that *A Portrait* was first published in book form (1916), another literary modernist in another British colony published a novel called *Ghare Baire* (translated into English as *The Home and the World*), which expressed a similar refusal of imperialism and authoritarian nationalism.[16] In language that virtually echoes Dedalus's determination to fly by the nets of nationality, language, and religion, Nikhil—the autobiographical protagonist of this other novel, written by the Indian Nobel laureate Rabindranath Tagore—speaks of the need to 'save the country from the thousand-and-one snares—of religion, custom and selfishness', which nationalist agitators were laying amongst the people.[17]

Although there is no evidence that Joyce and Tagore were influenced by each other's work, it is no coincidence that two novelists from Ireland and India crafted these fictional kindred spirits contemporaneously. Ireland and India were the two British colonies that already had relatively well-developed independence movements by the beginning of the twentieth century.[18] Both were largely bourgeois nationalist movements, closer to Garibaldi and Mazzini than Marx. Irish nationalists had been impressed by the Indian revolt of 1857 and they perceived in the Bengal famine of 1874 an echo of their own imperial history of the 1840s. Ireland in turn was a beacon for anti-colonial nationalist movements the world over, pioneering many of the techniques of agitation that would be attempted elsewhere (the term 'boycott', for example, comes from Captain Charles Boycott (1832–97), who was a land agent for the estate of Lord Erne in county Mayo during the Land League agitation of 1873).[19] In 1916, the Indian nationalist movement was radicalized by the creation of the Indian Home Rule League, modelled on the Irish equivalent, by the Irish theosophist Annie Besant. Her arrest by the British government in India the following year became a cause célèbre, precipitating the convergence of different factions of the nationalist movement. Following her release, Besant became president of the Indian National Congress. Early-twentieth-century Dublin and Bengal were characterized by remarkably similar conversations between distinct strands of anti-colonial resistance: constitutional agitation, a vigorous and articulate cultural nationalism, mass-based passive resistance in the form of strikes and boycotts, punctuated by more sporadic acts of revolutionary terrorism and insurrection. We should not, therefore, be surprised by the resonant sensibilities of novels located in such comparable discursive fields.[20]

Tagore was a vociferous critic of nationalism at a time when the vast majority of politically conscious Indians, rallying to Gandhi's call for non-cooperation and boycott, were deeply imbued with a nationalist fervour against British imperialism. Tagore's critique of nationalism was expressed forcefully in his fiction and essays, in a series of lectures delivered in Japan and the United States in 1916–17, and in a number of public disagreements with Gandhi in the 1920s and 1930s. This has made it easy for Tagore to be appropriated by the cosmopolitans, but I will argue in this section that this is a misappropriation. Tagore's awareness of the spatially dispersed nature of threats to freedom, exemplified in a deep and simultaneous antipathy towards both the brutal modernism of imperialism and the claustrophobia of authoritarian nationalism, induced him to occupy a space between cosmopolitanism and nationalism. This space is well illustrated by the narrative of *The Home and the World*. I shall therefore begin by offering a reading of the novel, before contextualizing it in relation to Tagore's political activism and writings.

The Home and the World is set against the backdrop of the Swadeshi movement, which convulsed Bengal from 1903 to 1908. The movement was provoked by the British government's announcement of its intention to partition Bengal into two provinces, one of which was to have a Hindu majority and the other a Muslim majority. Although justified on grounds of administrative convenience, the proposal was widely seen as an instance of the preferred imperial technique of 'divide and rule'. The anti-partition movement began rather meekly with *bhadralok* (middle-class) politicians writing petitions and making speeches, but by 1905 had moved well beyond its bourgeois origins to mobilize large numbers of people around a programme comprising a boycott of foreign goods and colonial educational and governmental institutions and a transfer of patronage to indigenous substitutes. Although the movement failed to avert the partition that had sparked it off, it was unprecedented in its ability to bridge the elite–subaltern divide, however briefly, and featured many of the tactics and idioms of protest that Gandhi was later to deploy more successfully.[21]

The Home and the World is the story of a love triangle comprising two men and a woman, which might be read as a metaphor for the relative attractions of cosmopolitanism and nationalism as seen from the vantage point of a nation attempting to wrest its freedom from imperial rule. The character of Nikhil, a wealthy but progressive zamindar (landlord) exemplifies a number of cosmopolitan tropes. Generally indifferent to tradition and custom, he is keen to relate to his wife Bimala on terms of equality—a determination that renders him 'absolutely modern' in her eyes.[22] His openness to external influences, including those that are the result of the imperial presence, is signified by the act of hiring a British governess for Bimala.[23] And he speaks a language of rural 'upliftment' and improvement that is emblematic of the Enlightenment spirit. Conversely, his friend Sandip is typically read as personifying the claims of nationalism. Passionately committed to the success of the Swadeshi movement, Sandip is acutely aware of the usefulness of symbolism and myth in mobilizing popular grievances and harnessing them to the nationalist cause—a politics that is anathema to Nikhil's rationalist sensibilities.

The progress of the Swadeshi movement occasions some of the sharpest disagreements between the two men. While sharing the ultimate goals of the movement (broadly, *swaraj* or self-rule), Nikhil is troubled by the uneven impact of the nationalist injunction to boycott foreign goods, correctly anticipating that poorer consumers who tended to purchase cheap imported goods in preference to expensive indigenous substitutes would suffer most.[24] He refuses to use his authority as a zamindar to enforce the boycott, remarking to Bimala that 'those who make sacrifices for their country's sake are indeed her servants...but those who compel others to make them in her name are her enemies. They would cut freedom at the root, to gain it at the top'[25]; and elsewhere, 'to tyrannize for the country is to tyrannize over the country'.[26] In a classically cosmopolitan gesture of rescue, when Panchu—the destitute tenant of a neighbouring landlord—is evicted by his nationalist zamindar as punishment for peddling foreign cloth to pay for his wife's funeral expenses, Nikhil offers to buy Panchu's landholding to keep a roof over his head. Meanwhile, Sandip's use of Hindu religious imagery has also alienated Muslims, who in addition, bear the commercial brunt of the boycott in their capacity as petty traders reliant on the sale of foreign cloth. Sandip urges his followers to show them no mercy: '...though we have shouted ourselves hoarse, proclaiming the Mussalmans to be our brethren, we have come to realise that we shall never be able to bring them wholly round to our side. So they must be suppressed altogether and made to understand that we are the masters.'[27]

Utilizing a common literary trope of the time, Tagore casts Bimala as the personification of Bengal, torn between the values espoused by the two men.[28] She is the terrain on which the two men duel and the prize for whose affections they compete. But she is also the arbiter of the novel, her modulating feelings towards the male characters functioning as a proxy for public perceptions of the political efficacy of their competing world views. On first meeting Sandip, Bimala is enamoured by his fiery rhetoric, which seems to offer a form of political agency that is more virile, potent, and immediately gratifying in its apparent ability to deliver the nation from imperialist subjugation. The eroticization of their relationship is a metaphor for the seductiveness of Swadeshi nationalism in the political arena. Conversely, Bimala becomes intellectually and emotionally estranged from Nikhil, whose less heroic social work, geared towards long-term social transformation and carried out in almost complete obliviousness of the British presence, seems less promising. Yet as the narrative progresses, Bimala is increasingly assailed by doubt. Sandip has persuaded her to steal money from her husband's safe for the nationalist cause—an act that she regrets almost immediately as it begins to vitiate her relationships with members of the household. In the world outside, the pernicious consequences of Sandip's political activism are beginning to unfold as the Muslims riot in protest. But Bimala's second thoughts may have come too late to save her relationship with Nikhil, who is wounded—possibly fatally[29]—in the course of trying to quell a communal riot.

Bimala's remorse at the end of the novel is usually read as a vindication of Nikhil's position, shot through with the deeply pessimistic sentiment that Sandip's views are politically more resonant in the world. Nussbaum, for example, has read the book as the 'tragic story of the defeat of a reasonable and principled cosmopolitanism by the forces of nationalism and ethnocentrism'.[30] This is too simple a reading particularly given the broader context of her article, which appears to set up an oppositional relationship between patriotism and cosmopolitanism. For Nikhil, these are not antinomic concepts. Early in the novel, we are told that he has long been an advocate of self-reliance—a central goal of the Swadeshi movement. As Bimala explains, 'from the time my husband had been a college student he had been trying to get the things required by our people produced in our own country'.[31] We are also informed, crucially, that Sandip's political activity is funded by Nikhil.[32] And when a smear campaign is mounted in the local press, branding Nikhil a collaborationist because of his refusal to enforce the nationalist boycott, he responds by attempting to redefine the patriotic space rather than ceding it to the Swadeshi activists:

> Our country... has been brought to death's door through sheer fear—from fear of the gods down to fear of the police; and if you set up, in the name of freedom, the fear of some other bogey, whatever it may be called; if you would raise your victorious standard on the cowardice of the country by means of downright oppression, then no true lover of the country can bow to your decision.[33]

Rather than depicting an opposition between patriotism and cosmopolitanism, the novel is therefore more productively read in the way that Ashis Nandy does, as a conflict between two forms of patriotism—one that is unreasoned, authoritarian, and demagogic, and another that is critical, reflective, and uncoerced.[34] Like Nussbaum, however, Nandy sees the novel as essentially a critique of Sandip's politics.

But *The Home and the World* is also a critique of Nikhil and the politics of cosmopolitanism. Indeed, in having both male protagonists exit the scene towards the end of the novel, one might argue that Tagore repudiates both cosmopolitanism and nationalism, leaving Bimala to contemplate her future in solitude. In silencing both male characters, Tagore was recommending neither of them. In a highly persuasive reading, Michael Sprinker has suggested that Nikhil's cosmopolitanism disappoints us because his proposed liberation is not some Kantian kingdom of ends in which all are equally empowered to realize their freedom, but is instead expressed in the deeply paternalistic mode of the enlightened and benevolent patriarch bestowing *his* conception of freedom on others.[35] We see this most clearly in his attempts to educate, modernize, and 'civilize' Bimala; indeed Nikhil himself sees this in a moment of acute self-awareness while introspecting about the causes of their estrangement:

> I have begun to suspect that there has all along been a vein of tyranny in me. There was a despotism in my desire to mould my relations with Bimala in a hard, clear-cut, perfect form. But man's life was not meant to be cast in a mould. And if we try to shape the good, as so much mere material, it takes a terrible revenge by losing its life... I did not realise all this while that it must have been this unconscious tyranny of mine which made us gradually drift apart... she could not be open with me, because she felt that, in certain things, I despotically differed from her.[36]

Elsewhere, writing about the importance of autonomous self-development, Tagore notes: 'I have learnt to fear the menace of the good-that-comes-in-the-form-of-improving-others more than evil itself.'[37] There is no corresponding awareness of the conservatism of Nikhil's rescue of Panchu, who is saved from one zamindar only to live out his days as the tenant of another. The novel contrasts the good zamindar (Nikhil) with the bad zamindar (Harish Kundu), but zamindari per se does not come under attack. Tanika Sarkar sees this as a deliberate choice rather than a failure of imagination on the part of Tagore: had Panchu enjoyed a meaningful degree of autonomy, he might have radically destabilized the class position of Nikhil.[38] As a zamindar in his own right, Tagore might have found this too close for comfort.

Notwithstanding these limitations, Tagore's critique of Nikhil suggests that *The Home and the World* is as much a criticism of the benevolent civilizing pretensions of imperialism and universalist modernization, as it is of nationalism. This alternative reading is borne out by Tagore's more didactic pronouncements on cosmopolitanism and nationalism, in which he distanced himself from both polarities. In an essay on nationalism published a year after *The Home and the World*, he declared that 'neither the colourless vagueness of cosmopolitanism, nor the fierce self-idolatry of nation-worship, is the goal of human history'.[39] Elsewhere, he concludes a reflection on identity politics in education with the hope that 'the institutions we are setting up today express both our national and our cosmopolitan consciousness'.[40] But what did this mean?

Tagore's attitude towards nationalism was shaped by his encounter with the Swadeshi movement, of which he was initially a leading personality[41] but later a severe critic. The change of heart seems to have been precipitated by his growing awareness of the extent to which the movement relied on coercion for its effectiveness. Such coercion typically took the form of destruction of property, physical intimidation and assault, social ostracism, or the use of caste sanctions against those found violating the nationalist injunction against patronizing foreign goods and institutions.[42] The result was a serious alienation of subaltern groups such as Muslims and lower-caste Namasudra peasants, and the eventual eruption of Hindu–Muslim riots in East Bengal in 1906–7, all of which were fictionalized in the violent denouement of *The Home and the World*.

This early awareness of the subaltern experience of nationalism developed into a more profound critique, expressed in a series of lectures delivered in Japan and the United States in 1916–17. Here, Tagore criticizes nationalism as 'one of the most powerful anaesthetics that man has invented', under the influence of which 'the whole people can carry out its systematic programme of the most virulent self-seeking without being in the least aware of its moral perversion'.[43] He accuses nationalism of fostering ill-will between nations and of curtailing individual freedom within nations, criticizing

> the voluntary submission of the whole people to the trimming of their minds and clipping of their freedom by their government, which through various educational agencies regulates their thoughts, manufactures their feelings, becomes suspiciously watchful when they show signs of inclining towards the spiritual, leading them through a narrow path not toward what is true but what is necessary for the complete welding of them into one uniform mass according to its own recipe.[44]

Tagore's critique exhibits a profound awareness of nationalism as an *international* phenomenon. Speaking directly to the experiences of his Japanese audience, he is full of admiration for that country's early attempts to learn from the West, but critical of its growing militarism and imperialism. Yet in an interesting twist, he holds international society (such as it existed then) partly responsible for encouraging the expression of political subjectivity in the form of militaristic nationalism. Referring to Japan's 'admission' into international society following its defeat of Russia in the war of 1905, he says:

> Japan had all her wealth of humanity, her harmony of heroism and beauty, her depth of self-control and richness of self-expression; yet the Western nations felt no respect for her till she proved that the bloodhounds of Satan are not only bred in the kennels of Europe but can also be domesticated in Japan and fed with man's miseries. They admit Japan's equality with themselves, only when they know that Japan also possesses the key to open the floodgates of hell-fire upon the fair earth whenever she chooses, and can dance, in their own measure, the devil dance of pillage, murder and ravishment of innocent women, while the world goes to ruin.[45]

These criticisms of nationalism recurred in a series of highly public disagreements with Gandhi, which offer a striking contrast between Tagore the philosopher, committed to a rationalistic transformation of social attitudes, and Gandhi the politician, given to harnessing social prejudices and popular beliefs for the purpose of nationalist mobilization.[46] Thus, Tagore was horrified by Gandhi's characterization of the 1934 Bihar earthquake as divine retribution for the practice of untouchability, even though he shared Gandhi's goal of eradicating that egregious social practice. He disagreed with Gandhi's attempt to persuade people to boycott and burn foreign cloth by describing it as 'impure'. He was irritated by Gandhi's exhortation to his followers to set aside a few hours every day to spin khadi on a charkha—an activity that Gandhi viewed as a collective egalitarian project symbolizing the dignity of labour, but that Tagore saw as promoting a mind-numbing uniformity that crushed individual creativity and rebellion. As he declared, somewhat heretically: 'If in any country we find no symptom of . . . rebellion, if we find its people submissively or contentedly prone on the dust, in dumb terror of some master's bludgeon, or blind acceptance of some guru's injunction, then indeed should we know that for such a country . . . it is high time to mourn.'[47] And he clashed with Gandhi repeatedly over the non-cooperation movement's rejection of Western learning.[48]

Tagore was well positioned to critique Gandhian hegemony because his anti-imperialism could never credibly be doubted. There were several key moments, particularly before Gandhi's assumption of the leadership of the national movement, when his voice led the anti-imperialist chorus. One thinks here particularly of his resignation of his knighthood following the Jallianwala Bagh massacre of 1919, an event that he described at the time as being 'without parallel in the history of civilised governments'.[49] Nonetheless, his criticisms of nationalism tended to be ignored by his compatriots, perhaps on account of his failure to articulate alternatives to the political structures that he was criticizing. At times it seemed as if he was not very interested in politics at all, with education and social reform being of much higher priority.[50] Far from constituting a retreat from politics, this attitude stemmed from an understanding of politics as a superstructural realm resting on a social base.[51] Tagore saw his primary work as that of building the social foundations on which emancipatory political systems could be constructed. In a view that is remarkably similar to Joyce's understanding of the relationship between 'London' and 'Rome' in threatening Irish freedom, Tagore sees imperialism as symptomatic of prior internal weaknesses such as casteism and social orthodoxy, rather than as the primary cause of India's ailments. The lectures on nationalism conclude with an indictment of Indian nationalists for their failure to recognize 'the patent fact that there were causes in our social organisation which made the Indian incapable of coping with the alien' and a warning that if England were driven away, 'we should simply be victims for other nations'.[52]

Culture, rather than politics, was therefore Tagore's primary arena of activity and it is here that we can see his commitment to both cosmopolitanism and nationalism. Tagore was passionately committed to enabling the interaction of cultures of the East and West, both from a normative conviction that universal truths could only be revealed through the comparative study of diverse cultures,[53] and from a historical appreciation of the inescapable hybridity of all cultures including 'Indian' culture.[54] He welcomed contact with British and European cultures as the latest in a long series of external influences that he likened to tributaries feeding the stream of Indian thought. He lauded these influences as 'providential' on account of their revitalizing effect on an Indian culture that had become stagnant and unreflective, insisting that India had much to learn from Europe. He writes that 'the East has instinctively felt, even through her aversion, that she has a great deal to learn from Europe, not merely about the materials of power, but about its inner source, which is of mind and of the moral nature of man'.[55] In this sense Tagore radically disrupts the split consciousness that Chatterjee describes as being typical of the bourgeois nationalist of the time, intent on mimicking the West in material respects but rejecting it in the domains of spirituality and culture.[56]

But Tagore was keen that cultural intercourse between East and West take place in an egalitarian fashion and painfully aware that this was not yet the case.[57] His argument for cultural cosmopolitanism is therefore qualified in the following way in an essay on education written in 1919:

> ... before we are in a position to face other world cultures, or cooperate with them, we must build up our own by the synthesis of the diverse elements that have come to India. When we take our stand at such a centre and turn towards the West, our gaze shall no longer be timid and dazed, our heads shall remain erect. For, we shall then be able to look at truth from our own vantage ground and open out a new vista of thought before the grateful world.[58]

Few modern Indian writers can be credited with doing more to 'build up our own' than Tagore. It is impossible in the course of a brief discussion such as this to do justice to his unparalleled and multifaceted contribution to the Bengali literary and artistic canon through the composition of novels, short stories, plays, and essays, not to mention thousands of songs, poems, and paintings.[59] His commitment to the revival of Bengali and other Indian languages was expressed in a strong emphasis on education in vernacular languages and an occasionally expressed worry that the excessive use of English would lead Indians to turn exclusively towards the West for inspiration.[60] In these and myriad other ways, Tagore played a central role in the production of a Bengali and an Indian identity—an immensely ironic achievement when juxtaposed with his political critique of nationalism. The irony is only heightened by the fact that two of his songs were selected as the national anthems of independent India and Bangladesh.

But Tagore saw the production of identity, not as an end in itself but as a prelude to a cosmopolitan cultural conversation. 'When we have the intellectual capital of our own', he writes, 'the commerce of thought with the outer world becomes natural and fully profitable', adding almost in the same breath that 'to say that such commerce is inherently wrong, is to encourage the worst form of provincialism, productive of nothing but intellectual indigence'.[61] Tagore repeatedly articulates a tension between openness and rootedness, often drawing on metaphors from the natural world, to make what sounds like a limited case for subaltern nationalism:

> The nursery of the infant should be secluded, its cradle safe. But the same seclusion, if continued after the infant has grown up, makes it weak in body and mind.[62]
>
> The butterfly will have to be persuaded that the freedom of the sky is of higher value than the shelter of the cocoon.[63]
>
> But now we are overtaken by the outside world, our seclusion is lost forever. Yet this we must not regret as a plant should never regret when the obscurity of its seed-time is broken ... we must not, in foolish pride, still keep ourselves fast within the shell of the seed and the crust of the earth which protected and nourished our ideals; for these, the shell and the crust, were meant to be broken, so that life may spring up in all its vigour and beauty, bringing its offerings to the world in open light.[64]

Tagore is not a cultural protectionist, for he remarks unsentimentally that when the barriers separating cultures are broken down, 'only that will survive which is basically consistent with the universal', and later, that cultures 'must pass the test of the world-market, if their maximum value is to be obtained'.[65] It is clear, though, that he believes seeds, cocoons, and cradles to be necessary—for a time—to provide the space within which to build the intellectual capital that makes intercultural exchange mutually profitable. In contrast to the cosmopolitans who have misappropriated Tagore, Isaiah Berlin was more insightful in describing him as an internationalist who understood the 'eternally valid element in nationalism'. For Berlin, this lay in the idea that 'those who are scattered, weak, humiliated, oppressed must first be collected, strengthened, liberated, given opportunity to grow and develop at least to some degree by their own natural resources, on their own soil, in their own languages, with unborrowed memories, and not wholly in perpetual debt, cultural or economic, to some outside benefactor'.[66] Tagore was not a political nationalist. But we might justifiably read him as making the case for cultural nationalism as a necessary, but necessarily temporary, stage through which subaltern cultures must pass before they could interact on equal terms with other cultures on the world stage.

4.2 EDWARD SAID

Edward Said uses Stephen Dedalus in his 1993 Reith lectures to illustrate what an intellectual life might look like: 'beset with numerous difficulties and temptations... a concrete experience constantly threatened by modern life itself... dependent on a kind of consciousness that is sceptical, engaged, unremittingly devoted to rational investigation and moral judgment'.[67] But it was not simply an affinity of temperament that drew Said to Dedalus. Elsewhere, he describes Joyce's literary alter ego as an 'Irish nationalist and an intellectual'—an ironic reading of Dedalus that parallels his own relationship with nationalism.[68]

Said's oeuvre, taken as a whole, is marked by a central tension between cosmopolitanism and nationalism. In a savage polemic against Said, the Marxist critic Aijaz Ahmad homes in on this tension, describing it in the following terms:

> In the years immediately following the publication of *Orientalism*, Said's position was indistinguishable from straightforward Third-Worldist cultural nationalisms, and what we used to get was an unselfcritical narrative of European guilt, non-European innocence. This has shifted dramatically, beginning in about 1984 and growing increasingly more strident in rejecting nationalism, national boundaries, nations as such, so that one now has reason to be equally alarmed by the extremity of this opposite stance. Characteristically, though, the most sweeping statements about 'nation' and 'state' as 'coercive identities' are frequently delivered alongside resounding affirmations of national liberation, of the Palestinian *intifada* in particular, and the right of the Palestinian people either to obtain a nation-state of their own or, alternatively, to live as coequals in a binational state. It is this growing ambivalence about nation and nationalism... which should bear some scrutiny.[69]

Ahmad does not offer the scrutiny he calls for, lamenting later: 'that a stateless Palestinian, longing always to have a state of his own, should describe the state—*all* states; the state *as such*—as a "coercive identity" signifies a paradox too painful to bear comment'.[70] Ahmad is right to point to the tension between Said's simultaneous advocacy of the Palestinian nationalist cause and criticism of nationalism per se. Yet far from being criticized on this account, I shall argue that Said's position should be appreciated for its sensitivity to the dispersed nature of threats to the freedom of the political community he was helping to imagine. It is this sensitivity that leads him to hold his cosmopolitan inclinations in tension with the nationalist imperatives of the Palestinian struggle. In his work as a literary theorist, Said insists that we eschew analytical essentialism and normative blame in the study of cultures. Yet as a Palestinian activist, he uses precisely these tools in the construction of a Palestinian identity. In this section, I elucidate this Saidian paradox that Ahmad flags but refuses to understand, before discussing the ways in which Said attempts to work through it.

Said expresses a cosmopolitan scepticism of stable, essentialized identities in a number of his writings.[71] His best known work *Orientalism* might be read as a critique of the discursive production of the 'Orient' in Western scholarship, as a monolithic space that was underdeveloped, barbaric, given to sensuality and despotism, and in all respects inferior to a 'West' that was rational, developed, and humane.[72] Critics like the Syrian philosopher Sadik Jalal al-'Azm argued that in positing an unchanging Western discursive tendency on these lines, stretching from Homer, Aeschylus, Euripides, and Dante, through Marx and the nineteenth-century British and French orientalists, *Orientalism* in effect performed a curious reverse-essentialism, reifying the very dichotomy between East and West that it had sought to deconstruct.[73] In an afterword to the 1995 edition of the book, Said regretted that it had been read as suggesting that the phenomenon of Orientalism was emblematic of the entire West, and insisted that the book was 'explicitly anti-essentialist, radically sceptical about all categorical designations such as Orient and Occident'.[74]

He also disavowed any interest in, or capacity for, demonstrating what more accurate representations of the Orient or Islam might look like, opening up a set of unresolved questions about his relationship to post-structuralist thought. There are deeply Foucauldian moments in *Orientalism*, when Said doubts that there can be 'true' representations of anything, given that all representations are embedded in the language, culture, institutions, and 'political ambience' of the speaker.[75] But there are also moments when he insists on the possibility of 'scholarship that is not as corrupt, or at least as blind to human reality' as Western orientalism.[76] In making these contradictory claims, Said borrows the Foucauldian notion of 'discourse' as policing or limiting what can be said within a discipline, without pushing it to the logical extremes that Foucault does. In Said's view, individual scholars can sometimes elude the constraints of discourse to have a transformational impact on the field. These views on representation will be relevant to my later discussion of Said as a spokesman for Palestinian self-determination.

Said's anti-essentialism is more clearly expressed in *Culture and Imperialism*, which argues that empire and imperialism were central to the production of modern European culture. Here, Said reveals the deep implication of the periphery in a number of cultural texts that are ostensibly 'about' the metropolis.[77] We are reminded, for example, that it is Australian wealth that enables the *Great Expectations* that Pip entertains, that the order and civility of Jane Austen's *Mansfield Park* are made possible by the profits generated by slave plantations in Antigua, and that it is impossible to make sense of Verdi's *Aida* without reference to the politics of its commissioning by the Khedive of Egypt for whom the opera was an integral element of his effort to gain admission into international society. In effect, Said demands that we see 'West' and 'non-West', not as separate worlds with their own distinct essences, but as mutually constitutive of one another. As a literary and cultural critic, Said frequently insists that essentialized identities are mythical abstractions, even lies: 'cultures are too intermingled, their contents and histories too interdependent and hybrid, for surgical separation into large and mostly ideological oppositions like Orient and Occident'.[78]

Yet as a prominent spokesman for Palestinian self-determination, Said has been described as 'an active and important producer of the evolving Palestinian identity'[79]—a task that seems to involve something akin to 'surgical separation'. Said introduces his book *The Question of Palestine* as an essay that attempts to put the 'reality' of the Palestinian people before the reader. In describing this reality, he speaks of:

> a plain and irreducible core of the Palestinian experience for the last hundred years: that on the land called Palestine there existed a huge majority for hundreds of years a largely pastoral, a nevertheless socially, culturally, politically, economically identifiable people whose language and religion were (for a huge majority) Arabic and Islam, respectively. This people—or, if one wishes to deny them any modern conception of themselves as a people, this *group* of people—identified itself with the land it tilled and lived on (poorly or not is irrelevant), the more so after an almost wholly European decision was made to resettle, reconstitute, recapture the land for Jews who were to be brought there from elsewhere ... such as it is, the Palestinian actuality is today, was yesterday, and most likely tomorrow will be built upon an act of resistance to this new foreign colonialism.[80]

In describing the Palestinian 'reality', the 'plain and irreducible core of the Palestinian experience', 'the Palestinian actuality', Said effectively distances himself from the more post-structuralist claims of *Orientalism*. In his early writing on Palestine, he seems to be engaged in the exercise of distilling the essentials of Palestinian identity. In this work, we are no longer reminded of the fluidity, murkiness, and imprecision of identity. Instead, Palestinian identity is posited as something distinct and discrete, part of a larger Arab identity admittedly, but different from Lebanese, Jordanian, Syrian, and other national identities in the region. 'I am Palestinian', Said reiterates; 'we have a collective identity that while Arab is not only generally Arab but specifically *Palestinian*, and an attachment to the actual land of Palestine antedates Zionism and Israel'.[81]

It is not difficult to appreciate why Said felt the need to play this role. *The Question of Palestine* was written in 1979, not ten years after Israeli Prime Minister Golda Meir had made her infamous remark denying the very existence of Palestinians. It was addressed to a Western and particularly a US audience, reared on a diet of media representations of Palestinians as terrorists and fanatics.[82] So rudimentary was the level of debate, so meagre the extent of awareness, and so hostile the nature of coverage, that Said could hardly begin to acknowledge what a complex and unstable formation Palestinian identity—like all identity—really is. That identity had first to be inserted into a Western public consciousness in a relatively clear and unambiguous fashion so as to obtain recognition for a people who had been expelled from and dispossessed of their land and therefore had a legitimate claim to redress, before it could begin to be deconstructed for other purposes. 'The first task', as Said puts it, 'was to get a place—literally anywhere—to say that we did exist'.[83] So while the nationalist Said appeared to be making the very essentializing moves that the cosmopolitan Said had savaged, we might see this as a case of what Gayatri Chakravorty Spivak has called 'a strategic use of positivist essentialism in a scrupulously visible political interest'.[84]

Benita Parry describes this tension running through Said's work as one between a 'cognitive recognition of cultural heterogeneity and the political need for solidarity'. In her view, Said recognizes the subject as decentred and culture as hybrid, but also acknowledges the potential of imaginary collectivities constructed under conditions of subjugation to confront and perhaps overcome those conditions.[85] This is correct, although I am not sure that Said experiences these tensions in separate realms—the cognitive and the political—as if Said the literary critic could afford to acknowledge the fluidity and hybridity of identity, while Said the political activist must insist on stability and solidarity. Even within the realm of the political, Said believed that political exigencies of different sorts pulled in both directions, demanding both split and united selves.

We can see this clearly in Said's view of nationalism as something that is both necessary and unfortunate. Nationalism is necessary, particularly 'for those of us just emerging from marginality and persecution' as a means of reclaiming identities that have long been denied or suppressed.[86] He insists that 'much of the early cultural resistance to imperialism on which nationalism and independence movements were built was salutary and necessary. I see it essentially as an attempt on the part of oppressed people who had suffered the bondage of slavery, colonialism, and—most important—spiritual dispossession, to reclaim their identity.'[87] Yet, in the paradoxical move that Ahmad draws our attention to, Said also relentlessly criticizes nationalism for its tendency to engender a politics of hierarchy and supremacism, for its reliance on myth-making and indoctrination and its laundering of the cultural past, and for its dangerous malleability in the hands of states, which are prone to abusing it as an ideology to legitimate various sorts of oppressions.[88] Unlike the other figures discussed in this chapter, Said dwells at length on the tension between the necessity for and misfortunes of nationalism, resorting to what I identify as three different sorts of manoeuvres—not all consistent with one another—to work through the contradictory potentials of nationalism.

First, in his most pessimistic moments, Said appears to view this dilemma as a tragedy incapable of resolution. This Said speaks in regretful tones of 'triumphant, achieved nationalisms' which 'consign truth exclusively to themselves and relegate falsehood and inferiority to outsiders', and which speak 'the encompassing and thumping language of national pride, collective sentiments, group passions'.[89] For this Said, nationalism's imperatives of surgical separation from larger worlds is so anathema to his cosmopolitan commitments that he wishes he did not have to be a nationalist at all, lamenting that 'it's the tragedy, the irony, the paradox of all anti-imperial or decolonising struggles that independence is the stage through which you must try to pass: for us independence is the only alternative to the continued horrors of the Israeli occupation, whose goal is the extermination of a Palestinian national identity'.[90]

Second, in more optimistic moments, Said appears to believe that the worst excesses of nationalism might be mitigated through a kind of methodological transparency and self-awareness. His writings on Palestinian nationalism frequently reflect on the tricks of the nationalist's trade, but in doing so, threaten to unmask the novelty, fragility, and instability of the very identity he is seeking to construct. Thus, even as he attempts to distinguish Palestinian identity from a more general Arab identity, he is humorously ironic about this endeavour—as in this narration of an encounter with a close friend and fellow Palestinian:

> In the morning we had breakfast, which included yoghurt cheese with a special herb, *za'tar*. This combination probably exists all over the Arab world, and certainly in Palestine, Syria, and Lebanon. But my friend said: 'There, you see. It's a sign of a Palestinian home that it has *za'tar* in it.' Being a poet, he then expiated at great and tedious length on Palestinian cuisine, which is generally very much like Lebanese and Syrian cuisine, and by the end of the morning we were both convinced that we had a totally distinct national cuisine.[91]

In a similar vein, reflecting on the mythic status in Palestinian national consciousness of the battle of Karameh, fought in 1968 between the Israeli army and forces of the Palestinian Liberation Organization (PLO) in Jordan, Said writes: 'All occurrences become events after they occur. In part events are mythic, but like all effective myths they record an important aspect of a real experience.'[92] He goes on to discuss and justify why Karameh has come to occupy such a significant place in Palestinian nationalist mythology, quite out of proportion to the strategic significance of the military encounter. There is a sympathetic appreciation of the myth and why it has been nurtured and handed down, but we are still reminded of the disjunction between occurrence and event, between what actually happened and the subsequent layers of meaning with which it became encrusted. Said's treatment of the *za'tar* conversation and the battle of Karameh both reveal a peculiar feature of his writing on nationalism, which frequently evinces a desire both to participate in the construction and reiteration of nationalist mythology and to remind his audience of the myth-making aspect of nationalism—in short, to both 'do' and unmask nationalism. As he writes, 'With regard to the consensus on group or national identity it is the intellectual's task to show how the group is a constructed, manufactured, even in some cases invented object, with a history of struggle and conquest behind it, that it is sometimes important to represent.'[93] But if successful nationalism requires the naturalization and primordialization of identity—or 'forgetting' as Ernst Renan put it more bluntly—it is not clear how the intellectual can draw attention to the invented nature of identity without being subversive of the nationalist project itself.[94]

Third, Said achieves greater clarity on the need for, but also the pitfalls of, nationalism, when he turns to Frantz Fanon, the foremost theorist of the Algerian revolution. Fanon's classic statement of resistance—*The Wretched of the Earth*—is concerned as much with independence from colonial oppression, as with liberation from a nationalist bourgeoisie that perpetuates the subjugation of subaltern classes. Resistance, for Fanon, is a bifocal enterprise in which the people must pass 'from total, undiscriminating nationalism to social and economic awareness'.[95] Without such a transition from nationalist to a universal humanist socio-economic consciousness, he argues, the oppressive nationalist bourgeoisie remains entrenched. Its dependence on the metropolitan bourgeoisie makes it both too weak to play the historic role of a true bourgeoisie (i.e. to generate the conditions conducive to the formation of an industrial proletariat), but also too strong to be easily dislodged. As a result, the post-colonial economy continues to be characterized by quasi-feudal productive relations and is consigned to a permanently peripheral position in the world system. Domestically, the revolutionary leader becomes 'a screen between the people and the rapacious bourgeoisie', using moral and political capital accrued from his leadership of the liberation struggle to obviate challenges from below.[96] The revolutionary party ossifies into an instrument of control and pacification. In such circumstances, a people who remain trapped within a nationalist mindset lack the necessary consciousness with which to challenge their own bourgeoisie.

Fanon appears to present the nationalist struggle against the colonial occupier and the universal struggle against the bourgeoisie as sequential stages, although there is room for debate on this point.[97] A recent biography reports that although he was extremely critical in private of elements of the Front de Libération Nationale (FLN) elite—particularly figures such as Boussouf and Bentobbal on account of their failure to develop a vision for Algeria beyond independence—he remained a loyal and disciplined militant of the organization in his public statements and writings, reluctant to distance himself from these men before the Algerian struggle had been won.[98] In contrast, without adopting his Marxist categories of analysis, Said reads Fanon as arguing that the two dimensions of the bifocal struggle must be contemporaneous, so that 'loyalty to the group's fight for survival cannot draw in the intellectual so far as to narcotise the critical sense, or reduce its imperatives, which are always to go beyond survival to questions of political liberation, to critiques of the leadership, to presenting alternatives that are too often marginalised or pushed aside as irrelevant to the main battle at hand'.[99]

In the years following the PLO's signing of what came to be known as the Oslo Accords in 1993, Said launched a scathing attack on the leadership of Yasir Arafat, denouncing him for his acquiescence in a 'peace process' that essentially perpetuated Israeli occupation while resulting in the transfer of a few sovereign powers over an archipelago of 'bantustans' that could hardly constitute a viable state. He wrote urgently and insistently about the lack of law, due process, freedom, and democracy under the newly constituted Palestinian Authority (PA),[100] bemoaning the inability of the Legislative Council to exercise any constitutional checks over Arafat—'a despot who controls the budget'—or over 'his twenty security services who torture, kill, imprison critics and ban their books at the whim of Palestine's overweening tyrant'.[101] He described the PA as 'at bottom a kind of mafia...operating all kinds of special deals...that profit the inner circle of Arafat appointees and "experts"'.[102] At times he even posited a rough moral equivalence between Israel and the PA, writing that 'the clamp down on expression and democratic practices [in post-Oslo Palestine] is as severe as under direct Israeli rule'[103] and speaking of 'the double occupation of the Israelis and the Palestinian Authority'.[104] As with Joyce and Tagore, we can see how Said's cognizance of the internal and external threats to the freedom of the political community he was helping to imagine, informed a simultaneous nationalist determination to construct unified collective agency against Israeli occupation and a cosmopolitan antipathy towards 'triumphant, achieved nationalisms'.

It is legitimate to ask whether the twofold struggle against imperialism and the nationalist bourgeoisie is better pursued sequentially or simultaneously in the context of a national liberation struggle. The argument for sequentiality was made by Lenin, who famously called for a tactical alliance against imperialism between communists and the nationalist bourgeoisies in the colonies (I discuss this in chapter 5). But proponents of simultaneity would argue that the postcolonial struggle for liberation is made more difficult by the hegemony acquired by a bourgeois nationalist leadership during the anti-colonial struggle. That hegemony must therefore be contested during the struggle itself, if liberation is not to be owned by its bourgeois leadership. In the context of Palestine, however, the debate over the sequentiality or simultaneity of independence and liberation is perhaps rendered moot by the fact that Said's major criticism of the Oslo Accords concerned the very incompleteness of the 'independence' from Israel that they heralded. The Accords, as he saw them, enabled Israel to defer negotiations on virtually all the difficult questions surrounding Palestinian statehood (borders, refugees, Jerusalem, settlements), perpetuating its hold over the Occupied Territories whilst absolving it of responsibility for the living conditions of Palestinians.[105] Conversely they gave the PA enough sovereignty to enable it to exercise coercive authority over its people, who were thereby robbed of the prospect of both independence and liberation.

Towards the end of his life, Said began to make the case for a bi-national one-state solution to the conflict in Palestine. This was prompted partly by a sense of the growing impossibility of the creation of a viable, territorially contiguous Palestinian state alongside Israel, thanks to the expansion of Jewish settlements, the construction of a mammoth 'Separation Barrier', the proliferation of checkpoints, and a complex apartheid-like regime that prohibits Palestinian movement and access to land and public infrastructure. But it was also prompted by a principled refusal of the notion of 'surgical separation' along ethnic and/or religious lines that underpins many nationalisms. As Said asks, and answers:

> What is it... that we have against Israel if we say that we want a 'pure' Palestine, free of Jews, free of everything that isn't pure Arab and Muslim and Palestinian? Nothing at all: we would be mimicking exactly what it is that we attack. And how ignorant and narrow-minded, how chauvinistic and racist it is to define a person not by his/her ideas and values, but by his racial origins, religion, or culture.[106]

Said condemns partition as 'the desperate and last-ditch efforts of a dying ideology of separation, which has afflicted Zionism and Palestinian nationalism, both of which have not surmounted the philosophical problem of the Other, of learning how to live with, as opposed to despite, the Other'.[107] We might see in Said's late advocacy of a one-state solution, a final attempt at reconciliation of his cosmopolitan and nationalist commitments.[108] Yet it is crucial to recognize that even the one-state solution does not dispense with the need for nationalist consciousness. For although the demand here is not

4.3 FRANTZ FANON

Looking at Fanon's work as a whole, one begins to suspect that Said's reading of his conception of liberation as entailing a two-stage struggle—first nationalist, then universalist—may have been a bit too neat. As Parry has convincingly argued: 'Fanon's writings function at a point of tension between cultural nationalism and transnationality, without "resolving" the contradiction and without yielding an attachment to the one or the aspiration to the other'.[109] The irony is that the same could be said of Said. It almost seems as if, in his more cosmopolitan moments, Said misappropriates Fanon through a very partial reading of his thought, in an effort to reconcile his competing commitments.

Parry draws attention to a curious phenomenon in Fanon's earlier work—*Black Skin, White Masks*—in which the narrative voice seems to take opposing stances with an equally passionate intensity, affirming an immediate need to construct an insurgent black subjectivity while insistently proclaiming a future beyond race and ethnicity. Although these are presented as sequential stages in *The Wretched of the Earth*, in this earlier work, Fanon indicts Jean-Paul Sartre for making exactly such a suggestion. In his 1948 essay 'Orphée Noir', Sartre describes Negritude—the black political and cultural nationalist movement of the 1930s—as an 'anti-racist racism'. Sartre saw Negritude as the antithesis of white supremacism in a Hegelian dialectic that would culminate in a universal non-racial future. This meant that Negritude was 'the minor term of a dialectical progression', a 'negative moment' that was insufficient by itself, 'a transition and not a conclusion, a means and not an ultimate end'.[110] For Fanon, Sartre's relegation of Negritude to the status of a passing phase seemed to forget that 'consciousness has to lose itself in the night of the absolute, the only condition to attain to consciousness of self'.[111] Fanon seems to be affirming here the need for pride in blackness for its own sake, as a way of overcoming the sense of degradation engendered by centuries of slavery and recovering a consciousness of self. Additionally, he is irritated by the teleological condescension of the European Marxist, authoritatively inscribing the dialectical course of history: 'Nothing is more unwelcome than the commonplace: "You'll change, my boy; I was like that too when I was young... you'll see, it will all pass".'[112] For Fanon, the Sartrean dialectic has shattered a moment that is whole and universal in itself:

> ...in terms of consciousness, black consciousness is immanent in its own eyes. I am not a potentiality of something, I am wholly what I am. I do not have to look for the universal. No probability has any place inside me. My Negro consciousness does not hold itself out as a lack. It *is*. It is its own follower.[113]

Notwithstanding this impassioned defence of Negritude, the last chapter of the same work takes on a much more universal humanistic tone. Here, Fanon asserts his attachment to all of human history, not merely that which pertains to the black man ('I am a man, and what I have to recapture is the whole past of the world. I am not responsible solely for the revolt in Santo Domingo.'[114]) He rejects the impulse to discover the black past, characteristic of Negritude ('In no way should I dedicate myself to the revival of an unjustly unrecognised Negro civilization.... I do not want to exalt the past at the expense of my present and of my future.'[115]) In a litany of almost Gandhian abnegation, he repudiates all thoughts of subaltern race pride, anger, or revenge ('I as a man of color do not have the right to hope that in the white man there will be a crystallization of guilt toward the past of my race. I as a man of color do not have the right to seek ways of stamping down the pride of my former master.'[116]) Indeed the book ends with a denial of the very notion of racial essences, expressing the hope 'that it may be possible for me to discover and to love man, wherever he may be. The Negro is not. Any more than the white man.'[117]

More intriguingly as we have already seen, in his later *The Wretched of the Earth*, Fanon adopts something very like the Sartrean dialectic that he criticizes so fiercely in *Black Skin, White Masks*, insisting on the transition from nationalist to a universal humanist consciousness. In an address to the Second Congress of Black Artists and Writers in Rome in 1959 two years before his death, Fanon reiterates the need for both nationalism and internationalism without establishing a clear sequential relationship between them. He warns that it is a mistake to skip the nationalist period, but hastens to add that the attainment of nationalist consciousness is a precondition for—rather than subversive of—internationalism. By this time, the relationship between these two forms of consciousness was not merely a metaphysical notion for him but a matter of political urgency. Alluding to the grim reality that every independent nation in an Africa where colonialism was still entrenched was an encircled nation, Fanon was essentially arguing that successful African nationalism required internationalist solidarity, just as a genuinely egalitarian internationalism presupposed the development of nationalist consciousness.[118] In this last address, the relationship is one of mutual constitution rather than dialectical sequentiality.

Fanon's political thinking is inseparable from his work as a psychiatrist—he saw both as addressing the problem of alienation—so it is instructive to observe his engagement with the relationship between universalism and particularism in the latter domain as well. He was firmly opposed to central tenets of prevailing approaches to psychiatry as it was practised in colonial Algeria, which tended to assume that the primitivism of the native's brain impeded higher functions. But ideas of cultural difference did play a role in his work. Alice Cherki tells an interesting and revealing story about Fanon's experiments with 'sociotherapy' at the Blida-Joinville hospital where he worked from 1953–7.[119] This was an approach that sought to humanize mental health institutions by transforming them into therapeutic environments where patients and staff worked in concert to construct a new social arena in which trauma could be accommodated and articulated in a more positive manner. This was done by introducing festivities, holiday celebrations, a Christmas party, music and film programmes, and activity groups into the life of the institution. The approach worked marvellously with the female European patients but not the Algerian men, who refused to engage with any of the collective games and other activities that had been introduced to resocialize them. Fanon was convinced that this failure had nothing to do with the purported backwardness of Muslims and more to do with the assumption that the modes of cultural expression of a technological Western society could be imposed on a rural Muslim one. The programme was modified to introduce new institutions for the Algerian male patients, including a teahouse, festivals to mark Muslim holidays, and events that featured indigenous musicians, with vastly improved results. Despite his own personal atheism, Fanon became increasingly interested in local mental health practices such as exorcisms and faith healing. He wanted to draw on referents that were culturally meaningful to his patients, without accepting orientalist assumptions of a relationship between cultures and hierarchies of mentalities. As Cherki puts it, Fanon saw culture 'as a point of temporal and spatial reference that is also a conduit to the universal'.[120]

In this chapter, I have been describing the protest sensibilities of thinkers associated with national liberation movements, who wished fervently for the success of these movements even as they were fierce critics of nationalism. This paradoxical attitude, I have argued, was in each case underpinned by a complex spatial imaginary of threat, in which the freedom of the political community was perceived to be threatened from both outside and within, from both an external other and an emerging self. As anti-imperialists, these thinkers made the case for a subaltern nationalism; but an anxiety about the oppressions inherent in nationalist mobilization also led them to a critique of nationalism. Tagore, Said, and Fanon attempted to square this circle by viewing nationalism as a transitory stage through which subaltern resistance must pass in order to recuperate the identity and sense of self that imperialist subjugation has trampled underfoot; but upon attaining its goal of recognition of equal worth, nationalism must subsume itself in universality. For these ironic nationalists, the progress of History seems to require the withering away of intense attachments to nation-states.[121] The question that needs to be posed is whether nationalism exhausts its progressive potential with the achievement of independent statehood. Does it have any place in the post-colonial utopias towards which subalterns strive, or do these take the essentially cosmopolitan vision of universal community in which national allegiances are less meaningful? Should it have a place in these utopias? These are questions for chapter 5, where I explore the afterlives of nationalism in the subaltern politics of the post-colonial Third World state.

5

Indigenous Insurgents and Rioting Ryots

'De majority of our people are honest, hardworking people. But dey are at de mercy of dese army bastards and dose tiefs in the IMF, de World Bank and de US', the King said.... 'Let me tell you, dere are no bigger tiefs dan dose World Bank people. Let me tell you how de World Bank helps us. Say dey offer us a ten-million-dollar loan for creating potable and clean water supply to rural areas. If we accept, dis is how dey do to us. First dey tell us dat we have to use de expertise of their consultants, so dey remove two million for salaries and expenses. Den dey tell us dat de consultants need equipment to work, like computer, jeeps or bulldozers, and for hotel and so on, so dey take another two million. Den dey say we cannot build new boreholes but must service existing one, so dey take another two million to buy parts. All dis money, six million of it, never leave de US. Den dey use two million for de project, but is not enough, so dey abandon it, and den army bosses take de remaining two million. Now we, you and I and all dese poor people, owe de World Bank ten million dollars for nothing. Dey are all tiefs and I despise dem—our people and de World Bank people!' the King ranted.

Chris Abani, *Graceland* (2004)

In Marxist spatial imaginaries of threat, the distinction between friends and enemies is marked not by the boundaries of nation-states, but by class lines. But class is a cosmopolitan category: the freedom of the workers of the world is threatened by a cosmopolitan bourgeoisie, whose agents are to be found both within and outside the political community that nationalists are invested in defending. Marxists associated with Third World national liberation struggles typically operated in uneasy alliance with bourgeois nationalists, acutely conscious of the need to direct their revolutionary energies against their bourgeois compatriots (and their international allies) once the colonial oppressor had been overthrown. In the post-colonial era, class-based resistance has continued to be complicated by the existence of state and national boundaries.

This chapter begins with a brief overview of the fraught theoretical and political relationship between class and nation in Marxist and Leninist thought, before going on to consider the articulation of these forms of consciousness in contemporary anti-capitalist protest. It takes as its point of departure Erica Benner's revisionist account of Marx's understanding of the relationship between class and national consciousness which suggests, contrary to the received reading, that he saw this ostensibly antagonistic relationship in a more subtle and complicated way than he is usually given credit for. It then goes on to demonstrate the conjunction of these forms of consciousness in the politics of two contemporary 'anti-globalization' movements. Notwithstanding the distance of these movements from the official Marxisms of their time and place, these conjunctions resonate strongly with Marx's understanding of the roles that class and national consciousness could play in anti-capitalist struggle.

5.1 CLASS AND NATION IN MARXIST AND LENINIST THOUGHT

In the conventional reading of the work of Marx and Engels, their insistence on the cosmopolitan character of the bourgeoisie and the working class is taken as positing class and national consciousness as mutually exclusive of one another. Where the working classes have identified with their respective nations, as on the eve of the First World War, mainstream Marxism is read as dismissing such identification as a form of 'false consciousness', foisted on workers by the bourgeoisie in an effort to blind them to their true interests in international solidarity against global capital. The founders of historical materialism are thought to have seriously underestimated the force of nationalism, which is seen to have always undermined international working class solidarity.

Benner's revisionist account of the place of nationalism in the thinking of the writers of *The Communist Manifesto* does much to unsettle this view. She demonstrates how, in both their theories of history and their thinking as political activists, they exhibited something very much like the sequential view of nationalism adopted by some of the figures studied in chapter 4. As historical materialists, Marx and Engels believed that if nationality and statehood were superstructural expressions of economic integration over particular areas, then economic globalization would see the withering away of those superstructural formations. As political activists, they advocated that the proletariat first close ranks with the bourgeoisie in its struggle against the vestiges of feudalism—in effect that they fight 'the enemies of their enemies'[1]—before turning against the bourgeoisie. As Benner explains it, Marx and Engels saw this preliminary struggle as an educative process whereby, in fighting the bourgeoisie's battles, the proletariat would come to understand the gulf between their own interests and those they were being used to defend.[2]

The case for sequentiality was not only pedagogical, but also political. In a number of places, the authors of the *Manifesto* suggest that the proletariat must first win the struggle at a national level against its bourgeoisie before it is in a position to take effective international action. As they put it, 'though not in substance, yet in form, the struggle of the proletariat with the bourgeoisie is at first a national struggle. The proletariat of each country must ... first of all settle matters with its own bourgeoisie'.[3] Even as they declared that 'the working men have no country', Marx and Engels clarified in the same paragraph that this settling of matters required that 'the proletariat must first of all acquire political supremacy, must rise to be the leading class of the nation, must constitute itself *the* nation'. As such, it is 'itself national, though not in the bourgeois sense of the word'.[4]

Far from positing a dogmatic opposition between working class internationalism and national identification, Benner takes these comments as suggesting a degree of flexibility on the part of Marx and Engels towards the concepts of state and nation. In insisting that 'the working men have no country', they were arguing that workers had no stake in the survival of national institutions and myths that reflected ruling-class interests. This did not mean that national consciousness was inherently reactionary; rather, it was objectionable in its contemporary manifestations because it had been captured by the bourgeoisie. The political task for the proletariat was to wrest the nation away from the bourgeoisie, by representing its own interests as those of the nation as a whole. In this way, it would be able to capture state power from the dominant classes and eventually use that power to further the goals of the international working class movement.[5]

As political activists addressing the metropolitan working classes, Marx and Engels advocated support for movements of national self-determination by demonstrating the links between national oppression abroad and class oppression at home. For example, Engels was keen to alert readers to the bargains underpinning the three-way partition of Poland between Russia, Prussia, and Austria, suggesting that in return for their membership in the Holy Alliance, Russia rewarded Prussia and Austria by supporting the feudal–aristocratic classes of those countries against their respective bourgeoisies. Participation in the oppression of Poland therefore committed these governments to reactionary policies at home. Opposing the Prussian incorporation of the Polish province of Posen, Engels declared that 'the fetters with which we have chained other nations will shackle our own freedom.... Germany will liberate herself to the extent to which she sets free neighbouring nations'.[6]

Benner cautions that Marx and Engels were highly discriminating in their support of nationalist movements, backing only those that appeared willing to challenge unjust class relations within the nation. Referring again to Poland, Engels was careful to point out that its subjection was also the result of internal class conflict, stemming specifically from the realization of the Polish aristocracy that partition by the Holy Alliance was the only way of buttressing its privileges against a rising bourgeoisie. Given this analysis of external oppression stemming from internal conflict, Engels took the view that non-reforming national movements that left intact the very class relations and institutions that invited foreign oppression, were not worth supporting.[7]

We can see a similar attitude of reluctance to support non-reforming nationalist movements in Marx's writings on India. On the one hand, he expresses a heartfelt sympathy for the 'misery inflicted by the British on Hindostan' and for the sense of disorientation experienced by colonized peoples as their civilization was trampled underfoot by a rampaging colonial modernity. But he had little patience for critics of colonialism who harked back to the 'golden age of Hindostan' or defended the perpetuation of the rule of native princes, reminding readers of the cruelties of India's villages, where the rigidities of caste and superstition condemned the vast majority to an 'undignified, stagnatory, and vegetative life'.[8] Marx saw British colonialism in India as playing a progressive role in sweeping away the remnants of 'Oriental despotism', in much the same way as he read capitalism as playing a progressive role in dismantling the vestiges of feudalism in Europe.[9] This did not mean that he denied Indians the right to resist colonialism. To the contrary, he saw the British bourgeoisie as simply laying the 'material premises' for the development of India's productive powers, the full realization of which would require their appropriation by the Indian people either via a proletarian revolution in Britain or at such time as 'the Hindus themselves shall have grown strong enough to throw off the English yoke altogether'.[10] Yet as his descriptions of pre-colonial India suggest, he believed that resistance to foreign oppression should not result in its replacement by earlier forms of indigenous oppression.

Although Marx and Engels never abandoned this stance of selective support to nationalist resistance, Benner detects what she calls an 'upgrading' of the importance of separatist nationalism and independent statehood in their thinking about the prospects for global proletarian revolution. If in the 1840s, the impetus for such revolution was seen to lie in the metropolitan working classes, by the 1860s—faced with the defeat of the 1848 revolutions, the expansion of European colonialism and, most importantly, a sense that there was no necessary identity of interests between the metropolitan working classes and colonized peoples—Marx and Engels came round to the view that national independence for the colonies could revitalize working-class internationalism.[11]

In his writings on Ireland, Marx argues that Irish freedom was a precondition for the emancipation of the English working classes for two reasons. The first was that the English landed oligarchy was considerably strengthened by the wealth accrued from its Irish possessions, making it difficult to dislodge on its home turf. Marx thought that once the Irish ruled themselves, it would be easier to abolish the landed aristocracy in Ireland because of the coincidence of class and national antagonisms in that country.[12] The second reason was that the working classes in England were a divided house. The ordinary English worker saw the Irishman as a competitor who lowered his standard of living. The Irish worker saw his English counterpart as being infected with the nationalist supremacism of his bourgeois compatriots ruling Ireland. This mutual antagonism, stoked by the ruling classes, was the source of the impotence of the working class in England. Marx saw England as the centre of global capitalism, and therefore of particular importance to worldwide proletarian struggle. Hence his conclusion that

> to hasten the social revolution in England is the most important object of the International Workingmen's Association. The sole means of hastening it is to make Ireland independent. Hence it is the task of the International everywhere to put the conflict between England and Ireland in the foreground, and everywhere to side openly with Ireland.[13]

If nationalism was previously seen as a means to the end of progressive internationalism, in the Irish writings it seems to become a prior condition for this end. As Benner puts it, 'the "nationalising" of internationalism was desirable... in so far as it involved a growing recognition of the practical interdependence of local and external needs'.[14]

We can see nationalism coming to the rescue of internationalism once again in the thinking of Lenin. Convinced that imperialism represented the most advanced stage of capitalism, Lenin took the view that the new revolutionary Soviet government that he had helped to establish ought to support anti-colonial struggles for national liberation. In doing so, he was also mindful of the strategic environment in which it found itself. When the Communist International (Comintern) was inaugurated in 1919 as an organization dedicated to the overthrow of the international bourgeoisie, the new Soviet state found itself virtually encircled by counter-revolutionary powers and undermined by the foreign assistance being given to its White Russian enemies in an ongoing civil war. The failure of revolutionary upheavals in Germany and Hungary also suggested that the prospects for communism in Europe were dim. It was in this context that Lenin proved receptive to the suggestion of Sultan-Galiev (the highest-ranking Muslim member of the Soviet Communist Party) that the countries of the East were of potentially more revolutionary significance.[15] Accordingly the 'colonial question' assumed centre stage at the 1920 Second Congress of the Comintern, where Lenin called for 'a union between revolutionary proletarians of the capitalist, advanced countries, and the revolutionary masses of those countries where there is no or hardly any proletariat, that is, the oppressed masses of colonial, Eastern countries'.[16] This foregrounding of the colonial question in effect made the Comintern (or Third International as it is sometimes called) the first global forum for the deliberation of anti-imperialist politics. If the First and Second Internationals were largely European affairs thanks to their identification of the industrial proletariat as the privileged revolutionary agent, the Comintern, with its more nuanced view of the 'combined and uneven development' of global capitalism and its consideration of the revolutionary potential of other social forces such as the peasantry, nationalist bourgeoisie, and petty bourgeoisie, attracted a substantial number of anti-colonial activists from the countries of what would later be called the Third World. In Colas's view:

> ...the Third International could claim to have been a more cosmopolitan organisation than its predecessors. It is significant, however, that a large part of this success came as a result of its support for *national* liberation struggles and the backing it received from the newly established Soviet *state*.[17]

Once again, support for national liberation had revived the fortunes of a flagging internationalism. But not all delegates to the Second Congress would agree with Lenin's articulation of the relationship between nationalism and internationalism. His view that communists should support and work with bourgeois nationalists in the colonies, wherever possible, was fiercely opposed by the Indian communist M. N. Roy, who saw bourgeois-led parties such as the Indian National Congress as pursuing narrow class interests under the banner of an inclusive nationalism. Both men agreed that anti-colonial struggle should not be content simply with overthrowing the colonial power, but should go further in challenging the oppression inherent within capitalism. Both also believed that bourgeois nationalist movements would establish state structures that appeared politically independent, even as they continued to remain economically, financially, and militarily dependent on metropolitan capital. But Lenin's call for cooperation with bourgeois nationalist movements stemmed from a pragmatic sense that in countries like India where such movements were more advanced and where (at the time of the debate with Roy) the communists had not yet succeeded in establishing a party, the overthrow of global capitalism would be furthered by assisting bourgeois nationalists in their struggle against imperialism.[18]

Over time, the official Comintern line on the relationship between communist internationalism and anti-colonial nationalism would fluctuate in response to a number of factors.[19] As the priorities of the Comintern shifted from the promotion of global proletarian revolution to the defence of the Soviet Union in accordance with Stalin's policy of 'socialism in one country', the importance accorded to the colonial question became contingent on the nature of the USSR's relations with the capitalist powers. When it sought accommodation with them, anti-colonial struggle faded from the agenda of the Comintern, as was the case during the Third and Fifth Congresses. Conversely, when relations with the capitalist powers deteriorated, the Comintern tended to be more supportive of anti-colonial nationalism, as was the case during the Fourth Congress. Even when the colonial question received due consideration, Comintern positions oscillated abruptly between recommendations of 'united front' tactics with bourgeois nationalists (Fourth and Seventh Congresses) and a more radical stance in favour of 'class against class' struggle (Sixth Congress). Both sorts of policies had deeply damaging consequences in practice. United front tactics, foisted on communists in Turkey and China (1922–7) in disregard of the advice of local party leaders culminated in the decimation of the communists by their bourgeois nationalist compatriots. On the other hand, the 'class against class' line resulted in the fragmentation of the left in places like Germany and Latin America, at a time when the forces of fascism were gathering strength. The key problem seems to have been that rather than being framed in response to local conditions and balances of forces within different countries, Comintern policies from around the time of the Third Congress in 1921 till the organization was disbanded in 1943 were distorted by the perceived imperatives of Soviet realpolitik. This was particularly true of the various positions that the organization adopted on the relationship between working class internationalism and anti-colonial nationalism.

5.2 CONTEMPORARY ANTI-CAPITALIST PROTEST

As one colony after another began to win its political independence, the banner of anti-imperialist revolt was increasingly held aloft by the states of the Third World—a political formation in which Lenin's accommodation between left internationalism and anti-imperialist bourgeois nationalism seemed to reach its apogee. The politics of Third Worldism as a project of states was always marked by a tension between the two tendencies that Lenin had identified as potentially progressive: on the one hand, a group of states that, while Communist in orientation, stood at varying political distances from the USSR (China, Yugoslavia, Vietnam, Cuba, etc.); on the other hand, a larger group of bourgeois nationalist states (India, Egypt, Indonesia, Brazil, etc.) that, while pursuing some version of capitalist development, were nonetheless considered anti-imperialist because they claimed to aspire to build a capitalism that was productive, egalitarian, and autonomous from metropolitan capital.[20] Whatever the actual prospects for autonomous capitalism in the Third World may have been, by the time the debt crisis pushed Latin American and sub-Saharan African countries into the arms of the international financial institutions (IFIs) in the 1980s, most regimes that could formerly have been described as 'bourgeois nationalist' within the terms described above, had given up even the pretence of pursuing autonomous capitalist development and had commenced the process of opening up their economies, with varying degrees of enthusiasm, to metropolitan capital. It was in this context that a new kind of anti-capitalist resistance became increasingly visible.

The story of the transformation of the anti-capitalist movement from one dominated by communist parties and coordinated to some degree by the Soviet Union, to something quite different, is far too complex to be recounted here in any detail.[21] Suffice it to say that the year 1968 is often seen as a pivotal moment in this transformation. The Soviet crushing of the 'Prague spring' severely undermined its credibility as the official agent of anti-capitalist resistance. The May student uprising in Paris signalled a deep discontent with both capitalism and the official left in France. The United States was rocked by massive demonstrations against the Vietnam War. More broadly, the Western left was increasingly pluralized (or, in the view of some Marxist critics, fragmented) by the emergence of the feminist, civil rights, environmental, and other 'new social movements' (NSMs) that contested the Marxist insistence on class as the primary antagonism in society, but nonetheless frequently theorized the oppressions they were fighting in relation to processes of contemporary capitalism. Critical of traditional hierarchical Marxist methods of organization, the NSMs seemed less interested in capturing state power and more invested in the transformation of social and political attitudes through acts of everyday resistance. This period also witnessed a proliferation of single-issue groups organizing around issues as diverse as housing, health care, education, immigration, animal rights, etc.

Meanwhile, structural transformations in global capitalism were also having an impact on the nature of anti-capitalist resistance in the Third World. Although Marx relegated accumulation by predation, fraud, and violence to an 'original' pre-capitalist phase, Harvey has suggested that such processes are a recurring phenomenon integral to the very survival of capitalism. As discussed in chapter 2, he argues that capitalism survives its crises of overaccumulation by devouring assets outside of itself in order to put overaccumulated capital to productive use. The crisis of over-accumulation experienced by metropolitan capital in the mid-1970s proved to be the catalyst for a drive towards accumulation by dispossession in the Third World, which manifested itself in a prising open of hitherto closed markets and myriad processes of privatization of the commons.[22] Anti-capitalist resistance in the Third World had already given up its single-minded focus on the industrial proletariat to take seriously the revolutionary potential of the peasantry, as a result of the influence of Maoism. With the renewal of capitalism's drive towards accumulation by dispossession in the Third World, the protest landscape diversified even further to incorporate movements of indigenous and tribal peoples protesting their displacement and the destruction of their habitats and livelihoods by 'development', struggles of the urban poor against the privatization of services and the downsizing of the state, etc. Crucially, some of these movements have an uneasy relationship with Marxism, expressing a romantic nostalgia for lost tradition rather than working towards the Marxist utopia of an alternative modernity in which the fruits of industrial capitalism are appropriated by the people.

In the 1980s and 1990s, under the shadow of debt-induced structural adjustment programmes, a bewildering array of anti-capitalist movements and organizations seemed to coalesce in what would be called, somewhat problematically, the 'anti-globalization movement'. Tormey argues that this convergence was aided by the identification of neo-liberal capitalism as a common enemy, and by the advent of communications technologies—chiefly the Internet—which enabled the rapid dissemination of information and the political affiliation of globally dispersed groups and organizations with shared concerns.[23] As the locus of economic policymaking was seen to shift from national capitals to the IFIs, the latter increasingly became targets of anti-capitalist contention. Meetings of the World Bank and the IMF and WTO ministerial conferences have now become familiar venues for such protest.

Since 2001, the World Social Forums (WSFs) have functioned as occasions for the deliberation of anti-capitalist strategy amongst activists from all over the globe.[24] It is tempting to view the Forums as successors to the Internationals, but there are a number of significant differences. As a consequence of the pluralization of the left, even formally constituted anti-capitalist spaces such as the WSFs are no longer colonized by Marxists but also attract liberals, anarchists, greens, religious groups, adherents of various indigenous belief systems, etc. Moreover, anti-capitalism no longer has a great power sponsor: there is no longer a 'centre' that disburses material and financial assistance or disseminates theoretical positions on the appropriate articulation of class internationalism and nationalism.

Much ink has been spilt on the issue of how contemporary anti-capitalist protest ought to be characterized. The description 'anti-globalization' is most frequently used in the mainstream media, but is unsatisfactory for a number of reasons. Many constituents of the so-called anti-globalization movement are critical of some aspects of the multidimensional phenomenon that is 'globalization', while being derivative of others (e.g. advances in transport and communication technologies, the emergence of institutions of global governance which serve as targets of contention and have in turn precipitated the formation of global public spheres such as the WSFs in opposition to them, etc.).[25] Further, many of these actors envisage global solutions to the problems generated by insufficiently regulated capital. Although I have been using the term frequently in this discussion, 'anti-capitalist' is also not an accurate description of this domain of contentious politics as a whole because it encompasses both 'reformists' (who are not opposed to capitalism per se, but typically to a particular 'neo-liberal' model of capitalism) and 'radicals' (who might be understood as genuine anti-capitalists).[26] 'Anti-neo-liberal capitalism' might capture the lowest common denominator underpinning this arena, but seems too anodyne to do justice to many actors whose critiques of capitalism and the state are rather more fundamental. The fractiousness of contention against contemporary capitalism has led some analysts to question whether its agents can be described as comprising a 'movement' at all,[27] and to prefer metaphors of space to describe their relationship to one another. Deploying Pierre Bourdieu's notion of 'fields' as 'sui generis social spaces, constituted by the objective relations which hold between specific agents, organisations and institutions, and organised around the common participation of these players in a historically and culturally specific social "game"', Nick Crossley has argued that anti-capitalist contention should be viewed as taking place in a 'protest field' constituted by a tacit minimalist agreement amongst players (opposition to a particular model of capitalism), which provides the axis around which they are able to disagree or compete.[28] My references to the space, domain, or arena of anti-capitalist politics (rather than to a movement, party, or actor) should be understood in this sense.

Analysts have devised a variety of typologies to classify actors within this space. Most of these distinguish between actors on the basis of their views on the role of boundaries in regulating or contesting capitalism and on the locus of power that is best placed to do this. For example, in the wake of the anti-WTO protests at Seattle in 1999, Patrick Bond identified a tension within the NSMs between a tendency that argued for a more robust regulation of capitalism by reinforcing existing institutions of global governance along the lines urged by post-Washington Consensus reformers such as Stiglitz, Jeffrey Sachs, and George Soros, and an opposing tendency that argued for the delegitimation of current sites of potential international regulation so as to reconstitute progressive politics at the national level, exemplified by voices such as the Filipino activist Walden Bello.[29] Hardt highlights two major positions in the political landscape of the WSF: on the one hand, national sovereigntists such as the Brazilian Partido dos Trabalhadores (PT), and the French Association pour la taxation des transactions pour l'aide aux citoyens (ATTAC); on the other hand, actors such as anarchist networks in the global North and the barrio-based movements in Argentina that strive towards 'a non-national alternative to the present form of globalization that is equally global'.[30] (Crucially, Hardt's anarchist 'globalists' are a world away from the global social democrats in Bond's typology, particularly in their antipathy towards state power, whether exercised at the national or global level.) Describing contemporary attitudes towards global capitalism, Meghnad Desai and Yahia Said speak of 'isolationists' attempting to delink from the global economy wherever possible, 'supporters' of global capitalism, 'reformists' seeking to humanize globalization in social democratic ways, and 'alternatives' who want to reclaim space from the market rather than to engage in direct confrontation with it.[31] Acknowledging the wider range of ideological positions arrayed against globalization, Manfred Steger divides these into the 'particularist protectionist right' which comprises critics of globalization who prioritize the welfare of members of their communities over outsiders (Pat Buchanan, Le Pen, and—rather less convincingly—Osama bin Laden and Hugo Chavez), and the 'internationalist egalitarian left' which works towards a more equitable relationship between the global North and South, refusing to prioritize the claims of citizens over strangers (Ralph Nader, the European greens, the Zapatistas, etc.).[32] Simon Tormey offers a more complex typology that does not use conventional IR levels of analysis or refer to attitudes towards boundaries. Instead, he maps actors within the anti-capitalist space along an 'x' axis that measures the strength of their contestation of capitalism (radical or reformist) and a 'y' axis that measures the extent to which their actions are driven by a coherent world view (ideological, post-, or non-ideological).[33] But even he occasionally distinguishes between nationalist and globalist tendencies.[34]

Each of these typologies goes some way towards helping us make sense of this enormously complex protest space. But in pigeonholing actors into distinct levels of analysis (local, national, global) or fixed attitudes towards boundaries (particularist, internationalist), they fail to adequately recognize the coexistence of cosmopolitan and communitarian sensibilities in the political thinking and practice of some actors that inhabit this space.[35] This coexistence of sensibilities is remarkably reminiscent of early Marxian and Leninist articulations of nationalism and internationalism, which should not come as a surprise. Notwithstanding the dramatically altered political and economic context of anti-capitalist protest today, Marxist spatial imaginaries of threat have remained remarkably consistent. Social classes are still imagined as cosmopolitan formations fractured by national boundaries, so that class enemies (and friends) are to be found both within and outside the nation-state. This poses challenges for the mobilization of anti-capitalist protest, particularly where the nation-state is seen to be a potentially valuable agent in such protest.

In the remainder of this chapter, I focus on two movements within the field of 'anti-globalization' protest. My main interest is in teasing out the cosmopolitan and communitarian registers within their discourse and in analysing the political work that each of these registers is intended to accomplish. Having described the terrain of 'anti-globalization' protest above, it should be obvious that in focusing on these two movements, I do not intend to make generalizations about this space as a whole. I only seek to foreground an important tendency that is not adequately highlighted in most typologies of this space. Nonetheless, one of the movements studied (the Zapatistas) was—at its height—one of the most visible icons of 'anti-globalization' protest, spawning a large international solidarity movement. This suggests that, for all its idiosyncrasies, its sensibility was widely shared beyond the immediate confines of the movement. The other movement studied here (the Karnataka State Farmers' Association) was the face of 'anti-globalization' protest in the southern Indian state of Karnataka, where I am from.

5.3 INDIGENOUS INSURGENTS

On 1 January 1994, the world awoke to news that between 2,000 and 3,000 members of a military organization calling itself the Ejército Zapatista de

Liberacion Nacional (Zapatista Army of National Liberation, hereafter EZLN) had occupied four large towns and hundreds of ranches in the state of Chiapas in southern Mexico, in a surprise armed uprising. Describing themselves as the 'product of five hundred years of struggle' of the indigenous peoples of Mexico and more pointedly claiming the ideological legacy of Emiliano Zapata—a leading figure of the Mexican Revolution of 1910—the rebels introduced their struggle as one for 'work, land, housing, food, healthcare, education, independence, freedom, democracy, justice and peace'.[36] Although taken by surprise, the Mexican military responded swiftly, bombing indigenous communities from the air and reportedly resorting to torture and extrajudicial execution to suppress the rebellion. More than 200 people lost their lives in the fighting that ensued.[37] By 6 January, the rebels had been dislodged from the municipalities they had occupied and were forced to retreat into the relative safety and obscurity of the Lacandon jungle.

Yet from the very outbreak of the rebellion, they had begun to employ a sophisticated communications strategy, explaining and justifying their actions in eloquent communiqués addressed variously 'to the people of Mexico', 'to the peoples and governments of the world', and 'to national and international civil society'. Issued under the authority of the 'General Command of the EZLN', but more frequently in the name of its enigmatic and erudite spokesman Subcomandante Marcos, the communiqués[38] are a curious blend of political and economic analysis, Mayan folklore, magical realism, satire, invective, and quasi-religious, almost messianic rhetoric that sketch incrementally a vision of a political project that has confounded, inspired, and intrigued observers in Mexico and elsewhere. Disseminated through a complex network[39] comprising indigenous communities, solidarity activists from Mexican and international civil society organizations, newspapers such as the Mexico City centre-left daily *La Jornada* and the Italian communist *Il Manifesto*, Internet listservs and web sites, the communiqués piqued such a high level of sympathetic interest in the rebellion both within Mexico and outside, that the government felt compelled to declare a unilateral ceasefire on 12 January 1994, despite its unquestionable ability to crush the rebellion decisively. A subsequent government military offensive in February 1995 was similarly halted by the glare of domestic and international publicity, made particularly embarrassing because it threw a spotlight on poverty and immiseration in Mexico not long after its government had invested much effort in breaking into First World clubs such as the North Atlantic Free Trade Agreement (NAFTA) and the Organisation for Economic Co-operation and Development (OECD).

That indigenous communities in Chiapas had chosen to rebel did not surprise informed observers of Latin American politics. The indigenous peoples of

Latin America have physically resisted European and *criollo* domination of the continent since the Conquest. That history of resistance includes hundreds of rebellions against minority rule in Bolivia, Peru, and Guatemala, participation in revolutionary coalitions in twentieth-century Mexico and Bolivia, and a half-millennium-long implicit contestation of hegemonic cultural practices through the use of indigenous languages, religions, dress, artistic expression, etc. Nor is it difficult to understand the motivations for such resistance. As Alison Brysk puts it starkly, 'Latin American Indians are the poorest, sickest, most abused, and most defenceless members of their societies'.[40] Chiapas (one of six states in Mexico with a high proportion of indigenous peoples) presents a classic instance of such deprivation, rendered still more unjust by the enormous natural wealth of the state. At the time of the rebellion, it produced 55% of Mexico's hydro-electricity for example, yet 33% of its homes were not electrified (compared with a national average of 12.5%). 41.6% of homes did not receive potable water (national average: 20.6%), and 58.8% lacked basic sanitation facilities (national average: 36.4%). Conversely, Chiapas accounted for 21% and 47% of Mexico's oil and natural gas production, respectively, and 35% of its coffee; it was also the second largest producer of beef and corn. Yet 70% of its population lived below Mexico's official poverty line and 31% of its people were illiterate (national average: 13%).[41]

Most observers of the conflict in Chiapas acknowledge that high levels of deprivation were exacerbated by tensions over land fuelled by the rapid penetration of capitalist relations in the region. Peasants were pushed off the land by a rapid expansion in cattle production during the 1970s, and pulled into urban areas by the oil boom of that decade. The growing demand for electricity from an expanding urban economy drove the establishment of hydroelectric projects, which resulted in further encroachment of land.[42] There followed a period of hyper-involvement of the state in the rural economy, particularly during the administration of Luis Echeverria Alvarez (1970–6) when, in an attempt to break the power of *caciques* and local middlemen who were seen as undermining the state's ability to siphon resources to the national level, government-run commercial institutions were set up to provide credit to, and purchase directly from, small farmers. Investment in rural development expanded further in the oil boom years under José López Portillo (1976–82), providing rural infrastructure, direct support to production and social welfare institutions. Extensive land distribution took place under the administration of Miguel de la Madrid (1982–8), although this was done in ways that undermined relatively independent *campesino* groups, whilst rewarding those that had been loyal to the ruling Partido Revolucionario Institucional (PRI).[43]

'Hyper-involvement' of the state in the rural economy induced a new dependence on the state, which in turn made the sudden withdrawal of state support in the wake of the Mexican debt crisis exceedingly difficult to adjust to. Determined to maintain Mexico's competitive position in the global economy, policy elites in the administrations of de la Madrid and Carlos Salinas de Gortari (1988–94) introduced a series of austerity measures in an effort to ensure that debt repayments were made on schedule. Two sets of policy initiatives sent seismic waves through the rural economy in Chiapas. First, maize and coffee growers were hurt by the phasing out of various forms of state support (guaranteed prices, input subsidies, etc.). Between 1989 and 1993, coffee productivity fell by 35% and small growers experienced a 65–70% drop in income; many in Chiapas were forced to abandon production entirely. Second, Article 27 of the Mexican Constitution, which had hitherto enabled the granting of communal use-rights over land (*ejidos*) to legally incorporated groups of peasants (*ejidatarios*), was reformed to allow a virtual free market in land.[44] Studies of the process of neo-liberal reform in Mexico suggest that these policy reforms were not externally imposed on the Mexican state by IFIs, but reflected ideas that insiders—particularly the 'technocrats' within the de la Madrid and Salinas administrations—had been advocating for some time. External crisis strengthened the hands of these insiders, enabling them to push through proposals that had previously encountered resistance from within the policymaking elite.[45]

Although the plight of indigenous communities in Chiapas was certainly exacerbated by the neo-liberal reforms of the Salinas administration, the roots of those grievances predate the advent of neo-liberalism by decades if not centuries and have more to do with the enduring alienation of indigenous peoples from the institutions and culture of a state that has consistently dispossessed them of their lands and livelihoods. It was therefore striking that from the very outset, the Zapatistas defined their rebellion in rather grandiloquent and presentist terms as one against '*neoliberalismo*'. The outbreak of the rebellion was timed to coincide with the coming into force of NAFTA, a powerful symbol of the tide of neo-liberal globalization that was seen to be engulfing the Third World. Zapatista communiqués contain frequent references to neo-liberalism, which Marcos describes as a 'Fourth World War' (the Cold War being the third), waged by 'the great financial centres' which are said to be engaged in a dual process: on the one hand, the destruction of the distinctive material, historic and cultural bases of nation-states and a 'qualitative depopulation' of their territories, which involves 'detaching all those who are useless to the new market economy'; on the other hand, a reconstruction of national states and their reorganization in accordance with the logic of the global market. This reconstruction and reorganization is said to produce 'a peculiar excess: left-over human-beings, not necessary for the "new world order", who do not produce, or consume, who do not use credit, in sum, who are disposable'.[46] In a number of communiqués, the Zapatistas speak a cosmopolitan language of solidarity with all those considered 'disposable' by the neo-liberal beast. Consider the following, in which Marcos casts himself as a metaphor for subaltern identities everywhere:

> Marcos is a gay person in San Francisco, a black person in South Africa, an Asian person in Europe, a Chicano in San Isidro, an anarchist in Spain, a Palestinian in Israel, an indigenous person in the streets of San Cristóbal, a gang-member in Neza, a rocker in the Ex-Soviet Union, a Jew in Germany.... In other words, Marcos is a human being in this world. Marcos is every untolerated, oppressed, exploited minority that is resisting and saying, 'Enough already!' He is every minority who is now beginning to speak and every majority that must shut up and listen. He is every untolerated group searching for a way to speak, their way to speak. Everything that makes Power and the good consciences of those in power uncomfortable—this is Marcos.[47]

The Zapatistas' cosmopolitan sensibility was expressed not only through this sort of rhetorical affiliation with distant struggles, but more significantly through the numerous ways in which they actively invited outsiders to be part of their struggle. In August 1994, the EZLN hosted a National Democratic Convention in Chiapas, which drew nearly 6,000 participants, mostly from Mexico, to discuss strategies for revitalizing Mexican democracy. It subsequently organized national and international *consultas* at periodic intervals as well as two extraordinary *encuentros*. The first of these, held in August 1996 in the jungles of Chiapas, brought together a few thousand activists from all over the world. The second, called by the European Zapatista support network, took place in Spain the following year and resulted in the creation in 1998 of Peoples' Global Action (PGA)—a network that has coordinated a number of global protest 'days of action' against the summits of the IFIs.[48] The *consultas* and *encuentros* have not only served as arenas for discussion but have also functioned as decision-making bodies, with delegates (both Mexican and foreign) voting on key strategic and tactical issues facing the movement including its decision to abandon the use of violence and to reconstitute itself as a political organization. These activities have, in a very tangible sense, contributed to the development of an extensive global solidarity network[49] that has brought an unending stream of international activists, observers, and solidarity-tourists to Chiapas, despite the state of siege and grinding poverty of the region.

Yet alongside these dramatic cosmopolitan gestures, the Zapatistas display a deeply nationalist streak in much of their political thinking and practice, which has tended to be ignored or downplayed in much of the sympathetic commentary on the movement offered by the Western left. In a number of communiqués, the Zapatistas cast themselves as patriots, as 'the inheritors of the true builders of our nation',[50] while successive federal administrations of Salinas, Ernesto Zedillo, and Vicente Fox are characterized as traitors and sell-outs that have betrayed the ideals of the 1910 revolution. 'Our fight is for the homeland, and the bad government dreams with a foreign flag and language.'[51] Laying claim to the ideological heritage of a long history of subaltern resistance in modern Mexico, the Zapatistas declare:

> We are a product of five hundred years of struggle: first, led by insurgents against slavery during the War of Independence with Spain; then to avoid being absorbed by North American imperialism; then to proclaim our constitution and expel the French empire from our soil; later when the people rebelled against Porfirio Diaz's dictatorship, which denied us the just application of the reform laws, and leaders like Villa and Zapata emerged, poor men just like us who have been denied the most elemental preparation so they can use us as cannon fodder and pillage the wealth of our country... we are millions, the dispossessed who call upon our brothers and sisters to join this struggle as the only path, so that we will not die of hunger due to the insatiable ambition of a seventy-year dictatorship led by a clique of traitors who represent the most conservative and sell-out groups. They are the same ones that opposed Hidalgo and Morelos, the same ones that betrayed Vicento Guerrero, the same ones that sold half our country to the foreign invader, the same ones that imported a European prince to rule our country, the same ones that formed the 'scientific' Porfirista dictatorship, the same ones that opposed the Petroleum Expropriation, the same ones that massacred the railroad workers in 1958 and the students in 1968, the same ones that today take everything from us, absolutely everything.[52]

Note how domestic opponents are accused of betraying the nation to 'the foreign invader' and are tarred by association with 'North American imperialism', 'the French empire', and 'a European prince'. Reinforcing this tirade against the state's facilitation of pillage by outsiders, the Zapatistas passionately embrace and reclaim nationalist imagery and symbols at every available occasion. They express allegiance to the national flag, which is displayed prominently alongside the EZLN flag in demonstrations and marches. Indeed one communiqué notes that although all are welcome to fly the EZLN flag, 'there is a much bigger and powerful [sic] flag with which we can all be covered. The flag of the national revolutionary movement where all the most diverse tendencies can fit....' The communiqué 'calls on Mexicans to fly that flag, not the EZLN flag, not the flag of armed struggle, but the flag that is the right of all thinking beings', and concludes that 'under that great flag we'll fly our Zapatista flag'.[53] The rebellion is even justified with reference to the national constitution,[54] with the Zapatistas casting themselves as guardians of the Constitution even as they take up arms against the state: 'As long as a new constitution is not created, we will uphold the 1917 Constitution as the true one. We will fight for it.'[55]

Commentators have offered a variety of tortuous interpretations of these strongly patriotic and nationalist inflections in a movement that has otherwise attracted attention for its cosmopolitan credentials. Massimo de Angelis argues that the invocation of 'nation' in Zapatista internationalism can be understood in four different ways.[56] First, 'nation' is said to refer to the 'ideal' or 'whole' that the indigenous communities feel a sense of belonging to. De Angelis is not explicit about what this 'whole' is in the context of the Zapatistas, but he seems disinclined to identify it with the Mexican nation. Gideon Baker displays a similar reluctance, preferring to read the Zapatistas' invocation of 'nation' as 'a metaphor for that self-determining political space from which they, and many other subaltern groups, are systematically excluded'.[57] Second, de Angelis argues that 'nation' as used by the Zapatistas is not defined by national borders or racial characteristics but more in terms of the 'subversive affinity' shared by actors in all parts of the world engaged in a common struggle. Third, the use of a nationalist discourse is said to enable the Zapatistas to challenge the state's claim to represent and protect the general interest against the competing clamours of special interests. Fourth, the Zapatista deployment of the term 'nation' is argued to be much closer to the rhetoric of liberation, autonomy, and identity pursued over the last two centuries by indigenous 'nations', whose claims to sovereignty have always been in direct opposition to those of nation-states. The third and fourth of these putative connotations of 'nation' in Zapatista discourse are most persuasive, yet what is notable about the discussion as a whole is the extreme reluctance to acknowledge the most obvious conclusion: that when the Zapatistas invoke the 'nation' and embrace symbols popularly associated with the *Mexican* nation, they use that term not as a metaphor for some other, quite different kind of political community, but in the way that it is commonly understood. One would hardly use 'nation' as a metaphor for some quite distinct notion of community, whilst wrapping oneself in the symbols of an actually existing nation-state.[58] Add to this the fact that much of the rhetoric of betrayal accuses domestic opponents of engaging in kleptocratic collaboration with foreigners, and one cannot help but be struck by the strongly nationalist currents in the political thought of the movement. One can only speculate that sympathetic commentators in the Western left are disinclined to acknowledge these nationalist currents because nationalism in post-war Europe is seen to have become irredeemably tainted by the evils of xenophobia and fascism.[59]

In Zapatismo, the commitment to nationalism is conjoined with an affirmation of state sovereignty, which has also been less remarked upon. As Marcos says very plainly:

> ... the Zapatistas think that, in Mexico (attention: in Mexico) the recuperation and defence of national sovereignty is part of an antineoliberal revolution.... The Zapatistas think that the defence of the national state is necessary in view of globalization, and that the attempts to slice Mexico to pieces comes from the governing group and not from the just demands for autonomy for the Indian Peoples. The EZLN, and the best of the national indigenous movement, does not want the Indian peoples to separate from Mexico, but to be recognized as part of the country with their differences.
> ... The paradoxes continue because while the EZLN struggles for the defence of national sovereignty, the Mexican Federal Army struggles against that defence and defends a government who has destroyed the material bases of national sovereignty and given the country, not just to powerful foreign capital, but to the drug traffickers...[60]

Elsewhere, the defence of national sovereignty is advanced with a clear awareness that the indigenous peoples of Chiapas, acting on their own, would have little chance of regulating the entry and operation of global capital:

> It hasn't escaped our notice that various international powers are nursing the idea of using the rich oil and uranium deposits under Zapatista soil for their own benefit. Those up above are making up complex accounts and calculations, entertaining the hope that the Zapatistas will make separatist proposals. It would be easier and cheaper to negotiate purchasing the subsoil with the cooperation of the Banana Republic (Mayan Nation, they call it). After all, it's well known that the indigenous are satisfied with small mirrors and glass beads... they certainly have made no headway, because—it just so happens—the Zapatistas take the 'National Liberation' part of the EZLN very much to heart and sword. We may be anachronistic, but we still believe in 'outmoded' concepts like 'national sovereignty' and 'national independence'.[61]

How do we square this resounding and rather traditional defence of national sovereignty with the cosmopolitan solidarity politics of a movement that has gone to the extent of inviting foreigners to shape key strategic and tactical decisions? In section 5.5, I will analyse the very distinct political functions performed by cosmopolitanism and nationalism in the discourse of the Zapatistas. Before that, I attempt to reveal an analogous juxtaposition of these forms of consciousness in the activism of the Karnataka State Farmers' Association.

5.4 RIOTING RYOTS

In June 1980, the Malaprabha irrigation project in the south Indian state of Karnataka became the focus of an agitation by farmers in the region against the state government. They were protesting the imposition of a 'betterment levy', water taxes, and irrigation cesses;[62] to add insult to injury, the water they were being charged for had not even been supplied to them.[63] Tensions were heightened after police fired at the protesters, resulting in five deaths. Beginning initially in the Dharwad and Gadag districts of Karnataka, the agitation had been led by a local coordination committee that included leaders of left political parties. By August, non-party *raitha sanghas* (farmers' associations) had sprung up in many districts, including Belgaum, Bijapur, Bellary, and Shimoga. These would eventually merge to form the Karnataka Rajya Raitha Sangha (Karnataka State Farmers' Association, hereafter KRRS).

The KRRS was not alone in organizing farmers. Other notable farmers' associations were Shetkari Sanghatana (SS) in Maharashtra state and the Bharatiya Kisan Union (BKU), based mainly in the northern state of Uttar Pradesh.[64] Unlike other contemporaneous social movements[65] such as those of women and dalits, which have tended to see themselves as pan-Indian, farmers' organizations were formed independently within the different linguistic states of the country. Although loosely federated with one another, each bears the stamp of the particular ethno-linguistic context from which it emerged (reflected in the word for 'farmer' in their names, which, in each case is taken from the regional language of their state of origin). The tendency towards localization is particularly evident in the case of the KRRS, which unlike the other two organizations, has not expanded beyond the state of Karnataka,[66] even though it has supported agitations elsewhere in India. Ironically, despite this intensely local orientation, the KRRS enjoys perhaps the highest international visibility of all the farmers' movements in India, particularly in 'anti-globalization' circles. It is a prominent member of La Via Campesina, an international network of small farmers' organizations, and played a central role in the creation of PGA, which, as mentioned earlier, was itself a product of the second Zapatista-inspired *encuentro* held in Spain in 1997.

At the local level, the KRRS has long been demanding better remuneration for agricultural produce, agitating against the increasing cost of agricultural inputs, and the consequent pressure on profit margins. This fundamental grievance has provoked a barrage of protest over the last three decades. Resorting to what Ramachandra Guha has described, in another context, as a 'Gandhian vocabulary of protest',[67] non-cooperation has been a favourite tactic. Farmers have refused to pay land revenue to land-development and commercial banks, evaded taxes on water and power and, on occasion, withheld agricultural produce from the market. When failure to pay land revenue has prompted attachment of land by the government, KRRS members have formed 'anti-attachment squads' to resist punitive action by the state, sometimes locking up or chasing away land revenue bureaucrats who approach their villages.[68] They have frequently refused to pay for electricity, returning electricity meters to officials in symbolic gestures of protest. They have demanded loan write-offs and have protested the 'unscientific' pricing policy of the government, accusing it of setting artificially low support prices even as (more recently) it has opened markets, in accordance with WTO obligations, to heavily subsidized foreign produce.[69]

These demands form part of what Gail Omvedt describes as an 'ideology of ruralism', which essentially calls for an improvement in the terms of trade between agriculture and industry, and between rural and urban areas.[70] The rallying cry is that of *grama swarajya* (village self-rule), in furtherance of which the movement has, in previous years, led boycotts of industrialized manufactured goods, insisted on the appropriation of natural resources in and around villages for the consumption of the rural populace, agitated against commercial eucalyptus plantations on environmental and economic grounds, demanded that social forestry programmes be managed by village panchayats (the lowest rung of local government in rural areas), etc. Many of these goals, it believes, are best advanced through a revitalization of Panchayati Raj institutions, primarily through programmes of mass education to raise awareness amongst the rural populace of their right to participate in local government.[71]

Alongside its tradition of Gandhian resistance through non-cooperation and civil disobedience, the KRRS began a gradual and hesitant engagement with party politics in the 1980s. It had adopted a resolute 'non-party, non-electoral politics' position till 1983, but ended its political neutrality and decided to support parties in opposition to the ruling Congress in elections to the state legislative assembly held that year. In 1984, it went back to rejecting all political parties and began a tentative non-party engagement with the electoral process by setting up *mathadarara vedike* (voters' forums) in each constituency. In 1987, it created a political party named Kannada Desha, distinct from the movement itself (the movement would reabsorb the party two years later). Finally, in 1990 and 1992, it contested elections in eleven constituencies of the Lok Sabha (lower house of the federal Parliament) and 111 constituencies of the Vidhana Sabha (lower house of the state legislative assembly), but won only two seats in the latter.[72] In addition to being spectacularly unsuccessful, this brief flirtation with the electoral sphere seems to have been a much-regretted affair. One issue of the movement's newsletter details how the lure of power led to the defection of several members, some to the right-wing Bharatiya Janata Party (BJP), in return for the promise of ministerial office. More broadly, entry into electoral politics is now seen to have bred hierarchical relations between the leadership and the rank and file of the movement, and to have demobilized the movement, robbing it of much of its activist zeal.[73]

Scholars of social movements in India have observed that interest-based movements tend to avoid electoral politics, while identity-based movements—particularly those organized around language, caste, and religion—have fared well in the electoral domain.[74] The reasons are not hard to fathom. Interest-based movements find it difficult to appeal to those outside the interest group, whereas identity claims can forge a sense of community amongst groups with different interests. Indeed, the particular issues taken up by identity-based movements are fungible: one can easily be replaced with another, so long as it does the work of securing recognition for the community's selfhood (think of the relative ease with which the Hindu right has used a number of different issues to consolidate its electoral base, from the construction of a Ram temple at Ayodhya to the promulgation of a uniform civil code or the ending of special constitutional status for Kashmir). It is difficult to estimate the size of the interest group that the KRRS represents, given that there has not been a numerical reckoning of the movement's base since at least 1995.[75] The estimate of 10 million, advanced in a 1999 newsletter[76] (equivalent to about 20% of the population of Karnataka),[77] appears to be a gross overestimate in light of its poor electoral performance. Nonetheless, its self-definition as an interest-based group might help us understand the difficulties it faced in widening its electoral appeal. At any rate, given this dismal failure in the electoral arena, it was time to try something different.

In December 1992, the KRRS hit the headlines when around seventy-five of its members occupied the Bangalore offices of the agro-multinational Cargill, threw much of its equipment out of the windows on to the street below and set fire to it. In July 1993, KRRS members destroyed a Cargill warehouse in the city of Bellary, 300 kilometres north of Bangalore. In August 1995, activists attacked the newly opened Bangalore outlet of Kentucky Fried Chicken, offering a battery of arguments in justification including health concerns over the possible carcinogenic effects of substances used to fatten chickens and economic and environmental concerns over the diversion of land use from food cropping to animal fodder.[78] Although the restaurant reopened soon after the attack and was well patronized by an urban middle-class clientele, it was given police protection for several months for fear of repeat attacks.[79] In 1998, KRRS activists sabotaged two of the three field trials of genetically engineered Bt cotton being conducted by Monsanto in Karnataka, setting the crop on fire (the action was called 'Operation Cremate Monsanto'). Throughout, the movement insisted that its actions were compatible with a Gandhian commitment to non-violence, on the understanding that 'one can only speak about violence when it is directed against living beings, not against inanimate objects. We hence consider the destruction of office material or buildings as perfectly non-violent actions, as long as no human being or other living beings are attacked.'[80] Less confrontationally, the KRRS had begun to engage in a number of awareness-raising activities. Working closely with the Malaysia-based Third World Network in 1992-3, it organized seminars to discuss the so-called Dunkel Draft, then still under negotiation, which would later become the basis for the agreement establishing the WTO.[81] In October 1993, it organized a convention of 'Third World peasantry' in Bangalore, attended by thousands of local farmers and representatives of farmers' organizations from other parts of India and from Indonesia, Malaysia, Nicaragua, Zimbabwe, Sri Lanka, and the Philippines.

As a consequence of the high level of global visibility that the KRRS had earned from its dramatic 'direct actions' against multinational corporations, its founding president M. D. Nanjundaswamy received an invitation to join La Via Campesina,[82] a global network of small farmer organizations.[83] The KRRS went on to become an active member of the network, organizing its third congress and first international women's meeting in Bangalore in 2000. It also participated actively in the second Zapatista-inspired *encuentro* held in Spain in August 1997 and in the process leading up to the creation of PGA—a network envisioned as an instrument for communication and coordination among, what its web site calls, 'clearly anti-capitalist (not just anti-neoliberal)' groups.[84] PGA's main activity has been the coordination of global 'days of action', chiefly in opposition to summits of the IFIs. On the first of these in May 1998, timed to coincide with the second ministerial conference of the WTO, the KRRS together with other Indian movements in a recently launched 'Joint Action Forum of Indian People against the WTO and Anti-People Policies', organized a rally reportedly attended by 200,000 people in the city of Hyderabad.[85] In the summer of 1999, in a highly unusual protest initiative, 400 Indian farmers (mostly from the KRRS) joined around 50 representatives of other Third World social movements in a month-long protest tour intended to travel through nine countries. Dubbed the Intercontinental Caravan of Solidarity and Resistance (ICCSR), it was an unprecedented initiative that brought members of Third World social movements at the forefront of resisting 'globalization', to protest for themselves en masse at First World venues of power—at the Cologne G8 summit and the headquarters of the WTO in Geneva, the EC in Brussels, and the OECD in Paris.[86] In addition of course, Nanjundaswamy saw it as an opportunity for coalition-building amongst like-minded farmer and peasant organizations.[87] Speaking at the demonstration against the G8 summit, the former law professor said:

> We have come here to build bridges between people who want to reclaim their future, to disobey the institutions that run the current, self-destructive system of global economic, political and military governance, and to take their own power in their hands in order to construct a different world. A world where local people are in control of their local economy, where centralised political and economic power disappear.... We do not want Western money, technologies or 'experts' to impose their development model on us.... We only want to organise our strength and combine it with the strength of other movements in the North and the South in order to regain control over our lives. We are not working for a place on the global table of negotiations, nor for a bloody revolution; we are just working on the long-term process of construction of a different world, a world which will come about from the local to the global, from a shift in the values and everyday choices of millions of persons.[88]

Looking at the KRRS's activities from 1992 onwards—its spectacular attacks on agents of global capitalism, its involvement in global anti-capitalist networks, and its participation in a discourse about the construction of an alternative world in alliance with like-minded international partners—it looks very much like an organization that should belong within Hardt's category of actors striving towards 'a non-national alternative to the present form of globalization that is equally global'.[89] Yet in parallel with this globalist discourse, the KRRS also speaks the language of national sovereignty (the very category that Hardt posits in opposition to his global anarchists).

The influence of Gandhian nationalism is apparent, both in the substantive ideological orientation of the movement (its ideology of ruralism and the championing of Panchayati Raj) and in its vocabulary of protest (the use of non-cooperation and other classic Gandhian tactics such as bandhs, hartals, and hunger strikes). In addition, Muzaffar Assadi has drawn attention to the influence of dependency theory on the political thinking of its leadership. In line with the dependentistas, the KRRS attributes the destitution of farmers and economic underdevelopment in the Third World more generally to the continuing dependence of these countries on metropolitan states at the core of the world economy. This state of affairs is reportedly perpetuated by the denial of technology and markets to Third World producers, resulting in the subordination of indigenous capitalism to metropolitan capital. Assadi argues that the KRRS has moved from a Gandhian conceptualization of indigenous capitalism as 'weak', to a more radical Marxist stance that sees it as 'comprador'. In addition, it has mapped caste relations on to its image of dependency, arguing that the periphery is itself divided into a core, dominated by Brahmins and other higher castes, who exert power over the periphery-within-the-periphery via an analogous denial of knowledge and property to the rest of society.[90] Yet this world view is replete with ambiguities. As I shall go on to suggest, the KRRS's anti-Brahminism is not necessarily a position against caste hierarchies per se. And its attitude towards technology is ambivalent:[91] even as it cites the denial of technology as a factor sustaining underdevelopment, it vigorously opposes the introduction of certain new technologies (such as genetically modified crops).[92] In a 1988 interview, Nanjundaswamy argued that dependence could only be ended by delinking from the global economy, an idea that he expressed through the metaphor of dropping a 'khadi curtain' between India and the rest of the world.[93] Ever since Gandhi's rousing call to every household to boycott foreign cloth and spin khadi during the struggle for independence, khadi has held connotations of indigeneity and self-sufficiency. But in contrast to the Churchillian phrase from which it derives, the 'khadi curtain' suggests a barrier that is softer and more porous than state-boundaries as traditionally conceived.

Indeed, the khadi curtain is an instructive metaphor for the KRRS's expectations of the role that the state ought to play. In its earlier Marxist-influenced phase when the state was seen as an instrument of the exploitative classes, the struggle was not against the state so much as for a state that would dispense *mridu rajya* (soft rule) in relation to farmers.[94] 'Soft rule' seemed to entail active state intervention in some respects (remunerative prices) and autonomy from the state in others (as Tom Brass writes, farmers' movements have tended to oppose state intervention to enforce land-ownership ceilings or payment of minimum wages to agricultural labour).[95] As far as relations with the outside world are concerned, the KRRS's criticism of the liberalized import regime which enables the dumping of foreign agricultural produce, suggests a desire for a stronger state that could better withstand pressure to open markets non-reciprocally. In effect, the demand seems to be for a state that is selectively soft on the inside, but hard on the outside.

Marxist critics like Brass have been deeply sceptical of the KRRS's invocations of nationalism, arguing that the use of nationalist discourse by such movements functions to obscure class differences between different categories of cultivators. Instead of providing a political critique of capitalism in general (whether foreign or indigenous), the movement focuses mainly on the noneconomic identities of alleged exploiters, who are identified as agents of 'foreign' or 'global' capital or as national high-caste allies thereof. It thereby instils a 'false' ethnic or national consciousness amongst poor peasants and agricultural labourers, who begin to perceive themselves as sharing an identity with wealthier farmers despite the antagonism of their class interests. The nationalist discourse of the KRRS therefore obviates challenges from below to the dominant position of wealthier farmers, ensuring that grievances are deflected towards other targets.[96]

To appreciate the force of the argument, we need to know more about the social composition of the KRRS. The literature on agrarian social movements makes a key distinction between 'peasants' and 'farmers', with the former being understood as cultivators whose livelihoods are centred primarily on subsistence and only secondarily on commodity production. 'Farmers', on the other hand, are understood as those who produce primarily for the market, often with advanced technology, hired labour, and formal credit.[97] Whatever their normative readings of these movements, most scholars agree that the major agrarian movements in India from the early 1980s onwards have been farmers' movements. Dipankar Gupta categorically describes the three most significant of these—the BKU, the SS, and the KRRS—as 'farmers' (not peasants')' movements, adding for good measure that although 'the agriculturalists present themselves as an undifferentiated phalanx... one should bear in mind that these farmers' movements distinguish their interests quite clearly from the interests of the agricultural labourers'.[98] This is borne out by Assadi's careful empirical work on the KRRS, which reveals that it is a movement primarily of landowners agitating against policies that have made landholdings uneconomical. It has never seriously taken up the issues of landless labour, whose participation in the movement, Assadi reports, has dwindled. Likewise in caste terms, the KRRS is heavily dominated by lingayats and vokkaligas.[99] It does not represent dalits in any meaningful sense and has been unable to form alliances with dalit organizations.[100]

Brass rightly highlights the very particular class (and caste) character of the KRRS that is obscured by its nationalist rhetoric, but his normative critique of the movement rests on the belief that the primary contradiction in agrarian relations is internal to cultivators (i.e. wealthier farmers—not the state or global capital—are the most crushing source of exploitation vis-à-vis the lowest class of cultivators). This is a controversial assertion. *Pace* Brass, Omvedt sees an 'unequal, caste-bound, but still cultivating peasantry... not being "differentiated" into agricultural labourers and capitalist farmers engaged in class struggle against each other, but rather pulled (with all their hierarchy and inequalities) into a new kind of capitalist enslavement to the market and the state'.[101] Omvedt criticizes 'old left' Marxists like Brass for conflating the possession of private property with exploitation—an assumption that leads them inexorably to conclude that only a landless labour-based movement on wage issues can be 'radical', while farmers' movements must be seen as reactionary. This perspective seems incapable of seeing cultivators as a whole, although it has no difficulty with a unitary conception of the 'working class', which is arguably equally hierarchical and fragmented. As Omvedt notes of traditional Marxists, 'the relationship of peasants as a group with supra-village exploitation (the state, the buyers of their produce, those who taxed them) and the struggles they organised against this—however militant and involving however many deaths—fell outside the scope of "class analysis" and "class struggle"'.[102]

The reference to death is apposite, although perhaps not in the way that Omvedt intends in her critique. Most informed observers—including liberalization's sympathetic interlocutors in the policy elite—acknowledge an agrarian crisis of serious proportions in south India, which has manifested itself in a spate of suicides by farmers. By one reckoning, 3,000 farmers in Karnataka took their lives in the period between 2000 and August 2003.[103] A 2005 Christian Aid report suggested that the situation in neighbouring Andhra Pradesh was even more acute: 2,115 farmers are estimated to have killed themselves in 2004 alone, bringing the toll since 1998 to 4,378.[104] These are mere regional snapshots of a nationwide phenomenon that has seen 86,922 farmers kill themselves in the period 2001–5, resulting in a national suicide mortality rate that is noticeably higher for farmers than non-farmers.[105]

Most of these suicides have been by small, landholding farmers producing for the market, driven to taking their lives by the crushing burden of debt. Small farmers find it difficult to access institutional credit because of the higher transaction costs of doing so given the extensive procedures and documentation involved, the requirement for tangible collateral security, etc. Bankers are likewise discouraged by the high transaction costs of making small loans to large numbers of people and, in addition, view small farmers as risky customers because of the lack of risk mitigation mechanisms on farms in the event of crop failure. Banking sector liberalization has resulted in the decline of preferential lending to agriculture. In such circumstances, small farmers are forced to borrow in the informal sector where transaction costs are lower, but rates of interest much higher.[106] Meanwhile, profit margins have been squeezed by the increase in cost of agricultural inputs, thanks in part to the withdrawal of state subsidies for fertilizers, water, and power (in many cases, these policy changes can be traced to World Bank pressure for the introduction of user fees).[107] Market prices have fallen, in part because the liberalization of the import regime has enabled the dumping of cheap (often heavily subsidized) foreign produce.[108]

Given this state of affairs, one is compelled to respond to Brass's criticism of the nationalist discourse of farmers' movements with the observation that it is not simply a distraction from intra-cultivator class contradictions. It is also a response to a crisis of existential proportions produced, in no small measure, by the liberalization of the agricultural sector and the entry of multinational capital. One could argue further that Brass's critique overlooks the progressive role that Marx assigned to nationalism in global anti-capitalist struggle and the possibility that it could continue to play this role, albeit in a post-colonial context. This would therefore be the appropriate juncture at which to analyse the political functions that cosmopolitanism and nationalism perform in the activism of the Zapatistas and the KRRS.

5.5 COSMOPOLITANISM AND NATIONALISM IN CONTEMPORARY ANTI-CAPITALIST PROTEST

Social movements confronting hostile or unresponsive states frequently seek to bypass those states and solicit the assistance of international allies in bringing pressure to bear on their states from the outside.[109] They are more likely to attract such allies if they are able to 'frame' their grievances in certain ways. The notion of 'framing' was originally proposed by sociologist David Snow and his collaborators, who argued that all societies use cognitive frames to organize experience and guide action. Social movements construct 'collective action frames' to attract supporters, signal their intentions, and gain media attention. Drawing on these ideas, Sidney Tarrow has argued that social movements are increasingly resorting to 'global framing', which he defines as 'the use of external symbols to orient local or national claims'.[110] In his incisive study of the strategies used by rebel movements to market themselves to solidarity and advocacy non-governmental organizations (NGOs) worldwide, Clifford Bob demonstrates the numerous ways in which global framing is achieved. Social movements tend to frame their grievances in terms of issue areas that resonate with powerful publics (usually in the developed world) that can be of assistance. They are likely to emphasize the universalistic aspects of parochial disputes and to point the finger of blame at globally notorious opponents in the hope of attracting support from the many enemies that such opponents might have.[111] To a large extent, the cosmopolitan rhetoric of the Zapatistas and the KRRS can be understood as attempts at global framing with a view to winning international allies who could be of assistance in their struggle.

As should be clear from the discussion of the rebellion above, Zapatista grievances centred on land inequality and poverty are indistinguishable from those that indigenous communities have had against the Mexican and other Latin American states for centuries. Although they may have been exacerbated by neo-liberal reforms such as the lifting of price controls on coffee and the amendment of Article 27, the roots of these grievances predate the advent of liberalization by a considerable period of time. In so far as liberalization was responsible for the plight of the Zapatistas, most studies of the liberalization process in Mexico have shown that the impetus for policy reform came from technocrats within the Mexican government rather than from foreign capital. So the framing of the rebellion as one against NAFTA, *neoliberalismo* and 'the great financial centres' requires some explanation.

Organized indigenous resistance in Chiapas is not a recent phenomenon. As far back as the 1960s, catechists preaching in indigenous languages had been urging people to articulate their experiences of oppression and to consider exercising their rights. Maoist student activists, particularly those influenced by the anti-Leninist–Stalinist Politica Popular tendency after 1968, had begun working with peasant groups in the state.[112] Formal campesino organizations had begun to emerge in the 1970s, three of which would merge to form the Alianza Campesina Independiente Emiliano Zapata (ACIEZ: Emiliano Zapata Independent Peasant Alliance), a direct precursor of the EZLN.[113] None of these early efforts at indigenous organization attracted much external support beyond a small circle of indigenous rights organizations.

In contrast, the EZLN was immensely successful at precipitating the rapid formation of a global solidarity network that exerted pressure on the Mexican government at key moments, halting military crackdowns on Zapatista enclaves in January 1994 and February 1995 and forcing the government to negotiate with the rebels instead. While its ability to do this stemmed from a number of factors, central among these was its framing of the rebellion as one against the depredations of neo-liberal capitalism exemplified by trade agreements such as NAFTA. This brought it the immediate support of a considerable transnational anti-NAFTA network of labour, environmental, and human rights groups, which in turn 'benefited' from the rebellion in the sense that it appeared to vindicate their own criticisms of NAFTA. By reframing resistance that had previously been articulated in terms of *campesino* or indigenous discontent against the Mexican state as a revolt against neo-liberal ideology, the EZLN had transformed what had previously been viewed as a local land dispute into a conflict that was relevant to the lives of distant audiences. Having linked their plight to the policies of foreign countries, the Zapatistas aroused in those audiences a sense of responsibility to act and gave them a set of targets within their own countries against which to vent their ire.[114] So persuasive was this reframing that activists in distant corners of the world were soon saying 'todos somos Marcos'.

Similar motivations could explain the turn to global rhetoric and activism in the case of the KRRS. The movement's spectacular 'direct actions' against agricultural multinational corporations from 1992 onwards have to be understood in the context of its failure to make any headway in the domestic electoral arena in the preceding years. In addition, the timing of the reframing of its grievances—from ones that were essentially local to a protest against neo-liberal capitalism—lent plausibility to the global frame. Coming barely a year after the Congress-led central government of P. V. Narasimha Rao had commenced a programme of structural adjustment in response to a severe balance of payments crisis, and amidst India's participation in the negotiation of the Dunkel Draft, the notion that Indian farmers were being hurt by the entry of foreign capital into the agricultural sector appeared plausible to domestic and international audiences.

In a scathing attack on 'global civil society' activists, David Chandler has argued that protest claims are typically transferred to global arenas when they fail to resonate with domestic publics. While Chandler suggests that such failure tends to be the result of a narcissistic unwillingness on the part of activists to engage with their own political communities, the broader assumption animating his argument seems to be that the failure of protest claims to take root domestically renders them illegitimate and unworthy of serious attention at the global level.[115] In the case of the KRRS, domestic failure was not for want of trying. Moreover, arguments often fail in the public sphere, not merely on their merits, but because structural inequalities might relegate the speaker to the position of a permanent minority. For example, adivasis are one of the most vulnerable communities in India, disproportionately likely to be displaced by dams and other development projects because they live in non-industrialized areas. Despite constituting 8.2% of the total population,[116] thanks to their geographical dispersion they are a miniscule minority in all but a few states. Inadequately served by the institutions of representative democracy and insufficiently protected by alternative institutions intended to mitigate the tyranny of the majority (such as the bureaucracy and judiciary), they have felt compelled to go global: the case of protest against the construction of the Sardar Sarovar dam in the Narmada valley provides perhaps the best known example of this.[117] Given the structural impediments to their effective participation in the domestic public sphere, we cannot assume that the failure of their arguments in that sphere somehow renders them illegitimate and unworthy of a second airing in other venues.

What did global framing do for the KRRS? As we have seen, it boosted the visibility of the KRRS at a time when its domestic fortunes were flagging. The movement's dramatic attacks on symbols of global opprobrium brought it to the attention of powerful publics in wealthy countries, winning it invitations to join important global anti-capitalist networks and enabling the externalization of its protest into new venues. And it generated a new cosmopolitan discourse in which the movement's leaders began to see themselves as part of a project to construct an alternative world in alliance with like-minded actors. But unlike in the case of the Zapatistas, the KRRS's attempts at global framing did not generate sufficient external pressure to induce the Indian state to change its agricultural policies. Indeed as the experience of other social movements has shown, global framing carries risks. In the case of the anti-dam movement, it invited a vicious backlash from the state, which sought to portray opponents of the dam as 'anti-national'. Going global also sometimes misdiagnoses the agency and extent of influence of external actors on the state. In focusing relentlessly on global targets such as the World Bank, the anti-dam movement successfully forced the Bank to withdraw funding for the Sardar Sarovar Project, but underestimated the determination and ability of the Indian state to continue work on the project with alternative sources of finance.[118]

Indeed, it is precisely the uncertainties and risks of global framing that necessitate the nationalist register in the discourse of 'anti-globalization' movements like the Zapatistas and the KRRS. Aimed primarily at domestic audiences, nationalist discourse is typically intended to obscure differences of interest and identity, forging alliances with other subaltern groups or across class lines. By portraying themselves as Mexican patriots, for example, the Zapatistas were able to reach out very effectively to other constituencies in Mexican civil society, which then rallied to their defence. Crucially, both movements are careful to distinguish their invocations of nationalism from official state-sponsored nationalism. In an open letter to President Zedillo, Marcos says:

> We do not want for Mexico your kind of unity, which will assure the permanence of the same system of oppression, now made up to look like a new administration. That is not the type of unity that Mexico needs. The one that our history reclaims is the *unity against the state-party system of government, which has the nation submerged in a poverty of body and spirit.*[119]

The KRRS has also gone to some lengths to differentiate its nationalism from that of the 'anti-globalization' wing of the Hindu right.[120] As it explains in a newsletter:

> We are obviously against capitalist globalisation and in favour of self-reliance, but this does not stop us from denouncing the neo-fascist use of the 'Swadeshi' concept, the originally very positive Gandhian concept of self-reliance that has been perverted and abused by the Hindu far-right of

> this country to boost the most stupid nationalism and intolerance with their xenophobe [sic] discourse on Swadeshi. We reclaim the internationalist roots of the Gandhian concept, which we do not see as an objective to achieve at the national level, but at community level. We have had enough years of over-bureaucratic, centralised, corrupt, inefficient and industry-biased 'national self-sufficiency'. Instead of the 'national Swadeshi' so loudly proclaimed by Hindu nationalist fanatics of BJP, we fight for the economic self-management and freedom of Village Republics...[121]

There are at least two significant things going on here. First, the attempt to distinguish 'good' left-wing internationalist nationalism from 'bad' right-wing xenophobic nationalism is motivated in part by a desire to render nationalist discourse directed at the domestic audience compatible with cosmopolitan 'global framing' rhetoric directed at international audiences. Second, the attempted separation of subaltern nationalisms from official and other putatively more privileged nationalisms should be viewed as an instance of what David Lloyd has called 'nationalisms against the state'.[122] Such nationalisms attempt to draw other constituents of the nation into a battle against the state, with a view to changing the fundamental goals or orientations of the state. Both movements studied here view their respective states as having prioritized their responsibilities to global capital (debt servicing, maintaining the state's competitive position in global markets) over their commitment to ensuring the socio-economic needs of their own citizens. Neo-Gramscian scholars have described this recalibration of priorities as a 'transnationalization' or 'internationalization' of the state.[123] In such circumstances, the nationalist discourse of protest movements aims at a 'renationalization' of the transnationalized state. Deploying a rhetoric of betrayal that accuses the post-colonial state of forgetting old heroes (Zapata, Gandhi) and abandoning the unfinished agendas of the revolutions that brought them into being, nationalisms against the state aim at repairing the disconnect between state and nation with a view to making the state representative of the nation. It should be emphasized that although directed against the current incumbents of the state apparatus, nationalisms against the state are not necessarily anti-state. Both movements studied here clearly envisage a role for the state as a defensive barrier against global capital, even if—like the Zapatistas—they do not aspire to occupy the apparatus of state themselves.

Although the movements studied in this chapter operate in vastly different contexts from those to which Marx, Engels, and Lenin were responding, there is at least one respect in which a comparison may be drawn: rather than positing an antithetical opposition between cosmopolitanism and nationalism, both forms of consciousness are seen as playing a mutually reinforcing role in the struggle for global social redistribution. Far from seeing nationalism as inescapably bourgeois, Marx and Engels exhorted the proletariat to infuse the concept of the nation with their interests so that they could wrest state power away from the dominant classes and use it to further the global proletarian revolution. Lenin's view of imperialism as the highest stage of capitalism gave him an appreciation of the role that anti-colonial nationalism could play in overthrowing the international bourgeoisie. In their more realist moments, all three saw support for anti-colonial nationalist struggles as having the potential to boost the fortunes of a flagging internationalism.

Writing in the context of post-colonial states that have become increasingly transnationalized, Pheng Cheah, following Samir Amin, has argued that 'uneven globalization makes the formation of popular nationalist movements in the periphery the first step on the long road to social redistribution'.[124] Recognizing that transnational networks need to work with and through popular nationalisms to achieve maximum political effectiveness, Cheah's description of the actors implicated in such a politics as 'nationalisms operating in a cosmopolitical force field'[125] seems more appropriate to the movements studied in this chapter than the nationalist–globalist categories adopted by conventional typologies of the 'anti-globalist' space. This view of the potential role of nationalism in contemporary anti-capitalist politics also offers a basis for critique of sequential or teleological views of the role of nationalism held by the authors discussed in chapter 4 and indeed sometimes by Marx and Engels themselves. Rather than relegating nationalism to a transitory phase through which subaltern or proletarian groups must pass on their way to cosmopolitan consciousness, we should see it as a recurring and potentially renewing discourse that might have the capacity to repair the unmooring of the state from the nation, thereby contributing to the project of global social redistribution.

Lest this chapter conveys too inflated a sense of the ethical credentials, prospects for success or representativeness of the movements under consideration, three sobering caveats are in order. First, the simultaneous articulation of cosmopolitan and national consciousness frequently generates embarrassing and potentially damaging dissonances, particularly where rhetorics directed at different audiences contradict one another. In this context, it is important to ask what resonance cosmopolitan 'global framing' rhetoric has for local audiences. (What does a Tzotzil Mayan peasant make of Marcos's identification with gay liberation? Should this matter?) Moreover, how familiar are global allies with the often deeply problematic local politics of a social movement? (How has a movement of petty capitalists like the KRRS become part of an anarchist network like PGA that advertises itself as being 'clearly anti-capitalist (not just anti-neoliberal)'?)[126]

These disjunctures also draw attention to the high degree of instrumentality in the choice of rhetoric and framing strategies. An entirely instrumentalist reading of the discourse of such movements would, however, be overly reductionist. Frames are not mere ploys, costumes donned for particular audiences. They typically correspond to real aspects of a conflict. Indeed they have to, if they are to be persuasive. Astute framing is about choosing from amongst the two or three most plausible ways of describing a conflict, the frame that would maximize media attention and solidarity. Further, the instrumental invocation of cosmopolitan or nationalist rhetorics is not a one-way street. Claims that are made for initially instrumental purposes can 'stick' to become constitutive of subjects, if they value their reputations, because their persuasiveness depends on a reasonable congruence between rhetoric and reality.[127]

A second caveat that should be borne in mind is that only actors who concede a role for the state in regulating capitalism are likely to be interested in renationalizing the state with a view to using it to regulate capitalism. Actors who see the state as irredeemably mortgaged to capital, and therefore disavow the project of capturing or reorienting the state, are unlikely to find nationalism useful in this way. As such, the movements described in this chapter should be understood as one major tendency within the anti-capitalist space rather than representative of that space as a whole.

Third, even amongst movements that concede a role for the state, those located in very weak states may not consider the recuperation of national sovereignty a worthwhile component of a global socialist politics, preferring instead to push for a reconstitution of sovereignty at a 'higher' regional or even global level. In this sense as well, the movements studied in this chapter may not be representative, located as they are in strong states like Mexico and India that possess a relatively greater ability to regulate capital than most Third World states. In very weak states where the prospects for regulation of capital rest on the reconstitution of sovereignty at regional or other levels, we may see cosmopolitanism conjoined with regional forms of consciousness such as pan-Africanism. The central point of this chapter about the political necessity and utility of the conjunction of such forms of consciousness would continue to hold, but in a suitably modified form.

6

Queer in the Time of Terror

> Some men like Jack
> And some like Jill;
> I'm glad I like
> them both; but still
> I wonder if
> this freewheeling
> really is an
> enlightened thing—
> or is its greater
> scope a sign
> of deviance from
> some party line?
> In the strict ranks
> of Gay and Straight
> what is my status?
> Stray? or Great?
>
> Vikram Seth, 'Dubious', *Mappings* (1981)*

Homosexual behaviour has been observed in virtually all cultures throughout recorded history. Yet the transformation of sexuality into an aspect of personal identity—the presumption, as akshay khanna puts it, 'that who I fuck or am attracted to says something about the type of person I am'—is both a more recent and culturally specific development.[1] Following Foucault,[2] scholars locate the emergence of homosexual identities in the West in the late nineteenth century and tend to explain this with reference to the operation of discourses of medicine and law. The dislocations produced by industrial capitalism and mass urbanization were simultaneously disrupting traditional family structures and providing the conditions—for some—of individual material self-sufficiency and anonymity that enabled the configuration of new forms of community around non-heteronormative identities. The expression of these identities in the Third World is said to have been made possible by the diffusion of these enabling conditions via the spread of capitalism and reinforced by the advent of AIDS, which opened up space for the political organization of sexual minorities considered to be particularly vulnerable to the disease.[3] Yet independently of

---

* © Vikram Seth, 1981.

these developments, there have long been transgendered groups in many Third World societies (e.g. *hijras* in India, *kathoeys* in Thailand), whose public transgressions of heteronormative behaviour have marked them out as visible sexual minorities.

As Third World activism around issues of concern to sexual minorities is increasingly articulated in terms of identity categories such as 'lesbian', 'gay', 'bisexual', and 'transgendered' (LGBT) that originated in the West, it has become possible to speak of a cosmopolitan discourse of 'LGBT rights'.[4] Such a discourse is constituted by self-identifying LGBT groups in most countries of the world including those that repress such identities, dedicated global LGBT advocacy organizations and networks such as the International Lesbian, Gay, Bisexual, Trans and Intersex Association (ILGA) set up in 1978 and the International Gay and Lesbian Human Rights Commission (IGLHRC) founded in 1990, LGBT advocacy sections within existing human rights organizations such as Amnesty International and Human Rights Watch (HRW), and the proliferation of national and international judicial decisions and 'soft law' instruments such as the 2006 Yogyakarta Principles on the Application of International Human Rights Law in Relation to Sexual Orientation and Gender Identity.[5]

Empowering as it has been for its participants, the construction of this discourse and a global politics of LGBT solidarity has not been an entirely benign development, free from questions of power and hierarchy. As LGBT communities have won political and legal battles in the West and have begun to assimilate ever more deeply into their respective societies, LGBT rights have become a marker of modernity, resulting in the creation of new hierarchies—what Jon Binnie calls 'a new racism'—in international politics.[6] States that fail to respect rights around sexual diversity are increasingly characterized as backward and uncivilized, with the internationalization of LGBT rights taking on the character of a modern day civilizing mission. Many have noted the historical irony here, in that while eighteenth- and nineteenth-century representations of the 'Orient' were replete with images of decadence and licentiousness (harems, concubines, pederasty, and so forth), the contemporary 'non-West' is castigated for its sexual repression. Importantly, this stigmatization is not directed solely at state functionaries who repress sexual minorities. As Neville Hoad has argued, much contemporary LGBT activism and scholarship is informed by a teleological developmental narrative in which sexual minorities who have not 'yet' made the transition from homosexual behaviour to identity are seen as occupying a preliminary stage in the hegemonic trajectory of sexuality activism as established in the West:

... we were like them, but have developed, they are like we were and have yet to develop. Space is temporalised and difference hierarchised, with the modern male homosexual taking the place of the normative white male heterosexual in an uninterrogated replication of the old evolutionary narrative.[7]

Third World feminists and feminists of colour in the West have long problematized assumptions of 'global sisterhood', alerting us to the hierarchies of race, class, and nationality that mark the global women's movement.[8] This chapter seeks to extend some of these insights to global queer activism, a task that has become politically urgent in the wake of recent controversies that have erupted around such activism in relation to the Middle East and Africa. The critique of the new cosmopolitan discourse of LGBT rights offered in this chapter will therefore be a contextual one, emerging out of a discussion of these controversies. It also comes out of my own involvement with queer movements in India, whose strategic and tactical dilemmas provide additional material for some of the arguments of this chapter.

Yet in being critical of global activism around sexual diversity, it is vital that we not lose sight of the reality of homophobia in the Third World (or indeed anywhere). In virtually all societies in which homosexuality is criminalized or socially stigmatized, cosmopolitan claims to LGBT rights are contested in a communitarian language that speaks to the preservation of a particular culture, religion, or 'way of life'.[9] Homosexuality is frequently cast as a corrupting, alien influence, imported from a decadent 'West'. Genealogical analyses of the institutionalization of homophobia in many Third World states have rendered the communitarian credentials of these claims deeply suspect. For example, Marc Epprecht has argued that while politicized homophobia in Zimbabwe (and other parts of Africa) does indeed have some roots in traditional African culture, 'it is also enormously indebted to Christian missionary propaganda, Western pseudo-science, and the demonstration effect of White Rhodesian "cowboy" culture'.[10] Building on the painstaking scholarship of Ruth Vanita and Saleem Kidwai on representations of same-sex love in Indian literary and historical texts, Arvind Narrain notes an amplification of homophobia in colonial India under the influence of Western discourses of law, medicine, and literature.[11] Both Epprecht and Narrain attribute the erasure of indigenous traditions of androgyny and same-sex behaviour to a perceived need to construct virile African and Indian nationalisms that countered colonial representations of the Orient as licentious, decadent, or childlike. Without valorizing the pre-colonial period, these scholars locate the institutionalization of homophobia in the colonial encounter, reminding us of its debts to both colonialism and nationalism. Yet notwithstanding these complicated genealogies, most contemporary articulations of homophobia are voiced in a self-consciously communitarian idiom that claims to uphold local norms of social morality against an imported vice.

A central preoccupation of this chapter is to find a language in which to criticize the hierarchies and supremacism that lurk within the cosmopolitan politics of LGBT solidarity without minimizing or ignoring the oppressiveness of communitarian homophobia. Joseph Massad's recent intervention in this field illustrates the dangers of failing to strike this balance. Massad is fiercely critical of Western LGBT solidarity politics as exemplified by the work of organizations such as ILGA, IGLHRC, and HRW. Their activities, in his view, take the form of an attempt to transform practitioners of same-sex conduct in the Arab world into subjects who identify as homosexual. Massad argues that the consequences of this push from behaviour to identity—what he calls, following Foucault, 'incitement to discourse'—are far from liberating.[12] He makes two claims: first, that by imposing a Western sexual ontology on Arab subjects, international LGBT activism is essentially an exercise in cultural imperialism, obliterating indigenous forms of sexual subjectivity; second, that the expression of sexual difference in the form of an LGBT identity politics renders sexual minorities increasingly visible, thereby inviting governmental repression which shuts down existing spaces for same-sex behaviour. This latter claim is evidenced with reference to incidents such as the arrest and prosecution of men alleged to be 'practising debauchery' (a veiled reference to same-sex conduct) aboard the floating Queen Boat discotheque in Cairo, Egypt, in May 2001. In Massad's view, such repression does not target same-sex sexual practices, as much as the socio-political identification of these practices with the Western identity of gayness.[13]

While there is much truth to Massad's claims about the aggressively orientalizing tendencies of some contemporary Western LGBT activism, there is also something deeply troubling about his denial of the agency and subjectivity of Arabs who are appropriating and reworking Western identities in their struggles for sexual self-determination. Massad dismisses such individuals as unrepresentative—'a miniscule minority', 'small groups of men in metropolitan areas such as Cairo and Beirut'[14]—but also, more ominously, as 'native informants' to Western activists, a phrase that is loaded with colonial memories of indigenous elites engaged in traitorous collaboration with colonizing powers. In addition, he assumes that their motivation for identification in terms of Western sexual identities is class-based: 'part of the package of the adoption of everything Western by the classes to which they belong'.[15] While class position certainly gives such individuals access to Western sexual ontologies, it cannot be assumed a priori that the motivation for identification in these terms is a consumerist one rather than, say, something that stems from a deep dissatisfaction with the 'traditional' sexual ontology. Rather than treating the question of motivation as an empirical one, Massad has in effect decided that coming out as gay in the Arab world is less about wanting to live in truth and more akin to buying the latest Calvin Klein underwear. While openly gay Arabs in the Middle East may be few in number, their characterization as faddish and traitorous amounts to a transhistorical normative claim about how Arabs ought to express non-heteronormative preferences. In effect, in criticizing cosmopolitan rescue politics and its local interlocutors, Massad slips into a reinforcement of communitarian authenticity narratives that police how sexual preferences ought to be expressed. There is something to his second, more tactical, criticism that the move from behaviour to identity invites governmental repression, and indeed many authors have made this argument.[16] Yet rather than shutting down activism around sexuality altogether, this begs the question of what sorts of activism are possible without identity politics, particularly in jurisdictions where sexual minority identities are criminalized.[17]

In contexts where rebellion against the 'traditional' sexual ontology has the potential to incur grave sanctions, it seems more reasonable to suppose that such rebellion is occasioned more by a sense of grievance against that ontology—a feeling of victimization by its patriarchal assumptions and expectations—than as part of an impulse to consume all things Western. If this is the case, then the question of global solidarity does not disappear: indeed, the task becomes one of making sure that we do not throw the baby of global solidarity out with the bathwater of imperialist activism. Section 6.1 attempts this task in the context of a recent controversy around Western LGBT activism vis-à-vis Iran. Massad's account of Western solidarity politics is an indiscriminate critique of the totality of international LGBT activism that emanates from the West, the institutions of which he collectively refers to as the 'Gay International' (reminiscent of W. H. Auden's 'homintern'). In contrast, I attempt to disaggregate the 'Gay International' into its constituent strands, bringing to light distinct manifestations of a gay rescue narrative on both the political right and left, produced by different actors with very different sorts of motivations (the focus here is on activists in the United States and the United Kingdom). Demonstrating that there is no single politics to this 'Gay International' is a first step towards deciding whether there is anything worth salvaging in its politics of putative solidarity with Third World sexual minorities. Section 6.2 considers the dilemmas and strategies of Third World queer activists and queer activists of colour in the West, who find themselves contesting both power hierarchies within cosmopolitan queer solidarity and communitarian homophobia claiming to uphold tradition. Section 6.3 considers the use of cosmopolitan and communitarian strategies by queer activists in India.

It would be disingenuous to pretend that my interest in the subject of this chapter had nothing to do with my positionality. Being explicit about positionality entails a certain transparency about one's motivations for pursuing particular lines of enquiry as well as about the prejudices and preconceptions with which one approaches them. On the one hand, as an upper-middle class, English-speaking, urban, gay man of Indian nationality who now lives in London and Bangalore, I suppose I am one of Massad's 'native informants'—part of that allegedly 'miniscule minority' in the Third World who identify in terms derived from a Western sexual ontology. Part of my antipathy towards his argument stems from his failure to problematize the 'traditional' sexual ontology from which I departed or to appreciate my reasons for doing so. As in many parts of the non-Western world, this ontology permitted some space for same-sex behaviour, but condemned any expression of homosexual identity. The physical, mental, and emotional costs that such an ontology exacts in the form of broken relationships, sham heterosexual marriages, suicides, lack of legal and social recognition of what are otherwise deeply fulfilling personal relationships, lack of access to health care, etc. are well documented in many countries, but remain unacknowledged in Massad's argument. These dissatisfactions mean that a considerable part of my activist energies are directed against the Indian state and the local communities to which I belong (family, neighbourhood, school, work, religion) with a view to reshaping a sexual ontology that condemns me to a sort of half-life, devoid of many of the pleasures and prerogatives that heterosexual people take for granted.

On the other hand, I have always been vexed by the geography of my 'coming out'—a process that began after I left India for Britain as a graduate student. One rather distressing social reading of the expression of my sexuality is that emigration to the West liberated me. Although rarely articulated in so many words, this reading is manifest in such well-meaning questions as 'Are you sure you want to go back to India?' The emigration-as-liberation narrative is irritating and incomplete, first because it fails to acknowledge the idiosyncrasies of my coming out process—*my* sexual and emotional history; *my* relationship with parents, family, and friends; *my* professional milieu, etc. Prior to any effort to obtain information about my specific circumstances (or perhaps to obviate the need to make any such effort), essentializations of what 'India' is like in these different respects assist in constructing a narrative that appears to account for the timing of my coming out. But the narrative chafes because it fails to acknowledge the deeply liberating influence of individuals, movements, and spaces[18] in India, without which coming out would have entailed not only a physical distancing from, but also a political and emotional jettisoning of, 'India'—a price that I would have considered too high to pay. In effect, both the 'traditional' sexual ontology and my well-meaning Western interlocutors have been complicit in producing 'India' as a homophobic space in which the assertion of homosexual identities is simply inconceivable. Yet notwithstanding my antipathy towards the 'emigration-as-liberation' reading of my sexual self-assertion, I am aware—from the increasing numbers of stories of people claiming asylum on grounds of persecution on the basis of sexual orientation—that for many people, emigration *is* liberation. Moreover, I have to remind myself that the elevation of autobiography to metanarrative is the worst kind of provincialism.

6.1 HANGINGS IN IRAN: DISAGGREGATING THE 'GAY INTERNATIONAL'

On 19 July 2005, two boys—Ayaz Marhoni and Mahmoud Asgari—variously reported to have been between 16 and 18 years of age, were hanged by the government of Iran in the city of Mashhad, for an alleged crime involving homosexual intercourse. Western activists were bitterly divided over how to respond.[19] Some regarded the boys as having been hanged on account of their sexuality and fiercely denounced the government of Iran, demanding that Western governments take punitive action. British activist Peter Tatchell, whose group OutRage! first brought the story to the attention of Western media, was quoted in a press release as saying 'This is just the latest barbarity by the Islamo-fascists in Iran . . . the entire country is a gigantic prison, with Islamic rule sustained by detention without trial, torture and state-sanctioned murder', before going on to claim that over 4,000 lesbians and gay men had been executed by the government since the 1979 revolution.[20] Conservative US commentator Andrew Sullivan echoed this language, repeating the claim that the boys had been hanged by the 'Islamo-fascist regime in Iran' for 'being gay'. Expressing disappointment that more gay organizations had not rallied to the war against 'Muslim religious fanatics', Sullivan emphasized: 'this is our war too'.[21] The linkage of Iran with fascism was reinforced by Doug Ireland, a journalist based in New York, who described the Ahmadinejad government as being engaged in a 'major anti-homosexual pogrom targeting gays and gay sex'.[22] The Human Rights Campaign, the largest LGBT civil rights organization in the United States, called upon the then Secretary of State Condoleezza Rice, to issue an 'immediate and strong condemnation' of Iran for its hanging of the teenagers who, it alleged, had been tortured and killed 'simply for being caught having consensual sex'. It urged that 'atrocities committed by foreign governments against all people must be condemned swiftly and forcefully by the world's greatest democracy'.[23] The Log Cabin Republicans, an organization of gay and lesbian members of the US Republican Party, issued a press release in which it noted that 'In the wake of news stories and photographs documenting the hanging of two gay Iranian teenagers, Log Cabin Republicans re-affirm their commitment to the global war on terror'. The group's President Patrick Guerriero is quoted as saying 'This barbarous slaughter clearly demonstrates the stakes in the global war on terror. Freedom must prevail over radical Islamic extremism'.[24]

It was not the first time that Western observers had expressed revulsion at the sexual mores of Iranian society. In an ironic reversal of contemporary attitudes, travelogues of Western visitors to Iran between the seventeenth and nineteenth centuries frequently record disgust at the observation of same-sex liaisons within aristocratic and court circles in Tehran. In her work on the 'gender and sexual anxieties of Iranian modernity', Afsaneh Najmabadi notes some dramatic and perplexing shifts in representation in Iranian culture and traces these to the encounter with the West. For example, while notions of beauty were largely undifferentiated by gender in early Qajar (1785–1925) paintings with beautiful men and women being depicted with very similar facial and bodily features, by the end of the nineteenth century the portrayal of beauty had become less androgynous and more gendered. In a similar vein, while biographical writing well into the nineteenth century contains numerous non-judgemental references to diverse sexual preferences, twentieth-century references to same-sex relationships are much more disapproving. Najmabadi attributes these shifts, in part, to a growing Iranian awareness of European disapproval of the homosociality of Iranian society and the same-sex practices that this engendered. This fuelled an anxiety on the part of Iranian elites to disavow the very practices that their European interlocutors considered vices.[25] If the heteronormalization of Iranian society was a marker of modernity in the late nineteenth century, the exact opposite has become true in the early twenty-first.

Returning to the events of 2005, Western voices of condemnation were divided in terms of the remedial action that they advocated. Some like Sullivan and the Log Cabin Republicans regarded incidents such as the Mashhad hangings as vindicating the use of force against 'radical Islam' wherever it manifested itself; others like Tatchell and OutRage! sought to clarify that their denunciation of the hangings did not amount to an endorsement of war against Iran.[26] Indeed, Tatchell appears incongruous amongst the many Republican Party-affiliated gay voices in the United States who happened to agree with him on this issue. He has long campaigned for quintessentially left-wing causes and is currently a member of the Green Party in Britain, which stands to the left of the Labour Party on virtually all issues. Although appearing to share a common position, these different reactions to the Iran hangings were underpinned by quite distinct sets of political considerations, which I discuss later in this section.

Larger organizations such as HRW and IGLHRC responded in a very different fashion, questioning the veracity of information about the case coming out of Iran and citing conflicting reports that the boys had been hanged for raping a 13-year-old boy. They sought to reframe the issue as one about the execution of minors—a violation of the UN Convention on the Rights of the Child and the International Covenant on Civil and Political Rights (both of which Iran has signed). One crucial implication of this reframing was that if Iran were to be censured for its execution of children, the US lacked the moral standing to do so. Of the nine countries that are known to have executed juvenile offenders between 1990 and 2009, while Iran topped the list with forty-six executions, the United States followed second with nineteen.[27] (The US Supreme Court declared the use of the death penalty against juvenile offenders unconstitutional in March 2005.[28]) In addition, activists at HRW and IGLHRC worried that vitriolic attacks on Iran by gay activists could legitimate the Bush administration's demonization of the Iranian regime at a time when tensions were already running high on account of its nuclear programme as well as the election of the conservative Ahmadinejad to the office of president only a few weeks before. Distancing themselves from protests organized by OutRage!, they convened a parallel event at the New York LGBT Community Centre together with groups such as the National Gay and Lesbian Task Force (NGLTF), at which the focus of discussion was changed to one of introspection for Westerners: 'How do we avoid reinforcing stereotypes and playing into hostilities prompted by our own government?'[29] I now turn to an examination of the politics of each of these responses.

In the wake of the July 2005 hangings in Iran, it was possible to discern the emergence of a discourse on right-wing gay web sites based in the United States and Europe, in which gay rights were pitted against the putative beliefs of 'Islamists'. A central feature of this discourse is that it placed LGBT rights at the heart of an enlightened Judaeo-Christian 'West', which confronted a uniformly homophobic 'non-West' 'sunk in ignorance, superstition, barbarism, and moral darkness',[30] evidenced by its failure to respect such rights. Indeed, the very purpose of the comparisons by means of which this narrative is constructed seems to be the extraction of a hierarchy in which the West is better than the non-West, Israel is superior to Palestine,[31] Christianity is preferable to Islam,[32] and so on. Spivak has characterized colonial feminism—

exemplified by such acts as the British abolition of sati in India in the nineteenth century—as a case of 'white men, seeking to save brown women from brown men'.[33] Through such gestures, imperialism represents itself as the establisher of the good society by espousing women as objects of protection from their own (racial and national) kind. Something similar appears to be at work in the contemporary eagerness of white gays to save brown gays from brown homophobes.

Although this rescue narrative represents itself in universalist categories as seeking to empower non-Western sexual minorities to express putatively universal sexual longings, it is worth marking out the specificity of these discourses by noting the particular conditions of their emergence. Jasbir K. Puar's notion of homonormative nationalism or 'homo-nationalism' is useful in understanding some of the impetus for rescue narratives, particularly as they operate in contemporary US political life. Borrowing from Lisa Duggan's idea of 'homonormativity' which refers broadly to the phenomenon of gay subjects becoming embroiled in a politics that does not contest dominant heteronormative forms but upholds and sustains them, Puar defines 'homo-nationalism' as a 'collusion between homosexuality and American nationalism that is generated both by national rhetorics of patriotic inclusion and by gay, lesbian, and queer subjects themselves'.[34] Contrary to conventional gendered readings of state and nation as being only supportive and productive of heterosexuality and always repressive and disallowing of homosexuality, Puar suggests that 'there is room for the absorption and management of homosexuality...when advantageous for US national interests'.[35]

From the perspective of the US state, such absorption might enable the co-option of LGBT rights as additional legitimation for the 'war on terror' and the project to reshape the Middle East.[36] The harnessing of 'Islamist persecution of LGBT rights' in this fashion is analogous to the use of the Taliban's persecution of Afghan women as justification for the war against Afghanistan launched in 2001.[37] Yet it might legitimately be asked whether a homophobic Republican US administration—such as the one in power in 2005—might have had any interest in using alleged LGBT persecution in the Middle East in this fashion. It might be thought, for example, that significant constituencies within the party base (evangelical Christians come to mind) would have been alienated by any advancement of LGBT rights either domestically or abroad. In what ways might the 'absorption and management of homosexuality' advantage the US state, particularly when it has been captured by the homophobic right?

Two quick responses are possible. First, the existence of a group such as the Log Cabin Republicans who, as mentioned earlier, regarded the Mashhad hangings as vindicating their commitment to the 'war on terror', testifies to the emergence of a gay rescue narrative within the party. Second, the global status of LGBT rights has become institutionalized as a matter of bipartisan concern to the US state. Since 1991, the State Department—under pressure from activists such as Michael Petrelis, Margaret Cantrell, and Barrett Brick—has included information about human rights abuses against sexual minorities on account of their sexual orientation in its Country Human Rights Reports.[38] In so far as the US government uses human rights instrumentally for the achievement of strategic objectives, LGBT rights are now fair game.

Yet the more significant motivations for the gay rescue narrative may lie not in the international interests of the US state so much as within the realm of US domestic politics. It is worth recalling that the narrative is produced, not by state functionaries, but by mostly right-wing non-governmental gay activists. It could be argued that it is the very incompleteness of their inclusion within the US nation and the Republican Party more specifically, which furnishes a powerful incentive for collusion between homosexuality and nationalism. Offering a 'gay' reason for supporting nationalist projects such as the 'war on terror', the gay rescue narrative becomes a means of expressing patriotic sentiment with a view to hastening assimilation into nation and party. Patriotism functions as what Puar calls a 'defensive and normalizing' gesture,[39] signalling proximity to a nation and party of which one is not (yet) a full member by emphasizing distance from ultimate others. Through the gay rescue narrative, the message that right-wing gay activists appear to be sending to a Republican Party whose acceptance they crave seems to be: 'you are against the terrorists; the terrorists are against gays; therefore you ought to be with gays'.

If assimilation at home rather than solidarity with distant others explains the predominant motivation behind the production of rescue narratives by right-wing constituents of the Gay International, how do we understand the politics of someone like Peter Tatchell, who would typically be seen as 'left-wing' in both the United States and the United Kingdom? Tatchell has been dismissive of the suggestion—which I put to him in an interview in 2007—that his activism against the Iranian regime might have played into the hands of warmongering neoconservatives, offering a decidedly anti-consequentialist argument for the position that he took. Hitting back at his critics (organizations such as HRW and IGLHRC, which distanced themselves from his protests), he says:

> They seem to take the view that because the United States is against Iran, we mustn't do anything that fuels the argument that Iran is a bad regime. My view is very simple. Human rights are universal and indivisible,

whether in Iran, Britain or the United States. There's no ifs, no buts. You defend the persecuted and oppose the oppressor... there's no qualifications, there's no exceptions, it's universal, for everyone, everywhere, in all circumstances, at all times... I'm fed up with leftwing—well what I call the rightwing left—who say, "I'm sorry, I sympathise with the execution of the Arabs in south-west Iran[40] but, I'm sorry, they'll have to die. The bigger picture is we've got to stop the war, we've got to stop the US attack on Iran." It's not either/or. The two things go hand in hand. The idea that sections of the far left, the sectarian left, are prepared to sacrifice the lives of other human beings for the greater good—that is the road to Stalinism and Pol Pot.... They're saying "those lives are expendable. They might in other circumstances be worthwhile protesting about, but not now. Because the greater good demands that we do everything to ensure that the neocons have no arguments or evidence to back their case".[41]

In a recent article, Scott Long of HRW has alleged that Tatchell's initial press releases—which alerted the Western world to the 2005 hangings—relied on mistranslated accounts of Iranian news reports. The erroneous translation reported that the boys had been executed for the crime of *lavat* (sodomy), rather than that of *lavat beh onf* (sodomy by force, i.e. rape). Long concedes that Tatchell may have been misled by Iranian dissident exiles, seeking to whip up protest against the Iranian regime for their own purposes. But he also suggests that Tatchell may have had his own reasons for reframing the issue as one about the execution of gay boys. Long offers a speculative account of what those reasons might have been, referring to Tatchell's need for new enemies after a long-running campaign against religious homophobia, primarily of the Anglican Church.[42] The specificities of these speculations need not detain us here, but they point to a broader and more fundamental set of motivations underpinning the activism of figures like Tatchell.

In appreciating these, it is vital to bear in mind that in comparison with conservative activists in the United States, Tatchell operates from a more gay-friendly jurisdiction in which LGBT citizens have won a number of significant victories, particularly since the election of a Labour government in 1997. Indeed for British and northern European activists, the fulfilment of much of the LGBT rights agenda at home has freed up time and resources and added a moral impetus for the internationalization of activism on behalf of distant others who are seen as less fortunate. This is not to suggest that sexual minorities in these countries have achieved all their aims, but with the 'great' victories of decriminalization, same-sex partnerships and—in some cases—marriage behind them, the existential crisis experienced by activists as a result of these achievements is alleviated to some extent by human rights abuses in the Third World that can be framed as gay rights violations. In his work on the 'marketing of rebellion' (discussed in Chapter 5), Bob reminds us that while it is easy to appreciate why Third World insurgencies need generous Western patrons, it is important to recognize that the latter derive significant non-material resources from their Third World interlocutors: a raison d'être, legitimation for international activism, proof that their agenda remains unfulfilled, symbols for broader campaigns, prestige with their support base, etc.[43] All of these may be plausible motivations for Tatchell's interest in framing human rights abuses abroad as gay rights violations.

Indeed, criticism of his activism is often met with the response that his interventions are explicitly requested by sexual minorities suffering oppression in distant parts of the world. This emphasis on the authorization or legitimation of activism parallels a phenomenon that is increasingly evident in the field of development, where a new orthodoxy insists that development must be 'owned' by its intended beneficiaries, an outcome that requires listening to the previously silenced voices of subalterns. Yet, critics of the modified development discourse of ownership have pointed out that the act of listening is in itself an exercise in power, with agents of development attempting to set the terms of their encounter with previously silent subalterns. As Cynthia Wood notes sceptically in the context of the 'women and development' literature:

> We decide to whom we will speak and which of the many silenced voices it is important to hear. We do not want to listen to anything unpleasant. It is unlikely that we will try to speak with someone we know is 'uncooperative' or unsupportive of development. Implicit in our new project is the demand that the third world woman perform for us, within the limits of our needs and desires.[44]

These problems are evident in Tatchell's relations with activists in other parts of the world. Arsham Parsi, a gay Iranian activist who obtained asylum in Canada from persecution on account of sexual orientation, is critical of Tatchell's brand of activism, arguing that his commemoration of the July 2005 hangings with protests outside Iranian embassies a year later was counterproductive and politically damaging.[45] When I put it to Tatchell that some Iranian activists appeared to be critical of what he was doing he was surprised at first, arguing that Parsi was initially supportive of the protests and changed his mind only after he had been influenced by Long. That Parsi was initially supportive appears to be true, given that he had himself incurred criticism from other Iranian activists for standing with Tatchell on the issue.[46] Tatchell is also quick to point out that Parsi does not speak for all Iranian homosexuals. He claims that there were five Iranian LGBT groups or magazines at the time of the commemorations, four of which supported his protests. He cites a letter of support issued by MAHA, an e-list which claims a subscription of 1,700 members and a readership of 3,000–5,000, which strongly endorsed the protests despite the controvery they generated.[47] Tatchell's claims of support are difficult to verify, given his unwillingness to reveal the identity of his interlocutors and the general difficulties of studying the political organization of homosexuals in Iran. Nonetheless, even if his claims are true, they do not elide the problems outlined by Wood. In a field apparently crowded with 'native informants', the Western solidarity activist seems to reach out to those who endorse his project, while ignoring the criticisms of those who do not.

These issues recur more starkly in Tatchell's relations with African activists. In January 2007, a group of African activists published an unprecedented 'statement of warning' which read: 'we strongly discourage the public from taking part in any LGBTI campaigns or calls to action concerning Africa that are led by Peter Tatchell or OutRage!'.[48] OutRage! was accused of a number of irregularities including the use of improperly verified information, quotation out of context, failure to consult with 'relevant local activists' and 'local genuine activists', and exaggeration of the violations committed by governments, etc. This last charge was underscored by the allegation that such exaggerations left local activists vulnerable to attack by governments for claims they had never made.

In background notes to the statement, which was signed by activists from over ten African countries, OutRage!'s activism in relation to Nigeria and Uganda were singled out for condemnation. In the case of Nigeria, the problem seems to have arisen out of differences over how to respond to a same-sex marriage prohibition bill that had been introduced in the federal legislature. Many activists were opposed to Tatchell's call for a public campaign against the Nigerian government, believing that this would revive governmental interest in a bill that was virtually dead thanks to behind-the-scenes pressure on Nigerian lawmakers. The public statement explains further:

> After being warned that the advice of Nigerian activists is to refrain from putting attention on the dormant bill, OutRage! looked for some individual in Nigeria to support them in the course they had already chosen to take. To serve this purpose, Leo Igwe's comments were quoted in . . . [a] press release and are being taken out of context. While Leo is a very courageous friend and ally of the movement, OutRage! should have contacted and requested

advice on strategy from the LGBTI Human Rights Defenders who led the original campaign against the bill from Nigeria.[49]

The charges in respect of Uganda are less delicately put, with the Chairperson of Sexual Minorities Uganda (SMUG), Juliet Victor Mukasa, accusing Tatchell of having made unverified allegations against the government which would ultimately hurt local activists: 'You will sit safely in London while our activists in Uganda pay the price for your deeds'.[50]

Tatchell reacts robustly to these charges, insisting that in both cases he was acting on instructions received from local activists. In the Ugandan case, he alleges further that SMUG's denunciation of OutRage! stems from petty local turf rivalries. In his view, SMUG resented the fact that OutRage! was publicizing and collaborating with other Ugandan groups such as Gay and Lesbian Alliance (GALA) and Makerere University Students' Lesbian Association (MUSLA), fearing that if these groups obtained a higher international profile, they would begin to compete with SMUG for external funding and assistance. Tatchell charges Mukasa with wanting to be 'the gatekeeper, the kingpin of the Ugandan lesbian-gay rights movement'.[51] In a press release following the publication of the African statement, OutRage! characterized its critics as well-funded reformist groups who mistrust the more radical volunteer grassroots activists with whom OutRage! has closer links. Tatchell insists that his activism continues to be legitimated by the support of many Nigerian and Ugandan activists.

As with Iran, it is impossible to verify many of these claims, given Tatchell's insistence on the need to maintain the confidentiality of his sources and local interlocutors. Nonetheless, these controversies illustrate the power struggles in which left-wing constituents of the Gay International are implicated, despite the rather different motivations that underpin their activism. Western solidarity activists gravitate towards local interlocutors who desire their presence, while ignoring those who do not. Often the choice of particular local interlocutors is made with reference to some externally imposed test of authenticity—thus, Tatchell argues that GALA and MUSLA are better interlocutors than SMUG 'because these people are on the ground. They're not in Cape Town or Johannesburg. They're on the ground in Uganda'.[52] It is possible that local interlocutors are being chosen on the basis of their claims to greater representativity, but one is left with the lingering suspicion that the choice of interlocutors may be guided more by considerations of who might serve as the most useful authenticators of international activism. The attempt to seek legitimation by authorization is complicated by the fact that local interlocutors are not abject, apolitical actors suffering oppression, but are complex subjects with interests and agendas of their own. The entry of resource-rich solidarity activists into an already fractious terrain can set off a competitive dynamic amongst local interlocutors competing with one another to be privileged informants in anticipation of the potential rewards that might flow from such relationships. Far from assisting in the creation of a united front against homophobia, the external activist can exacerbate local tensions and rivalries.

Finally, one has to consider the politics of the big organizations in the Gay International (Amnesty, HRW, IGLHRC, etc.). Such actors are vulnerable to many of the same criticisms they level at Tatchell. They too 'need' human rights violations abroad as a reason for being, and have an interest in framing power struggles in different parts of the world as 'rights violations' with a view to sustaining particular programmes and campaigns. They share the same sexual ontology as the right- and left-wing gay saviours discussed here. In this sense, Massad is not wrong to speak of the Gay International as a collectivity. In the context of their reactions to the 2005 executions in Iran, however, some crucial distinctions have to be made.

First, notwithstanding their common ontological premises, these organizations have tended to be wary of foisting a Western sexual ontology on subjects in countries like Iran in the absence of evidence of self-identification in these terms by those subjects. When Makwan Mouloudzadeh, a 21-year-old Iranian man, was sentenced to death in June 2007 on charges of having raped three boys when he was himself only 13, groups like OutRage! and the Italian collective Gruppo Everyone once again treated the case as one of gay persecution and lobbied the Iranian government vociferously in these terms, demanding that the sentence be lifted. In contrast Amnesty and HRW, following investigations which revealed no evidence of any sexual acts whatsoever, flatly denied that Mouloudzadeh was gay and sought to reframe advocacy around the issue as one about the execution of juveniles. Their position was based not only on evidentiary considerations, but also on the ground that it was tactically ill-advised to campaign for Mouloudzadeh as a 'gay' person in a country where homosexual conduct, whether consensual or not, carries the death penalty. Despite a brief window of hope in which the sentence was suspended by the head of Iran's judiciary pending an official investigation into allegations of trial irregularities, Mouloudzadeh was executed in December of that year. Long argues that the framing of advocacy on his behalf in terms of gay rights did real damage to his case, possibly inducing the Iranian authorities to carry out the sentence.[53] Given that key actors in the Gay International share Massad's tactical criticisms of gay rights campaigning, it seems wrong to tar the International as a whole with the same brush.[54]

Second, the larger human rights organizations have tended to be more sensitive to the possibility that rights advocacy can be co-opted by governments for purposes unrelated to the protection of human well-being. Here they seem to have learnt from the experience of Amnesty, whose research on rights abuses in Iraq during the Iran–Iraq war was dredged up fifteen years later in a UK government dossier to justify war on Iraq in an entirely different context.[55]

In sum, the Gay International is an extraordinarily fractious space. Its constituents span the entire political spectrum, from right-wing activists concerned about furthering their incomplete assimilation into party, nation, and state, to left-wing Greens looking for new causes to replenish spent agendas. It is united by a common Western sexual ontology, but its constituents disagree radically on whether, when and how to export this ontology to the rest of the world. And while some of its constituents seem eager to use gay rights as a means of consolidating the hegemony of Western states, others seem wary of contributing to such an outcome.

6.2 BETWEEN MALEVOLENT ENEMIES AND CONDESCENDING FRIENDS

In this section, I want to shift focus to consider the perspectives of Massad's 'native informants'—Third World queer activists as well as queer activists of colour within the West who are beginning to appropriate and rework Western identity categories in their struggles for sexual self-determination. This section considers the dilemmas and strategies of these activists as they manoeuvre between powerful interlocutors in the cosmopolitan Gay International on one side, and communitarian homophobic opponents at home on the other. The position of these activists can be read as a specific instantiation of the more general protest dilemma of Third World societies outlined in this book, sandwiched as they are between a coercive liberal solidarism supportive of Western hegemony, and a variety of authoritarian pluralisms that claim to contest this.

Ubaid Rehman and Asif Rashid, members of Imaan ('faith')—a support group for British LGBT Muslims—described to me in an interview how much of their work involved combating homophobia within the Muslim community, but also Islamophobia within the gay community.[56] The former entails providing support to Muslims struggling to come to terms with their sexuality under pressure from families and clerics. Islamophobia within the gay community reportedly manifests itself in a number of ways. Rehman narrated how members of the group who participated in the 2005 London Pride wearing hijab (so as to preserve their anonymity) were approached by Pride stewards enquiring if they were suicide bombers. More generally, the group responds to gay activists who occasionally attack Islam per se rather than particular interpretations of the religion—here Rehman mentioned a group called Gay and Lesbian Humanist Association (GALHA),[57] which once published material that was abusive of the Prophet.

One way in which Imaan attempts to fight homophobia within the Muslim community is to increase its visibility by inserting itself into discussions on subjects of concern to the community as a whole, such as racism and Islamophobia. In doing so, Imaan precipitates interactions with mainstream Muslim organizations such as the Muslim Council of Britain (MCB) regardless of whether or not those organizations recognize its legitimacy. The possibility of agreement on issues unrelated to sexuality seems to offer Imaan an opening into dialogue with the very elements within their faith community whose homophobia they must work so hard to change. The strident rhetoric of white, non-Muslim gay activists whenever Islam is implicated in homophobia, shows little awareness of these complex negotiating dynamics. Although Rehman personally has good relations with Tatchell and refuses to criticize him on any account, he displayed a fleeting exasperation with activists like Tatchell in an unguarded moment:

> ... [leading figures in the MCB] definitely [hold] homophobic views. But we still have to work with those people around issues like Islamophobia and racism and things like that, and it's only by working together that we can help change perspectives instead of knocking them and saying that we're different and we're not working with them because they hold these views. And that's the thing where Peter Tatchell and people like that fall down. They think just because you don't accept people being gay, I'm not accepting you.[58]

These dilemmas seemed familiar to Rauda Morcos, a lesbian Palestinian citizen of Israel, who ran an organization of Palestinian lesbians—Aswat ('voices')—at the time I interviewed her in November 2007. As a group for Palestinian lesbians run out of Haifa in Israel, Aswat is concerned primarily with providing a safe space for the discussion of issues associated with sexuality. But as an organization of and for Palestinians, it can hardly ignore the facts of Israeli Occupation and the struggle for Palestinian statehood. Indeed, the organization's mission statement mentions addressing the conflict between national and gendered identities as one of its key priorities.[59] It seems obvious that Israel's relative gay-friendliness gives Aswat the space within which to organize, so I asked Morcos how this complicated its members' identification as Palestinian.

Morcos described how although Aswat worked with a number of Israeli LGBT groups, none of them were actively anti-Occupation except for a group called Kvisa Shchora (Black Laundry).[60] She told me that when Aswat issued an anti-war statement during the 2006 Israeli attack on Lebanon, it was seen as an enemy by some Israeli LGBT organizations. Shortly thereafter, when the group's first conference held in March 2007 received threats from the Islamic Movement (an organization of Israeli Muslims), Israeli LGBT organizations flocked to support Aswat. 'This really annoys me', Morcos remarked. 'Are you my friend only when I am attacked by your enemy?' And virtually echoing the sentiments of my informants in Imaan, she said: 'As for the Islamic Movement, we don't want to see them as the enemy. They are our people, we want to work with them.' Morcos described how the Israeli media and some LGBT organizations, salivating at the prospect of conflict between a Palestinian lesbian organization and a Palestinian fundamentalist movement, egged Aswat on to a confrontation. Not wishing to pander to such voyeurism, the group hired a private security company to guard the conference venue, so as not to have to rely on the Israeli police for protection against fellow Palestinians. Ultimately, the protest by the Islamic Movement's Women's League was a muted affair, dwarfed by the conference which was, by all accounts, a success. But the experience seems to have pushed Aswat into that familiar, desolate space between orientalist LGBT allies and homophobic community members. As Morcos remarked:

> Sometimes in Israel you are put in a position where you have to defend your enemy. We have many problems within our community. Every time we want to criticize something in our community, Israel welcomes it. As if they don't have anything wrong with them. And then some Israelis say, 'if you were not in Israel, you would not have been able to do this'.[61]

In 1941, the political theorist Hannah Arendt published an angry open letter addressed to Jules Romains, then president of the international association of writers PEN. The letter was occasioned by Romains' complaint that he had been insufficiently thanked for his anti-fascist deeds, which included securing the release of numerous Jewish refugees from French concentration camps. Arendt notes pointedly that Romains' efforts were gestures performed 'for the sake of your own honor and the reputation of the organization you represent'. Jews, she said, regarded Romains 'as an ally and comrade-in-arms, rather than as a benefactor'. Arendt saw Romains' actions as basic obligations in a joint struggle—gratitude simply did not enter into the relationship. As she puts it:

> What concerns us Jews in all this and what makes us blush again for the hundredth time is our despairing question: Is our alternative truly only between malevolent enemies and condescending friends? Are genuine allies nowhere to be found, allies who understand, not out of either sympathy or bribery, that we were merely the first European nation on whom Hitler declared war? That in this war our freedom and our honor hang in the balance no less than the freedom and honor of the nation to which Jules Romains belongs? And that condescending gestures like the arrogant demand for gratitude from a protector cuts deeper than the open hostility of antisemites?[62]

Arendt's account of the Jewish predicament might well describe the position of queer activists caught between malevolent communitarian homophobia and condescending cosmopolitan rescue. The malevolence of homophobic opponents is expected, the condescension of putative allies much more startling. It is a condescension that comes out of being embedded in cultural contexts that are seen to be developmentally superior, by virtue of having already posed the questions, fought the battles, and won the liberties that distant sexual minorities now struggle for (the assumption being that they struggle for the *same* liberties). The satisfaction that white queers derive from saving brown queers from brown homophobes stems from the confirmation that this heroic gesture seems to provide for something that whites have always 'known': that 'whiteness' (and everything non-racial that this additionally signifies) is superior to 'brownness' and will always be so.

Without wishing to generalize about Third World queer activists and queer activists of colour in the West, the foregoing vignettes attempt to highlight a common protest dilemma that many of them face. Far from being simply 'native informants' to the Gay International as Massad would have us believe, it should be clear by now that their relationships with the International are in fact much more complex and conflictual. Although many have begun to appropriate Western identities in their struggles for sexual self-expression, this has not always amounted to a slavish endorsement of everything that emanates from the Gay International. In common with the other actors studied in Part II of this book, theirs is a protest sensibility underpinned by complex imaginaries of threat, in which the quest for self-determination has entailed a struggle against both homophobia within their communities as well as salvation by international or white LGBT allies. The latter struggle has been for power and resources but also, ironically, for recognition as equals. In part, what these activists have been trying to say to their purported rescuers is that they are not just gay, but other things as well—Palestinian, Arab, Muslim—and that gay liberation that does not respect those other identities is no liberation at all.

6.3 COSMOPOLITANISM AND COMMUNITARIANISM IN INDIAN QUEER ACTIVISM

Perhaps it is not surprising that the Middle East and Islam loom so large in Western gay rescue discourse, given that historically they have been primary sites for the discursive clash between the West and its Others. In comparison, sexual minority movements in places like India seem less buffeted by these forces and less penetrated by Western activism. There could be a number of additional reasons for this. State repression in India has tended to be less visible than in countries like Iran, and therefore less amenable to being framed in politically resonant ways. Persecution of sexual minorities in India typically takes the form of police harassment, blackmail, unreported custodial violence including rape, etc. In addition, the perception of India as a liberal democratic polity offering space for domestic political contention may induce Western activists to view Indian sexual minorities as less in need of assistance. Indeed, external assistance has acted as a catalyst for domestic activism in India mainly in the form of HIV AIDS funding, which opened up space for the discussion of sexuality and provided economic incentives and resources for political organization. Yet, notwithstanding its apparent relative autonomy from Western activism, queer activism in India has also had to operate within a force field constituted by the teleological pulls of cosmopolitan global activism and the ongoing reality of communitarian homophobia. Indian activists have responded in both a cosmopolitan and a communitarian idiom.

Providing a nuanced account of the Indian movement as a whole, its political objectives and the strategies that it has deployed to achieve these would take me well beyond the scope of this chapter.[63] Suffice it to say that the movement encompasses groups that identify in terms of a Western sexual ontology (LGBT), indigenous sexual minorities (*hijras* and *kothis*), as well as those doing advocacy on behalf of behavioural groups (MSM or men who have sex with men). It is a cross-class movement, though as Alok Gupta has written, one that is also deeply segregated by class, reflecting attitudes held more widely in Indian society.[64] One major point of convergence for this multi-identity cross-class movement has been the campaign against the criminalization of homosexual sex by section 377 of the Indian Penal Code, which was promulgated by the British colonial authorities in 1860. The legal campaign has been ongoing for nearly a decade, although it is seen by most activists as part of a broader strategy that includes social, cultural, medical, and other interventions aimed at provoking the attitudinal changes required for greater social acceptance of homosexuality. Without pretending to do justice to the complexity of this movement, the discussion here is confined to a single 'exhibit' that is revealing of the audiences to which it speaks and the languages in which it does so.

In September 2006, a glittering array of Indian celebrities led by the novelist Vikram Seth (with Nobel Laureate Amartya Sen writing independently in support) demanded the decriminalization of homosexual sex between consenting adults in an open letter addressed to the Government of India, members of the judiciary, and all citizens. This unprecedented elite civil society mobilization was timed to build public pressure for decriminalization in the run-up to a hearing by the Delhi High Court of a petition challenging the constitutional validity of section 377. The open letter and its list of signatories was accompanied by a meticulously researched press kit containing information about the situation of sexual minorities in India as well as global trends on the issue of sexual offences.[65] This press kit implicitly, and somewhat contradictorily, reinforces the narratives of communitarian authenticity and cosmopolitan rescue that this chapter has attempted to highlight.

On the one hand, section 377 is repeatedly characterized as 'a British-era law' and a 'colonial era monstrosity'[66]—in short as an alien, inauthentic imposition. This is in fact the activist response to the communitarian authenticity narrative that the Indian state typically articulates (gayness as an inauthentic Western preoccupation).[67] Activists contest this by pointing to the foreignness of criminalization, but in doing so they implicitly accept the state's terms of argument and the fundamental premise of the authenticity narrative: namely, that which is foreign has no place in the post-colonial community. Curiously, other parts of the press kit perform a reverse gesture, which appears to encode the cosmopolitan rescue narrative. After outlining the global position on the extent of criminalization of homosexual sex, readers are presented with a map in which countries that continue to criminalize sodomy are coloured orange, while those that do not remain white.[68] (This means, effectively, that Africa, the Middle East, South Asia, and a few states in the Caribbean are orange.) The map is captioned as follows: 'Only the Countries coloured in orange continue to criminalize sodomy. To which world must India belong?' The question is entirely rhetorical, relying for its persuasiveness on what it knows to be the predispositions of an Indian elite who are desperate to break away from the old Third World so as to take their rightful place at the table of great powers (it is not clear whether the map is trading on an elite aspiration to be part of the 'powerful' or 'civilized' world, but seeing as there is a substantial overlap between these two categories, perhaps the question does not matter very much). In this map and its accompanying caption, elite Indian activists (by no means representative of the movement as a whole) seem to have internalized the Western rescue narrative, reinforcing its assumption that progress means becoming like the West. In effect, pages 1, 2, and 3 of the press kit seem to say '*they* imposed this law on *us*, therefore we should get rid of it'; the map on page 11 seems to ask 'don't we *want* to become like them?'

It is possible that the incoherence is strategic, intended to speak to different audiences. Arguments insisting on the indigeneity of homosexuality and the foreignness of penalization are intended to appeal to communitarians, while those calling on the Indian state to join the ranks of the progressive, civilized West aim to appeal to elite cosmopolitans of the frequent-flying variety. Indeed, Stychin has argued that sexual minority activists must operate in different registers simultaneously, using cosmopolitan human rights claims as a kind of 'calling card' to enter civil and political societies from which they have been excluded, but also redeploying the very communitarian arguments that are used against them to produce revisionist same-sex histories of these communities with a view to embedding themselves within them.[69] There is a strong parallel here with the anti-globalization activists studied in the previous chapter, who also have incentives to operate simultaneously in these different registers.

We may never know exactly what impact the open letter had on the fate of the petition challenging section 377. On 2 July 2009, the Delhi High Court 'read down' section 377, so that—at the time of writing—it no longer penalizes consensual, adult, same-sex activity.[70] While steering clear of debates about Indian culture, the judgement is remarkably catholic in its sources of authority, referring to international conventions and judicial opinions, the 'almost unanimous medical and psychiatric opinion that homosexuality is not a disease',[71] decisions of courts in Canada, the United States, South Africa, Hong Kong, Fiji, and Nepal, but ultimately rooting its resounding affirmation of the freedom of sexual minorities in Indian constitutional jurisprudence guaranteeing the rights to life, equality, and non-discrimination, in the distinction between constitutional and public morality articulated by constitutional architect B. R. Ambedkar, and in Jawaharlal Nehru's vision of an inclusive India.[72] For the time being at least, both home and the world have conspired to play a part in my liberation.

7

Conclusion

> All games have morals; and the game of Snakes and Ladders captures, as no other activity can hope to do, the eternal truth that for every ladder you climb, a snake is waiting just around the corner; and for every snake, a ladder will compensate. But it's more than that; no mere carrot-and-stick affair; because implicit in the game is the unchanging twoness of things, the duality of up against down, good against evil; the solid rationality of ladders balances the occult sinuosities of the serpent; in the opposition of staircase and cobra we can see, metaphorically, all conceivable oppositions, Alpha against Omega, father against mother; here is the war of Mary and Musa, and the polarities of knees and nose . . . but I found, very early in my life, that the game lacked one crucial dimension, that of ambiguity—because, as events are about to show, it is also possible to slither down a ladder and climb to triumph on the venom of a snake . . .
>
> Salman Rushdie, *Midnight's Children* (1981)

Saleem Sinai's frustration with the lack of ambiguity between the polarities of Snakes and Ladders—'the unchanging twoness of things'—captures something of my own frustration with the duality of cosmopolitanism and communitarianism, which is at the heart of this book. Referring to this duality, Chris Brown once remarked that 'all variants of international relations theory can be seen as falling into one or the other camp without too much violence being done to the intentions of the theorist'.[1] Although he has subsequently retreated from this claim,[2] the distinction between what should properly be called 'bounded'[3] and 'universalist' ways of thinking—between the claim that it is permissible to prioritize citizens over strangers and the claim that it is not—continues to structure debate on issues as wide-ranging as humanitarian intervention, distributive justice, climate change, immigration, and asylum. But the question of how one relates to boundaries has an even wider significance beyond issues of public policy where the distribution of resources is at stake. We are forced to reflect on the meaning of boundaries when we try to make sense of the identities that we inhabit. The very act of 'identifying' as something or someone is an act of affiliation with some and disaffiliation with others. The question of how one relates to the other side of the boundary is therefore inescapable, both for states projecting power and for those resisting them.

One central intuition of this book is that attitudes towards boundaries expressed in the debate between cosmopolitanism and communitarianism are premised on assumptions about vital interests and the locus of threats to those interests. The relationship between space, threat, and boundaries is therefore a recurring theme through the book. Part I of the book explored hegemonic discourses of cosmopolitanism and communitarianism as expressed in the thinking and practices of states. It considered both the explicit invocation of these discourses by states to justify certain practices, as well as the sensibilities or subtext of these discourses evident in the inarticulate assumptions and spatial imaginaries of threat that underpin them. Chapter 2 argued that liberal cosmopolitanism is frequently invoked to justify practices that consolidate the hegemony of Western states. More particularly, it demonstrated how the consensual basis for such hegemony is constructed via spatial representations of political and economic crises—offered both within the Western academy and in the discourse of powerful states and international institutions—in which blame is attributed primarily to factors internal to the Third World state, with the culpability of the international being obscured. Chapter 3 argued that in Third World communitarian discourse, this spatial normativity is reversed, with the international being portrayed as a realm of neo-imperial predation from which the domestic has to be secured. Historical memories of empire as well as the ongoing experience of neo-imperial intervention are invoked to legitimate authoritarian state- and nation-building practices and to justify the construction of sovereignty as an impenetrable barrier between the domestic and the international. These discourses of cosmopolitanism and communitarianism are not straightforwardly false. Indeed they are hegemonic precisely because they capture widely held intuitions about sources of threat to the enjoyment of human rights and self-determination by Third World societies. Yet, each without the other is highly misleading because it provides a resolutely partial inventory of these threats. By juxtaposing critical accounts of both discourses, part I of the book attempted to set the stage for an exploration of protest sensibilities that recognize that the self-determination of Third World societies is under threat from sources external to the Third World state *and* from the state itself.

Part II of the book was an excursion through a series of such sensibilities in the context of resistance anchored primarily on three kinds of identities—nation, class, and gender. Thinking and writing in the high noon of nationalism in their respective communities, the 'ironic nationalists' of chapter 4 defended the need for subaltern nationalisms; yet their anxieties about the oppressions inherent in nationalist mobilization also led them to a critique of nationalism that was prescient. In these figures, we can see clearly the tension between a communitarian impulse to construct unified collective agency against external imperialist oppression and a simultaneous cosmopolitan inclination to deconstruct such communitarian fictions out of an acute awareness of their tendency to stifle the very freedoms they claimed to fight for. Their attempt to reconcile these tensions rests on the hope that nationalism might be a necessary but transitory stage through which subaltern cultures must pass as they attempt to recuperate identity and agency before they can join in the construction of postnational futures as equal participants.

Yet nationalism has persisted with a certain tenaciousness in post-colonial subaltern protest, reasserting its presence even in protest articulated around ostensibly universal categories like class and gender. As I argued in chapter 5, an important constituency within the 'anti-globalization' space regards the state as a potentially useful tool in regulating global capitalism. In the activism of such movements, one sees the conjunction of cosmopolitan claims made around grievances framed in global terms so as to mobilize transnational support against the targets of protest, and a simultaneous articulation of nationalism against the state with a view to shaming 'transnationalized' states into becoming more responsive to their nations. In a similar vein, the queer activists studied in chapter 6 have incentives to speak in both cosmopolitan and communitarian idioms. The appeal to a cosmopolitan discourse of queer rights challenges traditional patriarchal sexual ontologies and functions as a sort of calling card asserting one's humanity in communities in which such humanity has been denied. Yet acceptance within such communities seems to ride on a demonstration of indigeneity and belonging through the production of revisionist same-sex histories of those communities.

The political activism of the subjects of part II is animated by spatial imaginaries in which threats to vital interests in human rights and self-determination are seen to emanate both from outside and within the nation-state. The particular configurations of threat that these subjects confront vary: in chapters 4 and 6 external and internal threat are locked in Manichean confrontation that has disenfranchising effects on the subalterns trapped in between; in chapter 5 the relationship is collaborative, manifesting itself in the activities of a transnational bourgeoisie. Yet the awareness in each case that neither home nor the world is an entirely unthreatening space means that conceptions of the boundary between the two are contingent, shifting, and radically unstable. The fluidity of threat— the inability to fix threat in space across time—makes inflexible normative commitments to a particular view of boundaries politically suicidal. Instead, protest in the condition of post-coloniality demands a combination of cosmopolitan and communitarian sensibilities.

One important subsidiary theme of this book concerned the relevance of cosmopolitanism to the articulation of subaltern protest. Cosmopolitanism has often been criticized as an elite discourse enabled by circumstances of power and material privilege—at best, a normative world view that would be beneficial for subalterns if adopted by elites, but one that is ultimately inaccessible to subalterns themselves.[4] To the contrary, this book has shown that subaltern social movements have strong incentives to frame their grievances in global terms and to express their political utopias in cosmopolitan vocabularies. Yet, crucially, subaltern cosmopolitanism tends to operate in conjunction with a certain kind of communitarianism, with both forms of consciousness performing independent political work. Communitarianism, in such activism, tends to take the form of what is usually termed 'identity politics', concerned with the recuperation and reassertion of subaltern identities, frequently through the creation of alternative public spheres as a result of their exclusion from mainstream arenas. Cosmopolitanism aims at locating such subaltern struggles within larger contexts, so as to broaden support for them and to assist in the defence of the enclaves that they have carved out for themselves.

To some, this may look like a nakedly instrumental deployment of cosmopolitanism—one that does not necessarily imply that the subject self-identifies as cosmopolitan. This is certainly true, although—as constructivists have argued—rhetoric that is invoked for initially instrumental purposes can 'stick' to become constitutive of the subject, particularly in contexts where a loss of reputation as a result of discrepancies between rhetoric and reality could prove costly.[5] But even obviously instrumental invocations of cosmopolitanism do not detract from the argument here. Far from debasing cosmopolitanism as a normative ideal, such invocations attest to its enormous appeal to those who feel marginalized, excluded, forgotten. The enduring instrumental utility of cosmopolitanism might in fact be the most powerful evidence that could be cited in response to the arguments of critics who view it solely as a discourse of privilege. When domestic arenas for contention are blocked or unresponsive, the court of humanity is sometimes the only place to go. 'We are like you, our struggle is yours too', subaltern social movements are compelled to say. In such circumstances, cosmopolitanism looks more like a necessity than a luxury.

My argument that a combination of cosmopolitan and communitarian sensibilities is most appropriate to the condition of post-coloniality would seem to be aided by the body of literature that seeks to reconcile these concepts. Philosophers have long considered a tension in commonsense moral thought between 'general' obligations owed to all human beings and 'special' obligations owed to those with whom we stand in particular relationships (of family, friendship, nationality, etc.). This tension is sometimes described as one between equality and partiality. Taking the view that philosophy ought, as far as possible, to accommodate deeply held moral intuitions, some have attempted to justify partiality on the basis of universal principles that are equally applicable to all. For example, Alan Gewirth has justified familial partiality on the basis of a universal right to freedom of association.[6] Robert Goodin has argued that partiality to special others is merely an efficient means of discharging general responsibilities owed to all.[7] Others have argued that the attempt to derive special responsibilities from general obligations empties them of the actual motivations from which people favour those with whom they are in special relationships.[8] A number of participants in this debate have therefore argued for the accommodation of special relationships on their own terms, subject to limitations on the circumstances in which, and the extent to which, people may legitimately give priority to special others.[9]

While sympathetic to the motivations of this literature, my endeavour in this book is distinct in at least two ways. First, my concern has been to demonstrate the political urgency and necessity of combining cosmopolitan and communitarian sensibilities, given the architecture of threat that Third World societies confront in the current conjuncture. But second, in contrast to the philosophical literature referenced above, I am less sanguine about the prospects for a completely satisfactory theoretical reconciliation of these antagonistic sensibilities. Thus, even while asserting the political possibility of combining cosmopolitan and communitarian sensibilities with reference to the writing and practice of figures associated with Third World protest, I have offered a number of glimpses of unresolved paradoxes, contradictions, and fractures in the sketches that comprise part II. One thinks here of Tagore's disavowal of political nationalism but espousal of a limited cultural nationalism, of Said's attempt to both 'do' and unmask nationalism, of Fanon's deep ambivalence towards negritude, of the many conceivable disjunctures between the Zapatistas' cosmopolitan rhetoric and the lived beliefs and practices of the Mayan peasants that form their core constituency, of the relationship between the petty capitalists of the Karnataka Rajya Raitha Sangha (KRRS) and their global anarchist partners, of Indian queer activists' desire to both accede to and resist the teleological pull of Western culture. Kwame Anthony Appiah has written movingly about the possibility of 'cosmopolitan patriotism', insisting that 'you can be cosmopolitan—celebrating the variety of human cultures; rooted—loyal to one local society (or a few) that you count as home; liberal—convinced of the value of the individual, and patriotic—celebrating the institutions of the state (or states) within which you live'.[10] I could not agree more, but Appiah is sometimes in danger of making cosmopolitan patriotism, or what he calls elsewhere 'rooted cosmopolitanism', look easy.[11] In contrast, Berlin frequently reiterated the view that 'the ends of men are many, and not all of them are in principle compatible with each other', with the result that 'the possibility of conflict—and of tragedy—can never wholly be eliminated from human life'.[12] This book shares Appiah's belief in the need for a combination of cosmopolitan and particularist sensibilities, and argues that the attempt to do so has been constitutive of important strands of Third World protest. But it is also infused with Berlin's pessimism about the possibility of reconciling all human ends, paying close attention to the dissonances and schizophrenia of the endeavour to be both cosmopolitan and nationalist.

At least three sorts of responses are possible when one is confronted with polarities. First, one might choose to occupy one of these polarities and defend one's position accordingly. Second, one might seek some sort of Hegelian synthesis between these polarities, a middle path, a third way. Third, one might seek to hold these polarities in tension with one another, using each to provide critical perspective on the other but recognizing the kernel of truth in both. This book adopts the third approach. A final analogy may help to make the implications of this clearer. *The Twenty Years' Crisis* is typically read as a realist text, but its author was only reacting against what he perceived to be the idealist excesses of Wilsonian thinking. In fact, the book concludes with a rousing defence of both realism and utopianism, arguing that 'If... it is utopian to ignore the element of power, it is an unreal kind of realism which ignores the element of morality in any world order'.[13] Without dispensing with either realism or utopianism or conjuring up some spurious dialectical resolution of the tension between them, Carr affirms the indispensability of both and the inescapability of messy political compromise between them. In a similar vein, this book argues that normative theory that does not hold communitarianism and cosmopolitanism in tension with one another fails the needs of our non-ideal political lives. We need to be critical of both home and the world, never giving our unthinking allegiance to either.

Notes

CHAPTER 1

1. Power, 'A Problem From Hell', ch. 8.
2. Hardt & Negri, *Empire*, 211.
3. International Commission on Intervention and State Sovereignty (ICISS), *The Responsibility to Protect*.
4. Bellamy, 'Responsibility to Protect or Trojan Horse?'.
5. For a critique, see Shue, *Basic Rights*.
6. These included the Centre for Education and Communication (New Delhi); the Research Foundation for Science, Technology and Ecology (New Delhi); & the Narmada Solidarity Forum (Bangalore).
7. Power, 'A Problem From Hell', ch. 8; Mearsheimer & Walt, 'An Unnecessary War'.
8. *Oxford English Dictionary* (2009).
9. Ibid.
10. Austen, *Sense and Sensibility*.
11. For a brief statement of the differences between these two ways of thinking, see Jones, *Global Justice*, 15–16.
12. Pogge, *World Poverty and Human Rights*, 169; Caney, 'Review Article: International Distributive Justice', 977.
13. Beitz, 'Social and Cosmopolitan Liberalism', 519; Singer, *One World*, 1.
14. Bell, *Communitarianism and Its Critics*, 94.
15. Walzer, *Just and Unjust Wars*, 87.
16. Scheffler, *Boundaries and Allegiances*, 59, 103–8, 121.
17. The relationship between Parts I and II is elucidated more fully in a hinge section titled 'Intermezzo'.
18. Throughout the book, I treat nationalism as a particular kind of communitarianism. Communitarianism is the genus, nationalism the species.
19. Staying within the terms of Mehta's vignette, I use 'non-Gujarati' here as a metaphor for minorities of all kinds. Gujaratis themselves are a linguistic minority in Bombay, although Gujarati Hindus (whom Mehta is referring to) are part of Bombay's Hindu religious majority.
20. Gallie, 'Essentially Contested Concepts'.
21. Mill, *Principles of Political Economy with Some of Their Applications to Social Philosophy*, bk. 3, ch. 17, para. 1.
22. Marx & Engels, *The Communist Manifesto*, 7.
23. Nussbaum, 'Kant and Cosmopolitanism', 28–32, 46.
24. *Oxford English Dictionary*.
25. Beck, 'Cosmopolitical Realism'.

26. Beck is wrong to see normative cosmopolitanism 'in Kant's sense of the term' as 'an active task' and empirical-analytic cosmopolitanism as the result of 'uncontrollable liabilities...something that merely happens to us' (ibid., 135). While it is certainly the case that normative cosmopolitanism must be actively promoted by specific agents if its principles are to have any prospect of realization in world politics, the phenomena described by empirical-analytic cosmopolitanism are also the result of conscious human endeavour. The difference is that while the former is a project driven by explicitly moral motivations, empirical cosmopolitanism is the result of human activity driven by all sorts of motivations among which morality may or may not find a place.
27. Ibid., 137.
28. Pollock et al., 'Cosmopolitanisms', 10.
29. Ibid., 11.
30. Beck, 'Cosmopolitical Realism', 138.
31. Scheffler, *Boundaries and Allegiances*, 112. See also Appiah, *Cosmopolitanism*, xv.
32. Jones, *Global Justice*, 15–16.
33. Pollock et al., 'Cosmopolitanisms', 12.
34. Waldron, 'Minority Cultures and the Cosmopolitan Alternative', 751; Rushdie, 'In Good Faith', 394. See Guarnizo & Smith, 'The Locations of Transnationalism', 4, for a critical review of the cultural studies and social science literature that tends to celebrate transnationalism, hybridity, and other border-crossing practices as unqualifiedly emancipatory.
35. Miller, *Principles of Social Justice*, 18; Bell, *Communitarianism and Its Critics*, 32, 37–9, 94.
36. Walzer, *Thick and Thin*.
37. Pogge, *World Poverty and Human Rights*, 169; Caney, 'Review Article: International Distributive Justice', 977.
38. Colas, 'Putting Cosmopolitanism into Practice'.
39. Bajpai, 'Indian Conceptions of Order and Justice', 244–8.
40. Ibid., 248–53.
41. Hashmi, 'Islamic Ethics in International Society', 223. See also Hanafi, 'An Islamic Approach to Multilateralism', 118.
42. Bull, *The Anarchical Society*, 80–2.
43. Hovden & Keene, 'Introduction', 3. The authors argue that while liberalism in IR is often cast as a utopian and largely prescriptive theoretical approach, many of the so-called Westphalian rules of international society—relying on a view of the state as macrocosm of the human being—transpose thoroughly liberal beliefs about the rights and liberties of individuals to the level of the state.
44. Hurrell & Woods, 'Globalisation and Inequality', 447.
45. Hurrell, 'Order and Justice', 34, comments on the increasing intrusiveness of powerful states and international institutions in the affairs of Third World states, driven partly by moral (liberal cosmopolitan) concerns and partly by a functional need to manage problems created by globalization and interdependence.
46. Singer, 'Famine, Affluence, and Morality'; Singer, *Practical Ethics*.

47. Shue, *Basic Rights*.
48. O'Neill, *Bounds of Justice*, ch. 7.
49. Nussbaum, *Frontiers of Justice*.
50. Rawls, *A Theory of Justice*, 137.
51. Pogge, *Realizing Rawls*; Beitz, *Political Theory and International Relations*.
52. Bell, 'Communitarianism'.
53. Walzer, *Interpretation and Social Criticism*, 21.
54. Walzer, *Spheres of Justice*, 9–10, 28–9; Walzer, *Thick and Thin*, 34–6.
55. Miller, 'In Defence of Nationality', 4.
56. Miller, *On Nationality*, 90–8, 185; 'Nationality', 70. See also Tamir, *Liberal Nationalism*, 96, 115, 118.
57. Miller, *On Nationality*, 80; 'The Ethical Significance of Nationality', 661. See also Bell, *Communitarianism and Its Critics*, 137–8; Walzer, *Thick and Thin*, 81; the contributions by Barber, McConnell, & Pinsky in Cohen ed., *For Love of Country*. For my criticism of communitarian arguments from feasibility, see Rao, 'How to Make a Cosmopolitan'.
58. Pettit, *Republicanism*, 259.
59. Bohman, 'Republican Cosmopolitanism'.
60. Blake, 'Distributive Justice, State Coercion, and Autonomy'.
61. Nagel, 'The Problem of Global Justice', 128.
62. Sangiovanni, 'Global Justice, Reciprocity, and the State'.
63. Carr, *The Twenty Years' Crisis 1919–1939*, ch. 4, 5.
64. Morgenthau, *Politics Among Nations*, ch. 1.
65. Castells, *The Power of Identity*, 9.
66. Santos, *Toward a New Legal Common Sense*, 460, asks 'who needs cosmopolitanism?' and replies 'whoever is a victim of intolerance and discrimination needs tolerance; whoever is denied human dignity needs a community of human beings; whoever is a non-citizen needs world citizenship in any given community or nation'.
67. Freeman, 'Universalism, Particularism and Cosmopolitan Justice', 82.
68. Halliday, 'The potentials of Enlightenment', 108.
69. Pagden, 'Stoicism, Cosmopolitanism, and the Legacy of European Imperialism', 6.
70. Pagden, *Peoples and Empires*, 145.
71. Calhoun, 'The Necessity and Limits of Cosmopolitanism', 6.
72. Calhoun, 'The Class Consciousness of Frequent Travellers', 872.
73. Calhoun, '"Belonging" in the Cosmopolitan Imaginary', 545.
74. Sartre, 'Colonialism Is a System', 41, indicts French colonialism in Algeria for imposing 'an individualistic and liberal legal code in order to ruin the frameworks and the development of the Algerian community . . . it *fabricates* "natives" by a double movement which separates them from their archaic community by giving them or maintaining in them, *in the solitude of liberal individualism*, a mentality whose archaism can only be perpetuated in relation to the archaism of the society. It creates *masses* but prevents them from becoming a conscious proletariat by mystifying them with the caricature of their own ideology.'

75. Berlin, 'Nationalism', 349.
76. Scott, *Weapons of the Weak*.
77. Marx & Engels, *The Communist Manifesto*, 29.
78. Woolf, 'Three Guineas', 234.
79. Anderson, *Imagined Communities*.
80. Appadurai, *Modernity at Large*, 21.
81. Yeğenoğlu, 'Cosmopolitanism and Nationalism in a Globalized World', 111, 120.
82. Barkawi & Laffey, 'The Postcolonial Moment in Security Studies'.
83. Featherstone, 'Localism, Globalism, and Cultural Identity', 65, writes that the postmodern emphasis upon the mixing of codes, pastiche, fragmentation, incoherence, disjunction, and syncretism were characteristic of cities in colonial societies, decades or even centuries, before they appeared in the West. 'From this perspective, the first multicultural city was not London or Los Angeles but probably Rio de Janeiro, Calcutta or Singapore.'
84. Mignolo, 'The Many Faces of Cosmo-Polis', 157.
85. Prashad, *The Darker Nations*.
86. Bell, 'American Policy in the Third World, 1947–87'.
87. Escobar, *Encountering Development*.
88. The composition of the 'West' is an exceedingly complex issue. During the colonial era it was understood as comprising Europe and her white settler colonial offshoots. The relative positions of states within the 'West' has changed over time, with the United States coming to be seen as paramount, from the end of the Second World War if not earlier. The composition of the West is also a matter of perspective: following the Sino-Soviet split, Maoists in the Third World came to see the Soviet Union as part of the dominant core of international society. The position of the United States, Russia, and Latin American republics is further complicated by the fact that while all professed strong anti-colonial sentiments at various times, they were all built upon the subjugation—and often elimination—of indigenous peoples. To complicate matters still further, despite displaying many characteristics of Third Worldness, the Southern Cone states of Latin America have long thought of themselves as culturally European. Despite the constantly shifting nature of the boundaries of the 'West' and its relatively indeterminate penumbra, the core of the concept has been understood rather unambiguously since the end of the Second World War as encompassing the United States, Western Europe, Canada, Australia, and New Zealand. It is in this sense that I use the term. It should also be noted that 'West' has a cultural flavour, in contrast to the more economic connotations of 'First World' or 'developed countries' which are larger categories encompassing, in addition, the most industrialized economies of East Asia.
89. Bull, 'The Revolt Against the West'.
90. Westad, *The Global Cold War*.
91. Mortimer, *The Third World Coalition in International Politics*; Rothstein, *The Weak in the World of the Strong*; Cox, 'Ideologies and the NIEO'.

92. Independent Commission on International Development Issues, *North-South: A Programme for Survival*.
93. Prashad, *The Darker Nations*.
94. Woods, *The Globalizers*.
95. Patel & McMichael, 'Third Worldism and the Lineages of Global Fascism', 231.
96. See Hardt, 'Porto Allegre' and Mertes, 'Grass-Roots Globalism'.
97. Randall, 'Using and Abusing the Concept of the Third World', 43.
98. Acharya, 'Developing Countries and the Emerging World Order'.
99. Berger, 'The End of the "Third World"?'.
100. Hurrell & Woods, 'Globalisation and Inequality'.
101. 'Incompleteness' is a misleading term as no state- or nation-building endeavour is ever fully complete. Such institutions have constantly to be produced and reproduced over time in order to endure as social facts. I prefer the term 'incipience' to 'incompleteness' to indicate the relatively early stage of state- and nation-building in which Third World states are engaged, in which the legitimacy of actors attempting to acquire a monopoly over the use of force is contested to a relatively greater degree. This also avoids the problem of making Third Worldness a rigid and inflexible category from which its constituents have no possibility of escape. 'Incipience' places all states on a continuum along which they can move in either direction, as the state's monopoly over the legitimate use of force fluctuates.
102. Ayoob, *The Third World Security Predicament*, 15.
103. Centeno, *Blood and Debt*.
104. Waltz, *Theory of International Politics*, 88. For a critique, see Milner, 'The Assumption of Anarchy in International Relations Theory'.
105. O'Neill, *Bounds of Justice*, 68, 120.
106. See Hurrell, 'Norms and Ethics in International Relations', 140, for a critique of Rawls' use of empirical evidence; Stears, 'The Vocation of Political Theory'.
107. Hurrell, 'International Society and the Study of Regimes'; Dunne, *Inventing International Society*.
108. A rare exception is Keene, *Beyond the Anarchical Society*.
109. Bull & Watson, *The Expansion of International Society*.
110. Tickner, 'Seeing IR Differently'; Darby, 'Postcolonialism'.

CHAPTER 2

1. Keohane & Nye, *Power and Interdependence*; Keohane, *After Hegemony*.
2. Ruggie, *Constructing the World Polity*.
3. Bull, 'The Grotian Conception of International Society', 97; Alderson & Hurrell, 'Bull's Conception of International Society', 7–10; Hurrell, 'Society and Anarchy in the 1990s', 31.

4. Foucault, 'Governmentality'; Zanotti, 'Governmentalizing the Post-Cold War International Regime'.
5. Kennedy, *The Dark Sides of Virtue*, xvii.
6. Hurrell, *On Global Order*, 39.
7. Cox, *Approaches to World Order*, 99.
8. Teson, *Humanitarian Intervention*, 118; Teson, *A Philosophy of International Law*, 1, 40.
9. See for example ICISS, *The Responsibility to Protect*; Welsh ed., *Humanitarian Intervention and International Relations*; Holzgrefe & Keohane eds., *Humanitarian Intervention*.
10. Finnemore, *The Purpose of Intervention*, 58.
11. Bull, 'Intervention in the Third World', 138.
12. These are particularly evident in Articles 2(1), 2(4) and 2(7), which guarantee the sovereign equality and territorial integrity of states and prohibit intervention in 'matters which are essentially within the domestic jurisdiction of any state'.
13. See for example the Declaration on Granting Independence to Colonial Countries and Peoples; Declaration on the Inadmissibility of Intervention in the Domestic Affairs of States and the Protection of their Independence and Sovereignty.
14. India made a feeble attempt at invoking humanitarian claims, but rested the bulk of its argument on an alleged right of self-defence against 'refugee aggression' caused by the influx of nearly 10 million refugees from East Pakistan.
15. Wheeler, *Saving Strangers*, 8, ch. 2–4.
16. Foreign & Commonwealth Office, Foreign Policy Document No. 148, 614.
17. Lake, 'From Containment to Enlargement'.
18. Kaldor, *New and Old Wars*.
19. Berdal, 'How "New" are "New Wars"?'; Kalyvas, '"New" and "Old" Civil Wars'.
20. Woodward, *Balkan Tragedy*; Gagnon, Jr., 'Ethnic Nationalism and International Conflict';
21. Chandler, *From Kosovo to Kabul*, 63.
22. The relevant Security Council resolutions are 688 (Iraq), 794 (Somalia), 929 (Rwanda) and 770 and 836 (Bosnia). For an analysis of the diversity of motivations that shaped voting behaviour in the Security Council in each of these episodes, see Wheeler, *Saving Strangers*, 141–6 (Iraq), 182–7 (Somalia), 232 (Rwanda), 251–7 (Bosnia).
23. It is sometimes argued that interventions by ECOWAS in the Liberian civil war in 1990 and in Sierra Leone in 1997 were precedents for intervention by a regional organization without prior Security Council authorization. In both cases the Council was seen to have given retrospective authorization for intervention via resolutions 788 and 866 (Liberia) and resolution 1132 (Sierra Leone). However, ECOWAS actions in the Liberian civil war in 1990 and in Sierra Leone in 1997 were both invited by the then *de jure* heads of those states. In the case of Liberia, a beleaguered President Doe appealed to ECOWAS to introduce a peacekeeping force into Liberia 'to forestall increasing terror and tension' following the attack on his government's forces by the National Patriotic Front of Liberia led by

Charles Taylor. In the case of Sierra Leone, upon being deposed by a coup in May 1997, the democratically elected head of state—Ahmed Tijan Kabbah—requested Nigeria and ECOWAS to intervene to restore constitutional order (ICISS, *Responsibility to Protect*, 81, 105; see also Griffiths, Levine & Weller, 'Sovereignty and Suffering', 48.) On an understanding of 'intervention' as non-consensual, the ECOWAS actions do not qualify as interventions.

24. This appeared to be the view of the then NATO Secretary General Javier Solana who, in a letter to permanent representatives of NATO member-states dated 9 October 1998, sought to justify the legality of threatening or using force against the FRY with reference to the Security Council resolutions. However, the letter also mentions the unlikelihood of obtaining explicit Security Council authorization due to the threat of a Russian veto, thereby betraying a sense that such authorization was desirable, even if not strictly necessary (Simma, 'NATO, the UN and the Use of Force').
25. Robertson, *Crimes Against Humanity*, 431–2.
26. For an argument that the Security Council must expressly determine that military measures are necessary, see Lobel & Ratner, 'Bypassing the Security Council', 128.
27. Independent International Commission on Kosovo, *The Kosovo Report*, 4.
28. Habermas, 'Bestiality and Humanity', 268.
29. This assumption has to be tempered by the finding that NATO's aerial bombardment did little to stop ethnic cleansing by Serb forces and that Milosevic's eventual surrender was a result, not only of losses suffered as a result of the air war, but also of diplomatic desertion by Russia and the threat of a ground offensive (Daalder & O'Hanlon, *Winning Ugly*, 200, 210; Hosmer, *The Conflict over Kosovo*, 87).
30. Buchanan, 'Reforming the International Law of Humanitarian Intervention', 132. See also Buchanan, *Justice, Legitimacy, and Self-Determination*, ch. 11; Glennon, 'The New Interventionism', 5, 7. For a contrary view, with which I agree, see Byers & Chesterman, 'Changing the Rules About Rules?'.
31. For a similar view, see the work of W. Michael Reisman, especially, 'Coercion and Self-Determination', 642; 'Criteria for the Lawful Use of Force in International Law', 279; 'Sovereignty and Human Rights in Contemporary International Law', 875; 'Kosovo's Antinomies', 860.
32. Sands, *Lawless World*; Zunes, 'The United States'.
33. Schmitt, *The Concept of the Political*, 54.
34. Carr, *The Twenty Years' Crisis 1919–1939*, 58.
35. Zolo, *Invoking Humanity*, ch. 2.
36. Wheeler, *Saving Strangers*, 38.
37. Ignatieff, 'The Way We Live Now'. For a critique of consequentialist arguments, see Rao, 'The Empire Writes Back (to Michael Ignatieff)', 158–60.
38. For the importance of representational practices in shaping material relations between the First and Third Worlds, see Doty, *Imperial Encounters*.
39. Orford, *Reading Humanitarian Intervention*, 85.
40. Kaplan, 'The Coming Anarchy'.

41. Woodward, *Balkan Tragedy*, 17.
42. Furedi, *The New Ideology of Imperialism*, 98, 100, 106.
43. Jackson, *Quasi-States*, 140, 146–7, 151: 'Decolonisation did not result in a corresponding extension of human rights protection as was originally expected when independence was in the offing—instead, it increased the opportunity for human rights violations... before that time most governments of the non-Western world were under the authority of a few Western constitutional democracies... although it was far from perfect and serious abuses did most certainly occur there nevertheless was an institutional framework to discourage offences against the human rights of colonial subjects... most colonies were peaceful, orderly, lawful places by and large.... decolonisation was not only a liberation movement but also an enclosure movement: it confined populations within ex-colonial frontiers and subjected them to indigenous governments which often were not only untried and inexperienced but also unable or unwilling to operate in accordance with humanitarian standards.' For trenchant critiques of Jackson's views see Doty, *Imperial Encounters*, 153–6; Grovogui, 'Sovereignty in Africa'; Inayatullah, 'Beyond the Sovereignty Dilemma'.
44. Beitz, 'Human Rights and the Law of Peoples', 194–5.
45. Reisman, 'Kosovo's Antinomies', 861.
46. Franck, 'The Emerging Right to Democratic Governance'.
47. Rawls, *The Law of Peoples*, 108.
48. Miller, 'National Responsibility and International Justice'; 'Justice and Global Inequality'.
49. Bacevich, *American Empire*, 100.
50. The phrase is used by Bull, 'The Grotian Conception of International Society', 108, to describe the vanguardist behaviour of states that seek to advance a liberal solidarist agenda in international society. See also Moravcsik, 'Why Is US Human Rights Policy so Unilateralist?'.
51. White House (Office of the Press Secretary), 'Remarks by the President on Landmines'. Clinton did, however, seem sympathetic to some of the objectives of the treaty and announced a number of alternative measures that the United States would pursue unilaterally towards achieving those objectives.
52. Grossman, 'American Foreign Policy and the International Criminal Court'.
53. Rice, 'Promoting the National Interest', 47, 49, 50.
54. See also White House, The National Security Strategy of the United States of America (September 2002): '... in exercising our leadership, we will respect the values, judgment, and interests of our friends and partners. Still, we will be prepared to act apart when our interests and unique responsibilities require'.
55. The idea of the United States as the world's human rights arsenal finds echo in the work of Brilmayer, 'Transforming International Politics', 127–8: 'An ideal contemporary role for the powerful nations of the world—and the US, in particular—would be to assume the role of executive officer for the world community at large... the best that we can hope for in the near future is something akin to an unelected monarch working in conjunction with an elected legislature.'

56. Rothstein, *The Weak in the World of the Strong*, ch. 3–5.
57. Woods, *The Globalizers*, 48–52.
58. Williamson, 'In Search of a Manual for Technopols', 26–8.
59. Griffith-Jones ed., *Managing World Debt*; Biersteker ed., *Dealing with Debt*; Birdsall, Williamson & Deese, *Delivering on Debt Relief*.
60. Calhoun, '"Belonging" in the Cosmopolitan Imaginary', 545.
61. Locke, *Two Treatises of Government*, bk. 2, ch. 2, para. 6: 'And Reason... teaches all Mankind, who will but consult it, that being all equal and independent, no one ought to harm another in his Life, Health, Liberty, or Possessions.' For a contemporary invocation of the argument, see Wolf, *Why Globalization Works*, 25.
62. Korkman, 'The Vital String of Mankind', 25.
63. Hirschman, 'Rival Interpretations of Market Society', 1464–6.
64. Kant, *Perpetual Peace*, 114. For a discussion of Kant's view of the relationship between cosmopolitanism and capitalism, see Muthu, *Enlightenment Against Empire*, 195.
65. Kant, *Perpetual Peace*, 106–7.
66. Doyle, 'Kant, Liberal Legacies, and Foreign Affairs', 26–7. Note that Doyle defines 'liberal' states as those that recognize the institution of private property (including the ownership of the means of production) and where economic decisions are predominantly shaped by forces of supply and demand rather than by bureaucracies, indicating that these features of liberal states do quite a lot of work in his account (6).
67. White House, 'The National Security Strategy' (March 2006), section VI.
68. Gowan, *The Global Gamble*, 85.
69. Harvey, *The New Imperialism*, 109.
70. Gowan, *The Global Gamble*, 19–21; Harvey, *The New Imperialism* 62, 128.
71. Gowan, *The Global Gamble*, 49; Biersteker, *Dealing with Debt*, 10; Woods, *The Globalizers*, 53.
72. Griffith-Jones, *Managing World Debt*, 11.
73. Weisbrot, Naiman & Kim, 'The Emperor Has No Growth'.
74. Fishlow et al., *Miracle or Design?*
75. Rodrik, 'Trading in Illusions', 59.
76. Chang, *Kicking Away the Ladder*.
77. Harvey, *The New Imperialism*, 149–51.
78. Gowan, *The Global Gamble*, 41.
79. Harvey, *The New Imperialism*, 151.
80. Stiglitz, *Globalization and Its Discontents*, 95, 106–9, 207–13. Wade, 'Japan, the World Bank, and the Art of Paradigm Maintenance', makes the same argument in respect of the World Bank: 'the Bank's ability to borrow at the best rates and to act as a country rating agency depends on its reputation among financial capitalists, which in turn depends on its manifest commitment to *their* version of "sound" public policies'.
81. <http://go.worldbank.org/VKVDQDUC10>

82. <http://www.imf.org/external/np/exr/facts/quotas.htm>. In April 2008, the Board of Governors approved a package of reforms agreeing on ad hoc quota increases for 54 countries, a tripling of basic votes to enhance the voice of low-income countries and an additional Alternate Executive Director for the two Africa chairs at the Board in recognition of their heavy work load.
83. Rustomjee, 'Improving Southern Voice on the IMF Board'.
84. Woods, *The Globalizers*, 190–3.
85. Gowan, *The Global Gamble*, 41.
86. Woods, *The Globalizers*, 4, 82–3. Haggard and Kaufman have highlighted three sources of borrowing-country leverage in stabilization and adjustment negotiations: the size of the country's debt, the strategic significance of the country to the IFIs' most powerful shareholders, and the extent to which the country has access to other, non-conditional sources of funds (cited from Biersteker, *Dealing with Debt*, 6). It would therefore be wrong to see borrowing countries as completely lacking in agency.
87. Patnaik, 'On the Political Economy of Economic "Liberalisation"'.
88. Gowan, *The Global Gamble*, 57.
89. Woods, *The Globalizers*, 53–4, notes the significant numbers of senior staff at the IFIs with qualifications from North American and British universities. An analysis of economic policymakers in Mexico and India (the two countries studied in chapter 5) reveals a similar picture. The administration of Mexican President Carlos Salinas de Gortari (himself a Harvard-trained economist), which implemented a key package of reforms in the wake of the 1982 debt crisis, featured a significant number of North American-trained economists and was hailed by *The Economist* as 'probably the most economically literate group that has ever governed any nation anywhere'. Manmohan Singh and Montek Singh Ahluwalia, widely credited as architects of India's economic reforms, were educated at Oxford and Cambridge and have both worked for IFIs. See also Shastri, 'The Politics of Economic Liberalization in India'.
90. World Bank, *Accelerated Development in Sub-Saharan Africa*. See for example its conclusion that 'on balance, protectionism by developed countries had little effect on African growth in the last decade' (20) and its attribution of poor export performance purely to internal factors (21).
91. Ibid., 121.
92. See for example the United Nations Millennium Declaration, <http://www.un.org/millennium/declaration/ares552e.pdf>, clause 13: 'Success in meeting these objectives depends, *inter alia*, on good governance within each country. It also depends on good governance at the international level and on transparency in the financial, monetary and trading systems. We are committed to an open, equitable, rule-based, predictable and non-discriminatory multilateral trading and financial system.'
93. Krugman, 'Analytical Afterthoughts on the Asian Crisis', argues that the IMF ought to pay more attention to managing creditor panic through debt standstills and rollovers, instead of focusing solely on deep structural reform within debtor

countries. The latter course has the effect of reinforcing creditor panic by conveying the impression that 'things were out of control' within these countries. See also Sachs, 'Creditor Panics'.
94. Woods, *The Globalizers*, 42–3.
95. Hobson, *Imperialism*, 196–7.
96. Ibid., 197.
97. Ibid., 198.
98. Ibid., 54–5.
99. There is an extensive literature across the ideological spectrum that sees the United States as an empire, some examples of which are Bacevich, *American Empire*; Cox, 'The Empire's Back in Town'; Darwin, *After Tamerlane*; Ferguson, *Empire*; Haass, 'Imperial America'; Ignatieff, *Empire Lite*; Ikenberry, 'America's Imperial Ambition'; Johnson, *Blowback*; Johnson, *The Sorrows of Empire*; Kagan, 'The Benevolent Empire'; Lundestad, *The American 'Empire'*; Mallaby, 'The Reluctant Imperialist'; Prestowitz, *Rogue Nation*; Wade, 'The Invisible Hand of the American Empire'.
100. From the point of view of the indigenous inhabitants of settler colonies (Canada, Australia, New Zealand, the Latin American republics, etc.), these countries are not 'non-imperial'. There are significant variations between them of course. The Treaty of Waitangi or the creation of Nunavut might leave the Maoris of New Zealand and the First Nations of Canada respectively significantly better off than the aboriginals of Australia vis-à-vis their respective states. But these are still differences in the degree of colonization, not repudiations of the fact of it.
101. Sikkink, 'Explaining International Political and Civil Rights', reports that Argentina has been at the forefront of a developing international norm of domestic criminal prosecutions of individual state officials. Argentina's strong support for this norm most likely comes out of its historical experience of severe human rights abuse under military rule and a consequent desire on the part of liberal elites to lock the state into structures of international accountability that might make a relapse into authoritarianism less likely.
102. Wade, 'Japan, the World Bank, and the Art of Paradigm Maintenance'.
103. Foot, 'The Study of China's International Behaviour'; Levine, 'Perception and Ideology in Chinese Foreign Policy'.
104. Khalidi, *Resurrecting Empire*.
105. Nussbaum, 'Kant and Cosmopolitanism'.
106. Pagden, 'Stoicism, Cosmopolitanism, and the Legacy of European Imperialism', 5.
107. Calhoun, 'The Class Consciousness of Frequent Travellers', 887.
108. Muthu, *Enlightenment Against Empire*, 268.
109. Heater, *World Citizenship and Government*, 15, 24.
110. Douzinas, *Human Rights and Empire*, 156–9.
111. For a survey of English School views on the desirability of relying on states to act as agents of moral progress, see Wheeler, 'Guardian Angel or Global Gangster'.
112. Fukuyama, *The End of History and the Last Man*, 280.

113. Shaw, *Global Society and International Relations*, 181.
114. Doyle, 'Kant, Liberal Legacies and Foreign Affairs', 28: 'Farsighted and constitutive measures have only been provided by the liberal international order when one liberal state stood pre-eminent among the rest, prepared and able to take measures, as did the US following World War II, to sustain economically and politically the foundations of liberal society beyond its borders... the decline of US hegemonic leadership may pose dangers for the liberal world.' But importantly, Doyle is critical of the manner in which hegemonic leadership is exercised in relation to non-liberal states (30–48).
115. See Ignatieff, 'The Way We Live Now', for a consequentialist case for the 2003 war on Iraq: 'What tipped me in favour... was the belief that Hussein ran an especially odious regime and that war offered the only real chance of overthrowing him. This was a somewhat opportunistic case for war, since I knew that the administration did not see freeing Iraq from tyranny as anything but a secondary objective.... I supported an administration whose intentions I didn't trust, believing that the consequences would repay the gamble.'
116. Galtung, 'Violence, Peace, and Peace Research', 170–1.
117. Beitz, *Political Theory and International Relations*, 143–53; 'Cosmopolitan Ideals and National Sentiment', 595.
118. Pogge, *World Poverty and Human Rights*, 132–3.
119. Shue, *Basic Rights*, ch. 2.
120. Nussbaum, 'Patriotism and Cosmopolitanism', 14.
121. Singer, 'Famine, Affluence and Morality', 241.
122. Beitz, 'Cosmopolitan Liberalism and the States System', 124.
123. Ibid. See also Beitz, 'International Liberalism and Distributive Justice', 287. Pogge makes an identical distinction between what he calls 'legal' and 'moral' cosmopolitanism in 'Cosmopolitanism and Sovereignty', 90; *World Poverty and Human Rights*, 53.
124. Beitz, 'Cosmopolitan Liberalism and the States System', 125.
125. Ibid., 125–6.
126. Ibid., 127.
127. Ibid., endnote 3; Beitz, 'International Liberalism and Distributive Justice', 289; Nussbaum, *Frontiers of Justice*, ch. 5; Pogge, 'Cosmopolitanism and Sovereignty', 92; Shue, *Basic Rights*, 168–9.
128. Kant, *Perpetual Peace*, 113.
129. Shue, *Basic Rights*, 175; Appiah, *Cosmopolitanism*, 163.
130. Nussbaum, *Frontiers of Justice*, 257–8.
131. Pogge, 'Cosmopolitanism and Sovereignty', 90, appears to understand legal cosmopolitanism (his equivalent of Beitz's institutional cosmopolitanism) in this reductive fashion, defining it as 'a concrete political ideal of a global order under which all persons have equivalent legal rights and duties—are fellow citizens of a universal republic'.
132. Beitz, 'Cosmopolitan Liberalism and the States System', 124.

133. Pogge's recommendations for institutional reform—e.g. rescinding the international borrowing and resource extraction privileges of undemocratic governments, a global resources divided, etc.—are a noteworthy exception to this tendency (see *World Poverty and Human Rights*, ch. 6 and 8).
134. Nussbaum, *Frontiers of Justice*, 314–15.
135. Ibid., 318.
136. Shue, *Basic Rights*, 175.
137. Nussbaum, *Frontiers of Justice*, 314.
138. Held et al., *Global Transformations*, introduction.
139. Schmitt, *Political Theology*, 5.
140. Douzinas, *Human Rights and Empire*, 257.
141. Krisch, 'More Equal than the Rest?', 169.
142. Barkawi & Laffey, 'Retrieving the Imperial', 124.
143. Cited from Ikenberry, 'America's Imperial Ambition', 52.
144. Chimni, 'International Institutions Today'.
145. Hurrell, *On Global Order*, 292–8, offers a comprehensive argument for why a 'retreat to pluralism' is inconceivable in the current conjuncture.
146. For examples of this literature, see Archibugi & Held eds., *Cosmopolitan Democracy*; Archibugi, Held & Kohler eds., *Re-imagining Political Community*; Archibugi, 'Cosmopolitan Democracy'.
147. Calhoun, 'The Necessity and Limits of Cosmopolitanism', 13, 27–8; '"Belonging" in the Cosmopolitan Imaginary', 535.
148. Gowan, 'Neoliberal Cosmopolitanism', 92–3.
149. See for example, Falk, 'The World Order between Inter-State Law and the Law of Humanity'; Kaldor, *Global Civil Society*; Kaldor, 'Transnational Civil Society'; for criticisms of the use of 'global civil society', see Chandler, 'Building Global Civil Society "From Below"?'; Keane, 'Global Civil Society'.
150. Koskenniemi, *From Apology to Utopia*, 17, 20, 23, 602.

CHAPTER 3

1. Bull, *The Anarchical Society*, 13.
2. Brown, 'International Theory and International Society'.
3. Nardin, *Law, Morality, and the Relations of States*, 9.
4. Alderson & Hurrell, 'Bull's Conception of International Society', 7–10. Note that while solidarism entails convergence in the norms, rules, institutions, and goals of states, it does not imply a particular content to the norms and goals that they jointly pursue. As such, the theoretical category 'solidarism' can accommodate the solidarity of communist and Islamic states as easily as that of liberal states—different kinds of solidarism are possible (Buzan, *From International to World Society?*, 147).
5. Hurrell, 'Society and Anarchy in the 1990s', 31.

6. Jackson, *The Global Covenant*, 165.
7. Ibid., 163.
8. See Armstrong, *Revolution and World Order*, ch. 4, for an account of the USSR's movement towards 'increasingly state-like behaviour' as Lenin and others realized that worldwide proletarian revolution was not imminent.
9. Jackson, *The Global Covenant*, 374, 385, 409: '[T]he pluralist ethic was already evident in Europe in the Westphalian accommodation of religious differences between Protestant rulers and Catholic rulers. The global expansion of international society from Europe to the rest of the world can be understood as the universalisation of that same ethic of accommodation.'
10. Yasuaki, 'When Was the Law of International Society Born?', 30–2, 51–4.
11. This may strike some as a heretical assertion, yet if solidarism is understood as norm convergence it does not seem an unreasonable assertion given the extraordinary degree of norm convergence that an *international* society of *states* entailed. See Bull, 'The Emergence of a Universal International Society', 121–2: '[T]he coming together of numerous and extremely diverse political entities to form a single international society presupposed that these entities *had come to resemble one another* at least to the extent that they were all, in some comparable sense, states.... [T]he process by which Asian and African political communities did come to enter into such reciprocal relations and to enjoy full rights as members of international society was inseparable from domestic processes of political and social reform *which narrowed the differences between them and the political communities of the West, and contributed to a process of convergence*' (emphasis mine).
12. The degree of choice or coercion must obviously be assessed on a case-by-case basis. Uncolonized 'middle power' states such as Japan and Turkey exercised a greater degree of agency in this matter, engaging in pre-emptive defensive modernizations (the Meiji Restoration in Japan, the Tanzimat reforms in the Ottoman Empire) so as to better resist the encroachments of Western Powers. Even in colonized territories, native elites were always divided over questions of political subjectivity. Some embraced Western modes of subjectivity out of a genuine belief that these were superior to indigenous forms, others did so much more reluctantly and some not at all.
13. Thomas, *New States, Sovereignty and Intervention*, 22–51.
14. G. A. Res. 1514 (XV), U. N. Doc. A/4684 (1961).
15. G. A. Res. 2131 (XX), U. N. Doc. A/6014 (1965).
16. AHG/Res. 16(1), Resolutions adopted by the First Ordinary Session of the Assembly of Heads of State and Government, Cairo, 17–21 July 1964.
17. On the reasons for, and the implications of, the relative lack of interstate war between African states, see Herbst, 'War and the State in Africa'.
18. Clapham, *Africa and the International System*, 47.
19. See G. A. Res. 3379 (XXX), U. N. Doc. A/Res/3379 (1975), which determined that 'Zionism is a form of racism and racial discrimination' and was passed by a vote of 72 to 35 with 32 abstentions. The resolution remained in force for sixteen years and was revoked by G. A. Res. 4686 (1991).
20. Clapham, *Africa and the International System*, 113, 209–10.

21. Cited from Thomas, *New States, Sovereignty and Intervention*, 66.
22. Of course such regimes were not limited to Africa—think of 'Papa Doc' Duvalier in Haiti and Pol Pot in Cambodia, for example.
23. Thomas, *New States, Sovereignty and Intervention*, 73.
24. Ibid., 98. Despite his criticism of Amin's treatment of the Ugandan people, Nyerere justified Tanzania's intervention in Uganda in January 1979 on grounds of self-defence. He argued, somewhat disingenuously, that there was a second, parallel conflict—in which Tanzania was allegedly not involved—between the people of Uganda (including exile forces who had been organizing on Tanzanian territory) and Amin's regime.
25. Rothstein, *The Weak in the World of the Strong*, 110.
26. Mortimer, *The Third World Coalition in International Politics*, ch. 2–4.
27. Declaration on the Establishment of a New International Economic Order, G. A. Res. 3201 (S-VI), U. N. Doc. A/9559 (1974). See also Cox, 'Ideologies and the NIEO'.
28. Inayatullah, 'Beyond the Sovereignty Dilemma', 52. For the dependency literature, see Cardoso & Faleto, *Dependency and Development in Latin America*; Seers, *Dependency Theory*; Seligson & Passé-Smith, *Development and Underdevelopment*.
29. Wendt & Barnett, 'Dependent State Formation and Third World militarization', 332.
30. ICISS, *The Responsibility to Protect*, 16–18; Evans, 'The Responsibility to Protect', 285–6.
31. Final Document of the XIV Ministerial Conference of the Non-Aligned Movement, para. 8; Final Document of the XIII Conference of Heads of State or Government of the Non-Aligned Movement, para. 16; Final Document of the XII Summit, para. 7 (which, however, does not use the phrase 'humanitarian intervention').
32. Robinson, 'A Southern Perspective on Humanitarian Intervention?'.
33. Thakur, 'Developing Countries and the Intervention-Sovereignty Debate', 204.
34. Adebajo & Landsberg, 'The Heirs of Nkrumah'.
35. African Union, The Constitutive Act, Article 4(h).
36. See ch. 2, footnote 23.
37. Nel, 'South Africa', 257–8.
38. See R2PCS, 'What Governments said about R2P at 2005 World Summit', and 'Chart on Government Positions on R2P'.
39. But see 'The Common African Position on the Proposed Reform of the United Nations', para. B(i), which suggests a willingness to contemplate intervention by regional organizations with *post hoc* Security Council authorization.
40. 'Final Communiqué: African Mini-Summit on Darfur'.
41. Nkrumah, 'Darfur in Flames'.
42. Serrano, 'Latin America', 232.
43. R2PCS, 'Chart on Government Positions on R2P', mentions Argentina, Chile, Colombia, Mexico, Panama, and Peru as having embraced the 'responsibility to

protect', Brazil as having an unclear position, and Cuba and Venezuela as being opposed.
44. On the definition of 'regions' see Hurrell, 'Regionalism in Theoretical Perspective'.
45. Final Declaration of the Regional Meeting for Asia of the World Conference on Human Rights, para. 8.
46. See for example its very strong statements against the NATO intervention in Kosovo, quoted in Nambiar, 'India', 263, 265, 267–8. See also Kumar, 'Sovereignty and Intervention'.
47. Wheeler, *Saving Strangers*, 186.
48. Griffiths et al., 'Sovereignty and Suffering', 48.
49. This is not a regional group, but I discuss it here because some of the most powerful Muslim-majority states are in Asia.
50. Wheeler, *Saving Strangers*, 280.
51. Karawan, 'The Muslim World', 219–20.
52. R2PCS, 'Chart on Government Positions on R2P'.
53. Robinson, 'A Southern Perspective on Humanitarian Intervention?', 71.
54. Bellamy, 'Responsibility to Protect or Trojan Horse?', 52.
55. Cited from Evans, 'The Responsibility to Protect', 288.
56. For a concise snapshot of what remained of the economic pluralist space in the early post-Cold War years, see Williamson, 'Democracy and the "Washington Consensus"', 1329–36.
57. Final Document of the XIV Ministerial Conference of the Non-Aligned Movement, para. 214–18.
58. For an overview, see Bell, *Communitarianism*.
59. Walzer, *Spheres of Justice*, 9–10, 28–9; Walzer, *Thick and Thin*, 34–6.
60. Bell, *Communitarianism and Its Critics*, 94.
61. Miller, *On Nationality*, 90–8, 185; 'Nationality', 70. See also Tamir, *Liberal Nationalism*, 96, 115, 118.
62. Pettit, *Republicanism*, 259.
63. Miller, *On Nationality*, ch. 4. The argument is qualified, crucially, by a recognition of the practical infeasibility of the principle of 'a state for every nation' (115).
64. Walzer, 'The Moral Standing of States', 228.
65. Cunliffe, 'Sovereignty and the Politics of Responsibility', 52–3.
66. Der Derian et al., 'How Should Sovereignty Be Defended?', 189–92. See also Kingsbury, 'Sovereignty and Inequality'.
67. Ayoob, 'The Security Problematic of the Third World', 266.
68. Ayoob, *The Third World Security Predicament*, 30.
69. Ibid., 34.
70. Ibid., 39, 40.
71. See Jackson, *Quasi-States*, ch. 7, where lack of readiness is a prominent theme in the explanation for why 'quasi-states' have failed to develop the requisites for 'positive sovereignty'.
72. Ayoob, *The Third World Security Predicament*, 29.
73. Ayoob, 'Humanitarian Intervention and State Sovereignty', 94.

74. Ayoob, *The Third World Security Predicament*, 173.
75. Ayoob, 'Subaltern Realism', 40.
76. Barnett, 'Radical Chic?', 61. For an argument emphasizing the moral dimension of this objection, see Makinda, 'The Global Covenant as an Evolving Institution', 113, 120.
77. Tilly, *Coercion, Capital, and European States, AD 990–1990*, 224.
78. Ibid., 16, 206, 211, 220.
79. Taylor & Botea, 'Tilly Tally', argue that war is more likely to contribute to state-formation in Third World states that are ethnically homogeneous and led by revolutionary regimes. On the basis of these variables, they find that war was state-making in Vietnam, but state-destroying in Afghanistan.
80. Barnett, 'Radical Chic?', 61.
81. Walzer, *Just and Unjust Wars*, 98, suggests that legitimacy criteria should become more stringent after a 'period of grace': 'What is the test of popular support in a country where democracy is unknown and elections are routinely managed? The test, for governments as for insurgents, is self-help ... one assumes the legitimacy of new regimes; there is, so to speak, a period of grace, a time to build support.'
82. Ayoob, *The Third World Security Predicament*, 173.
83. For a discussion of the distinction between utilitarian and deontological approaches to international ethics, see Donaldson, 'Kant's Global Rationalism' and Ellis, 'Utilitarianism and International Ethics'.
84. Ayoob, *The Third World Security Predicament*, 39, 40.
85. Bardhan, 'Symposium on Democracy and Development', 45, 46.
86. Haggard, *Pathways from the Periphery*, 262. Haggard mentions a number of policy reforms that could be modelled as collective action problems, which authoritarian elites are able to solve by command. These include stabilization, devaluation, trade liberalization, opening to foreign direct investment, rationalization of fiscal incentives, tax reform, financial market reform, shifts in the composition of government spending, etc.
87. Scott, *Seeing Like a State*, 94.
88. Haggard, 'Politics and Institutions in the World Bank's East Asia', 104.
89. Clapham, *Africa and the International System*, 58, writes that 'in terms of their willingness to use coercion, there was little to choose between Samuel Doe of Liberia and Mengitsu Haile-Mariam of Ethiopia, but whereas Doe's was merely a personal dictatorship, Mengitsu sought through Marxism-Leninism (however counter-productively) to establish a powerful and centralized Ethiopian state and a planned economy'.
90. Przeworski & Limongi, 'Political Regimes and Economic Growth', 64.
91. Przeworski et al., *Democracy and Development*, 271.
92. Sen, *Development as Freedom*, 152–3.
93. Ayoob, *The Third World Security Predicament*, 195; 'Humanitarian Intervention and State Sovereignty', 94.
94. Jackson, *The Global Covenant*, 179.
95. Gellner, *Nations and Nationalism*, 57.

96. Ibid.
97. I do not use 'citizen' here in a legal sense. Formal legal equality is often a veneer for a more differentiated experience of belonging in which the membership of dominant groups is not in question, but marginalized groups must continually bend over backwards to demonstrate their fealty to the nation.
98. Anderson, *Imagined Communities*, 43.
99. Ibid., 44, 45.
100. Hobsbawm, *Nations and Nationalism Since 1780*, 60. Eugen Weber has suggested in the case of France, that the imposition of a single official language should be viewed as a process of domestic colonization in which various foreign provinces such as Brittany and Occitanie are linguistically subdued and culturally incorporated (cited from Scott, *Seeing Like a State*, 72).
101. Anderson, *Imagined Communities*, 86.
102. Hobsbawm, *Nations and Nationalism Since 1780*, 90.
103. Scott, *Seeing Like a State*, 81–2.
104. Harding, 'The Money that Prays', 8.
105. Reanda, 'The Commission on the Status of Women', 286.
106. Clark, 'The Vienna Convention Reservations Regime and the Convention on Discrimination Against Women', 283.
107. Compare reservations to the CERD, <http://www.unhchr.ch/html/menu3/b/treaty2_asp.htm>, with those to CEDAW, <http://www.un.org/womenwatch/daw/cedaw/reservations-country.htm>.
108. Charlesworth & Chinkin, 'The Gender of Jus Cogens', 67. The appropriate test of a norm's 'jus cogens' status is universal acceptance 'as a legal rule by states and recognition of it as a rule of jus cogens by an overwhelming majority of states, crossing ideological and political divides' (Shaw, *International Law*, 97).
109. Affidavit filed by the Government of India in Special Leave Petition (Civil) No. 7217–7218 of 2005, in the matter of *Naz Foundation* v. *Government of Delhi*, <http://humanrights-india.blogspot.com/2005_10_01_humanrights-india_archive.html>.
110. *Narmada Bachao Andolan* v. *Union of India* (2000) 10 SCC 664, per Justice Kirpal.
111. Chatterjee, *Nationalist Thought and the Colonial World*, 50.
112. Chatterjee, *The Nation and Its Fragments*, 6, 119–20.
113. Ibid., 120, 126, 130.
114. The colonial state no doubt intervened heavily in areas that nationalists regarded as part of the 'spiritual' domain, but when these interventions threatened the 'essence' of national identity, the nationalist response often took the form of establishing institutions in parallel with those created by the state (one thinks of educational institutions in particular here).
115. The phrase is borrowed from Naipaul, *The Mimic Men*.
116. Yet the story is not that simple, for even the post-colonial state faces difficulty in entering this domain. Because, for so long in the nationalist imagination, it was conceived as a domain off limits to the colonial state, the 'spiritual' gradually

begins to be seen as off limits to the state *per se*, so that post-colonial states attempting reform in these areas now encounter the hostility and resistance of their own societies, or at least elements thereof (think of the Indian state's attempts at law reform in the domain of family law).
117. Chatterjee, *The Nation and Its Fragments*, 6.
118. Zakaria, 'Culture Is Destiny', quotes Singapore's first Prime Minister Lee Kuan Yew as saying: 'We have left the past behind, and there is an underlying unease that there will be nothing left of us which is part of the old.'
119. The thesis was most forcefully articulated at the time of the Bangkok Declaration prior to the 1993 World Conference on Human Rights; the debate had waned by the end of the 1990s, with the onset of the Asian financial crisis.
120. See for example Final Declaration of the Regional Meeting for Asia of the World Conference on Human Rights, para. 5.
121. Engle, 'Culture and Human Rights', 329. See also Dallmayr, '"Asian Values" and Global Human Rights'.
122. Cited from Pritchard, 'The Jurisprudence of Human Rights'.
123. Bell, *East Meets West*, 8, 15, 34, 90–3.
124. Wedeen, *Ambiguities of Domination*, 7, 41, 43.
125. BBC, 'Tsvangirai "Leads" Zimbabwe Vote'; See Mamdani, 'Lessons of Zimbabwe', for an analysis of the roots of Mugabe's domestic support; but see also the debate in the letters column of the *London Review of Books* (vol. 30, no. 24 and vol. 31, no. 1).
126. Phimister & Raftopoulos, 'Mugabe, Mbeki & the Politics of Anti-Imperialism', 385. See also the exchange in Chan & Patel, 'Zimbabwe's Foreign Policy'.
127. It would be simplistic to view internal conflicts in straightforwardly 'state versus society' terms, for they often reflect deep divisions within societies themselves. These may manifest themselves as state versus society struggles if the state is largely appropriated by one or a few societal groups. In more representative states, they will manifest themselves as conflicts within the state apparatus between different factions.

INTERMEZZO

1. On levels of analysis, see Singer, 'The Level-of-Analysis Problem in International Relations'.
2. Tarrow, *The New Transnational Activism*, 104.
3. Subaltern studies first emerged as a distinct approach to Indian historiography (see Guha, 'On Some Aspects of the Historiography of Colonial India', 40). Works from a subaltern perspective in other disciplines include Hobsbawm, *Primitive Rebels*; Scott, *Weapons of the Weak*; Rajagopal, *International Law from Below*; Colas, *International Civil Society*, especially ch. 4.

4. For an influential account of the dangers of reading subaltern agency from elite texts, see Spivak, 'Can the Subaltern Speak?'.
5. Soueif, *In the Eye of the Sun*, 63.

CHAPTER 4

1. Joyce, *A Portrait of the Artist as a Young Man*, 219.
2. Ibid., 221.
3. Howes, 'Joyce, Colonialism, and Nationalism', 265.
4. Joyce, *A Portrait of the Artist as a Young Man*, 276.
5. Ibid., 261.
6. Barry, 'Introduction', xxx.
7. Nolan, *James Joyce and Nationalism*, 38.
8. Cited from Deane, 'Joyce the Irishman', 37.
9. Ibid., 36–7.
10. Joyce, *Dubliners*, 49.
11. Howes, 'Joyce, Colonialism, and Nationalism', 262.
12. Joyce, 'Ireland: Island of Saints and Sages', 119.
13. Ibid., 116.
14. Ibid., 125.
15. Deane, 'Joyce the Irishman', 41.
16. *A Portrait* was first serialized in *The Egoist* from 1914–15 and was published in book form in 1916. *Ghare Baire* was serialized in the Bengali journal *Sabuj Patra* from May 1915 to February 1916, and appeared as a book in 1916. It was published in English translation serially as *At Home and Outside* in the Calcutta monthly *Modern Review* over 1918–19, and as a book called *The Home and the World* by Macmillan in 1919. All references here are from the English book translation, so I use this last title.
17. Tagore, *The Home and the World*, 136.
18. Young, *Postcolonialism*, 168, 302, 313, 318; Sarkar, *The Swadeshi Movement in Bengal*, ch. 2.
19. Joyce, 'Home Rule Comes of Age', footnote 7.
20. It is surprisingly difficult to locate work in comparative literature on Joyce and Tagore (for one example see Livingstone, 'Global Tropes/Worldly Readings'). This may be due to the fact that while Joyce is read as the quintessential modernist, Tagore in English translation reads like a Victorian writer. Readers of Tagore in the original Bengali are better able to appreciate his stylistic innovations (see for example, Radice, 'Preface', x, who writes that *Ghare Baire* was the first Bengali novel written in *chalit* (colloquial) Bengali, rather than in the more Sanskritized, high-vernacular *sadhu bhasha*).
21. Sarkar, *The Swadeshi Movement in Bengal*, ch. 2.
22. Tagore, *The Home and the World*, 18.

23. Ibid., 19, 27–8.
24. This relative price disparity was very likely a consequence of colonial tariff policy, although we are not told this in the novel.
25. Tagore, *The Home and the World*, 94.
26. Ibid., 109.
27. Ibid., 120.
28. Sarkar, 'Many Faces of Love', 34.
29. We are left in some doubt as to his fate in the novel, but in the film adaptation of the book by Satyajit Ray, it is very clear that Nikhil has died.
30. Nussbaum, 'Patriotism and Cosmopolitanism', 5.
31. Tagore, *The Home and the World*, 26.
32. Ibid., 27.
33. Ibid., 129.
34. Nandy, *The Illegitimacy of Nationalism*, 13–14.
35. Sprinker, 'Homeboys', 114, 120.
36. Tagore, *The Home and the World*, 197–8.
37. Cited from Nandy, *The Illegitimacy of Nationalism*, 75.
38. Sarkar, 'Many Faces of Love', 41.
39. Tagore, *Nationalism*, 5.
40. Tagore, 'Hindu University', 156.
41. Sarkar, '*Ghare Baire* in Its Times', 145; Dutta & Robinson, *Rabindranath Tagore*, 145.
42. Guha, 'Discipline and Mobilize', 82, 89; Sarkar, *The Swadeshi Movement in Bengal*, ch. 8.
43. Tagore, *Nationalism*, 42.
44. Ibid., 26.
45. Ibid., 83.
46. For a sense of these disagreements, see the following essays by Tagore: 'The Call of Truth', 'The Cult of the Charkha', 'Striving for Swaraj'; and the replies by Gandhi: 'The Great Sentinel', 'The Poet and the Charkha'.
47. Tagore, 'The Cult of the Charkha', 100.
48. See Tagore, 'Tagore's Reflection on Non-cooperation and Cooperation', and the following essays by Gandhi: 'The Poet's Anxiety', 'The Poet and the Charkha', 'The Poet and the Wheel'; On this exchange, see also Guha, 'The Independent Journal of Opinion'.
49. Tagore, Letter to Lord Chelmsford, 187.
50. Dutta & Robinson, *Rabindranath Tagore*, 123, 145, 299. I am reminded of Waiyaki, the protagonist of Kenyan novelist Ngũgĩ wa Thiong'o's *The River Between*, who, in trying to mediate between colonialist and nativist influences, hesitates to enter politics but throws himself into education.
51. Tagore, 'The Congress', 174.
52. Tagore, *Nationalism*, 113.
53. Tagore, 'East and West', 212–13.
54. Tagore, *Nationalism*, 14.

55. Tagore, *Nationalism*, 89, 109. See also Tagore, 'The Changing Age', 342; 'The Problem of India', 239.
56. Chatterjee, *Nationalist Thought and the Colonial World*, 50–1.
57. Tagore, *Nationalism*, 14.
58. Tagore, 'The Centre of Indian Culture', 220.
59. Kabir, 'Introduction', 7.
60. Tagore, 'The Vicissitudes of Education'; 'The Centre of Indian Culture'.
61. Tagore, 'Tagore's Reflection on Non-cooperation and Cooperation', 62.
62. Tagore, 'The Centre of Indian Culture', 220.
63. Tagore, 'Tagore's Reflection on Non-cooperation and Cooperation', 55.
64. Tagore, *Nationalism*, 67.
65. Ibid., 219–20.
66. Berlin, 'Rabindranath Tagore and the Consciousness of Nationality', 264.
67. Said, *Representations of the Intellectual*, 15.
68. Said, *Culture and Imperialism*, 228.
69. Ahmad, *In Theory*, 200.
70. Ibid., 215.
71. Recall Scheffler's understanding of cosmopolitanism as a doctrine about culture and the self, explained in chapter 1, this volume.
72. Said, *Orientalism*, 3, 205, 300–01.
73. Lockman, *Contending Visions of the Middle East*, 196.
74. Said, *Orientalism*, 331.
75. Ibid., 272.
76. Ibid., 326.
77. Said, *Culture and Imperialism*, 52, 137.
78. Said, *Representations of the Intellectual*, xi.
79. JanMohamed, '"Worldliness-Without-World, Homelessness-As-Home"', 104.
80. Said, *The Question of Palestine*, 7.
81. Said, *The Politics of Dispossession*, xvi.
82. Said, *Covering Islam*.
83. Said, *The Politics of Dispossession*, xvi.
84. Spivak, 'Subaltern Studies', 13.
85. Parry, 'Overlapping Territories and Intertwined Histories', 20, 30.
86. Said, *Reflections on Exile and Other Literary and Cultural Essays*, 402.
87. Ibid., 377.
88. Ibid., 421–5.
89. Ibid., 176–7.
90. Wicke & Sprinker, 'Interview with Edward Said', 236–7.
91. Said, *The Politics of Dispossession*, 115–16. On the construction of an Indian 'national cuisine', see Appadurai, 'How to Make a National Cuisine'.
92. Said, *The Politics of Dispossession*, 9.
93. Said, *Representations of the Intellectual*, 24.
94. Renan, 'What Is a Nation?', 45.
95. Fanon, *The Wretched of the Earth*, 115.

96. Ibid., 135.
97. On the one hand, Fanon's sensitivity to different strands of anti-colonial resistance (tensions between urban and rural, moderates and radicals, legal and illegal tendencies within the party) suggests that social and economic consciousness develops—and needs to develop—in the thick of struggle against the colonial oppressor. On the other hand, he calls for struggle against the national bourgeoisie *after* independence from the colonialists, even suggesting at one point that 'what can be dangerous is when [the people] reach the stage of social consciousness before the stage of nationalism. If this happens, we find in underdeveloped countries fierce demands for social justice which paradoxically are allied with often primitive tribalism' (ibid., 164). Yet the very fact that Fanon offered this analysis *before* Algeria had won its independence suggests that he was keen to foster the development of social and economic consciousness even before the nationalist struggle had been won.
98. Cherki, *Frantz Fanon*, 104–5, 112, 159.
99. Said, *Representations of the Intellectual*, 30.
100. Said, *The End of the Peace Process*, 19.
101. Ibid., 162.
102. Ibid., 22. See also in the same collection, the essays entitled 'Post-Election Realities' and 'Are There No Limits to Corruption?'.
103. Ibid., 110.
104. Ibid., 67.
105. For an account of why the PLO signed the Oslo Accords despite the lack of any meaningful concessions to Palestinian demands, see Shehadeh, 'Analyzing Palestine', 100–1; Khalidi, *The Iron Cage*, ch. 5, 6.
106. Said, *The End of the Peace Process*, 264.
107. Ibid., 330.
108. See in ibid., the essays entitled 'Art, Culture and Nationalism', 'What Can Separation Mean?' and 'Truth and Reconciliation'.
109. Parry, 'Resistance Theory/Theorizing Resistance or Two Cheers for Nativism', 186–7.
110. Cited in Fanon, *Black Skin, White Masks*, 133.
111. Ibid., 134.
112. Ibid., 135.
113. Ibid.
114. Ibid., 226. He is referring here to the Haitian revolution (1791–1804) led by Toussaint L'Ouverture, which established Haiti as the first independent black republic (see James, *The Black Jacobins*).
115. Ibid.
116. Ibid., 228.
117. Ibid., 231.
118. Fanon, *The Wretched of the Earth*, 198–9.
119. Cherki, *Frantz Fanon*, 67–72.
120. Ibid., 34.
121. Gandhi, *Postcolonial Theory*, 109.

CHAPTER 5

1. Marx & Engels, *The Communist Manifesto*, 14.
2. Benner, *Really Existing Nationalisms*, 48.
3. Marx & Engels, *The Communist Manifesto*, 18.
4. Ibid., 29.
5. Benner, *Really Existing Nationalisms*, 50–5.
6. Cited from ibid., 149.
7. Ibid., 154.
8. Marx, 'The British Rule in India'.
9. Ahmad, *In Theory*, 225.
10. Marx, 'The Future Results of British Rule in India', 365.
11. Benner, *Really Existing Nationalisms*, 197, 199.
12. Marx, 'Letter to Kugelmann, 29 November 1869', 639.
13. Marx, 'Letter to Meyer and Vogt, 9 April 1870', 640.
14. Benner, *Really Existing Nationalisms*, 200.
15. Young, *Postcolonialism*, 129.
16. Cited from ibid., 130.
17. Colas, 'Putting Cosmopolitanism into Practice', 526.
18. Young, *Postcolonialism*, 131–4.
19. The discussion in this paragraph is taken from ibid., ch. 11.
20. Desai, 'From National Bourgeoisie to Rogues, Failures and Bullies', 171.
21. For a good overview, see Tormey, *Anti-Capitalism*, ch. 2.
22. Harvey, *The New Imperialism*, 143–5.
23. Tormey, *Anti-Capitalism*, 61–7.
24. Sen et al., *World Social Forum*.
25. Graeber, 'The New Anarchists', 204; Klein, *Fences and Windows*, 4; Laffey & Weldes, '"Anti-Globalization" Protests and the Future of Democracy'.
26. Desai & Said, 'The New Anti-Capitalist Movement'; Tormey, *Anti-Capitalism*, 74–8.
27. Many commentators view the lack of a linking metanarrative as a strength rather than a weakness, enabling coalition-building among radically different actors without a consequent subsumption of individuality (Klein, *Fences and Windows*, 16; Kingsnorth, *One No, Many Yeses*). This lack of coherence has given rise to the occasional usage 'movement of movements' (Mertes ed., *A Movement of Movements*).
28. Crossley, 'Global Anti-Corporate Struggle', 674–6.
29. Cited from Callinicos, 'Where Now?', 393.
30. Hardt, 'Porto Allegre', 232.
31. Desai & Said, 'The New Anti-Capitalist Movement', 65–9.
32. Steger, *Globalism*, 93–4.
33. Tormey, *Anti-Capitalism*, 76.
34. Ibid., 91–102.

35. There are exceptions to this trend in the typologies discussed above (see e.g. Desai & Said's description of the 'schizophrenic relationship to globalisation' of the category of actors labelled 'alternatives' (69); see also Tormey's discussion of 'national internationalists' (91)).
36. General Command of the EZLN, 'War! First Declaration of the Lacandon Jungle', 15.
37. Human Rights Watch, *World Report 1995: Mexico*.
38. The communiqués are the key textual primary sources from which the political theory of the Zapatistas might be abstracted. I focus mainly on the 1994–2001 period, a highpoint in the global visibility of the movement, during which much of its initial political and philosophical world view was elucidated. As a movement that is ongoing, a great deal of this world view may change in response to events on the ground. The difficulties of chasing a moving target have compelled me to confine the analysis to a defined period.
39. For a description of this network, see Olesen, 'The transnational Zapatista solidarity network'; for a sense of the Internet presence of the solidarity network, see <http://www.eco.utexas.edu/faculty/Cleaver/zapsincyberwebsites.html>; for a description of the process of diffusion of Zapatista propaganda, see Tarrow, *The New Transnational Activism*, 113–17.
40. Brysk, 'Turning Weakness into Strength', 40.
41. All figures cited from Wager & Schulz, 'Civil-Military Relations in Mexico', 3–4. For Marcos' recitation of these facts, see Marcos, 'A Storm and a Prophecy: Chiapas—The Southeast in Two Winds', 22–9.
42. Gonzalez, 'The Zapatistas', 63.
43. Burbach, 'Roots of the Postmodern Rebellion in Chiapas', 118–20.
44. Harvey, 'Rural Reform and the Zapatista Rebellion', 192–3; Grindle, 'Reforming Land Tenure in Mexico', 42–3, 46, 49.
45. Woods, *The Globalizers*, 86; Grindle, 'Reforming Land Tenure in Mexico', 47–50.
46. Marcos, 'The Seven Loose Pieces of the Global Jigsaw Puzzle'.
47. Marcos, 'The Streams, When They Descend, Have No Way of Returning to the Mountains Except Beneath the Ground'. Other texts are less personalized, with the 'Zapatistas' functioning as universal metaphor for exclusion. See for example, General Command of the EZLN, 'Opening Remarks at the First Intercontinental *Encuentro* for Humanity and against Neoliberalism', 103–4; 'Mexico City', 155.
48. For archives of the two encuentros, see <http://www.nadir.org/nadir/initiativ/agp/chiapas1996/en/encounter1dx.html> and <http://www.nadir.org/nadir/initiativ/agp/chiapas1996/en/index.htm>. For more on PGA, see <http://www.nadir.org/nadir/initiativ/agp/en/>.
49. See Olesen, 'Globalising the Zapatistas', 260, who argues that the Zapatista solidarity network has a stronger claim to being 'global' and reflects a more intense sense of mutuality because, in contrast to older internationalisms where there was often a clear distinction between providers and beneficiaries of solidarity along North–South lines, the Zapatistas serve as a source of inspiration and ideas and not merely as an object of solidarity. But see Johnston & Laxer,

'Solidarity in the Age of Globalization', 76, who argue that the Zapatista solidarity network cannot be considered 'global' because its participants come primarily from a limited number of Western countries. Johnston & Laxer fail to consider the extent to which elements of Zapatista ideology have come to influence the social forum process, thereby travelling far beyond Western and Latin American left circles.

50. General Command of the EZLN, 'War! First Declaration of the Lacandon Jungle', 13.
51. General Command of the EZLN, 'Fourth Declaration of the Lacandon Jungle', 79.
52. Ibid.
53. General Command of the EZLN, 'We Want All Who Walk with the Truth to Unite in One Step'.
54. Specifically, Article 39 of the constitution, which provides that 'National Sovereignty essentially and originally resides in the people. All political power emanates from the people and its purpose is to help the people. The people have, at all times, the inalienable right to alter or modify their form of government'. General Command of the EZLN, 'First Declaration of the Lacandon Jungle', 14; 'Second Declaration of the Lacandon Jungle', 43.
55. Marcos, 'Mr. Zedillo, Welcome to the Nightmare', 69.
56. de Angelis, 'Globalization, New Internationalism and the Zapatistas', 20–1. The author makes the argument that whereas in the 'old internationalism', the international dimensions of struggle were subordinated to the strategic objectives of the national dimension, in the 'new internationalism' the national–international distinction has lost its sharpness. I disagree with de Angelis' view that 'this new internationalism is definitively losing the "national" dimension as the referent of social transformation' (16).
57. Baker, *Civil Society and Democratic Theory*, 144.
58. This is not intended to suggest that 'nation' can never be used as a metaphor in political communication. One frequently hears the term 'queer nation', where 'nation' is intended to arouse strong feelings of loyalty and allegiance to an identity without carrying the territorial connotations that national identities tend to. The phrase is understood easily enough, but confusions would certainly arise if queer advocacy on behalf of queer people worldwide were carried out under the banner of, say, the US flag.
59. Laxer, 'The Movement That Dare Not Speak Its Name'.
60. Marcos, 'The Seven Loose Pieces of the Global Jigsaw Puzzle'.
61. Marcos, 'For Maurice Najman, Who Keeps Feigning Death', 201. This seems to echo Eric Hobsbawm's observation that 'the most convenient world for multinational giants is one populated by dwarf states or no states at all', cited in Laxer, 'The Movement That Dare Not Speak Its Name', 7.
62. Omvedt, *Reinventing Revolution*, 111.
63. Mohan, 'A Powerful Voice that Espoused Farmers' Cause'.
64. Other major farmers' organizations are the Bharatiya Kisan Sangh in Gujarat and the Tamilaga Vyavasavavigal Sangham (Tamil Nadu Agriculturalists' Association) in Tamil Nadu.

65. For overviews of the social movement landscape in India, see Kothari, 'Social Movements and the Redefinition of Democracy'; Jayal, 'Reinventing the State'; Parajuli, 'Power and Knowledge in Development Discourse'; Shah ed., *Social Movements and the State*.
66. Assadi, *Peasant Movement in Karnataka*, 143.
67. Guha, 'The Environmentalism of the Poor', 28.
68. Assadi, *Peasant Movement in Karnataka*, 59–61.
69. Interview, Chukki Nanjundaswamy, who informed me that 'dumping' facilitated by the liberalized import regime had significantly undercut local prices in the market for sugarcane, paddy, coconut, maize, jowar, and wheat.
70. Omvedt, *Reinventing Revolution*, 111.
71. Interview, A. Somalingayya.
72. This account is summarized from Assadi, *Peasant Movement in Karnataka*, ch. 2; Assadi, '"Khadi Curtain", "Weak Capitalism" and "Operation Ryot"'.
73. KRRS, *News from KRRS*.
74. Katzenstein, Kothari, & Mehta, 'Social Movement Politics in India', 244, 252.
75. Interview, Chukki Nanjundaswamy.
76. KRRS, *News from KRRS*. An internet search revealed that this claim had been picked up and disseminated, uncritically and without verification, by the movement's international allies.
77. Census of India, 2001.
78. Assadi, '"Chickens", "Greens", and "Ragi Balls"', 204.
79. The attack on KFC took place four years before the more widely reported dismantling of a McDonald's outlet by French farmers led by José Bové, suggesting that KRRS may have been playing something of a pedagogic role in the 'anti-globalization' movement.
80. KRRS, *News from KRRS*.
81. Assadi, '"Chickens", "Greens", and "Ragi Balls"', 211.
82. <http://viacampesina.org/main_en/index.php>. For an overview of Via Campesina and other efforts at organizing small farmers globally, see Edelman, 'Transnational Peasant and Farmer Movements and Networks'.
83. Interview, Chukki Nanjundaswamy.
84. PGA, 'Brief history of PGA'.
85. KRRS, *News from KRRS*.
86. For critical discussions of the InterContinental Caravan which illustrate the challenges and ambiguities of international solidarity activism that draws together movements from very different social milieus, see Featherstone, 'Spatialities of Transnational Resistance to Globalization'; Ainger, 'Life Is Not Business'.
87. Raj, 'Indian Farmers Take the War to Europe'.
88. Nanjundaswamy, Statement at the Demonstration Against the World Economic Summit.
89. Hardt, 'Porto Allegre', 232.
90. Assadi, *Peasant Movement in Karnataka*, 125–8; Assadi, '"Khadi Curtain", "Weak Capitalism" and "Operation Ryot"', 219–21.

91. Omvedt, *Reinventing Revolution*, 117, sees this as characteristic of Indian farmers' movements, which embraced and profited from 'green revolution' technology, but also recognized the destructive effects of the new seeds and chemical inputs and looked for alternatives.
92. But see Nanjundaswamy, Interview with Fred de Sam Lazaro, where he clarifies that the issue is not the provenance of technology (*indigenous* versus *imported*), but the high degree of scientific uncertainty inherent in new technologies and the need to minimize these uncertainties before introducing them into farmers' fields.
93. Assadi, '"Khadi Curtain", "Weak Capitalism" and "Operation Ryot"', 221, and endnote 22.
94. Assadi, 'Globalisation and the State', 49.
95. Brass, 'The Politics of Gender, Nature and Nation in the Discourse of the New Farmers' Movements', 35.
96. This argument is condensed from a selection of Brass' writings. See ibid., 32; Brass, 'Introduction', 12–18; Brass, 'Moral Economists, Subalterns, New Social Movements, and the (Re-)Emergence of a (Post-)Modernized (Middle) Peasant', 180–5.
97. Edelman, 'Transnational Peasant and Farmer Movements and Networks', 187.
98. Gupta, 'Farmers' Movements in Contemporary India', 195. See also Omvedt, *Reinventing Revolution*, 100, 114, who agrees that these movements are composed, not of sharecroppers or poor peasants fighting landlords, but of independent commodity producers engaged in market production.
99. Both communities are found in the Government of India's list of 'other backward classes', making them eligible for various forms of affirmative action, unless they are excluded by a complicated set of criteria used to define the elite 'creamy layer' within each eligible caste on grounds such as property holdings. See <http://ncbc.nic.in/backward-classes/karnataka.html>. Both are, however, unambiguously above dalits in the caste hierarchy.
100. Assadi, *Peasant Movement in Karnataka*, ch. 3.
101. Omvedt, *Reinventing Revolution*, 103.
102. Ibid., 104.
103. Guttal, 'Farmers' Suicides in Karnataka State'.
104. Christian Aid, *The Damage Done*.
105. Mishra, 'Risks, Farmers' Suicides and Agrarian Crisis in India', 41–2. The suicide mortality rate (SMR, suicide deaths per 100,000 persons) for male farmers in India increased from 12.3 in 1996 to 19.2 in 2004 and then fell to 18.2 in 2005. SMR figures for male non-farmers were 11.9 in 1996, rising to a peak of 14.2 in 2000 and then declining to 13.4 in 2005.
106. Sidhu & Gill, 'Agricultural Credit and Indebtedness in India', 24.
107. Menon, 'The Rural Anger in Karnataka'.
108. These connections are traced in Jeromi, 'Impact of Agricultural Trade Liberalisation'; Mohanty, '"We Are Like the Living Dead"'; Menon, 'From Debt to

Death'; Sainath, 'No Sugar-Coated Pills for Cotton Farmers'; Rao, 'Blenheim and Bangalore'.
109. Keck & Sikkink, *Activists Beyond Borders*, 12; Risse & Sikkink, 'The Socialization of International Human Rights Norms into Domestic Practices', 18.
110. Tarrow, *The New Transnational Activism*, 60–1.
111. Bob, *The Marketing of Rebellion*, 29–32.
112. Gonzalez, 'The Zapatistas', 69. Articulated in a document entitled 'Hacia una Politica Popular' ('Towards a Popular Politics'), written by Adolfo Orive, a lecturer at Mexico City's Universidad Nacional Autónoma de Mexico, this tendency was critical of armed struggle and sceptical of the Leninist conception of a vanguardist party, calling instead for a 'politica de dos caras' (politics on two fronts). This entailed political organization on the margins, away from the threat of state repression and immersed within mass movements; the method of organization was called 'una politica asambleista', entailing direct democracy through mass meetings.
113. Morton, 'Mexico, Neoliberal Restructuring and the EZLN', 262.
114. Bob, *The Marketing of Rebellion*, 158–9.
115. Chandler, 'Building Global Civil Society "From Below"?'.
116. Census of India, 2001, <http://www.censusindia.gov.in/Census_Data_2001/India_at_glance/scst.aspx>.
117. For studies of the movement against the Narmada dam, see Khagram, *Dams and Development*; Fisher ed., *Toward Sustainable Development?*; Drèze, Samson & Singh eds., *The Dam and the Nation*.
118. Interview, Ramachandra Guha.
119. Marcos, 'Mr. Zedillo, Welcome to the Nightmare', 64.
120. For more on right-wing anti-globalization rhetoric, see Nigam, 'Radical Politics in the Times of Globalization', 157.
121. KRRS, *News from KRRS*.
122. Lloyd, 'Nationalisms Against the State'.
123. Johnston, 'Pedagogical Guerrillas, Armed Democrats, and Revolutionary Counterpublics', 472; Cox, *Production, Power, and World Order*, 253.
124. Cheah, *Inhuman Conditions*, 38–9. See also Amin, 'The Social Movements in the Periphery'.
125. Ibid., 43.
126. PGA, 'Brief history of PGA'. There are at least two possible reasons for this: a conscious theoretical open-endedness within PGA that sees the condition of even petty capitalists in some parts of the world as so abject that their exclusion would be an act of unjustifiable theoretical dogmatism; or more prosaically, the weakness of PGA verification mechanisms thanks to the lack of gatekeeping actors with authority to verify the political credentials of potential affiliates in a network that prides itself on non-hierarchical organization.
127. Risse & Sikkink, 'The Socialization of International Human Rights Norms into Domestic Practices'.

CHAPTER 6

1. Khanna, 'Us "Sexuality Types": A Critical Engagement with the Postcoloniality of Sexuality', 167.
2. Foucault, *The History of Sexuality* I, 43.
3. Altman, *Global Sex*, 86; Altman, 'Rupture or Continuity?', 87–8; Altman, 'On Global Queering'; Drucker, 'In the Tropics There Is No Sin'.
4. I use the term 'LGBT' to refer to an essentially liberal identity politics that aims at the inclusion of sexual minorities within the political community. 'Queer' refers to a more radical politics that challenges the deep structures of heteronormativity, rather than seeking inclusion within them (see Warner, 'Introduction', xiii). At the risk of oversimplifying, the LGBT paradigm is hegemonic within activist circles, while queer thinking has been much more influential in the academy. In this chapter, I also use the term 'queer' as an umbrella category encompassing non-Western sexual minorities, such as *hijras* and *kothis*, that cannot easily be accommodated within a Western-style LGBT identity politics.
5. Kollman & Waites, 'The Global Politics of Lesbian, Gay, Bisexual and Transgender Human Rights'.
6. Binnie, *The Globalization of Sexuality*, 68–76.
7. Hoad, 'Arrested Development or the Queerness of Savages', 148.
8. See for example Mohanty, *Feminism Without Borders*.
9. Stychin, 'Same-Sex Sexualities and the Globalization of Human Rights Discourse', 955.
10. Epprecht, 'Black Skin, "Cowboy" Masculinity', 263.
11. Narrain, *Queer*, 41–5; Vanita & Kidwai, *Same-Sex Love in India*, 200.
12. Massad, *Desiring Arabs*, 163, 174.
13. Ibid., 182–3.
14. Massad, 'Re-Orienting Desire', 373.
15. Massad, *Desiring Arabs*, 173.
16. Phillips, 'Zimbabwean Law and the Production of a White Man's Disease', 484.
17. See for example El Menyawi, 'Activism from the Closet', who appears to share Massad's tactical criticisms of Western responses to the Queen Boat incident, but advances a number of alternative indirect strategies for enhancing the space for sexual diversity.
18. For an account of one such space, see the section on National Law School of India University in D'Penha & Tarun, 'Queering the Campus'.
19. For comprehensive accounts of the controversy see Kim, 'Witnesses to an Execution'; Schindler, 'The Battle Over Iran'.
20. OutRage!, 'Execution of Gay Teens in Iran'.
21. Cited from Kim, 'Witnesses to an Execution'.
22. Ireland, 'Iran's Anti-Gay Pogrom'.
23. Human Rights Campaign, 'Secretary Rice Urged to Condemn execution of Gay Iranian Teens'.

24. Log Cabin Republicans, 'Log Cabin Republicans Denounce Execution of Gay Youth by Iran'.
25. Najmabadi, *Women with Mustaches and Men Without Beards*, ch. 1, 2.
26. OutRage!, 'Iranian Gay Group Backs 19 July Protests'.
27. Amnesty International, 'Executions of juveniles since 1990'.
28. BBC News, 'US Court Bans Juvenile Executions'.
29. Cited from Rosendall, 'No Excuses for Iran', who is strongly critical of this change of focus.
30. Varnell, 'Toward a Gay Foreign Policy'.
31. There is a considerable orientalist discourse, which uses the closeted status of many gay Palestinians as a means of undermining support for Palestinian self-determination per se. See for example, Halevi, 'Tel Aviv Dispatch'; Bernstein, 'Gay Palestinians Suffer Under Arafat'; Varnell, 'Israel, Palestine, and Gays'; Goodwin, 'Palestine's Oppression of Gays Should Not Be Ignored'; Kirchik, 'Palestine and Gay Rights'; for an excellent critique of this literature, see Kuntz, '"Queer" as a Tool of Colonial Oppression'.
32. See for example the comparative religious writings of Paul Varnell at <www.indegayforum.org>. While he acknowledges the universality of bigotry and homophobia across the major monotheistic religions, Christian proscriptions of homosexuality are rationalized and contextualized, even if they are ultimately criticized, while Islam's lack of pluralism and internal contestation is emphasized. For a remarkably different treatment of Islam, stressing its indeterminacy and contingency and the consequent scope for reconciliation of sexuality and faith, see Whitaker, *Unspeakable Love*, 113–42.
33. Spivak, 'Can the Subaltern Speak?', 296.
34. Puar, 'Mapping US Homonormativities', 67–8.
35. Ibid., 72.
36. For an instance of linkage between gay solidarity and support for the war on Afghanistan, see Varnell, 'Bombing for Justice'.
37. For an instance of linkage between feminist solidarity and the war on Afghanistan, see Bush, 'Radio Address by Mrs. Bush'.
38. Rosendall, 'The State Department's Gay Rights Tool'; Ireland, 'LGBT Advocates Needn't Cozy Up to State Department'.
39. Puar, 'Mapping US Homonormativities', 70.
40. Tatchell is currently campaigning on behalf of the Ahwaz Arabs, an ethnic minority in south-west Iran, who allegedly suffer various forms of state-sanctioned discrimination and persecution. The boys executed at Mashhad in 2005 are thought to have belonged to this community (Whitaker, *Unspeakable Love*, 128).
41. Interview with Peter Tatchell.
42. Long, 'Unbearable Witness', 122–7.
43. Bob, *The Marketing of Rebellion*, 15.
44. Wood, 'Authorizing Gender and Development', 435.

45. Telephone interview with Arsham Parsi: 'When I met Peter Tatchell at ILGA I asked him why do you organize a protest in front of the Iranian embassy? You have to choose a good way. Why organize a political action? We know our culture. If it's political, people are not interested to support. There are no political parties. And gay people beg us, please don't start a political action. We would have lost credibility with our supporters. We are not political. We are not going to change the regime. That is not our role. Some people want to mix all these issues.'
46. See for example Roshan & Shemirani, 'Gays in Iran'.
47. MAHA, 'The Need for Continued International Solidarity with Iranian LGBTs'.
48. 'African LGBTI Human Rights Defenders Warn Public against Participation in Campaigns Concerning LGBTI Issues in Africa Led by Peter Tatchell and Outrage!' (hereafter African LGBTI statement).
49. African LGBTI statement.
50. Ibid.
51. Interview with Peter Tatchell.
52. Ibid. This seems a somewhat unfair criticism, given that SMUG's Mukasa moved to South Africa because of concerns for her safety and that of her partner.
53. Long, 'Unbearable Witness', 120–2.
54. Ironically, Long is one of the Western activists whom Massad singles out for especially harsh criticism, in the context of advocacy around the Queen Boat case (Massad, *Desiring Arabs*, 182, 185–7).
55. For Amnesty's bitter reaction to this, see Amnesty International, 'Iraq: UK Government Dossier on Human Rights Abuses'.
56. Interview with Ubaid Rehman and Asif Rashid.
57. <http://www.galha.org/>.
58. Interview with Ubaid Rehman and Asif Rashid.
59. Aswat, 'Our Mission and Aims'.
60. <http://www.blacklaundry.org/eng-index.html>.
61. Telephone interview with Rauda Morcos.
62. Arendt, 'The House of Judah's Gratitude?', 134–6.
63. Two excellent collections that provide an overview of the movement are Narrain & Bhan eds., *Because I Have a Voice*; Bose & Bhattacharyya eds., *The Phobic and the Erotic*.
64. Gupta, 'Englishpur ki Kothi'.
65. Open Letters Against Sec 377.
66. Ibid., 1–3.
67. See, for example, Affidavit filed by the Government of India in Special Leave Petition (Civil) No. 7217–7218 of 2005, in the matter of *Naz Foundation* v. *Government of Delhi*.
68. Open Letters Against Sec 377, 11.
69. Stychin, 'Same-Sex Sexualities and the Globalization of Human Rights Discourse', 958–60, 967.
70. *Naz Foundation* v. *Government of NCT of Delhi and Others*, WP(C) No. 7455/2001.

CHAPTER 7

1. Brown, *International Relations Theory*, 27.
2. Brown, *Sovereignty, Rights and Justice*, 17.
3. As I argued in section 1.3, communitarianism is one variety of bounded thinking but one that I choose to focus on because its justification rests on the value of the goods enabled by a life in community, including the value of community for political protest.
4. See section 1.4.
5. Risse & Sikkink, 'The Socialization of International Human Rights Norms into Domestic Practices'.
6. Gewirth, 'Ethical Universalism and Particularism', 292–8.
7. Goodin, 'What is So Special about Our Fellow Countrymen?', 678. See also Nussbaum, 'Patriotism and Cosmopolitanism', 13; Nussbaum, 'Kant and Cosmopolitanism', 32.
8. McMahan, 'The Limits of National Partiality', 118.
9. Scheffler, *Boundaries and Allegiances*, 108–9; Shue, *Basic Rights*, 118, 122; Shue, 'Eroding Sovereignty', 347; Tan, *Justice Without Borders*, 150–7.
10. Appiah, 'Cosmopolitan Patriots', 106.
11. Appiah, *The Ethics of Identity*, 214: 'my sisters and I reside in four different countries—I in America, and they in Namibia, Nigeria, and Ghana—but wherever we live, we are connected to Ghana and England, our family roots, and to other places by love and friendship and experience. And what strikes me about these trajectories—apart from the fact that they are reproduced in many, many families today—is not the difficulty of these relocations but how easy they have largely been.' This apparently innocuous remark becomes more troubling when one considers that the class privileges that accompany descent from both the Ghanaian and English aristocracies may account, in no small part, for the ease with which Appiah and his siblings are able to live their rooted cosmopolitanism. Elsewhere in the same chapter he writes of rooted cosmopolitanism that 'One might suppose this is easier said than done. In fact, it is easier done than said' (223).
12. Berlin, 'Two Concepts of Liberty', 214.
13. Carr, *The Twenty Years' Crisis 1919–1939*, 302.

References

Articles and Books

Abani, Chris, *Graceland* (Johannesburg: Picador Africa, 2004).
Acharya, Amitav, 'Developing Countries and the Emerging World Order: Security and Institutions', in *The Third World Beyond the Cold War: Continuity and Change*, eds. Louise Fawcett & Yezid Sayigh (Oxford: Oxford University Press, 2000).
Achebe, Chinua, *Anthills of the Savannah* (London: Penguin, 2001 [1987]).
Adebajo, Adekeye & Chris Landsberg, 'The Heirs of Nkrumah: Africa's New Interventionists', *Pugwash Occasional Papers* 2:1 (2001), <http://www.pugwash.org/reports/rc/como_africa.htm>.
African LGBTI statement, 'African LGBTI Human Rights Defenders Warn Public against Participation in Campaigns Concerning LGBTI Issues in Africa Led by Peter Tatchell and Outrage!' (African LGBTI statement), *Monthly Review*, 31 January 2007, <http://mrzine.monthlyreview.org/increse310107.html>.
Ahmad, Aijaz, *In Theory: Classes, Nations, Literatures* (London: Verso, 1994).
Ainger, Katharine, 'Life Is Not Business: The Intercontinental Caravan', in *We Are Everywhere: The Irresistible Rise of Global Anticapitalism*, ed. Notes from Nowhere (London: Verso, 2003).
Alderson, Kai & Andrew Hurrell, 'Bull's Conception of International Society', in *Hedley Bull on International Society*, eds. Kai Alderson & Andrew Hurrell (Basingstoke, UK: Macmillan, 2000).
Altman, Dennis, 'On Global Queering', *Australian Humanities Review* 2 (1996a), <http://www.australianhumanitiesreview.org/archive/Issue-July-1996/altman.html>.
—— 'Rupture or Continuity: The Internationalization of Gay Identities', *Social Text* 48, 14:3 (1996b), 77–94.
—— *Global Sex* (Chicago, IL: University of Chicago Press, 2001).
Amin, Samir, 'The Social Movements in the Periphery: An End to National Liberation?', in *Transforming the Revolution: Social Movements and the World-System*, eds. Samir Amin, Giovanni Arrighi, Andre Gunder Frank & Immanuel Wallerstein (New York: Monthly Review Press, 1990).
Amnesty International, 'Executions of Juveniles Since 1990', <http://www.amnesty.org/en/death-penalty/executions-of-child-offenders-since-1990>.
—— 'Iraq: UK Government Dossier on Human Rights Abuses', 2 December 2002, <http://www.amnesty.org/en/library/info/MDE14/031/2002>.
Anderson, Benedict, *Imagined Communities: Reflections on the Origin and Spread of Nationalism* (London: Verso, 1991 [1983]).
Appadurai, Arjun, 'How to Make a National Cuisine: Cookbooks in Contemporary India', *Comparative Studies in Society and History* 30:1 (1988), 3–24.
—— *Modernity at Large: Cultural Dimensions of Globalization* (Minneapolis, MN: University of Minnesota Press, 1997).

Appiah, Kwame Anthony, 'Cosmopolitan Patriots', in *Cosmopolitics: Thinking and Feeling Beyond the Nation*, eds. Pheng Cheah & Bruce Robbins (Minneapolis, MN: University of Minnesota Press, 1998).
—— *The Ethics of Identity* (Princeton, NJ: Princeton University Press, 2005).
—— *Cosmopolitanism: Ethics in a World of Strangers* (New York: W.W. Norton, 2006).
Archibugi, Daniele, 'Cosmopolitical Democracy', *New Left Review* 4 (2000), 137–50.
—— & David Held eds., *Cosmopolitan Democracy: An Agenda for a New World Order* (Cambridge: Polity Press, 1995).
—— —— & Martin Kohler eds., *Re-imagining Political Community* (Cambridge: Polity Press, 1998).
Arendt, Hannah, 'The House of Judah's Gratitude? Open Letter to Jules Romains' (1941), in *The Jewish Writings*, eds. Jerome Kohn & Ron H. Feldman (New York: Schocken Books, 2007).
Armstrong, David, *Revolution and World Order: The Revolutionary State in International Society* (Oxford: Clarendon Press, 1993).
Assadi, Muzaffar H., '"Khadi Curtain", "Weak Capitalism" and "Operation Ryot": Some Ambiguities in Farmers' Discourse, Karnataka and Maharashtra 1980–93', in *New Farmers' Movements in India*, ed. Tom Brass (Ilford, UK: Frank Cass, 1995).
—— *Peasant Movement in Karnataka: 1980–94* (Delhi: Shipra Publications, 1997).
—— '"Chickens", "Greens", and "Ragi Balls": A Discourse on Kentucky Fried Chickens', in *Contemporary Social Movements in India: Achievements and Hurdles*, eds. Sebasti L. Raj & Arundhuti Roy Choudhury (New Delhi: Indian Social Institute, 1998).
—— 'Globalisation and the State: Interrogating the Farmers' Movement in India', *Journal of Social and Economic Development* 4:1 (2002), 42–54.
Aswat, 'Our Mission and Aims', <http://www.aswatgroup.org/english/about.php?category=24>.
Austen, Jane, *Sense and Sensibility* (London: Penguin, 2006 [1811]).
Ayoob, Mohammed, 'The Security Problematic of the Third World', *World Politics* 43:2 (1991), 257–83.
—— *The Third World Security Predicament: State Making, Regional Conflict, and the International System* (Boulder, CO: Lynne Rienner, 1995).
—— 'Subaltern Realism: International Relations Theory Meets the Third World', in *International Relations and the Third World*, ed. Stephanie G. Neuman (New York: St. Martin's Press, 1998).
—— 'Humanitarian Intervention and State Sovereignty', *International Journal of Human Rights* 6:1 (2002), 81–102.
Bacevich, Andrew J., *American Empire: The Realities and Consequences of U.S. Diplomacy* (Cambridge, MA: Harvard University Press, 2002).
Baker, Gideon, *Civil Society and Democratic Theory: Alternative Voices* (London: Routledge, 2002).
Bajpai, Kanti, 'Indian Conceptions of Order and Justice: Nehruvian, Gandhian, Hindutva, and Neo-Liberal', in *Order and Justice in International Relations*, eds. Rosemary Foot, John Lewis Gaddis & Andrew Hurrell (Oxford: Oxford University Press, 2003).
Bardhan, Pranab, 'Symposium on Democracy and Development', *Journal of Economic Perspectives* 7:3 (1993), 45–9.

Barnett, Michael, 'Radical Chic? Subaltern Realism: A Rejoinder', *International Studies Review* 4:3 (2002), 49–62.

Barkawi, Tarak & Mark Laffey, 'Retrieving the Imperial: *Empire* and International Relations', *Millennium: Journal of International Studies* 31:1 (2002), 109–27.

—— 'The Postcolonial Moment in Security Studies', *Review of International Studies* 32:2 (2006), 329–52.

Barry, Kevin, 'Introduction', in *Occasional, Critical, and Political Writing*, ed. James Joyce (Oxford: Oxford University Press, 2000).

BBC News, 'US Court Bans Juvenile Executions', 1 March 2005, <http://news.bbc.co.uk/1/hi/world/americas/4308881.stm>.

—— 'Tsvangirai "leads" Zimbabwe vote', 1 May 2008, <http://news.bbc.co.uk/1/hi/world/africa/7378829.stm>.

Beck, Ulrich, 'Cosmopolitical Realism: On the Distinction Between Cosmopolitanism in Philosophy and the Social Sciences', *Global Networks* 4:2 (2004), 131–56.

Beitz, Charles R., *Political Theory and International Relations* (Princeton, NJ: Princeton University Press, 1999 [1979]).

—— 'Cosmopolitan Ideals and National Sentiment', *Journal of Philosophy* 80: 10 (1983), 591–600.

—— 'International Liberalism and Distributive Justice: A Survey of Recent Thought', *World Politics* 51:2 (1999*a*), 269–96.

—— 'Social and Cosmopolitan Liberalism', *International Affairs* 75:3 (1999*b*), 515–29.

—— 'Cosmopolitan Liberalism and the States System', in *Political Restructuring in Europe: Ethical Perspectives*, ed. Chris Brown (London: Routledge, 2002).

—— 'Human Rights and the Law of Peoples', in *The Ethics of Assistance: Morality and the Distant Needy*, ed. Deen K. Chatterjee (Cambridge: Cambridge University Press, 2004).

Bell, Coral, 'American Policy in the Third World, 1947–87', in *The West and the Third World—Essays in Honour of J. D. B. Miller*, eds. Robert O'Neill & R. J. Vincent (Basingstoke, UK: Macmillan, 1990).

Bell, Daniel, *Communitarianism and Its Critics* (Oxford: Clarendon Press, 1993).

—— *East Meets West: Human Rights and Democracy in East Asia* (Princeton, NJ: Princeton University Press, 2000).

—— 'Communitarianism', in *The Stanford Encyclopaedia of Philosophy*, ed. Edward N. Zalta (2009), <http://plato.stanford.edu/entries/communitarianism/>.

Bellamy, Alex J., 'Responsibility to Protect or Trojan Horse? The Crisis in Darfur and Humanitarian Intervention after Iraq', *Ethics & International Affairs* 19:2 (2006), 31–54.

Benner, Erica, *Really Existing Nationalisms: A Post-Communist View from Marx and Engels* (Oxford: Clarendon Press, 1995).

Berdal, Mats, 'How "New" are "New Wars"? Global Economic Change and the Study of Civil War', *Global Governance* 9:4 (2003), 477–502.

Berger, Mark, 'The End of the "Third World"?', *Third World Quarterly* 15:2 (1994), 257–75.

Berlin, Isaiah, 'Two Concepts of Liberty' (1958), in *Liberty*, ed. Henry Hardy (Oxford: Oxford University Press, 2008).

—— 'Nationalism: Past Neglect and Present Power', in *Against the Current: Essays in the History of Ideas*, ed. Henry Hardy (London: Hogarth Press, 1980).

Berlin, Isaiah, 'Rabindranath Tagore and the Consciousness of Nationality', in *The Sense of Reality: Studies in Ideas and Their History*, ed. Henry Hardy (London: Pimlico, 1997).

Bernstein, Davi J., 'Gay Palestinians Suffer Under Arafat', *The Yale Herald*, 13 September 2002, <http://www.yaleherald.com/article.php?Article=933>.

Biersteker, Thomas J., ed., *Dealing with Debt: International Financial Negotiations and Adjustment Bargaining* (Boulder, CO: Westview Press, 1993).

Binnie, Jon, *The Globalization of Sexuality* (London: Sage, 2004).

Birdsall, Nancy, John Williamson & Brian Deese, *Delivering on Debt Relief: From IMF Gold to a New Aid Architecture* (Washington, DC: Institute for International Economics & Centre for Global Development, 2002).

Blake, Michael, 'Distributive Justice, State Coercion, and Autonomy', *Philosophy & Public Affairs* 30:3 (2002), 257–96.

Bob, Clifford, *The Marketing of Rebellion: Insurgents, Media, and International Activism* (New York: Cambridge University Press, 2006).

Bohman, James, 'Republican Cosmopolitanism', *Journal of Political Philosophy* 12:3 (2004), 336–52.

Bose, Brinda & Subhabrata Bhattacharyya eds., *The Phobic and the Erotic* (Oxford: Seagull, 2007).

Brass, Tom, 'Moral Economists, Subalterns, New Social Movements, and the (re-) Emergence of a (Post-)Modernized (Middle) Peasant', *Journal of Peasant Studies* 18:2 (1991), 173–205.

—— 'Introduction: The New Farmers' Movements in India', in *New Farmers' Movements in India*, ed. Tom Brass (Ilford, UK: Frank Cass, 1995).

—— 'The Politics of Gender, Nature and Nation in the Discourse of the New Farmers' Movements', in *New Farmers' Movements in India*, ed. Tom Brass (Ilford, UK: Frank Cass, 1995).

Brilmayer, Lea, 'Transforming International Politics: An American Role for the Post Cold War World', *University of Cincinnati Law Review* 64:1 (1995), 119–42.

Brown, Chris, *International Relations Theory: New Normative Approaches* (Hemel Hempstead, UK: Harvester Wheatsheaf, 1992).

—— 'International Theory and International Society: The Viability of the Middle Way?', *Review of International Studies* 21:2 (1995), 183–96.

—— *Sovereignty, Rights and Justice: International Political Theory Today* (Cambridge: Polity Press, 2002).

Brysk, Alison, 'Turning Weakness Into Strength', *Latin American Perspectives* 23:2 (1996), 38–57.

Buchanan, Allen, 'Reforming the International Law of Humanitarian Intervention', in *Humanitarian Intervention: Ethical, Legal, and Political Dilemmas*, eds. J. L. Holzgrefe & Robert O. Keohane (Cambridge: Cambridge University Press, 2003).

—— *Justice, Legitimacy, and Self-Determination: Moral Foundations for International Law* (Oxford: Oxford University Press, 2004).

Bull, Hedley, 'The Grotian Conception of International Society' (1966), in *Hedley Bull on International Society*, eds. Kai Alderson & Andrew Hurrell (Basingstoke, UK: Macmillan, 2000).

—— *The Anarchical Society: A Study of Order in World Politics* (London: Macmillan, 2002 [1977]).

Bull, Hedley, 'Intervention in the Third World', in *Intervention in World Politics*, ed. Hedley Bull (Oxford: Clarendon Press, 1984*a*).

—— 'The Emergence of a Universal International Society', in *The Expansion of International Society*, eds. Hedley Bull & Adam Watson (Oxford: Clarendon Press, 1984*b*).

—— 'The Revolt Against the West', in *The Expansion of International Society*, eds. Hedley Bull & Adam Watson (Oxford: Clarendon Press, 1984*c*).

Burbach, Roger, 'Roots of the Postmodern Rebellion in Chiapas', *New Left Review* 205 (1994), 113–24.

Bush, Laura, 'Radio Address by Mrs. Bush', 17 November 2001, <http://georgewbush-whitehouse.archives.gov/news/releases/2001/11/20011117.html>.

Buzan, Barry, *From International to World Society? English School Theory and the Social Structure of Globalisation* (Cambridge: Cambridge University Press, 2005).

Byers, Michael & Simon Chesterman, 'Changing the Rules About Rules? Unilateral Humanitarian Intervention and the Future of International Law', in *Humanitarian Intervention: Ethical, Legal, and Political Dilemmas*, eds. J. L. Holzgrefe & Robert O. Keohane (Cambridge: Cambridge University Press, 2003).

Calhoun, Craig, 'The Necessity and Limits of Cosmopolitanism: Local Democracy in a Global Context', paper presented to the UNESCO/ISSC Conference 'Identity and Difference in the Global Era', Candido Mendes University, Rio de Janeiro, 20–23 May 2001.

—— 'The Class Consciousness of Frequent Travellers: Toward a Critique of Actually Existing Cosmopolitanism', *South Atlantic Quarterly* 101:4 (2002), 869–97.

—— '"Belonging" in the Cosmopolitan Imaginary', *Ethnicities* 3:4 (2003), 531–68.

Callinicos, Alex, 'Where Now?', in *Anti-Capitalism: A Guide to the Movement*, eds. Emma Bircham & John Charlton (London: Bookmarks Publications, 2001).

Caney, Simon, 'Review Article: International Distributive Justice', *Political Studies* 49:5 (2001), 974–97.

Cardoso, Fernando Henrique & Enzo Faletto, *Dependency and Development in Latin America*, trans. Marjory Mattingly Urquidi (Berkeley, CA: University of California Press, 1979).

Carr, E. H., *The Twenty Years' Crisis 1919–1939: An Introduction to the Study of International Relations* (London: Macmillan, 1942 [1939]).

Castells, Manuel, *The Power of Identity* (Oxford: Blackwell Publishers, 1997).

Centeno, Miguel Angel, *Blood and Debt: War and the Nation-State in Latin America* (University Park, PA: Pennsylvania State University Press, 2002).

Chan, Stephen & Hasu Patel, 'Zimbabwe's Foreign Policy: A Conversation', *The Round Table* 95:384 (2006), 175–90.

Chandler, David, *From Kosovo to Kabul: Human Rights and International Intervention* (London: Pluto Press, 2002).

—— 'Building Global Civil Society "From Below"?', *Millennium: Journal of International Studies* 33:2 (2004), 313–39.

Chang, Ha-Joon, *Kicking Away the Ladder: Development Strategy in Historical Perspective* (London: Anthem Press, 2002).

Charlesworth, Hilary & Christine Chinkin, 'The Gender of Jus Cogens', *Human Rights Quarterly* 15:1 (1993), 63–76.

Chatterjee, Partha, *The Nation and Its Fragments: Colonial and Postcolonial Histories* (Princeton, NJ: Princeton University Press, 1993).
—— *Nationalist Thought and the Colonial World: A Derivative Discourse?* (Oxford: Oxford University Press, 1999).
Cheah, Pheng, *Inhuman Conditions: Cosmopolitanism and Human Rights* (Cambridge, MA: Harvard University Press, 2006).
Cherki, Alice, *Frantz Fanon: A Portrait*, trans. Nadia Benabid (Ithaca, NY: Cornell University Press, 2006).
Chimni, B. S., 'International Institutions Today: An Imperial Global State in the Making', *European Journal of International Law* 15:1 (2004), 1–37.
Christian Aid, *The Damage Done: Aid, Death and Dogma* (2005), <http://www.christianaid.org.uk/Images/damage_done.pdf>.
Clapham, Christopher, *Africa and the International System* (Cambridge: Cambridge University Press, 1999).
Clark, Belinda, 'The Vienna Convention Reservations Regime and the Convention on Discrimination Against Women', *American Journal of International Law* 85:2 (1991), 281–321.
Cohen, Joshua ed., *For Love of Country: Debating the Limits of Patriotism* (Boston, MA: Beacon Press, 1996).
Colas, Alejandro, 'Putting Cosmopolitanism into Practice: The Case of Socialist Internationalism', *Millennium: Journal of International Studies* 23:3 (1994), 513–34.
—— *International Civil Society* (Cambridge: Polity Press, 2002).
Conrad, Joseph, *Heart of Darkness* (Harmondsworth, UK: Penguin, 1982 [1902]).
Cox, Michael, 'The Empire's Back in Town: Or America's Imperial Temptation—Again', *Millennium: Journal of International Studies* 32:1 (2003), 1–27.
Cox, Robert W., 'Ideologies and the NIEO', *International Organization* 33:2 (1979), 257–302.
—— *Production, Power, and World Order: Social Forces in the Making of History* (New York: Columbia University Press, 1987).
—— *Approaches to World Order* (Cambridge: Cambridge University Press, 1999).
Crossley, Nick, 'Global Anti-corporate Struggle: A Preliminary Analysis', *British Journal of Sociology* 53:4 (2002), 667–91.
Cunliffe, Philip, 'Sovereignty and the Politics of Responsibility', in *Politics Without Sovereignty: A Critique of Contemporary International Relations*, eds. Christopher J. Bickerton, Philip Cunliffe & Alexander Gourevitch (Abingdon, UK: UCL Press, 2007).
D'Penha, Mario & Tarun, 'Queering the Campus: Lessons from Indian Universities', in *Because I Have a Voice*, eds. Arvind Narrain & Gautam Bhan (New Delhi: Yoda Press, 2005).
Daalder, Ivo H. & Michael E. O'Hanlon, *Winning Ugly: NATO's War to Save Kosovo* (Washington, DC: Brookings Institution Press, 2000).
Dallmayr, Fred, '"Asian Values" and Global Human Rights', *Philosophy East & West* 52:2 (2002), 173–89.
Darby, Phillip, 'Postcolonialism', in *At the Edge of International Relations: Post-colonialism, Gender & Dependency*, ed. Phillip Darby (Pinter: London, 1997).
Darwin, John, *After Tamerlane: The Global History of Empire* (London: Penguin, 2007).

De Angelis, Massimo, 'Globalization, New Internationalism and the Zapatistas', *Capital & Class* 70 (2000), 9–35.

Deane, Seamus, 'Joyce the Irishman', in *The Cambridge Companion to James Joyce*, ed. Derek Attridge (Cambridge: Cambridge University Press, 2006).

Der Derian, James, Michael W. Doyle, Jack L. Snyder & David Kennedy, 'How Should Sovereignty Be Defended?', in *Politics Without Sovereignty: A Critique of Contemporary International Relations*, eds. Christopher J. Bickerton, Philip Cunliffe & Alexander Gourevitch (Abingdon, UK: UCL Press, 2007).

Desai, Meghnad & Yahia Said, 'The New Anti-Capitalist Movement: Money and Global Civil Society', in *Global Civil Society 2001*, eds. Helmut Anheier, Marlies Glasius & Mary Kaldor (Oxford: Oxford University Press, 2001).

Desai, Radhika, 'From National Bourgeoisie to Rogues, Failures and Bullies: 21st Century Imperialism and the Unravelling of the Third World', *Third World Quarterly* 25:1 (2004), 169–85.

Donaldson, Thomas, 'Kant's Global Rationalism', in *Traditions of International Ethics*, eds. Terry Nardin & David R. Mapel (Cambridge: Cambridge University Press, 1992).

Doty, Roxanne Lynn, *Imperial Encounters* (Minneapolis, MN: University of Minnesota Press, 1996).

Douzinas, Costas, *Human Rights and Empire: The political philosophy of cosmopolitanism* (Abingdon, UK: Routledge-Cavendish, 2007).

Doyle, Michael, 'Kant, Liberal Legacies and Foreign Affairs', in *Debating the Democratic Peace*, eds. Michael E. Brown, Sean M. Lynn-Jones & Steven E. Miller (Cambridge, MA: The MIT Press, 1996).

Drèze, Jean, Meera Samson & Satyajit Singh eds., *The Dam and the Nation: Displacement and Resettlement in the Narmada Valley* (Delhi: Oxford University Press, 1997).

Drucker, Peter, '"In the Tropics There Is No Sin": Sexuality and Gay-Lesbian Movements in the Third World', *New Left Review I* 218 (1996), 75–101.

Dunne, Tim, *Inventing International Society: A History of the English School* (Basingstoke, UK: Macmillan, 1998).

Dutta, Krishna & Andrew Robinson, *Rabindranath Tagore: The Myriad-Minded Man* (New Delhi: Rupa, 2005).

Edelman, Marc, 'Transnational Peasant and Farmer Movements and Networks', in *Global Civil Society 2003*, eds. Mary Kaldor, Helmut Anheier & Marlies Glasius (Oxford: Oxford University Press, 2003).

El Menyawi, Hassan, 'Activism from the Closet: Gay Rights Strategising in Egypt', *Melbourne Journal of International Law* 7(1) 28–51 (2006), <http://www.austlii.edu.au/au/journals/MelbJIL/2006/3.html>.

Ellis, Anthony, 'Utilitarianism and International Ethics', in *Traditions of International Ethics*, eds. Terry Nardin & David R. Mapel (Cambridge: Cambridge University Press, 1992).

Engle, Karen, 'Culture and Human Rights: The Asian Values Debate in Context', *New York University Journal of International Law and Politics* 32:2 (2000), 291–333.

Epprecht, Marc, 'Black Skin, "Cowboy" Masculinity: A Genealogy of Homophobia in the African Nationalist Movement in Zimbabwe to 1983', *Culture, Health & Sexuality* 7:3 (2005), 253–66.

Escobar, Arturo, *Encountering Development: The Making and Unmaking of the Third World* (Princeton, NJ: Princeton University Press, 1995).

Evans, Gareth, 'The Responsibility to Protect: An Idea Whose Time Has Come ... and Gone?', *International Relations* 22:3 (2008), 283–98.

Falk, Richard, 'The World Order Between Inter-State Law and the Law of Humanity: The Role of Civil Society Institutions', in *Cosmopolitan Democracy: An Agenda for a New World Order*, eds. Daniele Archibugi & David Held (Cambridge: Polity Press, 1995).

Fanon, Frantz, *Black Skin, White Masks*, trans. Charles Lam Markmann (London: Pluto Press, 1986 [1952]).

—— *The Wretched of the Earth*, trans. Constance Farrington (London: Penguin, 2001 [1961]).

Featherstone, David, 'Spatialities of Transnational Resistance to Globalization: The Maps of Grievance of the Inter-Continental Caravan', *Transactions of the Institute of British Geographers* 28:4 (2003), 404–21.

Featherstone, Mike, 'Localism, Globalism, and Cultural Identity', in *Global/Local: Cultural Production and the Transnational Imaginary*, eds. Rob Wilson & Wimal Dissanayake (Durham, NC: Duke University Press, 1996).

Ferguson, Niall, *Empire: How Britain Made the Modern World* (London: Penguin, 2003).

Finnemore, Martha, *The Purpose of Intervention: Changing Beliefs About the Use of Force* (Ithaca, NY: Cornell University Press, 2004).

Fisher, William F. ed., *Toward Sustainable Development? Struggling over India's Narmada River* (Armonk, NY: M. E. Sharpe, 1995).

Fishlow, Albert, Catherine Gwin, Stephan Haggard & Dani Rodrik, *Miracle or Design? Lessons from the East Asian Experience* (Washington, DC: Overseas Development Council, 1994).

Foot, Rosemary, 'The Study of China's International Behaviour: International Relations Approaches', in *Explaining International Relations Since 1945*, ed. Ngaire Woods (Oxford: Oxford University Press, 1997).

Foreign & Commonwealth Office, Foreign Policy Document No. 148, *British Yearbook of International Law* 57 (1986): 614.

Foucault, Michel, 'Governmentality', in *The Foucault Effect: Studies in Governmentality with Two Lectures by and an Interview with Michel Foucault*, eds. Graham Burchell, Colin Gordon & Peter Miller (Chicago, IL: University of Chicago Press, 1991).

—— *The Will to Knowledge: The History of Sexuality, Volume 1* (London: Penguin, 1998 [1976]).

Franck, Thomas M., 'The Emerging Right to Democratic Governance', *American Journal of International Law* 86:1 (1992), 46–91.

Freeman, Michael, 'Universalism, Particularism and Cosmopolitan Justice', in *International Justice*, ed. Tony Coates (Aldershot, UK: Ashgate, 2000).

Fukuyama, Francis, *The End of History and the Last Man* (London: Penguin, 1992).

Furedi, Frank, *The New Ideology of Imperialism: Renewing the Moral Imperative* (Boulder, CO: Pluto Press, 1994).

Gagnon, Jr., V. P., 'Ethnic Nationalism and International Conflict: The Case of Serbia', *International Security* 19:3 (1994–95), 130–66.

Gallie, W. B., 'Essentially Contested Concepts', *Proceedings of the Aristotelian Society* 56 (1955–56), 167–98.

Galtung, Johan, 'Violence, Peace, and Peace Research', *Journal of Peace Research* 6:3 (1969), 167–91.

Gandhi, Leela, *Postcolonial Theory: A critical introduction* (Edinburgh: Edinburgh University Press, 1998).

Gandhi, Mohandas, 'The Great Sentinel' (1921), reprinted in *The Mahatma and the Poet: Letters and Debates Between Gandhi and Tagore 1915–1941*, ed. Sabyasachi Bhattacharya (New Delhi: National Book Trust, 1999*a*).

—— 'The Poet's Anxiety' (1921), reprinted in *The Mahatma and the Poet: Letters and Debates Between Gandhi and Tagore 1915–1941*, ed. Sabyasachi Bhattacharya (New Delhi: National Book Trust, 1999*b*).

—— 'The Poet and the Charkha' (1925), reprinted in *The Mahatma and the Poet: Letters and Debates Between Gandhi and Tagore 1915–1941*, ed. Sabyasachi Bhattacharya (New Delhi: National Book Trust, 1999*c*).

—— 'The Poet and the wheel' (1926), reprinted in *The Mahatma and the Poet: Letters and Debates Between Gandhi and Tagore 1915–1941*, ed. Sabyasachi Bhattacharya (New Delhi: National Book Trust, 1999*d*).

Gellner, Ernest, *Nations and Nationalism* (Oxford: Blackwell, 1983).

General Command of the EZLN, 'We Want All Who Walk with the Truth to Unite in One Step', 20 January 1994, <http://flag.blackened.net/revolt/mexico/ezln/ccri_unite.html>.

—— 'War! First Declaration of the Lacandon Jungle' (1994), in *Our Word Is Our Weapon*, ed. Juana Ponce de León (London: Serpent's Tail, 2001*a*).

—— 'Fourth Declaration of the Lacandon Jungle' (1996), in *Our Word Is Our Weapon*, ed. Juana Ponce de León (London: Serpent's Tail, 2001*b*).

—— 'Opening Remarks at the First Intercontinental *Encuentro* for Humanity and against Neoliberalism' (1996), in *Our Word Is Our Weapon*, ed. Juana Ponce de León (London: Serpent's Tail, 2001*c*).

—— 'Mexico City: We Have Arrived. We Are Here: The EZLN' (2001), in *Our Word Is Our Weapon*, ed. Juana Ponce de León (London: Serpent's Tail, 2001*d*).

Gewirth, Alan, 'Ethical Universalism and Particularism', *The Journal of Philosophy* 85:6 (1988), 283–302.

Glennon, Michael J., 'The New Interventionism: The Search for a Just International Law', *Foreign Affairs* 78: 3 (1999), 2–7.

Gonzalez, Mike, 'The Zapatistas: The Challenges of Revolution in a New Millennium', *International Socialism* 89 (2000), 59–80.

Goodin, Robert E., 'What Is So Special About Our Fellow Countrymen?', *Ethics* 98:4 (1988), 663–86.

Goodwin, William, 'Palestine's Oppression of Gays Should Not Be Ignored', *Daily Trojan*, 13 March 2003, <http://www.sodomylaws.org/world/palestine/pseditorials001.htm>.

Gowan, Peter, *The Global Gamble: Washington's Faustian Bid for World Dominance* (London: Verso, 1999).

—— 'Neoliberal Cosmopolitanism', *New Left Review* 11 (2001), 79–93.

Graeber, David, 'The New Anarchists', in *A Movement of Movements: Is Another World Really Possible?*, ed. Tom Mertes (London: Verso, 2004).

Griffith-Jones, S. ed., *Managing World Debt* (Hemel Hempstead, UK: Harvester Wheatsheaf, 1988).

Griffiths, Martin, Iain Levine & Mark Weller, 'Sovereignty and Suffering', in *The Politics of Humanitarian Intervention*, ed. John Harriss (London: Pinter, 1995).

Grindle, Merilee S., 'Reforming Land Tenure in Mexico: Peasants, the Market, and the State', in *The Challenge of Institutional Reform in Mexico*, ed. Riordan Roett (Boulder, CO: Lynne Rienner, 1995).

Grovogui, Siba N., 'Sovereignty in Africa: Quasi-Statehood and Other Myths in International Theory', in *Africa's Challenge to International Relations Theory*, eds. Kevin C. Dunn & Timothy M. Shaw (Basingstoke, UK: Macmillan, 2001).

Guarnizo, Luis Eduardo & Michael Peter Smith, 'The Locations of Transnationalism', in *Transnationalism from Below*, eds. Michael Peter Smith & Luis Eduardo Guarnizo (New Brunswick, NJ: Transaction Publishers, 1999).

Guha, Ramachandra, 'The Environmentalism of the Poor', in *Between Resistance and Revolution: Cultural Politics and Social Protest*, eds. Richard G. Fox & Orin Starn (New Brunswick, NJ: Rutgers University Press, 1997).

—— 'The Independent Journal of Opinion', *Seminar* 481 (1999).

Guha, Ranajit, 'On Some Aspects of the Historiography of Colonial India', in *Selected Subaltern Studies*, eds. Ranajit Guha & Gayatri Chakravorty Spivak (Oxford: Oxford University Press, 1988).

—— 'Discipline and Mobilize', in *Subaltern Studies VII*, eds. Partha Chatterjee & Gyanendra Pandey (Delhi: Oxford University Press, 1997).

Gupta, Alok, '*Englishpur ki Kothi*: Class Dynamics in the Queer Movement in India', in *Because I Have a Voice: Queer Politics in India*, eds. Arvind Narrain & Gautam Bhan (New Delhi: Yoda Press, 2005).

Gupta, Dipankar, 'Farmers' Movements in Contemporary India', in *Social Movements and the State*, ed. Ghanshyam Shah (New Delhi: Sage, 2002).

Guttal, Shalmali, 'Farmers' Suicides in Karnataka State', *Focus on the Global South*, 14 September 2004, <http://focusweb.org/farmers-suicides-in-karnataka-state.html?Itemid=92>.

Haass, Richard N., 'Imperial America', *Monthly Review*, February 2003.

Habermas, Jürgen, 'Bestiality and Humanity: A War on the Border Between Legality and Morality', *Constellations* 6:3 (1999), 263–72.

Haggard, Stephan, *Pathways from the Periphery: The Politics of Growth in the Newly Industrializing Countries* (Ithaca, NY: Cornell University Press, 1994).

—— 'Politics and Institutions in the World Bank's East Asia', in *Miracle or Design? Lessons from the East Asian Experience* (Washington, DC: Overseas Development Council, 1994).

Halevi, Yossi Klein, 'Tel Aviv Dispatch: Refugee Status', *The New Republic*, 19 & 26 August 2002.

Halliday, Fred, 'The Potentials of Enlightenment', *Review of International Studies* 25:5 (1999), 105–25.

Hanafi, Hassan, 'An Islamic Approach to Multilateralism', in *The New Realism: Perspectives on Multilateralism and World Order*, ed. Robert W. Cox (Basingstoke, UK: Macmillan, 1997).

Harding, Jeremy, 'The Money that Prays', *London Review of Books* 31:8 (2009), 6–10.

Hardt, Michael, 'Porto Allegre: Today's Bandung?', *New Left Review* 14 (2002), 112–18.

—— & Antonio Negri, *Empire* (Cambridge, MA: Harvard University Press, 2000).

Harvey, David, *The New Imperialism* (Oxford: Oxford University Press, 2005).

Harvey, Neil, 'Rural Reform and the Zapatista Rebellion: Chiapas, 1988–1995', in *Neo-liberalism Revisited: Economic Restructuring and Mexico's Political Future*, ed. Gerardo Otero (Boulder, CO: Westview Press, 1996).

Hashmi, Sohail H., 'Islamic Ethics in International Society', in *International Society: Diverse Ethical Perspectives*, eds. David R. Mapel & Terry Nardin (Princeton, NJ: Princeton University Press, 1998).

Heater, Derek, *World Citizenship and Government* (London: Macmillan, 1996).

Held, David, Anthony McGrew, David Goldblatt & Jonathan Perraton, *Global Transformations* (Cambridge: Polity Press, 1999).

Herbst, Jeffrey, 'War and the State in Africa', *International Security* 14:4 (1990), 117–39.

Hirschman, Albert O., 'Rival Interpretations of Market Society: Civilizing, Destructive, or Feeble?', *Journal of Economic Literature* 20:4 (1982), 1463–84.

Hoad, Neville, 'Arrested Development or the Queerness of Savages: Resisting Evolutionary Narratives of Difference', *Postcolonial Studies* 3:2 (2000), 133–58.

Hobsbawm, Eric, *Primitive Rebels: Studies in Archaic Forms of Social Movement in the 19th and 20th Centuries* (Manchester, UK: Manchester University Press, 1963).

——*Nations and Nationalism Since 1780: Programme, Myth, Reality* (Cambridge: Cambridge University Press, 2005 [1990]).

Hobson, J. A., *Imperialism: A Study* (New York: Cosimo, 2005 [1902]).

Holzgrefe, J. L. & Robert O. Keohane eds., *Humanitarian Intervention: Ethical, Legal, and Political Dilemmas* (Cambridge: Cambridge University Press, 2003).

Hosmer, Stephen T., *The Conflict over Kosovo: Why Milosevic Decided to Settle When He Did* (Santa Monica, CA: RAND, 2001).

Hovden, Eivind & Edward Keene, 'Introduction', in *The Globalization of Liberalism*, eds. Eivind Hovden & Edward Keene (New York: Palgrave, 2002).

Howes, Marjorie, 'Joyce, Colonialism, and Nationalism', in *The Cambridge Companion to James Joyce*, ed. Derek Attridge (Cambridge: Cambridge University Press, 2006).

Human Rights Campaign, 'Secretary Rice Urged to Condemn Execution of Gay Iranian Teens', 22 July 2005, <http://www.hrc.org/1945.htm>.

Human Rights Watch, *World Report 1995: Mexico*, <http://www.hrw.org/reports/1995/WR95/AMERICAS-09.htm#P490_177020>.

Hurrell, Andrew, 'International Society and the Study of Regimes: A Reflective Approach', in *International Rules: Approaches from International Law and International Relations*, eds. Robert J. Beck, Anthony C. Arend & Robert D. Vander Lugt (Oxford: Oxford University Press, 1996).

——'Society and Anarchy in the 1990s', in *International Society and the Development of International Relations Theory*, ed. Barbara Roberson (London: Pinter, 1998).

——'Norms and Ethics in International Relations', in *Handbook of International Relations*, eds. Walter Carlsnaes, Thomas Risse & Beth Simmons (London: Sage, 2002).

——'Order and Justice: What Is at Stake?', in *Order and Justice in International Relations*, eds. Rosemary Foot, John Lewis Gaddis & Andrew Hurrell (Oxford: Oxford University Press, 2003).

——'Regionalism in Theoretical Perspective', in *Regionalism in World Politics*, eds. Louise Fawcett & Andrew Hurrell (Oxford: Oxford University Press, 2004).

Hurrell, Andrew, *On Global Order: Power, Values, and the Constitution of International Society* (Oxford: Oxford University Press, 2007).

—— & Ngaire Woods, 'Globalisation and Inequality', *Millennium: Journal of International Studies* 24:3 (1995), 447–70.

Ignatieff, Michael, *Virtual War: Kosovo and Beyond* (London: Vintage, 2001).

—— *Empire Lite* (London: Vintage, 2003).

—— 'The Way We Live Now: The Year of Living Dangerously', *New York Times Magazine*, 14 March 2004.

Ikenberry, G. John, 'America's Imperial Ambition', *Foreign Affairs* 81:5 (2002), 44–60.

Inayatullah, Naeem, 'Beyond the Sovereignty Dilemma: Quasi-states as Social Construct', in *State Sovereignty as Social Construct*, eds. Thomas J. Biersteker & Cynthia Weber (Cambridge: Cambridge University Press, 1996).

Independent Commission on International Development Issues, *North-South: A programme for survival* (London: Pan Books, 1980).

Independent International Commission on Kosovo, *The Kosovo Report: Conflict, International Response, Lessons Learned* (Oxford: Oxford University Press, 2000).

International Commission on Intervention and State Sovereignty (ICISS), *The Responsibility to Protect: Research, Bibliography, Background* (Ottawa: International Development Research Centre, 2001).

Ireland, Doug, 'Iran's Anti-Gay Pogrom', *In These Times*, 4 January 2006, <http://www.inthesetimes.com/article/2458/>.

—— 'LGBT Advocates Needn't Cozy Up to State Department', *Gay City News*, 5 April 2007, <http://gaycitynews.com/site/news.cfm?newsid=18173976&BRD=2729&PAG=461&dept_id=569346&rfi=6>.

Jackson, Robert H., *Quasi-States: Sovereignty, International Relations, and the Third World* (Cambridge: Cambridge University Press, 1990).

—— *The Global Covenant: Human Conduct in a World of States* (Oxford: Oxford University Press, 2000).

James, C. L. R., *The Black Jacobins: Toussaint L'Ouverture and the San Domingo Revolution* (London: Penguin, 2001 [1938]).

JanMohamed, Abdul R., 'Worldliness-Without-World, Homelessness-As-Home': Toward a Definition of the Specular Border Intellectual', in *Edward Said: A Critical Reader*, ed. Michael Sprinker (Oxford: Blackwell Publishers, 1992).

Jayal, Niraja Gopal, 'Reinventing the State: The Emergence of Alternative Models of Governance in India in the 1990s', in *Democratic Governance in India: Challenges of Poverty, Development, and Identity*, eds. Niraja Gopal Jayal & Sudha Pai (New Delhi: Sage, 2001).

Jeromi, P. D., 'Impact of Agricultural Trade Liberalisation: Farmers' Indebtedness and Suicides in Kerala', *Indian Journal of Agricultural Economics* 62:2 (2007), 159–75.

Johnson, Chalmers, *Blowback: The Costs and Consequences of American Empire* (London: Time Warner, 2002).

—— *The Sorrows of Empire: Militarism, Secrecy, and the End of the Republic* (New York: Metropolitan Books, 2004).

Johnston, Josée, 'Pedagogical Guerrillas, Armed Democrats, and Revolutionary Counterpublics: Examining Paradox in the Zapatista Uprising in Chiapas Mexico', *Theory and Society* 29:4 (2000), 463–505.

Johnston, Josée & Gordon Laxer, 'Solidarity in the Age of Globalization: Lessons from the Anti-MAI and Zapatista Struggles', *Theory and Society* 32:1 (2003), 39–91.

Jones, Charles, *Global Justice: Defending Cosmopolitanism* (Oxford: Oxford University Press, 2001).

Joyce, James, 'Home Rule Comes of Age' (1907), in *James Joyce: Occasional, Critical, and Political Writing*, ed. Kevin Barry (Oxford: Oxford University Press, 2000*a*).

——'Ireland: Island of Saints and Sages' (1907), in *James Joyce: Occasional, Critical, and Political Writing*, ed. Kevin Barry (Oxford: Oxford University Press, 2000*b*).

——*Dubliners* (London: Penguin, 1956 [1914]).

——*A Portrait of the Artist as a Young Man* (London: Penguin, 1965 [1916]).

KRRS (Karnataka Rajya Raitha Sangha), *News from KRRS* 1 (1999), <http://www.rfb.it/icc99/krrsnews/news1.htm>.

Kabir, Humayun, 'Introduction', in *Towards Universal Man* (London: Asia Publishing House, 1962).

Kagan, Robert, 'The Benevolent Empire', *Foreign Policy* 111 (1998), 24–35.

Kaldor, Mary, 'Transnational Civil Society', in *Human Rights in Global Politics*, eds. Tim Dunne & Nicholas J. Wheeler (Cambridge: Cambridge University Press, 1999).

——*New and Old Wars: Organized Violence in a Global Era* (Cambridge: Polity Press, 2002).

——*Global Civil Society: An Answer to War* (Cambridge: Polity Press, 2003).

Kalyvas, Stathis N., '"New" and "Old" Civil Wars: A Valid Distinction?', *World Politics* 54:1 (2001), 99–118.

Kant, Immanuel, *Perpetual Peace: A Philosophical Sketch*, ed. Hans Reiss (Cambridge: Cambridge University Press, 1991 [1795]).

Kaplan, Robert D., 'The Coming Anarchy', *The Atlantic*, February 1994.

Karawan, Ibrahim A., 'The Muslim World: Uneasy Ambivalence', in *Kosovo and the Challenge of Humanitarian Intervention: Selective Indignation, Collective Action, and International Citizenship*, eds. Albrecht Schnabel & Ramesh Thakur (Tokyo: United Nations University Press, 2000).

Katzenstein, Mary, Smitu Kothari & Uday Mehta, 'Social Movement Politics in India: Institutions, Interests, and Identities', in *The Success of India's Democracy*, ed. Atul Kohli (Cambridge: Cambridge University Press, 2001).

Keane, John, 'Global Civil Society', in *Global Civil Society 2001*, eds. Helmut Anheier, Marlies Glasius & Mary Kaldor (Oxford: Oxford University Press, 2001).

Keck, Margaret E. & Kathryn Sikkink, *Activists Beyond Borders: Advocacy Networks in International Politics* (Ithaca, NY: Cornell University Press, 1998).

Keene, Edward, *Beyond the Anarchical Society: Grotius, Colonialism and Order in World Politics* (Cambridge: Cambridge University Press, 2002).

Kennedy, David, *The Dark Sides of Virtue: Reassessing International Humanitarianism* (Princeton, NJ: Princeton University Press, 2004).

Keohane, Robert O., *After Hegemony: Cooperation and Discord in the World Political Economy* (Princeton, NJ: Princeton University Press, 1984).

——& Joseph S. Nye, *Power and Interdependence: World Politics in Transition* (Boston, MA: Little, Brown, 1977).

Khagram, Sanjeev, *Dams and Development: Transnational Struggles for Water and Power* (Ithaca, NY: Cornell University Press, 2004).

Khalidi, Rashid, *Resurrecting Empire: Western Footprints and America's Perilous Path in the Middle East* (London: I. B. Tauris, 2004).
——*The Iron Cage: The Story of the Palestinian Struggle for Statehood* (Boston, MA: Beacon Press, 2007).
Khanna, Akshay, 'Us "Sexuality Types": A Critical Engagement with the Postcoloniality of Sexuality', in *The Phobic and the Erotic*, eds. Brinda Bose & Subhabrata Bhattacharyya (Oxford: Seagull, 2007).
Kim, Richard, 'Witnesses to an Execution', *The Nation*, 7 August 2005, <http://www.thenation.com/doc/20050815/kim>.
Kingsbury, Benedict, 'Sovereignty and Inequality', in *Inequality, Globalization, and World Politics*, eds. Andrew Hurrell & Ngaire Woods (Oxford: Oxford University Press, 2000).
Kingsnorth, Paul, *One No, Many Yeses: A Journey to the Heart of the Global Resistance Movement* (London: Free Press, 2003).
Kirchik, James, 'Palestine and Gay Rights', *Advocate.com*, 11 July 2006, <http://www.advocate.com/exclusive_detail_ektid33587.asp>.
Klein, Naomi, *Fences and Windows: Dispatches from the Front Lines of the Globalization Debate* (London: Flamingo, 2002).
Kollman, Kelly & Matthew Waites, 'The Global Politics of Lesbian, Gay, Bisexual and Transgender Human Rights: An Introduction', *Contemporary Politics* 15:1 (2009), 1–17.
Korkman, Petter, 'The Vital String of Mankind—Sociability and the Foundation of Natural Law and Universal Rights', in *Universalism in International Law and Political Philosophy*, eds. Petter Korkman & Virpi Mäkinen (Helsinki: Helsinki Collegium for Advanced Studies, 2008).
Koskenniemi, Martti, *From Apology to Utopia: The Structure of International Legal Argument* (Cambridge: Cambridge University Press, 2005).
Kothari, Smitu, 'Social Movements and the Redefinition of Democracy', in *India Briefing 1993*, ed. Philip Oldenburg (Boulder, CO: Westview Press, 1993).
Krisch, Nico, 'More Equal than the Rest? Hierarchy, Equality and US Predominance in International Law', in *United States Hegemony and the Foundations of International Law*, eds. Michael Byers & George Nolte (Cambridge: Cambridge University Press, 2003).
Krugman, Paul, 'Analytical Afterthoughts on the Asian Crisis', <http://web.mit.edu/krugman/www/MINICRIS.htm>.
Kumar, Radha, 'Sovereignty and Intervention: Opinions in South Asia', *Pugwash Occasional Papers* 2:1 (2001), <http://www.pugwash.org/reports/rc/como_india.htm>.
Kuntz, Blair, '"Queer" as a Tool of Colonial Oppression: The Case of Israel/Palestine', *ZNet*, 13 August 2006, <http://www.zmag.org/content/showarticle.cfm?ItemID=10756>.
Laffey, Mark & Jutta Weldes, '"Anti-Globalization" Protests and the Future of Democracy', in *Democracy and Globalization*, ed. Charles Nieman (Kent: Kent State University Press, 2004).
Laxer, Gordon, 'The Movement That Dare Not Speak Its Name: The Return of Left Nationalism/Internationalism', *Alternatives* 26:1 (2001), 1–32.
Levine, Steven I., 'Perception and Ideology in Chinese Foreign Policy', in *Chinese Foreign Policy: Theory and Practice*, eds. Thomas W. Robinson & David Shambaugh (Oxford: Clarendon Press, 1994).

Livingstone, Rick, 'Global Tropes/Worldly Readings: Narratives of Cosmopolitanism in Joyce, Rich, and Tagore', *Narrative* 5:2 (1997), 121–34.

Lloyd, David, 'Nationalisms against the State', in *The Politics of Culture in the Shadow of Capital*, eds. Lisa Lowe & David Lloyd (Durham, NC: Duke University Press, 1997).

Lobel, Jules & Michael Ratner, 'Bypassing the Security Council: Ambiguous Authorizations to Use Force, Cease-fires and the Iraqi Inspection Regime', *American Journal of International Law* 93:1 (1999), 124–54.

Locke, John, *Two Treatises of Government*, ed. Peter Laslett (New York: The New American Library, 1965 [1689]).

Lockman, Zachary, *Contending Visions of the Middle East: The History and Politics of Orientalism* (Cambridge: Cambridge University Press, 2005).

Log Cabin Republicans, 'Log Cabin Republicans Denounce Execution of Gay Youth by Iran', 26 July 2005, <http://online.logcabin.org/news_views/log-cabin-republicans-denounce-execution-of-gay-youth-by-iran.html>.

Long, Scott, 'Unbearable Witness: How Western Activists (Mis)Recognize Sexuality in Iran', *Contemporary Politics* 15:1 (2009), 119–36.

Lundestad, Geir, *The American 'Empire'* (Oxford: Oxford University Press, 1992).

MAHA, 'The Need for Continued International Solidarity with Iranian LGBTs', 15 August 2006, <http://www.ilga.org/news_results.asp?LanguageID=1&FileCategory=9&ZoneID=3&FileID=879>.

Mallaby, Sebastian, 'The Reluctant Imperialist: Terrorism, Failed States, and the Case for American Empire', *Foreign Affairs* 81:2 (2002), 2–7.

Mamdani, Mahmood, 'Lessons of Zimbabwe', *London Review of Books* 30:23 (2008), 17–21.

Makinda, Samuel M., 'The Global Covenant as an Evolving Institution', *International Journal of Human Rights* 6:1 (2002), 113–26.

Marcos, Subcomandante Insurgente, 'The Streams, When They Descend, Have No Way of Returning to the Mountains Except Beneath the Ground', 28 May 1994, <http://www.spunk.org/texts/places/mexico/sp000655.txt>.

—— 'A Storm and a Prophecy—Chiapas: The Southeast in Two Winds' (1994), in *Our Word Is Our Weapon: Selected Writings*, ed. Juana Ponce de León (London: Serpent's Tail, 2001).

—— 'Mr. Zedillo, Welcome to the Nightmare' (1994), in *Our Word Is Our Weapon*, ed. Juana Ponce de León (London: Serpent's Tail, 2001).

—— 'The Seven Loose Pieces of the Global Jigsaw Puzzle', June 1997, <http://flag.blackened.net/revolt/mexico/ezln/1997/jigsaw.html>.

—— 'For Maurice Najman, Who Keeps Feigning Death' (1999), in *Our Word Is Our Weapon: Selected Writings*, ed. Juana Ponce de León (London: Serpent's Tail, 2001).

Marx, Karl, 'The British Rule in India', *New York Daily Tribune*, 25 June 1853, <http://www.marxists.org/archive/marx/works/1853/06/25.htm>.

—— 'The Future Results of British Rule in India' (1852–53), in *Karl Marx: selected writings*, ed. David McLellan (Oxford: Oxford University Press, 2000*a*).

—— 'Letter to Kugelmann' (1869), in *Karl Marx: selected writings*, ed. David McLellan (Oxford: Oxford University Press, 2000*b*).

—— 'Letter to Meyer & Vogt' (1870), in *Karl Marx: selected writings*, ed. David McLellan (Oxford: Oxford University Press, 2000*c*).

Marx, Karl & Friedrich Engels, *The Communist Manifesto* (London: Penguin, 2004 [1848]).
Massad, Joseph A., 'Re-Orienting Desire: The Gay International and the Arab World', *Public Culture* 14:2 (2002), 361–85.
—— *Desiring Arabs* (Chicago, IL: University of Chicago Press, 2008).
McMahan, Jeff, 'The Limits of National Partiality', in *The Morality of Nationalism*, eds. Robert McKim & Jeff McMahan (Oxford: Oxford University Press, 1997).
Mearsheimer, John J. & Stephen Walt, 'An Unnecessary War', *Foreign Policy* 134 (2003): 51–9.
Mehta, Suketu, *Maximum City: Bombay Lost and Found* (New York: Vintage, 2005).
Menon, Parvathi, 'From Debt to Death', *Frontline* 20:20 (2003), <http://www.flonnet.com/fl2020/stories/20031010003810800.htm>.
—— 'The Rural Anger in Karnataka', *Frontline* 21:12 (2004), <http://www.frontlineonnet.com/fl2112/stories/20040618003303500.htm>.
Mertes, Tom, 'Grass-Roots Globalism: Reply to Michael Hardt', *New Left Review* 17 (2002), 101–10.
Mignolo, Walter D., 'The Many Faces of Cosmo-Polis: Border Thinking and Critical Cosmopolitanism', in *Cosmopolitanism*, eds. Carol A. Breckenridge, Sheldon Pollock, Homi K. Bhabha & Dipesh Chakrabarty (Durham, NC: Duke University Press, 2002).
Mill, John Stuart, *Principles of Political Economy with Some of Their Applications to Social Philosophy*, ed. Sir William Ashley (Fairfield, CA: Augustus M. Kelly, 1976 [1848]).
Miller, David, 'The Ethical Significance of Nationality', *Ethics* 98:4 (1988), 647–63.
—— 'In Defence of Nationality', *Journal of Applied Philosophy* 10:1 (1993), 3–16.
—— *On Nationality* (Oxford: Clarendon Press, 1995).
—— 'Nationality: Some Replies', *Journal of Applied Philosophy* 14:1 (1997), 69–82.
—— *Principles of Social Justice* (Cambridge, MA: Harvard University Press, 1999).
—— 'Justice and Global Inequality', in *Inequality, Globalization and World Politics*, eds. Andrew Hurrell & Ngaire Woods (Oxford: Oxford University Press, 2000).
—— 'National Responsibility and International Justice', in *The Ethics of Assistance: Morality and the Distant Needy*, ed. Deen K. Chatterjee (Cambridge: Cambridge University Press, 2004).
Milner, Helen, 'The Assumption of Anarchy in International Relations Theory: A Critique', *Review of International Studies* 17:1 (1991), 67–86.
Mishra, Srijit, 'Risks, Farmers' Suicides and Agrarian Crisis in India: Is There a Way Out?', *Indian Journal of Agricultural Economics* 63:1 (2008), 38–54.
Mohan, M. Madan, 'A Powerful Voice That Espoused Farmers' Cause', *The Hindu*, 4 February 2004, <http://www.hindu.com/2004/02/04/stories/2004020401530500.htm>.
Mohanty, B. B., '"We Are Like the Living Dead": Farmer Suicides in Maharashtra, Western India', *Journal of Peasant Studies* 32:2 (2005), 243–76.
Mohanty, Chandra Talpade, *Feminism Without Borders: Decolonizing Theory, Practicing Solidarity* (Durham, NC: Duke University Press, 2003).
Moravcsik, Andrew, 'Why Is US Human Rights Policy So Unilateralist?', in *Multilateralism & US Foreign Policy: Ambivalent Engagement*, eds. Stewart Patrick & Shepard Forman (Boulder, CO: Lynne Rienner, 2002).

Morgenthau, Hans J., *Politics Among Nations: The Struggle for Power and Peace* (New York: McGraw-Hill, 1993 [1948]).

Mortimer, Robert A., *The Third World Coalition in International Politics* (Boulder, CO: Westview Press, 1984).

Morton, Adam David, 'Mexico, Neoliberal Restructuring and the EZLN: A Neo-Gramscian Analysis', in *Globalization and the Politics of Resistance*, ed. Barry K. Gills (New York: Palgrave, 2001).

Muthu, Sankar, *Enlightenment Against Empire* (Princeton, NJ: Princeton University Press, 2003).

Nagel, Thomas, 'The Problem of Global Justice', *Philosophy & Public Affairs* 33:2 (2005), 113–47.

Naipaul, V. S., *The Mimic Men* (London: Penguin, 1969 [1967]).

Najmabadi, Afsaneh, *Women with Mustaches and Men without Beards: Gender and Sexual Anxieties of Iranian Modernity* (Berkeley, CA: University of California Press, 2005).

Nambiar, Satish, 'India: An Uneasy Precedent', in *Kosovo and the Challenge of Humanitarian Intervention: Selective Indignation, Collective Action, and International Citizenship*, eds. Albrecht Schnabel & Ramesh Thakur (Tokyo: United Nations University Press, 2000).

Nandy, Ashis, *The Illegitimacy of Nationalism: Rabindranath Tagore and the Politics of Self* (New Delhi: Oxford University Press, 1994).

Nardin, Terry, *Law, Morality, and the Relations of States* (Princeton, NJ: Princeton University Press, 1983).

Narrain, Arvind, *Queer: Despised Sexuality, Law and Social Change* (Bangalore, India: Books for Change, 2004).

—— & Gautam Bhan eds., *Because I Have a Voice: Queer Politics in India* (New Delhi: Yoda Press, 2005).

Nel, Philip, 'South Africa: The Demand for Legitimate Multilateralism', in *Kosovo and the Challenge of Humanitarian Intervention: Selective Indignation, Collective Action, and International Citizenship*, eds. Albrecht Schnabel & Ramesh Thakur (Tokyo: United Nations University Press, 2000).

Nigam, Aditya, 'Radical Politics in the Times of Globalization: Notes on Recent Indian Experience', in *Democratic Governance in India: Challenges of Poverty, Development, and Identity*, eds. Niraja Gopal Jayal & Sudha Pai (New Delhi: Sage, 2001).

Nkrumah, Gamal, 'Darfur in Flames', *Al-Ahram Weekly Online* 688 (29 April-5 May 2004), <http://weekly.ahram.org.eg/2004/688/fr3.htm>.

Nolan, Emer, *James Joyce and Nationalism* (London: Routledge, 1995).

Nussbaum, Martha C., 'Patriotism and Cosmopolitanism', in *For Love of Country: Debating the Limits of Patriotism*, ed. Joshua Cohen (Boston, MA: Beacon Press, 1996).

——'Kant and Cosmopolitanism', in *Perpetual Peace: Essays on Kant's Cosmopolitan Ideal*, eds. James Bohman & Matthias Lutz-Bachmann (Cambridge, MA: The MIT Press, 1997).

——*Frontiers of Justice: Disability, Nationality, Species Membership* (Cambridge, MA: Harvard University Press, 2006).

O'Neill, Onora, *Bounds of Justice* (Cambridge: Cambridge University Press, 2000).

Olesen, Thomas, 'Globalising the Zapatistas: From Third World Solidarity to Global Solidarity?', *Third World Quarterly* 25:1 (2004), 255–67.
—— 'The Transnational Zapatista Solidarity Network: An Infrastructure Analysis', *Global Networks* 4:1 (2004), 89–107.
Omvedt, Gail, *Reinventing Revolution* (Armonk, NY: M. E. Sharpe, 1993).
Orford, Anne, *Reading Humanitarian Intervention: Human Rights and the Use of Force in International Law* (Cambridge: Cambridge University Press, 2004).
OutRage!, 'Execution of Gay Teens in Iran', 27 July 2005, <http://www.petertatchell.net/international/iranexecution.htm>.
—— 'Iranian Gay Group Backs 19 July Protests', 14 July 2006, <http://www.petertatchell.net/international/irandemo.htm>.
PGA (Peoples' Global Action), 'Brief History of PGA', <http://www.nadir.org/nadir/initiativ/agp/en/pgainfos/history.htm>.
Pagden, Anthony, 'Stoicism, Cosmopolitanism, and the Legacy of European Imperialism', *Constellations* 7:1 (2000), 3–22.
—— *Peoples and Empires: Europeans and the Rest of the World, From Antiquity to the Present* (London: Phoenix Press, 2002).
Parajuli, Pramod, 'Power and Knowledge in Development Discourse: New Social Movements and the State in India', in *Democracy in India*, ed. Niraja Gopal Jayal (Oxford: Oxford University Press, 2001).
Parry, Benita, 'Overlapping Territories and Intertwined Histories: Edward Said's Postcolonial Cosmopolitanism', in *Edward Said: A Critical Reader*, ed. Michael Sprinker (Oxford: Blackwell Publishers, 1992).
—— 'Resistance Theory/Theorizing Resistance or Two Cheers for Nativism', in *Colonial Discourse/Postcolonial theory*, eds. Francis Barker, Peter Hulme & Margaret Iversen (Manchester, UK: Manchester University Press, 1994).
Patel, Rajeev & Philip McMichael, 'Third Worldism and the Lineages of Global Fascism: The Regrouping of the Global South in the Neoliberal Era', *Third World Quarterly* 25:1 (2004), 231–54.
Patnaik, Prabhat, 'On the Political Economy of Economic "Liberalisation"', *Social Scientist* 13:7/8 (1985), 3–17.
Pettit, Philip, *Republicanism: A Theory of Freedom and Government* (Oxford: Oxford University Press, 1999).
Phillips, Oliver, 'Zimbabwean Law and the Production of a White Man's Disease', *Social & Legal Studies* 6:4 (1997), 471–91.
Phimister, Ian & Brian Raftopoulos, 'Mugabe, Mbeki & the Politics of Anti-Imperialism', *Review of African Political Economy* 31:101 (2004), 385–400.
Pogge, Thomas, *Realizing Rawls* (Ithaca, NY: Cornell University Press, 1989).
—— 'Cosmopolitanism and Sovereignty', in *Political Restructuring in Europe: Ethical Perspectives*, ed. Chris Brown (London: Routledge, 2002).
—— *World Poverty and Human Rights* (Cambridge: Polity Press, 2002).
Pollock, Sheldon, Homi K. Bhabha, Carol A. Breckenridge & Dipesh Chakrabarty, 'Cosmopolitanisms', in *Cosmopolitanism*, eds. Carol A. Breckenridge, Sheldon Pollock, Homi K. Bhabha & Dipesh Chakrabarty (Durham, NC: Duke University Press, 2002).

Power, Samantha, 'A Problem from Hell': America and the Age of Genocide (New York: Harper Perennial, 2007).

Prashad, Vijay, The Darker Nations: A People's History of the Third World (New York: The New Press, 2007).

Prestowitz, Clyde, Rogue Nation: American Unilateralism and the Failure of Good Intentions (New York: Basic Books, 2003).

Pritchard, Sarah, 'The Jurisprudence of Human Rights: Some Critical Thought and Developments in Practice', Australian Journal of Human Rights 2:1 (1995), 3–38.

Przeworski, Adam & Fernando Limongi, 'Political Regimes and Economic Growth', Journal of Economic Perspectives 7:3 (1993), 51–69.

——— Michael E. Alvarez, José Antonio Cheibub & Fernando Limongi, Democracy and Development: Political Institutions and Well-Being in the World, 1950–1990 (Cambridge: Cambridge University Press, 2002).

Puar, Jasbir K., 'Mapping US Homonormativities', Gender, Place and Culture 13:1 (2006), 67–88.

Radice, William, 'Preface', in The Home and the World, trans. Surendranath Tagore (London: Penguin, 2005).

Raj, Ranjit Dev, 'Indian Farmers Take the War to Europe', Inter Press Service, 24 May 1999, <http://squat.net/caravan/articles/en-ips-24-5.htm>.

Rajagopal, Balakrishnan, International Law from Below (Cambridge: Cambridge University Press, 2003).

Randall, Vicky, 'Using and Abusing the Concept of the Third World: Geopolitics and the Comparative Political Study of Development and Underdevelopment', Third World Quarterly 25:1 (2004), 41–53.

Rao, Rahul, 'How to Make a Cosmopolitan: The Problem of Moral Motivation Across Boundaries', M. Phil. thesis, University of Oxford, Oxford, 2003.

——— 'The Empire Writes Back (to Michael Ignatieff)', Millennium: Journal of International Studies 33:1 (2004), 145–66.

——— 'Blenheim and Bangalore', New Internationalist 382 (2005), <http://newint.org/columns/essays/2005/09/01/blenheim_and_bangalore/>.

Rawls, John, A Theory of Justice (Cambridge, MA: Harvard University Press, 1971).

——— The Law of Peoples (Cambridge, MA: Harvard University Press, 1999).

Reanda, Laura, 'The Commission on the Status of Women', in The United Nations and Human Rights, ed. Philip Alston (Oxford: Clarendon Press, 1996).

Reisman, W. Michael, 'Coercion and Self-Determination: Construing Charter Article 2(4)', American Journal of International Law 78:3 (1984), 642–5.

——— 'Criteria for the Lawful Use of Force in International Law', Yale Journal of International Law 10:2 (1985), 279–85.

——— 'Sovereignty and Human Rights in Contemporary International Law', American Journal of International Law 84:4 (1990), 866–76.

——— 'Kosovo's Antinomies', American Journal of International Law 93:4 (1999), 860–62.

Renan, Ernest, 'What Is a Nation?' (1882), in Becoming National: A Reader, eds. Geoff Eley & Ronald Grigor Suny (New York: Oxford University Press, 1996).

Rice, Condoleezza, 'Promoting the National Interest', Foreign Affairs 79:1 (2000), 45–62.

Risse, Thomas & Kathryn Sikkink, 'The Socialization of International Human Rights Norms into Domestic Practices: Introduction', in The Power of Human Rights:

International Norms and Domestic Change, eds. Thomas Risse, Stephen C. Ropp & Kathryn Sikkink (Cambridge: Cambridge University Press, 2001).

Robertson, Geoffrey, *Crimes Against Humanity: The Struggle for Global Justice* (London: Penguin Books, 2002).

Robinson, Sarah L., 'A Southern Perspective on Humanitarian Intervention?: Rhetoric and Practice of Developing States, 1992–2000', M. Phil. thesis, University of Oxford, Oxford, 2004.

Rodrik, Dani, 'Trading in Illusions', *Foreign Policy* 123 (2001): 54–62.

Rosendall, Richard J., 'No Excuses for Iran', *Independent Gay Forum*, <http://www.indegayforum.org/news/show/31019.html>.

——'The State Department's Gay Rights Tool', *Independent Gay Forum*, <http://www.indegayforum.org/news/show/27346.html>.

Roshan, Mitra & Kourosh Shemirani, 'Gays in Iran', *Gay City News*, 3 August 2006, <http://gaycitynews.com/site/index.cfm?newsid=17334376&BRD=2729&PAG=461&dept_id=568864&rfi=8>.

Rothstein, Robert L., *The Weak in the World of the Strong: The Developing Countries in the International System* (New York: Columbia University Press, 1977).

Ruggie, John Gerard, *Constructing the World Polity: Essays on International Institutionalization* (London: Routledge, 1998).

Rushdie, Salman, *Midnight's Children* (London: Picador, 1982 [1981]).

——'In Good Faith', in *Imaginary Homelands: Essays and Criticism 1981–1991* (London: Granta, 1991).

Rustomjee, Cyrus, 'Improving Southern Voice on the IMF Board: Quo Vadis Shareholders?', in *Accountability of the International Monetary Fund*, eds. Barry Carin & Angela Wood (Aldershot, UK: Ashgate, 2005).

R2PCS (Responsibility to Protect-Engaging Civil Society), 'Chart on Government Positions on R2P', 11 August 2005a, <http://www.responsibilitytoprotect.org/index.php/civil_society_statements/294>.

——'What Governments Said About R2P at 2005 World Summit', 15 September 2005b, <http://www.responsibilitytoprotect.org/index.php/government_statements/>.

Said, Edward W., *Orientalism: Western Conceptions of the Orient* (London: Penguin, 1995 [1978]).

——*The Question of Palestine* (London: Vintage, 1992).

——*Culture and Imperialism* (London: Vintage, 1994a).

——*Representations of the Intellectual: The 1993 Reith Lectures* (London: Vintage, 1994b).

——*The Politics of Dispossession: The Struggle for Palestinian Self-Determination 1969–1994* (London: Vintage, 1994c).

——*Covering Islam: How the Media and the Experts Determine How We See the Rest of the World* (London: Vintage, 1997).

——*Reflections on Exile and Other Literary and Cultural Essays* (London: Granta Books, 2001).

——*The End of the Peace Process* (New Delhi: Penguin Books India, 2003).

Sainath, P., 'No Sugar-Coated Pills for Cotton Farmers', *The Hindu*, 13 December 2006, <http://www.hindu.com/2006/12/13/stories/2006121303801000.htm>.

Sands, Philippe, *Lawless World: Making and Breaking Global Rules* (London: Penguin, 2006).

Sangiovanni, Andrea, 'Global Justice, Reciprocity, and the State', *Philosophy & Public Affairs* 35:1 (2007), 3–39.

Santos, Boaventura de Sousa, *Toward a New Legal Common Sense: Law, Globalization, and Emancipation* (London: Butterworths, 2002).

Sarkar, Sumit, *The Swadeshi Movement in Bengal: 1903–1908* (New Delhi: People's Publishing House, 1973).

—— '*Ghare Baire* in Its Times', in *Rabindranath Tagore's* The Home and the World: *A Critical Companion*, ed. P. K. Datta (Delhi: Permanent Black, 2003).

Sarkar, Tanika, 'Many Faces of Love: Country, Woman and God in *The Home and the World*', in *Rabindranath Tagore's* The Home and the World: *A Critical Companion*, ed. P. K. Datta (Delhi: Permanent Black, 2003).

Sartre, Jean-Paul, 'Colonialism Is a System', in *Colonialism and Neocolonialism*, trans. Azzedine Haddour, Steve Brewer & Terry McWilliams (London: Routledge, 2001).

Scheffler, Samuel, *Boundaries and Allegiances: Problems of Justice and Responsibility in Liberal Thought* (Oxford: Oxford University Press, 2001).

Schindler, Paul, 'The Battle over Iran', *Gay City News*, 20 July 2006, <http://gaycitynews.com/site/index.cfm?newsid=17334312&BRD=2729&PAG=461&dept_id=568864&rfi=8>.

Schmitt, Carl, *Political Theology: Four Chapters on the Concept of Sovereignty*, trans. George D. Schwab (Chicago, IL: University of Chicago Press, 2005 [1922]).

—— *The Concept of the Political*, trans. George D. Schwab (New Brunswick, NJ: Rutgers University Press, 1976 [1927]).

Scott, James C., *Weapons of the Weak: Everyday Forms of Peasant Resistance* (New Haven, CT: Yale University Press, 1985).

—— *Seeing Like a State: How Certain Schemes to Improve the Human Condition Have Failed* (New Haven, CT: Yale University Press, 1998).

Seers, Dudley, *Dependency Theory: A Critical Reassessment* (London: Frances Pinter, 1981).

Seligson, Mitchell A. & John T. Passé-Smith eds., *Development and Underdevelopment: The Political Economy of Global Inequality* (Boulder, CO: Lynne Rienner, 2003).

Sen, Amartya, *Development as Freedom* (Oxford: Oxford University Press, 2001).

Sen, Jai, Anita Anand, Arturo Escobar & Peter Waterman eds., *World Social Forum: Challenging Empires* (New Delhi: Viveka, 2004).

Serrano, Monica, 'Latin America: The Dilemmas of Intervention', in *Kosovo and the Challenge of Humanitarian Intervention: Selective Indignation, Collective Action, and International Citizenship*, eds. Albrecht Schnabel & Ramesh Thakur (Tokyo: United Nations University Press, 2000).

Seth, Vikram, *Mappings* (New Delhi: Viking, 2005 [1981]).

Shah, Ghanshyam, 'Introduction', in *Social Movements and the State*, ed. Ghanshyam Shah (New Delhi: Sage, 2002).

Shastri, Vanita, 'The Politics of Economic Liberalization in India', *Contemporary South Asia* 6:1 (1997), 27–56.

Shaw, Malcolm N., *International Law* (Cambridge: Cambridge University Press, 1998).

Shaw, Martin, *Global Society and International Relations* (Cambridge: Polity Press, 1994).

Shehadeh, Raja, 'Analyzing Palestine: Post-Mortem or Prognosis?', in *Waiting for the Barbarians: A Tribute to Edward W. Said*, eds. Müge Gürsoy Sökmen & Basak Ertür (London: Verso, 2008).

Shue, Henry, *Basic Rights: Subsistence, Affluence, and US Foreign Policy* (Princeton, NJ: Princeton University Press, 1996).

—— 'Eroding Sovereignty: The Advance of Principle', in *The Morality of Nationalism*, eds. Robert McKim & Jeff McMahan (Oxford: Oxford University Press, 1997).

Sidhu, R. S. & Sucha Singh Gill, 'Agricultural Credit and Indebtedness in India: Some Issues', *Indian Journal of Agricultural Economics* 61:1 (2006), 11–35.

Simma, Bruno, 'NATO, the UN and the Use of Force: Legal Aspects', *European Journal of International Law* 10:1 (1999), 1–22.

Singer, J. David, 'The Level-of-Analysis Problem in International Relations', in *International Politics and Foreign Policy: A Reader in Research and Theory*, ed. James N. Rosenau (New York: The Free Press, 1969).

Singer, Peter, 'Famine, Affluence, and Morality', *Philosophy & Public Affairs* 1:3 (1972), 229–43.

—— *Practical Ethics* (Cambridge: Cambridge University Press, 1995).

—— *One World: The Ethics of Globalization* (New Haven, CT: Yale University Press, 2004).

Soueif, Ahdaf, *In the Eye of the Sun* (London: Bloomsbury, 1999).

Spivak, Gayatri Chakravorty, 'Can the Subaltern Speak?', in *Marxism and the Interpretation of Culture*, eds. Cary Nelson & Lawrence Grossberg (Basingstoke, UK: Macmillan, 1988).

—— 'Subaltern Studies: Deconstructing Historiography', in *Selected Subaltern Studies*, eds. Ranajit Guha & Gayatri Chakravorty Spivak (Oxford: Oxford University Press, 1988).

Sprinker, Michael, 'Homeboys: Nationalism, Colonialism, and Gender in *The Home and the World*', in *Rabindranath Tagore's* The Home and the World: *A Critical Companion*, ed. P. K. Datta (Delhi: Permanent Black, 2003).

Stears, Marc, 'The Vocation of Political Theory: Principles, Empirical Inquiry and the Politics of Opportunity', *European Journal of Political Theory* 4:4 (2005), 325–50.

Steger, Manfred B., *Globalism: Market Ideology Meets Terrorism* (Lanham, MD: Rowman & Littlefield, 2005).

Stiglitz, Joseph, *Globalization and Its Discontents* (London: Penguin, 2002).

Stychin, Carl F., 'Same-Sex Sexualities and the Globalization of Human Rights Discourse', *McGill Law Journal* 49 (2004), 951–68.

Tagore, Rabindranath, 'The Vicissitudes of Education' (1892), in *Towards Universal Man* (London: Asia Publishing House, 1962*d*).

—— 'The Problem of India' (1909), in *Rabindranath Tagore: An Anthology*, eds. Krishna Dutta & Andrew Robinson (London: Picador, 1997*b*).

—— 'Hindu University' (1911), in *Towards Universal Man* (London: Asia Publishing House, 1962*a*).

—— *Nationalism*, trans. Surendranath Tagore (London: Macmillan, 1917).

—— 'Letter to Lord Chelmsford' (1919), reprinted in *The Mahatma and the Poet: Letters and Debates Between Gandhi and Tagore 1915–1941*, ed. Sabyasachi Bhattacharya (New Delhi: National Book Trust, 1999*a*).

Tagore, Rabindranath, 'The Centre of Indian Culture' (1919), in *Towards Universal Man* (London: Asia Publishing House, 1962*b*).
—— *The Home and the World*, trans. Surendranath Tagore (London: Penguin, 2005 [book version 1919]).
—— Tagore's reflection on non-cooperation and cooperation (1921), reprinted in *The Mahatma and the Poet: Letters and Debates Between Gandhi and Tagore 1915–1941*, ed. Sabyasachi Bhattacharya (New Delhi: National Book Trust, 1999*b*).
—— 'The Call of Truth' (1921), reprinted in *The Mahatma and the Poet: Letters and Debates Between Gandhi and Tagore 1915–1941*, ed. Sabyasachi Bhattacharya (New Delhi: National Book Trust, 1999*c*).
—— 'East and West' (1922), in *Rabindranath Tagore: An Anthology*, eds. Krishna Dutta & Andrew Robinson (London: Picador, 1997*a*).
—— 'Striving for Swaraj' (1925), reprinted in *The Mahatma and the Poet: Letters and Debates Between Gandhi and Tagore 1915–1941*, ed. Sabyasachi Bhattacharya (New Delhi: National Book Trust, 1999*d*).
—— 'The Cult of the Charkha' (1925), reprinted in *The Mahatma and the Poet: Letters and Debates Between Gandhi and Tagore 1915–1941*, ed. Sabyasachi Bhattacharya (New Delhi: National Book Trust, 1999*e*).
—— 'The Changing Age' (1933), in *Towards Universal Man* (London: Asia Publishing House, 1962*c*).
—— 'The Congress' (1939), reprinted in *The Mahatma and the Poet: Letters and Debates Between Gandhi and Tagore 1915–1941*, ed. Sabyasachi Bhattacharya (New Delhi: National Book Trust, 1999*f*).
Tamir, Yael, *Liberal Nationalism* (Princeton, NJ: Princeton University Press, 1993).
Tan, Kok-Chor, *Justice Without Borders: Cosmopolitanism, Nationalism and Patriotism* (Cambridge: Cambridge University Press, 2004).
Tarrow, Sidney, *The New Transnational Activism* (Cambridge: Cambridge University Press, 2005).
Taylor, Brian D. & Roxana Botea, 'Tilly Tally: War-Making and State-Making in the Contemporary Third World', *International Studies Review* 10:1 (2008), 27–56.
Teson, Fernando R., *Humanitarian Intervention: An Inquiry into Law and Morality* (Irvington-on-Hudson, NY: Transnational Publishers, 1997).
—— *A Philosophy of International Law* (Boulder, CO: Westview Press, 1998).
Thakur, Ramesh, 'Developing Countries and the Intervention-Sovereignty Debate', in *The United Nations and Global Security*, eds. Richard M. Price & Mark W. Zacher (New York: Palgrave Macmillan, 2004).
Thomas, Caroline, *New States, Sovereignty and Intervention* (Aldershot, UK: Gower, 1985).
Tickner, Arlene, 'Seeing IR Differently: Notes from the Third World', *Millennium: Journal of International Studies* 32:2 (2003), 295–324.
Tilly, Charles, *Coercion, Capital, and European States, AD 990–1990* (Oxford: Basil Blackwell, 1990).
Tormey, Simon, *Anti-Capitalism: A Beginner's Guide* (Oxford: Oneworld Publications, 2004).

Vanita, Ruth & Saleem M. Kidwai, *Same-Sex Love in India: Readings from Literature and History* (Basingstoke, UK: Palgrave, 2001).

Varnell, Paul, 'Bombing for Justice', *Independent Gay Forum*, <http://www.indegayforum.org/news/show/27137.html>.

—— 'Israel, Palestine, and Gays', *Independent Gay Forum*, <http://www.indegayforum.org/news/show/27154.html>.

—— 'Toward a Gay Foreign Policy', *Independent Gay Forum*, <http://www.indegayforum.org/news/show/27139.html>.

Wade, Robert, 'Japan, the World Bank, and the Art of Paradigm Maintenance: The East Asian Miracle in Political Perspective', *New Left Review* I217 (1996), 3–36.

—— 'The Invisible Hand of the American Empire', *Ethics & International Affairs* 17:2 (2003), 77–88.

Wager, Stephen J. & Donald E. Schulz, 'Civil-Military Relations in Mexico: The Zapatista Revolt and Its Implications', *Journal of Interamerican Studies and World Affairs* 37:1 (1995), 1–42.

Waldron, Jeremy, 'Minority Cultures and the Cosmopolitan Alternative', *University of Michigan Journal of Law Reform* 25:3 (1992), 751–93.

Walzer, Michael, *Just and Unjust Wars: A Moral Argument with Historical Illustrations* (Harmondsworth, UK: Penguin, 1980).

—— 'The Moral Standing of States: A Response to Four Critics', *Philosophy & Public Affairs* 9:3 (1980), 209–29.

—— *Interpretation and Social Criticism* (Cambridge, MA: Harvard University Press, 1987).

—— *Spheres of Justice: A Defence of Pluralism and Equality* (Oxford: Blackwell Publishers, 1995).

—— *Thick and Thin: Moral Argument at Home and Abroad* (Notre Dame, IN: University of Notre Dame Press, 2001).

Waltz, Kenneth, *Theory of International Politics* (Reading, MA: Addison-Wesley, 1979).

Warner, Michael, 'Introduction', in *Fear of a Queer Planet: Queer Politics and Social Theory*, ed. Michael Warner (Minneapolis, MN: University of Minnesota Press, 1993).

Wedeen, Lisa, *Ambiguities of Domination: Politics, Rhetoric, & Symbols in Contemporary Syria* (Chicago, IL: University of Chicago Press, 1999).

Weisbrot, Mark, Robert Naiman & Joyce Kim, 'The Emperor Has No Growth: Declining Economic Growth Rates in the Era of Globalization' (Centre for Economic and Policy Research, 2000).

Welsh, Jennifer M. ed., *Humanitarian Intervention and International Relations* (Oxford: Oxford University Press, 2004).

Wendt, Alexander & Michael Barnett, 'Dependent State Formation and Third World Militarization', *Review of International Studies* 19:4 (1993), 321–47.

Westad, Odd Arne, *The Global Cold War: Third World Interventions and the Making of Our Times* (Cambridge: Cambridge University Press, 2005).

Wheeler, Nicholas J., 'Guardian Angel or Global Gangster: A Review of the Ethical Claims of International Society', *Political Studies* 44:1 (1996), 123–35.

—— *Saving Strangers: Humanitarian Intervention in International Society* (Oxford: Oxford University Press, 2000).

Whitaker, Brian, *Unspeakable Love: Gay and Lesbian Life in the Middle East* (London: Saqi, 2006).

Wicke, Jennifer & Michael Sprinker, 'Interview with Edward Said', in *Edward Said: A Critical Reader*, ed. Michael Sprinker (Oxford: Blackwell Publishers, 1992).

Williamson, John, 'Democracy and the "Washington Consensus"', *World Development* 21:8 (1993), 1329–36.

—— 'In Search of a Manual for Technopols' (Appendix), in *The Political Economy of Policy Reform*, ed. John Williamson (Washington, DC: Institute for International Economics, 1994).

Wolf, Martin, *Why Globalization Works: The Case for the Global Market Economy* (New Haven, CT: Yale University Press, 2005).

Wood, Cynthia A., 'Authorizing Gender and Development: "Third World Women", Native Informants, and Speaking Nearby', *Nepantla: Views from South* 2:3 (2001), 429–47.

Woods, Ngaire, *The Globalizers: The IMF, the World Bank and Their Borrowers* (Ithaca, NY: Cornell University Press, 2006).

Woodward, Susan L., *Balkan Tragedy: Chaos and Dissolution After the Cold War* (Washington, DC: The Brookings Institution, 1995).

Woolf, Virginia, 'Three Guineas', in *A Room of One's Own/Three Guineas* (Oxford: Oxford Paperbacks, 1998 [1938]).

World Bank, *Accelerated Development in Sub-Saharan Africa* (Washington, DC: World Bank, 1982).

Yasuaki, Onuma, 'When Was the Law of International Society Born?—An Inquiry of the History of International Law from an Intercivilizational Perspective', *Journal of the History of International Law* 2 (2000), 1–66.

Yeğenoğlu, Meyda, 'Cosmopolitanism and Nationalism in a Globalized World', *Ethnic and Racial Studies* 28:1 (2005), 103–31.

Young, Robert J. C., *Postcolonialism: An Historical Introduction* (Oxford: Blackwell, 2001).

Zakaria, Fareed, 'Culture Is Destiny: A Conversation with Lee Kuan Yew', *Foreign Affairs* 73:6 (1994), 189–94.

Zanotti, Laura, 'Governmentalizing the Post-Cold War International Regime: The UN Debate on Democratization and Good Governance', *Alternatives* 30:4 (2005), 461–87.

Zolo, Danilo, *Invoking Humanity: War, Law and Global Order*, trans. Federico Poole & Gordon Poole (London: Continuum, 2002).

Zunes, Stephen, 'The United States: Belligerent Hegemon', in *The Iraq War: Causes and Consequences*, eds. Rick Fawn & Raymond Hinnebusch (Boulder, CO: Lynne Rienner, 2006).

Conventions, Declarations, Resolutions, and Other Textual Primary Sources

Affidavit filed by the Government of India in Special Leave Petition (Civil) No. 7217–7218 of 2005, in the matter of *Naz Foundation* v. *Government of Delhi*, <http://

humanrights-india.blogspot.com/2005/10/text-of-government-reply-in-s-377-case.html>.
African Union, The Constitutive Act, <http://www.africa-union.org/root/au/AboutAu/Constitutive_Act_en.htm>.
Census of India, 2001, <http://www.censusindia.net/>.
Declaration on Granting Independence to Colonial Countries and Peoples, G. A. Res. 1514 (XV), U. N. Doc. A/4684 (1961).
Declaration on the Establishment of a New International Economic Order, G. A. Res. 3201 (S-VI), U. N. Doc. A/9559 (1974).
Declaration on the Inadmissibility of Intervention in the Domestic Affairs of States and the Protection of Their Independence and Sovereignty, G. A. Res. 2131 (XX), U. N. Doc. A/Res/2131 (XX)/Rev. 1 (1966).
Final Communiqué: African Mini-Summit on Darfur, Tripoli, 17 October 2004, <http://www.issafrica.org/AF/profiles/sudan/darfur/minisumoct04.pdf>.
Final Declaration of the Regional Meeting for Asia of the World Conference on Human Rights, Bangkok, 29 March–2 April 1993, <http://www.unhchr.ch/html/menu5/wcbangk.htm>.
Final Document of the XII Summit of Heads of State or Government of the Non-Aligned Movement, Durban, 2–3 September 1998, <http://www.nam.gov.za/xiisummit/chap1.htm>.
Final Document of the XIII Conference of Heads of State or Government of the Non-Aligned Movement, Kuala Lumpur, 20–25 February 2003, <http://www.nam.gov.za/media/030227e.htm>.
Final Document of the XIV Ministerial Conference of the Non-Aligned Movement, Durban, 17–19 August 2004, <http://www.nam.gov.za/media/040820.pdf>.
Narmada Bachao Andolan v. *Union of India* (2000) 10 SCC 664.
Naz Foundation v. *Government of NCT of Delhi and Others*, WP(C) No. 7455/2001, <http://lobis.nic.in/dhc/APS/judgement/02–07–2009/APS02072009CW74552001.pdf>.
Open Letters Against Sec 377, <www.nytimes.com/packages/pdf/international/open_ letter.pdf>.
Resolutions adopted by the First Ordinary Session of the Assembly of Heads of State and Government of the Organisation of African Unity, Cairo, 17–21 July 1964.
'The Common African Position on the Proposed Reform of the United Nations: "The Ezulwini Consensus"', 7th Extraordinary Session of the Executive Council of the African Union, Addis Ababa, 7–8 March 2005, Ext/EX.CL/2 (VII).
United Nations Millennium Declaration, <http://www.un.org/millennium/declaration/ares552e.pdf>.
White House, 'The National Security Strategy of the United States of America', September 2002, <http://georgewbush-whitehouse.archives.gov/nsc/nss/2002/>.
—— 'The National Security Strategy', March 2006, <http://georgewbush-whitehouse.archives.gov/nsc/nss/2006/>.
'Zionism Is a Form of Racism and Racial Discrimination', G. A. Res. 3379 (XXX), U. N. Doc. A/Res/3379 (1975).

Lectures, Seminars, and Speeches

Grossman, Marc, 'American Foreign Policy and the International Criminal Court', Address to the Centre for Strategic and International Studies, Washington, DC, 6 May 2002, <http://www.amicc.org/docs/Grossman_5_6_02.pdf>.

Lake, Anthony, 'From Containment to Enlargement', Address to the School of Advanced International Studies (Johns Hopkins University), Washington, DC, 21 September 1993, <http://www.mtholyoke.edu/acad/intrel/lakedoc.html>.

Nanjundaswamy, M. D., Statement at the demonstration against the World Economic Summit, Cologne, 19 June 1999, <http://www.rfb.it/icc99/discorso_Nanjundaswamy.htm>.

——Interview with Fred de Sam Lazaro, Twin Cities Public Television (2002), <http://www.mindfully.org/GE/GE4/M-D-Nanjundaswamy-02.htm>.

Sachs, Jeffrey D., 'Creditor Panics: Causes and Remedies', Prepared for the Cato Institute's 16th Annual Monetary Conference, 22 October 1998, <http://www.cato.org/events/monconf16/sachs.pdf>.

Sikkink, Kathryn, 'Explaining International Political and Civil Rights', Global Economic Governance Research Seminar, University of Oxford, 26 May 2006.

White House, 'Remarks by the President on Landmines', 17 September 1997, <http://www.fas.org/asmp/resources/govern/withdrawal91797.html>.

Interviews

Ekine, Sokari, Queer feminist blogger, London, 2 October 2007.

Guha, Ramachandra, Writer, Bangalore, 22 September 2005.

Khaitan, Tarunabh, Queer rights activist, Oxford, 23 August 2005.

Morcos, Rauda, Co-founder of Aswat (Palestinian lesbian group), Haifa (telephone interview), 12 November 2007.

Nanjundaswamy, Chukki, Working president of the Karnataka Rajya Raitha Sangha, Bangalore, 20 September 2005.

Narrain, Arvind, Legal Researcher/Advocate, Alternative Law Forum, Bangalore, 16 September 2005.

Narrain, Siddharth, Journalist (*Frontline/The Hindu*), New Delhi, 5 September 2005.

Parsi, Arsham, Queer activist and founder of Iranian Queer Organization (IRQO), Toronto (telephone interview), 18 October 2007.

Rehman, Ubaid & Asif Rashid, Members of Imaan (British Muslim LGBTQ support group), London, 17 November 2007.

Somalingayya, A., Karnataka Rajya Raitha Sangha member, Bangalore, 20 September 2005.

Tatchell, Peter, Human rights activist and founding member of OutRage!, London, 23 October 2007.

Trasgu, Peoples' Global Action activist, Bangalore, 20 September 2005.

Index

A Portrait of the Artist as a Young Man (Joyce) 113–5
Abani, Chris 139
Achebe, Chinua 69
adivasi 99, 168
Aeschylus 128
Afghanistan 26, 65, 88, 182
Africa 47, 51, 53, 54, 136, 146, 175, 186–8, 194
  modernity and 100–1
  non-intervention and 75–6, 80–1, 207–8n
African Union (AU) 80, 81, 83
Ahmad, Aijaz 127, 128, 130
Ahmadinejad, Mahmoud 179, 181
Aida (Verdi) 129
AIDS 173, 193
al-Asad, Hafiz 103
al-Qaeda 11
al-'Azm, Sadik Jalal 128
Alexander III (of Macedon) 21
Algeria 83, 133, 137
Alvarez, Luis Echeverria 152
Ambedkar, B. R. 195
Amin, Idi 76
Amin, Samir 171
AMIS (African Union Mission in Sudan) 81
Amnesty International 88, 174, 188–9
anarchy 19, 29, 88
Anderson, Benedict 23, 95
Andhra Pradesh 165
de Angelis, Massimo 156
Angola 26
anti-globalization movements 84, 147–72, 195, 198
  sovereignty and 3–4, 73
  see also capitalism
Antigua 129

apartheid 76, 134
Appadurai, Arjun 24
Appiah, Kwame Anthony 200–1, 234n
Arab League 83
Arafat, Yasir 133
Arendt, Hannah 191–2
Argentina 57, 81, 149
Asia 75
  Asian values 82, 102
  modernity and 100–1
  non-intervention and 81–3
Asian Tigers 26, 27, 84
Assadi, Muzaffar 162–3, 164
Aswat 190–1
Auden, W. H. 177
Aurelius, Marcus 21
Austen, Jane 5, 129
Australia 57
Austria 141
authoritarianism 71, 92–3, 102–4
authority 93, 104
  of the international 19, 44–5, 55, 80
  of the state 61, 71, 90, 91, 101
  see also hegemony
Ayodhya 160
Ayoob, Mohammed 28, 86–94, 95

Bacevich, Andrew 45
Bahrain 82
Bajpai, Kanti 13
Baker, Gideon 156
Baku 25
Ban Ki-moon 83
Bandung 25, 27
Bangalore 160, 161, 178
Bangkok Declaration 82
Bangladesh 125
Bardhan, Pranab 92
Barkawi, Tarak 66

Barnett, Michael 89, 90
Barry, Kevin 115
Beck, Ulrich 11, 12, 203n
Beirut 176
Beitz, Charles 43, 61–2
Belarus 82
Bell, Daniel 85, 102
Bellamy, Alex 83
Bellary 160
Bello, Walden 149
Bengal 118, 119, 123
Benner, Erica 140–3
Bentobbal, Lakhdar 133
Berlin, Isaiah 22, 126, 201
Besant, Annie 118
Bharatiya Kisan Union 158, 164
Biafra 80
Bihar 124
Black Skin, White Masks (Fanon) 135–6
Blair, Tony 1, 2, 103
Blake, Michael 17, 19
Bob, Clifford 166, 185
Bohman, James 17
Bokassa, Jean-Bédel 76
Bolivia 81, 152
Bombay 9, 10
Bond, Patrick 149
Bosnia 40
Botswana 80
boundaries 4, 5–7, 75, 86–7, 88, 101, 105–6, 108, 196–7, 198
  subaltern resistance and 20, 22–3, 149–50, 156
  see also identity; threat
Bourdieu, Pierre 148
Boussouf, Abdelhafid 133
Boycott, Captain Charles 118
Brasilia 97
Brass, Tom 163–6
Brazil 27, 65, 81, 146
Brezhnev Doctrine 38
Brick, Barrett 183
Britain 1, 178, 184
Brown, Chris 196

Brussels 25, 162
Brysk, Alison 152
Buchanan, Allen 41
Buchanan, Pat 149
Bull, Hedley 13, 25, 38, 39
Bush, George W. 1, 2, 45, 66, 181

Cairo 1, 75, 176
Calhoun, Craig 22, 48, 59
Calvo, Carlos 74
Calvo Doctrine 74
Cambodia 26, 38
Canada 57, 185, 195
Cantrell, Margaret 183
Cape Town 187
capitalism 44, 47, 50, 52, 55, 57, 98, 143–5, 146, 147, 163, 171, 173, 198
  anti-capitalism 139–50, 162, 169, 172
  liberal cosmopolitanism and 22–4, 48–50, 59
  neo-liberal capitalism 147, 148, 153, 154, 167, 168
  print capitalism 95–6
  see also anti-globalization movements; class; Marx; Marxism
Cargill 160
Caribbean 194
Carr, E. H. 42, 45, 201
caste 20, 122–3, 124, 142, 160, 163–4
Castells, Manuel 20
Central African Republic 76
Central America 81
Central Asia 11
Chandigarh 97
Chandler, David 40, 168
Chang, Ha-Joon 51
Chatterjee, Partha 100–2, 125
Chavez, Hugo 81, 84, 149
Cheah, Pheng 171
Cherki, Alice 137
Chiapas 7, 151, 152, 153, 154, 157, 167
  see also Zapatistas
Chile 55, 57, 81
China 40, 49, 51, 58, 72, 82, 83, 145, 146

Christianity 56, 71, 115, 117, 175, 181, 182
Cicero 21
circumstances of justice 15
civil society 67–8, 168
civilizing mission 59, 97, 174
Clapham, Christopher 75
class 7, 9, 13, 20, 23, 54, 55, 59, 77, 79, 106, 119, 122, 132, 152, 161, 197, 198
   class basis of KRRS 163–6
   nation and 139–50, 169–71
   sexuality and 175, 176–8, 193
   see also anti-globalization movements; capitalism; Marx; Marxism
Clinton, Bill 45
Colas, Alejandro 144
colonialism 3, 38, 57, 75, 86–7, 130, 136, 175
Comintern (Communist International) 144–5
communism 98
communitarianism 6, 16–17, 44, 103, 105–8, 196–201
   pluralism and 85–6, 89, 94–7
   sexuality and 175–6, 177, 178, 189, 192, 193–5
   subaltern resistance and 20, 22–3
   see also nationalism; pluralism
community 6, 16, 85, 86, 102
Comoros 80
conditionality 82, 102
   see economic conditionality
Condorcet, Nicolas 49
Congo-Brazzaville 80
Connolly, James 115
Conrad, Joseph 35
containment 38
cosmopolis 13–14
cosmopolitanism 5, 6, 8, 105–8, 196–201
   as anti-imperialist 59–60, 68
   definitions of 5, 10–16
   Edward Said and 128–9
   elitism and 20–4
   empire and 21–2, 59–60
   everyday conceptions of 9–10

   KRRS and 161–2, 168–9, 170–2
   LGBT rights and 174, 175, 176, 177, 178, 189, 192, 193–5
   Rabindranath Tagore and 122, 124–6
   socialist cosmopolitanism 13, 139–72
   subalterns and 24, 199
   Zapatistas and 153–4, 166–8, 170–2
   see also liberal cosmopolitanism
Côte d'Ivoire 80
Cox, Robert 37
Crossley, Nick 148
Cuba 81, 146
Culture and Imperialism (Said) 128
Cunliffe, Philip 86

dalits 164
Dante 128
Dar-es-Salaam 75
Darfur 3, 81
Deane, Seamus 115–6, 117
debt crisis 26, 46, 50–1, 57, 146, 153
Declaration of a New International Economic Order 26
decolonization 43, 91, 101, 209n
democracy 44, 60, 81, 85, 102, 133, 151, 154, 168, 180
   cosmopolitan democracy 67–8
   democratic peace theory 49
   state- and nation-building and 87–101
Democratic Republic of Congo 65, 80
   Zaire 76, 88
deontological 91
dependence 26, 76–7, 78–9, 162–3
Desai, Meghnad 149
developing world 25, 28
   see also Third World
development 26, 28, 29, 43, 44, 51, 58, 77, 82, 86, 98, 185, 192
   authoritarianism and 92–3, 102
   displacement and 3, 147, 168
   underdevelopment 44
Diaz, Porfirio 155
dictatorship 44, 93
Diderot, Denis 59

difference principle 16, 61
Diogenes 9, 10, 59
domestic 35, 43–4, 54–5, 67, 78, 103, 105, 197
   see also authority; economic conditionality; humanitarian intervention
Douzinas, Costas 60, 65
Doyle, Michael 60, 86
Drago Doctrine 74
Drago, Luis 74
Dublin 116, 118
Dubliners (Joyce) 116
Duggan, Lisa 182
Durban 84

East Asia 51, 52, 55, 58, 92, 93, 102, 103
East Timor 40
economic conditionality 92
   advent of 46–8, 50–1
   as hegemonic practice 54–5, 84
   effects of 51–3
   historical memory and 56–8
   moral justification of 48–50
   see also structural adjustment
ECOWAS (Economic Community of West African States) 40, 80, 82, 207–8n
egalitarianism 10, 11, 14, 18, 21
Eglinton, John 115
Egypt 57, 80, 82, 108, 129, 146, 176
El Salvador 81
Eliot, T. S. 5
empire 21–2, 58–60, 66, 96, 128, 197
   see also imperialism
Engels, Friedrich 23, 140–3, 170–1
England 116, 143
English School 31
   see also international society
Enlightenment 21, 59, 119
Epprecht, Marc 175
Eritrea 80
Erne, Lord 118
Ethiopia 75, 80
Euripides 128

Europe 42, 98, 114, 125, 142, 144, 154, 181
   European imperialism 21, 38, 59, 73, 180
   European society of states 31, 68, 71–3
   state- and nation-building in 86–90, 92, 95
European Community 162
European Union (EU) 57

Fanon, Frantz 7, 132–3, 135–7, 138, 200
fascism 179
feminism 99, 175
Fiji 195
Foucault, Michel 128, 173, 176
Fourth World 65
Fox, Vicente 155
France 57, 95, 116, 146
Franck, Thomas 44
French Revolution 25
Front de Libération Nationale (FLN) 133
Fukuyama, Francis 60

GALA (Gay and Lesbian Alliance) 187
GALHA (Gay and Lesbian Humanist Association) 190
Gallie, W. B. 10
Galtung, Johan 60
Gandhi, Mohandas 118, 119, 163, 170
   disagreements with Tagore 123–4
   Gandhian ideology 13, 159, 161, 162, 163, 169–170
Garibaldi 118
gay see homosexuality; Lesbian, Gay, Bisexual, Transgendered
Gellner, Ernest 94
gender 23, 98–9
   see also homosexuality; Lesbian, Gay, Bisexual, Transgendered; queer
Geneva 162
Germany 142, 144, 145, 154
Gewirth, Alan 200
globalization 65, 84, 87, 148, 149, 162, 169, 171
   see also anti-globalization movements

Golan Heights 103
Goodin, Robert 200
de Gortari, Carlos Salinas 153, 155
Gowan, Peter 49, 52, 53
Great Expectations (Dickens) 128
Green Party (UK) 181
Gregory, Lady 115
Grossman, Marc 45
Grotius, Hugo 48
Group of 8 : 27
Group of 77 : 25, 77
Gruppo Everyone 188
Guatemala 81, 152
Guerrero, Vicente 155
Guerriero, Patrick 180
Guha, Ramachandra 159
Gupta, Alok 193
Gupta, Dipankar 164

Haass, Richard 66
Habermas, Jürgen 41
Haggard, Stephan 93
Haifa 190
Haiti 40
Halabja 2
Halliday, Fred 21
Hardt, Michael 2, 66, 149, 162
Harvey, David 50, 52, 147
Hashmi, Sohail 13
Heater, Derek 59
Heavily Indebted Poor Countries 27, 53
hegemony 37, 42, 54, 66, 124, 134, 197
  US hegemony 27, 50, 52, 53, 55, 60
  Western hegemony 7, 36, 42, 68, 189, 197
  see also authority; economic conditionality; humanitarian intervention
Held, David 65, 67
Herder, Johann Gottfried 59
Hidalgo, Miguel 155
hijra 174, 193, 231n
Hinduism 13, 14, 73, 120
  Hindu Right 160, 169–70

Hirohito (Emperor Showa) 71
Hirschman, Albert 49
Hitler, Adolf 71, 192
Hoad, Neville 174
Hobsbawm, Eric 95
Hobson, J. A. 56
Homer 128
homophobia 175–6, 179, 182, 184, 188, 189–90, 191, 192, 193
homosexuality 99, 173–95
Hong Kong 93, 195
Howes, Marjorie 115, 116
human rights 3, 15, 43–4, 60, 62, 81, 106, 197, 209n
  cultural relativism and 82, 97–102
  LGBT rights 173–95, 198
  state- and nation-building and 87–101
Human Rights Campaign 179
Human Rights Watch 174, 176, 181, 183, 184, 188–9
humanitarian intervention 2–4
  Cold War practice of 38
  historical memory and 56–8
  liberal cosmopolitanism and 37–8
  post-Cold War practice of 39–42
  Third World states and 3, 38, 79–84, 88–9
  Western hegemony and 42–6
humanity 10, 15, 38, 42, 44, 48, 56, 59, 76, 80, 198, 199
  inhumanity 45–6
Hume, David 49
Hungary 116, 144
Hurrell, Andrew 37, 70
Hussein, Saddam 2, 4, 8, 88, 92
hybrid 12
  hybridity 24, 125
Hyderabad 161

Ibrahim, Anwar 102
identity 12, 75, 90, 127, 128, 129, 196, 198
  resistance and 20, 57, 100–1, 125–6, 130–8, 156, 160, 169, 199

identity (*cont.*)
    sexual identity 173–9, 189, 192, 193
    see also boundaries; threat
ideology 92, 102
IGLHRC (International Gay and Lesbian Human Rights Commission) 174, 176, 181, 183, 188–9
Ignatieff, Michael 42, 60
Igwe, Leo 186
ILGA (International Lesbian, Gay, Bisexual, Trans and Intersex Association) 174, 176
Imaan 189–90, 191
imperialism 56–8, 130, 133, 134, 143, 155, 171, 176, 182
    anti-imperialism 103, 143–5, 146
    neo-imperialism 58, 69, 87, 103, 104, 105, 197
    see also empire
In The Eye of the Sun (Soueif) 108
India 27, 38, 65, 125, 146, 172, 182
    cultural relativism in 99–101
    economic liberalization in 3, 165–6
    Marx on 145
    nationalist movement in 118
    non-intervention and 82
    sexual minorities in 174, 175, 178–9, 193–5
    social movements in 3–4, 158, 159, 161, 168–9, 193–5
    see also Karnataka Rajya Raitha Sangha; Tagore
Indian National Congress 118, 144, 159, 168
indigenous peoples 101, 147
    see also Zapatistas
Indonesia 83, 93, 102, 146, 161
international 35, 43–4, 54–5, 67, 103, 105, 197
    see also authority; economic conditionality; humanitarian intervention
International Commission on Intervention and State Sovereignty 79

International Court of Justice (World Court) 64, 114
International Criminal Court 45, 64
international financial institutions (IFIs) 3, 27, 44, 47, 49, 51–5, 65, 67, 92, 104, 146, 147, 153, 154, 161
International Labour Organization (ILO) 64
International Monetary Fund (IMF) 3, 47, 51–5, 58, 64, 147
international normative theory 6, 14, 30–1, 105, 108, 201
international order 13, 14
international relations theory 29, 31
international society 35, 58, 69–70, 83, 91
    culture and 58, 94–101
    expansion of 31, 123, 129
    relationship between solidarism and pluralism in 71–4
    theory of 31
    see also pluralism; solidarism
internationalism 136–7, 156, 170
    class-based 23, 143, 145, 171
    gender-based 23
    see also cosmopolitanism
Iran 4, 83, 98, 177, 179–89
Iraq 1, 4, 8, 40, 41, 42, 56, 58, 65, 81, 83, 88, 91, 92, 189
Ireland 114, 115, 116, 117, 118, 143
Ireland, Doug 179
Islam 13, 14, 98, 128, 129, 179, 180, 182, 190, 193
    Islamophobia 189–90
Islamic Movement 191
Israel 103, 129, 134, 154, 181, 190–1

Jackson, Robert 43, 71, 94
Japan 49, 58, 72, 83, 123
Jerusalem 134
Jews 191–2
Johannesburg 187
Jordan 83, 131
Joyce, James 7, 113–7, 118, 124, 127, 133
Judaism 181

jus cogens 99
justice 6, 151
   distributive justice 16, 85
   institutions and 62–8
   order and 88–9, 94
   state- and nation-building and 87–101

Kaldor, Mary 39
Kampala 76
Kant, Immanuel 49, 59, 60, 63
Karameh 131, 132
Karnataka 150, 158, 160, 161, 165
Karnataka Rajya Raitha Sangha (Karnataka State Farmers' Association) 7, 150, 200
   cosmopolitanism in thought and practice of 161–2, 168–9, 170–2
   nationalism in thought and practice of 162–6, 169–72
   origins of 158
   demands and tactics of 158–61
Kashmir 160
Katanga 80
kathoey 174
Kennedy, David 36
Kettle, Thomas 115
Kidwai, Saleem 175
Kohl, Helmut 26
Korea 72
Koskenniemi, Martti 36, 68
Kosovo 40, 41, 42, 65, 80, 82
kothis 193, 231n
Krisch, Nico 65–6
Kurds 2, 4, 91
Kvisa Shchora 191

La Via Campesina 158, 161
labour 24, 50, 92
   labour standards 4, 64
Labour Party (UK) 181, 184
bin Laden, Osama 149
Laffey, Mark 66
Lake, Anthony 39, 45
Landes, David 44

Latin America 29, 47, 51, 57, 145, 146, 151, 152, 167
   non-intervention and 74–5, 81
Le Pen, Jean-Marie 149
Lebanon 88, 131, 191
Lee Kuan Yew 102
legitimacy 88, 89, 101, 185, 187–8, 190
   authoritarianism and 102–4
   state- and nation-building and 90–4
   see also authority; hegemony
Lenin, Vladimir 71, 134, 143–5, 146, 170–1
Lesbian, Gay, Bisexual, Transgendered (LGBT) 173–95, 231n
Lesotho 80
levels of analysis 106, 149, 150
liberal cosmopolitanism 13, 14, 15–6
   apologist liberal cosmopolitans 60–1, 68
   capitalism and 22–4, 48–50, 59
   cosmopolitan democracy 67–8
   empire and 21–22, 59–60
   historical memory and 56–8
   institutional liberal cosmopolitanism 61–8, 213n
   international law and 41–2
   moral liberal cosmopolitanism 61–8
   sensibility of 6, 43–4, 48, 59
   subaltern resistance and 22
   utopian liberal cosmopolitans 61–8
   Western hegemony and 36, 37–8, 42–6, 60, 197
Liberia 40, 65, 80, 82, 88, 207n
Libya 83
Lloyd, David 115, 170
Locke, John 48
Log Cabin Republicans 180, 182
London 1, 117, 178, 187, 190
Long, Scott 184, 185, 188
Loria, Achille 57
Louis XIV: 71
Luck, Edward 83
Lusaka Manifesto 76
Lynd, R. W. 115

McDonagh, Thomas 115
de la Madrid, Miguel 152, 153
Maharashtra 158
Malaysia 55, 82, 83, 93, 102, 161
Mali 75
Mansfield Park (Austen) 129
Maoism 147, 167
Marcos, Subcomandante 151, 153, 154, 157, 169, 171
Marx, Karl 10, 23, 118, 128, 140–3, 147, 170–1
Marxism 139–50, 163–6, 170–1
Mashhad 179, 182
Massad, Joseph 176–9, 188, 189, 192
Mauritius 80
Mazzini, Giuseppe 118
Mehta, Suketu 1, 9
Meir, Golda 130
Mexico 7, 27, 57, 74, 81, 151, 152, 153, 154, 155, 157, 167, 169, 172
  see also Zapatistas
Middle East 29, 58, 177, 182, 193, 194
Mill, John Stuart 10
Miller, David 16–17, 20, 44, 85
Milosevic, Slobodan 80, 82, 83
mimicry 98, 100–1, 125
Mistry, Rohinton 9
Mobutu Sésé Seko 76
modernism 92, 97, 99
  Third World and modernity 100–2
Mohamad, Mahathir 102
Monroe Doctrine 57, 74
Monsanto 161
Montesquieu 49
Morales, Evo 81, 84
Morcos, Rauda 190–1
Morelos, José Maria 155
Mouloudzadeh, Makwan 188
Movement for Democratic Change 103
Mugabe, Robert 103
Mukasa, Juliet Victor 187
multiculturalism 10, 11
multinational corporations 64

MUSLA (Makerere University Students' Lesbian Association) 187
Muslim Council of Britain (MCB) 190
Muslims 189–90, 192
Mussolini, Benito 71
Muthu, Sankar 59

Nader, Ralph 149
NAFTA (North American Free Trade Agreement) 151, 153, 167
Nagel, Thomas 18, 19
Najmabadi, Afsaneh 180
NAM (Non-Aligned Movement) 3, 25, 77, 79, 84
Namibia 82, 103
Nandy, Ashis 121
Nanjing 72
Nanjundaswamy, M. D. 161, 162, 163
Napoleon 71
Nardin, Terry 70
Narmada dams (Sardar Sarovar Project) 99, 168, 169
Narrain, Arvind 175
Nasser, Gamal Abdel 108–9
nation
  class and 139–50, 169–71
  justification of 16–17, 85
  sexuality and 190–2
  statehood and 85–6
nation-building 86–101
National Alliance of Peoples' Movements 3
National Gay and Lesbian Task Force 181
nationalism 23, 94–6
  anti-colonial nationalism 98, 100–1, 175
  economic nationalism 77, 84
  Edward Said and 129–30
  homo-nationalism 182–3
  KRRS and 162–6, 169–72
  Marxism and 139–50, 170–1
  necessity for and pitfalls of 130–8
  Rabindranath Tagore and 122–4

subaltern nationalism 22, 126, 138, 170–1, 197–8
   Zapatistas and 154–7, 169–72
   see also communitarianism; pluralism
native informants 176, 178, 186, 188, 189, 192
NATO (North Atlantic Treaty Organization) 40, 41, 42, 80, 82, 83
Negri, Antonio 2, 66
Negritude 135–6, 200
Nehru, Jawaharlal 195
Nepal 195
Nero 21
New Social Movements (NSMs) 146, 147, 149
New York 179
New Zealand 57
Neza 154
Nicaragua 26, 81, 161
Nicholas II, Tsar 114
NIEO (New International Economic Order) 77
Nigeria 40, 80, 103, 186–7, 208n
Nixon, Richard 50
Nolan, Emer 115
non-alignment 25–6, 77
non-intervention 71, 73
   Third World and 74–84
Nussbaum, Martha 61, 62, 64, 65, 121
Nyerere, Julius 76, 81

O'Neill, Onora 30
Obama, Barak 66
Omvedt, Gail 159, 164–5
OPEC 47
Orford, Anne 43
Organisation for Economic Cooperation and Development (OECD) 151, 162
Organization of African Unity (OAU) 75, 80
orientalism 89, 137, 176, 191
Orientalism (Said) 127, 128, 129
OutRage! 179, 180, 181, 186–8
OXFAM 64

Pagden, Anthony 21, 58
Paine, Thomas 49
Pakistan 38, 83
Palestine 25, 75, 129, 131, 133, 134, 181, 190–1, 192
Palestinian Authority 133, 134
Palestinian Liberation Organization (PLO) 131
Paris 146, 162
Paris Club 26
Parry, Benita 130, 135
Parsi, Arsham 185
partiality
   communitarian justifications of 16–17
   equality and 199–200
   institutionalist justifications of 17–19
   realist justifications of 19
Partido dos Trabalhadores (PT) 149
Partido Revolucionario Institucional (PRI) 152
patriotism 56, 96, 121, 183, 200–1
Peoples' Global Action (PGA) 154, 158, 161
Perpetual Peace (Kant) 49
Peru 152
Petit, Philip 17, 20, 85
Petrelis, Michael 183
Philippines 161
pluralism 35, 70–4
   authoritarian pluralism 102–4, 105, 106, 189
   communitarianism and 85–6, 89, 94–7
   critique of 89–104
   cultural relativism and 97–101
   Third World state preference for 73–84
   moral justification of 85–9
   nation-building and 86–101
   state-building and 86–101
   see also solidarism
Pogge, Thomas 61, 62
Pol Pot 184
Poland 141, 142
Portillo, José López 152

postcolonial 43, 73, 96, 104, 198, 199
  literature 31, 108
  modernity and 97–101
  theory 31
postnational 24, 198
Prashad, Vijay 25
predatory state 44, 90, 91, 93
  predation of the international 7, 44
proletariat 2, 13, 25, 132, 141, 144, 147, 171
  see also capitalism; class; Marx; Marxism
Prussia 141, 142
Puar, Jasbir K. 182–3
public goods 92
Pufendorf, Samuel 48

Qajar 180
Qing 72
'quasi-states' 43
queer 99, 173–95, 198, 200, 231n

race 100, 103, 135–6, 156
  racial discrimination/racism 98, 99, 186
  racial equality 25
  racial solidarism 76, 78, 81
  sexuality and 174–5, 182, 189–90, 192
  see also Negritude
Rao, P. V. Narasimha 168
Rashid, Asif 189
Rawls, John 15, 16, 30, 44, 61
Reagan, Ronald 26
realism 19, 37, 201
Rehman, Ubaid 189–90
Reisman, Michael 44
religion 56, 99
Renan, Ernst 132
rent-seeking 55, 92
Republican Party (US) 180, 182–3
republicanism 17, 85
responsibility to protect 3, 5, 86
  Third World states and 79–84
  see also humanitarian intervention
Ricardo, David 48

Rice, Condoleezza 45, 179
Richards, Grant 116
Robertson, William 49
Robinson, Sarah 83
Rodrik, Dani 51
Romains, Jules 191–2
Rome 117, 136
Rothstein, Robert 77
Roy, M. N. 144–5
Rushdie, Salman 9, 196
Russell, George 'A. E.' 115
Russia 40, 82, 114, 123, 141
Rwanda 40, 43, 80

Sachs, Jeffrey 149
Sacranie, Iqbal 190
SADC (Southern African Development Community) 80
Said, Edward 7, 138, 200
  as cosmopolitan 128–9
  as nationalist 129–30
  tension between cosmopolitanism and nationalism in work of 127–8, 130–5
Said, Yahia 149
San Cristóbal 154
San Francisco 154
San Isidro 154
Sangiovanni, Andrea 18–19
Santo Domingo 136
Sarkar, Tanika 122
Sartre, Jean-Paul 135–6
Sauvy, Alfred 25
Scheffler, Samuel 12, 22
Schmitt, Carl 42, 45, 65, 76
scope of justice 9, 16, 19–20
Scott, James 23, 92, 96, 97
Seattle 149
self-determination 6, 76, 106, 176, 189, 192, 197, 198
  see also democracy; human rights
Sen, Amartya 93, 194
Seneca 21
Sense and Sensibility (Austen) 5

sensibilities 6, 197
  of communitarianism 7, 44
  of liberal cosmopolitanism 6, 43–4, 48, 59
  protest sensibilities 4–5, 7–8, 106, 107, 108, 137–8, 192
Serbia 40
Serrano, Monica 81
Seth, Vikram 173, 194
Shanghai 11
Shaw, George Bernard 115
Shaw, Martin 60
Shetkari Sanghatana 158, 164
Shue, Henry 61, 62, 63, 65
Sierra Leone 40, 65, 80, 207–8n
Singapore 83, 93, 102
Singer, Peter 61
Sinn Fein 117
Smith, Adam 49
SMUG (Sexual Minorities Uganda) 187
Snow, David 166
social contract 91
socialism 13, 14, 92
  see also anti-globalization movements; capitalism; class; Marx; Marxism
Socrates 59
solidarism 35, 71–4, 81, 82, 214n
  coercive solidarism 70, 73, 104, 105, 106, 189
  in Third World state behaviour 75–9
  solidarist vanguard 58, 60
  see also pluralism
Somalia 39, 40, 75, 82, 88
Soros, George 149
Soueif, Ahdaf 105, 108
South (global) 26, 28, 162
South Africa 25, 65, 75, 76, 80, 103, 154, 195
South America 81
South Asia 194
South China Sea 11
South Korea 52, 83, 93
sovereignty 5, 44, 63, 65–67, 70, 71, 73, 197
  justification of state sovereignty 86
  nation and 85–6
  social movements and 3–4, 156–7, 162, 172
  Third World state insistence on 74–84
  see also boundaries; identity; threat
Soviet Union 38, 39, 50, 97, 145, 146, 154
Spain 154, 155, 158, 161
Spivak, Gayatri Chakravorty 130, 181
Sprinker, Michael 121
Sri Lanka 83, 161
Stalin, Joseph 71, 145
  Stalinism 184
state-building 72–3, 86–101
Steger, Manfred 149
Stiglitz, Joseph 52, 149
structural adjustment 27, 47, 51–5, 92, 147, 168
Stychin, Carl 195
Sudan 83
Sudanese National Democratic Alliance 81
Sudanese Peoples' Liberation Army 81
Sullivan, Andrew 179, 180
Sultan-Galiev, Mirza 144
Swadeshi movement 119, 169–70
Synge, J. M. 115
Syria 88, 103, 131

Tagore, Rabindranath 7, 133, 138, 200
  as critic of cosmopolitanism and nationalism 122
  critique of political nationalism 122–4
  espousal of cultural cosmopolitanism and nationalism 124–6
  see also *The Home and the World*
Taiwan 93
Taliban 182
Tanzania 38, 76, 80, 97
Tarrow, Sidney 166
Tatchell, Peter 179, 180, 183–8, 190
Tehran 180
terrorism 66, 183
Thailand 174

Thakur, Ramesh 80, 81
Thatcher, Margaret 26
The Communist Manifesto (Marx & Engels) 140–1
The Dark Sides of Virtue (Kennedy) 36
The Home and the World (Ghare Baire) (Tagore) 117, 119–123
The Law of Peoples (Rawls) 30
The Question of Palestine (Said) 129, 130
The Twenty Years' Crisis (Carr) 201
The Wretched of the Earth (Fanon) 132, 135–6
Third World 3, 7, 153, 161, 162, 172, 194, 197, 200, 201
  analytical utility of 28–30
  as political project 25–6, 146
  cultural relativism and 97–101
  death of 26–7
  economic demands of 76–7
  historical memory and resistance of 56–8
  modernity and 100–2
  nation-building in 86–101, 206n
  pluralist preference of states in 74–84
  political relevance of 27
  sexual minorities in 173–95
  solidarist behaviour of 75–9
  state-building in 86–101, 206n
  structural position of 29, 78–9, 105
  threat (spatial imaginaries of) 4, 6–8, 105–8, 137–8, 197, 198, 200
    Edward Said and 133
    James Joyce and 116–7
    Marxism and 139–40, 150
    Rabindranath Tagore and 118–9, 124
    Third World sexual minorities and 192
    see also boundaries; identity
Tilly, Charles 89–90
Tormey, Simon 149
tradition 12, 16, 85, 99, 102
Tripoli 81
Tunis 57
Turkey 145

Uganda 38, 76, 186–8
United Kingdom 41, 42, 46, 177, 183, 189
United Nations 11, 25, 64, 74, 83
  General Assembly 75, 84
  Human Rights Commission 88
  Security Council 40, 41, 82, 88, 207–8n
United States 5, 37, 38, 39, 41, 42, 43, 46, 57, 60, 83, 116, 123, 146, 177, 180–4, 195
  as world sovereign 65–6, 209n
  material basis of power of 50–55
  unilateralism and 45–6
universalism 12, 13, 59, 60, 137
utilitarianism 15, 19, 91
Uttar Pradesh 158

Vanita, Ruth 175
Vattel, Emerich 48
veil of ignorance 15
Venezuela 74, 81
Verdi, Giuseppe 129
Vietnam 38, 83, 146
Villa, Pancho 155

Walzer, Michael 16, 17, 85
'war on terror' 79, 180, 182, 183
Washington Consensus 47–8, 51, 54, 55, 149
Wedeen, Lisa 103
West
  as agent 25, 37, 38, 43, 45, 60, 100, 123, 125
  as cultural formation 25, 100, 123, 125, 128, 129, 175, 177, 180, 181, 193, 195, 200
  as place 178, 184, 189, 192
  definition of 205n
  Western conception of human rights 102
  Western hegemony 7, 36, 42, 68, 189, 197
  Western imperialism 2, 58, 61, 68
  Western intervention 27, 37–9, 81, 83

Western knowledge 100, 124, 128, 175, 176, 178, 188, 189, 193
Western left 2, 146, 155, 156
Western modernity 98–101
Western states 2, 4, 12, 26, 31, 38, 40, 43, 44, 47, 60, 61, 70, 71, 84, 89, 123, 179
Westphalia 71, 72, 73, 98
Wheeler, Nicholas 38, 42, 82
Wilde, Oscar 115
Williamson, John 47
Wood, Cynthia 185, 186
Woods, Ngaire 54
Woodward, Susan 43
Woolf, Virginia 23
World Bank 4, 47, 53, 54, 58, 64, 147, 165, 169
world citizenship 22, 59–60
World Conference on Human Rights (1993) 82
world orders 13, 201
World Social Forum 27, 148, 149
world state 10, 59–68,
World Summit (2005) 80, 81, 83
World Trade Organization (WTO) 51, 147, 148, 159, 160, 161, 162

Yasuaki, Onuma 72
Yeats, W. B. 115
Yogyakarta Principles 174
Yugoslavia 39, 40, 43, 146

Zambia 75
Zanu-PF 103
Zapata, Emiliano 151, 155, 170
Zapatistas 7, 149, 200
  causes of rebellion 152–3
  cosmopolitanism in thought and practice of 153–4, 166–8, 170–2
  nationalism in thought and practice of 154–7, 169–72
  outbreak of rebellion 150–1
Zedillo, Ernesto 155, 169
Zeno 21, 59
Zimbabwe 80, 103, 161, 175
Zionism 103, 129
Zolo, Danilo 42